· REVIEWS FOR BOOKS BY TROY TAYLOR ·

HAUNTED ILLINOIS is truly another top-notch, in-depth look at the Land of Lincoln. I highly recommend this book to anyone interested in Illinois ghost stories, as it goes to show that ghosts can be found anywhere throughout the state!
DALE KACZMAREK, author of WINDY CITY GHOSTS

Troy Taylor has done it yet again. In HAUNTED ILLINOIS, the author has hit that rare (and delightful) middle ground between fascinating paranormal research and compelling storytelling. His stories will put you on the edge of your seat and his insights into the supernatural will keep you there…a must-read from one of the best ghost authors writing today.
MARK MARIMEN, author of HAUNTED INDIANA Series

We have read all the books on Civil War haunts and SPIRITS OF THE CIVIL WAR is the best one ever! It has it all from the history to the hauntings and both familiar and little-known ones. This is a must-read for any Civil War buff and for anyone who believes the war continues on in the afterlife! We're not sure how Troy Taylor's going to top this one… but we'll be waiting!
ROB AND ANNE WLODARKSI, authors of HAUNTED ALCATRAZ & Others

HAUNTED ILLINOIS is a generous introduction to the resident wraiths of one of the nation's most haunted states, from its most prolific ghost writer. This book is a must for natives, ghost hunters and aficionados of Americana and holds captive anyone with an interest in the wonderful experiences so often omitted from the "proper" historical record.
URSULA BIELSKI, author of CHICAGO HAUNTS

GHOST BOOKS BY TROY TAYLOR

Haunted Illinois (1999 / 2001)
Spirits of the Civil War (1999)
The Ghost Hunter's Guidebook (1999 / 2001)
Season of the Witch (1999)
Haunted Alton (2000)
Haunted New Orleans (2000)
Beyond the Grave (2001)
No Rest for the Wicked (2001)
Haunted St. Louis (2002)

The History & Hauntings Series
I. The Haunting of America (2001)

The Haunted Decatur Series
Haunted Decatur (1995)
More Haunted Decatur (1996)
Ghosts of Millikin (1996 / 2001)
Where the Dead Walk (1997)
Dark Harvest (1997)
Haunted Decatur Revisited (2000)
Flickering Images (2001)

Ghosts of Springfield (1997)
The Ghost Hunter's Handbook (1997)
Ghost Hunter's Handbook (Second Edition - 1998)
Ghosts of Little Egypt (1998)

HAUNTED ST. LOUIS

History & Hauntings Along the Mississippi

BY TROY TAYLOR

~ A Whitechapel Productions Press Publication ~

As with all of the other books that I have written, this book is dedicated to the most inspiring person to ever enter my life.. my wife, Amy. But I would also like to add another dedication to my children, Orrin, Anastasia and (as of this writing) "the baby to be named later". I'll have to save another dedication for that one later on!

I would also like to dedicate this book in memoriam to Richie Lampertz, a good friend who was lost just as it was going to publication. I could always say that she was there with us from the beginning.. and she always knew how to make me laugh! We'll miss you!

Original Cover Artwork Designed by
Michael Schwab, M & S Graphics & Troy Taylor
Visit M & S Graphics at www.msgrfx.com
Back Cover Photograph by Michael Schwab

This Book is Published by
~ Whitechapel Productions Press ~
A Division of the History & Hauntings Book Co.
515 East Third Street ~ Alton, Illinois ~62002
(618) 465~1086 / 1~888~GHOSTLY
Visit us on the Internet at www.prairieghosts.com

First Printing ~ January 2002
ISBN: 1~892523~20~5

Printed in the United States of America

The first time I ever saw St. Louis, I could have bought it for six million dollars, and it was the mistake of my life that I did not do it.

MARK TWAIN

"First in booze, first in shoes and last in the American League..." Any slick-paper writer knows that this is sure-fire way to start a piece about St. Louis. Garnish with a few paragraphs about packet boats on the Mississippi. and some South Side Germans enjoying beer, rose gardens and Gemuetlichkeit, and the job is done. The trouble, though, is that what you read about St. Louis "ain't necessarily so".

ERNEST KIRSCHTEN

St. Louis ghost stories have been around almost as long as St. Louis...

JIM LONGO

After visiting here, you can almost understand why the dead are so reluctant to leave St. Louis. It is a city of great diversity and amazing beauty, nestled on the banks of the Mississippi River and stretching back into the forests and hills of Missouri. It is home to a great number of hauntings, including a house that tops the list as one of the "most haunted" in America. The city is also home to two of the greatest mysterious in the annals of the supernatural. It is a very haunted place!

From AMONG THE SHADOWS

- TABLE OF CONTENTS -

WELCOME TO HAUNTED ST. LOUIS

Ghost stories have always been a part of the history of St. Louis. Tales of wandering ghosts, women in black and the suicidal spirits of beer-brewing millionaires have always held great appeal to those with a taste for the macabre.

Growing up in Illinois, I have always been fascinated with both St. Louis, the Mississippi River and the hauntings centered around them. For years I had hoped to write an account of not only the unusual history of St. Louis but the unsolved mysteries, the paranormal happenings and the mysterious legends of the region as well. The book that you hold in your hands is the end product of those desires. Having said this though, it is not my intention to say that I have written the final word on St. Louis ghosts. There have been several wonderful books written about the city and this is certainly not the first (and will most likely not be the last) to be written about her spirits and hauntings. This book was not written to be better than any of the others, merely different. In fact, as someone who is writing about the local haunts from the perspective of an "outsider", I think that you will find a different take on the city than any that you have read before.

So, what prompted me to write a book like "Haunted St. Louis", you might ask?

For one thing, I have long been fascinated with ghosts, hauntings and legends and throughout my life, it had been my dream to someday live along the Mississippi River. The lore of the river had always appealed to me and in 1998, I found myself living atop a bluff in the city of Alton, Illinois. My writings soon turned to river towns in Illinois, ghost stories of Alton itself and even the history and haunts of New Orleans. It seemed to me a natural progression to turn my attentions to the resident spirits of St. Louis. But this book is not only about ghosts, it also encompasses my love of history as well. I have always been of the mind that a good ghost story cannot exist without a history behind it. The events of yesterday, you see, are what create the hauntings of today.

However, this is not some dry textbook of mere St. Louis dates and facts. I am fascinated with the darker side of the history of the city, but I am no historical expert or collegiate scholar. I simply collected a history of the city and highlighted the stories, incidents and accounts that most intrigued me. This book is meant to be a journey into the past, a trip back through St. Louis history that also includes the ghosts, spooks and specters of this haunted city.

So, ghosts are what may have brought you to this book but if you are looking for nothing more than breathless first-hand accounts of waking up in the middle of the night to see Aunt Gertrude standing at the foot of the bed, then this may not be the book for you! Those kinds of stories, lacking the already mentioned history, have never been of much interest to me. I have always had the need to "tell" the story and I like to let the documented accounts speak for themselves. You'll discover what I mean in the pages ahead...

And while this book does contains much in the way of history and hauntings, it still falls short when it comes to collecting every single story to "haunt" this city. I don't think that you will be disappointed though because I have managed to collect stories of hauntings and of dark history that are both familiar and unfamiliar, have been forgotten by time and most of all, are uniquely a part of the history of St. Louis. There are all sorts of tales of ghosts and strange events, including stories of haunted houses, terrifying locations, bizarre legends, bloody history and some that are not ghost stories at all but were so unusual they had to be included anyway.

Even with that said though, I am sure that there are tales that have still managed to elude me. There are haunted places here that have remained unknown since the first settlers came to the region and these spots remain hidden, or forgotten, today. I do not claim to have uncovered every ghost tale of St. Louis but I do think that I can entertain and thrill you in a way that perhaps no other book has done before.

But can I tell you that every one of the stories in this book is true? Can I vouch for their complete authenticity? No, I cannot do that. What I can tell you though is that each of them was told to me, or was documented, as being the truth. The stories that are included in this book are presented as "real" stories that have been told by "real" people. The truth of each story is up to the reader to decide.

But consider these questions before you begin this book...
Do you believe in ghosts? Could St. Louis really be a haunted and mysterious place?
There are many readers who do believe that ghosts are real and who have had their own strange experiences over the years. Like many of us, they have tried to explain them away, but cannot. These folks are quick to accept the possibility that ghosts exist but many readers are not so open-minded.

Those who do not believe in ghosts say that spirits are merely the figments of our imagination. Ghost stories, these readers insist, are the creations of fools, drunkards and folklorists. Such a reader will most likely finish this book and will still be unable to consider the idea that ghosts might exist. In that case, I can only hope to entertain this person with the history and horrific tales from eerie past of St. Louis.

If you are such a person though, I hope that you will not be too quick to assume that you have all of the answers. Can you really say for sure that ghosts aren't real? Are you completely convinced that spirits do not wander the streets of St. Louis? Those are questions that you should ask yourself, but before you immediately reply, try answering them while walking down some fog-shrouded street in the Soulard district some night.

Is that moaning sound that you hear really just the wind whispering in your ear, or could it be the voices of the dead, crying for eternal peace?

Is that merely a patch of fog that you see darting around a corner, or the spirit of a forgotten wanderer searching for the ghost of a long ago lover?

Are those lights in the distance merely the reflection of passing cars, or are they the restless souls of the city's dead?

Is that rustling in the leaves really just a passing breeze, or is it the ominous sound of footsteps coming up behind you?

If you suddenly turn to look, then you might realize that, despite the fact that there is no living person around you, you just might not be alone! Perhaps you are not as sure as you thought you were about the existence of ghosts. Perhaps they are not simply a part of fanciful fiction after all. Perhaps no one person among us has all of the answers....

Remember that there are stranger things, to paraphrase the poet, than are dreamt of in our philosophies. Some of these strange things are lurking just around the corner, in the dark shadows of St. Louis!

Happy Hauntings!
Troy Taylor
Holidays 2001- 02

HAUNTED ST. LOUIS
- PART ONE -

GHOSTS BY GASLIGHT
The History & Hauntings of Old St. Louis

WELCOME TO THE MOUND CITY

As stated already in these pages, it is impossible for us to understand and appreciate the hauntings that occur in St. Louis without first understanding the city's past. Time has woven a rich tapestry here alongside the Mississippi River and has left behind an incredible legacy of supernatural legend and lore. It is the history of the city that has created its hauntings. As even the most hesitant readers can attest, ghosts and hauntings are often born from violence, murder, bloodshed and tragedy. Even from its very beginnings, St. Louis was a region where death was commonplace and mysteries thrived.

The first explorers and settlers who came to this area found Native Americans who roamed the land, with no written language and no real communities or culture. However, scattered across the region, they discovered strange mounds, altars and burial sites and what appeared to be ruins where towns and villages once stood. It seemed that a civilization, far advanced of the current natives, had once prospered in the Mississippi River Valley.

Who these mysterious dwellers may have been remains a mystery. They have been called the "Mound Builders", thanks to the monuments of earth they left behind, but the people have so utterly disappeared that their true identity will never be known. They left only silent graves and magnificent mounds in their wake.

At Cahokia, across the river near present-day Collinsville, Illinois, are the remains of the region's most ancient city. The site boasts a number of mounds, but has one main centerpiece. It is sometimes called "Monk's Mound", after Trappist monks who farmed the terraces of the structure sometime in the early 1800's. It is a stepped pyramid that covers about 16 acres and one that was apparently rebuilt several times in the distant past. At the summit of the mound are the buried remains of some sort of temple, further adding to the mystery of the site. The settlers who later came to the area were intrigued by the mounds and they believed them to be evidence of some long vanished and forgotten culture. As they dug into the mounds, they found extraordinary artifacts like pottery, carved pipes and stone trinkets, effigies of birds and serpents made from copper and mica and vast numbers of human bones.

During the Middle Ages, Cahokia was a larger city than London was and yet today, it is an abandoned place about which we know almost nothing. Centuries ago, there were more than 120 mounds at the Cahokia site, though the locations of 106 have been recorded. Many of them have been destroyed or altered because of modern farming or construction, although 68 have been preserved inside of Illinois State historic boundaries.

Across the river, within the bounds of present-day St. Louis, another 27 such mounds also existed. A military officer named Major Long made a drawing of the St. Louis mound locations near the river before many buildings were constructed around them. It shows a circle of mounds near the center of the future town, a large square mound to the circle's southeast, groupings of small mounds, a few mounds to the west and a large mound on the north. A map that was made from his drawing was later included in a Smithsonian report from 1861. The drawing was not to scale, but it did show that the mounds were man-made and were not formations created by the Mississippi River.

The St. Louis mounds were very similar to the mounds as Cahokia and are believed to have been by the Mound Builder society. Years later, St. Louis would even gain the nickname of the "Mound City" by river travelers who used the two largest mounds as landmarks. The largest of them, La Grange de Terre (which means "earthen barn") was located on land that was surrounded by Broadway, Second Street, Mound Street and Brooklyn Street.

As St. Louis grew, all of the mounds were chipped away and destroyed to make way for buildings and streets. The early residents did not see any importance to these antiquities at all and were indifferent to their destruction. They were only used as vantage points and seen as curiosities. In fact, in 1844, a local man leveled off the top of La Grange de Terre and built a small tavern on top of it! The view was great but the business soon failed and the building was razed.

In 1855, new streets cut through the north and south ends La Grange Terre and in 1866, Archbishop Peter Kenrick sold most of the site to some New York investors for $18,000. The remainder of it was later sold to a blacksmith for an additional $12,000. The mound's destruction came in 1868 when workers began carrying away wagons filled with dirt, bones and artifacts to be used as fill in a construction project by the Northern Missouri Railroad.

The mounds located west of the city were also destroyed. One, located near Kingshighway and Martin Luther King, was known as Cote Brilliante (or "shining hill") and was destroyed in 1877 to make way for Christian Brothers College. Two smaller mounds, located within the bounds of Forest Park, were destroyed during the construction for the 1904 World's Fair.

As one writer noted in 1868, "to all intents and purposes the Mound is gone. What should have been purchased by the City and preserved inviolate, will soon be known only in local tradition." And so it is... the mysterious structures are now vanished forever, although the city's nickname of the "Mound City" still remains today.

THE FRENCH COME TO ST. LOUIS

No one will ever know who the first white man to set foot where St. Louis now stands actually was. It is possible that some French adventurer arrived here first, but recorded history really begins with the arrival of Louis Jolliet and Father Jacques Marquette in 1673.

Jolliet was a young Canadian from France who was an explorer and map-maker, while Marquette was a Jesuit priest who longed to bring his religion to the native people of the wilderness. These two men, along with several Indians and nineteen white men, began a treacherous journey that would take them down the Mississippi River. The concluded the journey at the mouth of the river, finally realizing that the waterway did not turn west toward the Pacific Ocean.

This expedition began the French exploration of North America. In that era, the British claimed much of the eastern seaboard, while the French claimed the southern and eastern reaches of Canada and the Great Lakes. The Spanish had conquered Mexico, the southwest and California. All of these European powers battled to claim more territory in the New World and to find a water passage across the continent that would make for faster travel to the Far East.

The future site of St. Louis would be claimed for France by Robert Cavalier, who was better known as the flamboyant promoter, sieur de LaSalle. He was the first of the early arrivals to comprehend the economic importance of the territory and also became the first to explore many of the waterways and forests of the region. In spite of his courage and his brilliance, LaSalle was regarded by most as haughty, arrogant and rude. He was often referred to as a "man of magnificent failures" as he brutalized the Indian tribes, borrowed huge sums of money and squandered fortunes.

LaSalle had been born into a noble French family in 1643. He came to America two decades later and took up exploration as a means of creating his fortune. On his first trip, seeking the Ohio River, he encountered the explorer Louis Jolliet, who was returning from Illinois. Jolliet's fortunes would never be made, LaSalle believed, because he was unable to get land grants from the French government. Because of his friendship with Marquette, the explorer would always be linked to the Jesuit order of the Catholic Church. LaSalle did not have such a problem, he despised the Jesuits, and thanks to this he was able to gain a grant that gave him control of the fur trade south of the Great Lakes. In return for it, he agreed to explore the lower Mississippi Valley and try to discover a water passage to the Pacific Ocean.

In the spring of 1682, LaSalle made his first journey down to the mouth of the Mississippi River. When he arrived, LaSalle claimed all of the land for France and dubbed the region "Louisiana". In so doing, he created a vast territory that stretched from the Appalachians to the Rocky Mountains.

LaSalle left the region after only five years. He returned home to France, where he was considered a hero. He was asked again to serve his country, as France was now at war with Spain, and LaSalle promised to set up a base of operations at the mouth of the Mississippi River. He departed with two hundred colonists but somehow managed to miss Louisiana and land in Texas instead. He conducted several expeditions in search of the Mississippi but he never found it again. While on the fourth mission, he was shot and killed by one of his own men. It was a rather strange, but somehow fitting, end for the "man of magnificent failures".

From 1698 to 1722, the French expanded throughout the Lower Mississippi Valley. In 1700, Jesuit missionaries briefly established a village with some Kaskaskia Indians north of River Des Peres but aside from this, France stayed mostly to the south, founding Mobile, Alabama in 1702 and New Orleans in 1722. A few years later, more settlements began to appear in the north at Kaskaskia, Cahokia, St. Genevieve and Fort de Chartres.

Finally in 1763, the stage was set for St. Louis to appear. Between 1756 and 1763, France had been embroiled in the Seven Year's War (or the French and Indian War as it was known in the colonies) and this had curtailed much of the exploration that had started in decades past. The war had created a poor economy in New Orleans and in other parts of French North America, so in an effort to generate money, the governor of the Louisiana colony, Jean Jacques Blaise d' Abbadie, granted six-year monopolies in various commodities to several New Orleans businessmen. Exclusive fur trading rights with Indians of the Missouri River and the western banks of the Mississippi were granted to Gilbert Antoine Maxent and his partner, Pierre Laclede de Liguest. Maxent was the wealth behind the operation and Laclede's job was to establish a trading post and manage it with the expectation that the post would become a settlement.

In 1763, Laclede left New Orleans with a party of 30 men, including his young lieutenant, Auguste Chouteau, who was then just 14 years-old. They traveled north up the Mississippi River to the confluence of the Missouri in search of the ideal location for the trading post. They had briefly considered setting up shop in St. Genevieve but as it had a history of flooding and of disease, they moved on in favor of a place closer to the Missouri River. They wintered that season at Fort de Chartres and scouted the western banks of the river while they waited for spring. It was here that Laclede learned of the 1763 Treaty of Paris, which ended the war and ceded all territory east of the Mississippi River to the British. France retained, Laclede thought, all its claims to land west of the Mississippi River, along with New Orleans. Because of this, the settlers and soldiers from Fort De Chartres followed Laclede to the new settlement in the spring, fearing British rule. Unfortunately, what none of them knew at the time, was that France had already secretly deeded the western lands to Spain in 1762.

Laclede found the site for his trading post below the confluence of the Missouri and Mississippi Rivers. It was a gently sloping area that ended at a limestone bluff, safely above the flood plain. A gap in the bluff provided easy access to the river. There was an abundance of wood here for building, stones for construction, clean water and plenty of room for expansion.

Laclede sent his lieutenant, Auguste Chouteau, to the site and he landed here on February 15, 1764. The men began to clear the area and to lay out streets according to Laclede's detailed instructions. The plans provided for wide north and south streets called La Grande Rue (First Street), Rue d' Eglise (Second Street) and Rue de la Grange (Third Street). Several streets were also laid out to run from the river, including today's Walnut, Market and Chestnut Streets. The area formed a large grid and an area was left open for a gathering place and military drilling field. There was also land set aside for cattle grazing and for farming. The crew also started construction on warehouses for tools and supplies and on living quarters.

Laclede returned to the chosen site in April 1764 and named it St. Louis, after King Louis XV, whose patron saint was the Crusader King, Louis IX.

After Laclede departed, a party of 150 Missouri Indians arrived at the settlement and asked to become permanent residents. The eastern bank families, who had come from Fort De Chartres and the Illinois lands, quickly moved back across the river. Chouteau sent for Laclede, who persuaded the Indians to go elsewhere.

In addition to the construction of the city itself, the work crews also began construction on a large house that would serve as Laclede's home and as the business center for the settlement. Laclede's house stood on the block between Rue d'Eglise and the public market. The stone basement, which extended ten feet above ground in New Orleans fashion, was dug by Indian laborers and was lined to cool the interior during the summer months. The first floor consisted of a large center room, with two smaller rooms on each side. Government and trading business was conducted in the center room and the others were used as living quarters.

The place was luxurious by the standards of the frontier, with plastered and whitewashed walls and polished black walnut floors that had been looted from Fort de Chartres before the British took over. The house was also surrounded by a stockade fence, as were all residences at the time. This was part of Laclede's defensive plan for St. Louis. If the city was attacked, the homes would be sheltered and only the streets would need to be closed off to repel an army.

While Laclede's house was large, it was also crowded. Laclede had sent for Chouteau's mother, Madame Marie Therese Bourgeois Chouteau, to come to St. Louis from New Orleans with her four other children. She was estranged from her husband, Rene Auguste Chouteau, and there were whispers as to the paternity of her three younger children. In spite of this, Laclede never acknowledged any of the children as being his own. So, Laclede, Marie and all of the children occupied the house, as did Louis St. Ange de Bellerive, the last French governor of the Louisiana Territory. It would be six years before the Spanish would send their own governor to St. Louis and he would also live in Laclede's home.

Probably because of the close quarters and also in thanks for the services of young Auguste Chouteau, Laclede had a second and equally impressive home built for Marie. This house was built in typical French style and Laclede deeded it, along with his original house, to his old partner Maxent to keep him from financial ruin.

Apparently, Laclede was more of a soldier and explorer than a businessman. To attract new settlers to the area, he gladly shared his trading rights with others. Because of this, he did not share much in the early prosperity of the region. He died on June 20, 1778 while bringing cargo by boat up the Mississippi River from New Orleans. He was buried on shore near the mouth of the Arkansas but the grave site has long been washed away by floods and changing channels of the river.

In 1789, Auguste Chouteau bought the Laclede House and purchased his friend's share of the business from Maxent. He began to repair and improve the house, making it the showplace of the growing city. He added a second floor and a garret to the house and added to the thickness of the walls. The wooden stockade fence was replaced by one made of stone and stables, slave cabins and other buildings were constructed on the grounds. He also sank a well near the house, the first in St. Louis.

The house became much more than a slightly improved frontier dwelling. The furniture was also imported from France, along with fine china and silver. Chouteau's home boasted a library of more than 500 volumes and while there were no schools, the children of the city leaders were well-read and educated.

Chouteau died in 1829 but his widow lived on the house for several more years. The house was finally torn down in 1841, despite pleas to save it. The land was cleared for commercial enterprises that followed. As author Mary Bartley stated, "It was the first of the grand St. Louis homes to meet that fate, but certainly not the last."

Chouteau is considered by many to be the real founder of St. Louis and so it's no wonder that his name is still familiar today thanks to street names and an area once called Chouteau's Pond. The pond was formed in 1765 when Joseph Tallion built a flour mill and dammed the La Petite Riviere to provide power for it. Pierre Laclede later purchased the mill and upon his death, the mill, the pond and the surrounding land became the property of Chouteau. In 1770, he built a larger mill and expanded the size of the pond. Each time the dam was raised, it enlarged the lake and eventually, it was bounded roughly by Eighth Street, Market Street, Gratiot Avenue and Twenty-Second Street.

Chouteau's Pond was a favorite location for many St. Louisans and became popular for fishing, boating and swimming. In 1821, a boathouse was established here and it was also used for fireworks displays and for religious services and baptisms. By this time, the mill and pond were owned by Chouteau's sons, Henri and Gabriel. Henri Chouteau had been born in 1805 and was Auguste's third child. In 1827, he was appointed clerk of the county court and became recorder of St. Louis County. He also married Clemence Coursault of Baltimore and together, they raised ten children.

In 1830, Henri built a grand home on a hill overlooking Chouteau's Pond, at a site that is now the corner of Tucker Boulevard and Clark Street. The Greek Revival style mansion had a prominent portico with stone columns, double chimneys and a number of rooms. He was now well established and soon resigned his county office and established a mercantile firm called Chouteau and Riley, later Chouteau and Valle. He became one of the largest coffee and sugar merchants along the Mississippi and he spent his winters on a plantation in the south.

In 1845, George Collier located his Collier White Lead Co. on the shores of Chouteau Pond and was soon joined in the area by a slaughterhouse. The destruction of the pond's natural environment was soon underway. The industries here began using the pond as an open sewer. There were no zoning restrictions to prevent this and no regulations to prevent the dumping of waste or to force the companies to clean it up. The 1849 cholera epidemic (see later section) that decimated the St. Louis population was thought to be caused by these horrible conditions. The public soon demanded that the pond be drained for health reasons and by 1852, it was no more. Later, suspicions were raised that the pond was actually drained because nearby land was ideal for much-needed rail and switching yards.

Henri Chouteau died in 1855 in the Gasconade River Disaster. This inaugural trip for the Missouri Pacific Railroad, celebrating the completion of the line as far as Jefferson City, turned into a horrific event that claimed some 30 lives. Rain had undermined the stability of a rail bridge over the Gasconade River and it collapsed when the loaded train crossed over it. Henri Chouteau was one of those killed.

After Chouteau's death, the magnificent Chouteau Mansion was torn down and its location became the site of the Four Courts Building. It was completed in 1871 and housed St. Louis' four municipal courts, the Police Department and the jail. (see later chapter for more details)

In July 1803, more news came to St. Louis. They discovered that in 1800, Spain had secretly returned the Lower and Upper Louisiana Territories to France by the Treaty of Ildefenso. While this was a great surprise to the residents, there was still more news to come. They discovered that France had in turn sold all of the land to the United States for about $15 million.

The people of St. Louis were outraged! They had been abandoned by the French, but had been left alone by the Spanish. They didn't appreciate becoming a part of the United States without their knowledge or consent. They feared being ruled over by the nation across the Mississippi and their fears were shared by the Americans who had come west to find land and freedom and to escape from taxes and an interfering government. It was a time of great uncertainty for the early settlers of St. Louis and most dreaded the changes to come.

THE "BOSTONS" COME TO ST. LOUIS

The American flag was raised over St. Louis on March 10, 1804. Captain Amos Stoddard conducted the act of transfer between nations. He and a company of men oversaw the lowering of the Spanish flag and the raising of the French flag on March 9. It was said that the cheers of the city's inhabitants were so loud that they drowned out the bugles, drums and guns that had accompanied the flag raising. Stoddard allowed the flag of France to fly throughout the night and an honor guard was formed around it. The people danced and celebrated and the stories go that no Frenchmen in St. Louis slept that night.

The following morning, Stoddard lowered the flag and raised the Stars and Stripes in its place. Again, the bugles called, the drums rolled and the guns fired, but the cheers were not as loud or as enthusiastic as they had been the day before. The American flag meant that St. Louis now stood to be invaded by the "Bostons", which was the local slur for any Americans from east of the Mississippi. Stoddard had been ordered by President Thomas Jefferson to make as few changes in St. Louis as possible and this may have been the reason why the transition went as smoothly as it did. Local leaders like Auguste Chouteau and others simply went about their business and looked for ways to continue making money in the new nation.

As for Thomas Jefferson, he was anxious to discover just what he had acquired for the United States and what was located between the Mississippi and the Pacific Ocean. He soon authorized an expedition to the west to be led by his secretary, a young man named Meriwether Lewis. He eagerly accepted the commission and began buying scientific instruments, studying medicine and even ordered the Harper's Ferry arsenal to build him a collapsible iron boat. Most importantly, he requested the help his friend William Clark to accompany him on his journey. Clark knew the wilderness and was good with a drawing pencil and would make a perfect companion for the expedition. Clark quickly accepted and replied in a letter to Lewis that "no man lives with whom I would prefer to undertake and share the difficulties of such a trip than yourself. My friend, I join you with hand and heart." With that said, the two men began to embark on a journey that would make them prominent in St. Louis for years and would create a legend that still lingers today.

William Clark & Meriwether Lewis (courtesy Independence National Historical Park Collection)

St. Louis became the base of operations for the expedition. It was the "Gateway to the West" and the place to find mountain men and trappers like Manuel Lisa, who were full of information about the western lands. Many of them had traveled far up the Missouri River and had lived among the Indians. Lewis and Clark prepared their boats and supplies at Camp Du Bois, near the site of present-day Wood River, Illinois, and gathered information in St. Louis, all the while attending dinners and parties held in their honor.

Clark departed from St. Louis on May 14, 1804 and started up the Missouri River, arriving in St. Charles in two days. Here, the boats were reloaded and Clark went to meet with Daniel Boone, who lived nearby and with whom Clark had consulted over the last few months. Lewis joined the expedition in St. Charles. He had been delayed in St. Louis bidding farewell to some Osage Indian chiefs who were on their way to Washington to meet with Jefferson. A group of citizens had accompanied him to St. Charles and another party was held in honor of he and Clark. Finally, the expedition was underway again by the following afternoon.

The adventures experienced by these two men during the expedition is another story altogether but their departure and return to St. Louis caused the city to become known as the Capital of the West. From this point on, those who sought to make a name or a fortune for themselves in the west passed through St. Louis on their way to points beyond. The city became a thriving market for the growing fur trade, as it was the only large city where pelts could be sold and shipped to the east. The Chouteau's and other French merchants had begun to develop a profitable trade in buffalo, deer, beaver, fox, otter, muskrat and other skins and furs. Traders exchanged cloth, blankets, knives, beads, kettles, tin cups and more with the Indians for the pelts that had been trapped along the Missouri River.

Perhaps the most influential of those in the St. Louis fur trade was a Spaniard named Manuel Lisa. He had come to St. Louis in the late 1790's and quickly made a place for himself among the local merchants. He was young and aggressive and began competing for fur trade against the Chouteau's. While he did not fare well at first, he later became close with the Omaha, Ponca, Teton and Yankton Sioux, Mandan and Arikara tribes. Lisa was bold and fearless and never backed down in an argument or hesitated to use the brass cannons that he kept at ready. The Indians respected him for this and soon would do business with no one else. He took an Omaha woman as his wife and dominated the fur trade for more than two decades.

While in St. Louis, Lisa made more enemies than friends but his reputation began to improve during the War of 1812 when he used his influence with the Santee Sioux, and other tribes allied with the British, and kept them from attacking St. Louis. He gained more respectability in 1818 when he married Mary Hempstead, the widowed daughter of a Presbyterian minister.

Shortly after this, Lisa constructed a building to hold his expanding commercial enterprise. Completed in 1818, the large stone warehouse was located at Main and Chestnut Streets. The structure, which became known as the Old Rock House, had many uses during its long life. It was first used to store furs and supplies for the military and later, after Lisa was killed in 1820 during a brawl, the warehouse was taken over by other fur trading companies until the trade died out. After that it was used for warehouse space until the late 1880's, when an odd mansard roof was added to it and it was turned into a saloon. When the National Park Service purchased it in 1936, there was a barroom on the first floor, a night club on the second and the third floor, which had been created when the mansard roof was added, was divided into small bedrooms and used as a bordello.

In 1939, the Old Rock House was dismantled, restored and reconstructed as a piece of authentic St. Louis history. In the 1950's, it was taken down again to make way for some railroad tracks needed for the construction of the Gateway Arch. When the structure was completed, the

Old Rock House had nowhere to go, as stairs for the Arch occupied its former site. The Park Service then incorporated the stones from the house into an exhibit in the northwest gallery of the Old Courthouse.

The Old Rock House (courtesy of Missouri Historical Society)

Some have wondered if perhaps the history contained in these stones is what has caused rumors of hauntings to plague the Old Courthouse for many years. The building was completed in 1828 and served the city until it was retired from service in 1930. It is now owned by the National Park Service, which conducts tours and special activities and events here. However, it was not until after the stones from the Old Rock House were moved into the building that the "activity" reported here began to be more than just historical in nature. It has been suggested that perhaps the violence and history of the Old Rock House was impressed upon the stones of the building and began to manifest itself at its new home in the Old Courthouse.

According to a former employee of the building, there have been many occasions when security guards have been frightened by strange noises and by footsteps that are heard in otherwise empty rooms. The staff member stated that lights have been known to turn on and off in the building, doors have opened and closed and occasionally, the sounds of men laughing, shouting and talking have been heard. When a guard has checked to see who is there, he finds the area deserted. One security guard was even so frightened that he called the St. Louis Police Department one night. When they checked for intruders, no one was there.

Perhaps the history of St. Louis lives on in this way as well!

MYSTERIOUS DEATH OF MERIWETHER LEWIS

In September 1806, the Lewis and Clark Expedition returned to St. Louis after an absence of two years and four months. The men had crossed more than 6,000 miles of wilderness and arrived in the city to much celebration. The welcoming festivities were even more joyous than the ones that had marked their departure. The adventurers of the expedition crew were mustered out and Lewis departed for Washington, followed by Clark a short time later.

Lewis was welcomed into the home of President Jefferson and managed to obtain both extra money and land grants for his men. He was also appointed as Governor of the Louisiana Territory, with Clark serving as the region's Indian agent and being promoted to the rank of Brigadier General. Clark was the first to depart for St. Louis and there, the general married and moved into a new home. He invited Lewis to stay with he and his family but the governor refused, not wanting to impose on the Clark's. Instead, he moved in with Auguste Chouteau and took over his duties as governor. He soon found much to dislike about the office, such as sitting behind a desk all day long and dealing with politicians, which he despised. There were abuses with the fur trade and problems with land titles, all of which were brought to Lewis.

In spite of this, he seemed to be the man for the job. He was well acquainted with the Louisiana Territory, an experienced military officer and popular in the city. The closest post office at that time was in Illinois and it took weeks for mail to reach the city. With that in mind, he opened the city's first post office and encouraged newspaper publishers to open in St. Louis as well. This news was met with enthusiasm, but Lewis' early initiatives would not last.

In order to keep the peace and intimidate the Indians, he demanded more money and troops than Washington could afford to send him. War seemed to be coming with England once again, as British ships were seizing sailors on the high seas. Lewis also became involved in several local quarrels and made an enemy of his subordinate, Frederick Bates. A heated argument at a ball one night resulted in Bates humiliating Lewis in public. The furious governor sent Clark to invite Bates to a private meeting. Clark refused to go, convinced that the two men would end up involved in a duel if he did. Bates soon became the governor's tormentor, spreading rumors about Lewis and reporting the mistakes that he made to men in Washington.

Lewis' administration began to fail and as it did, his personal life began to deteriorate as well. Land speculating drained his finances. He became careless about his clothing and his appearance. He began to drink too much, complaining that he was unable to sleep unless he took laudanum. To make matters worse, Thomas Jefferson left the presidency and a new administration took over in Washington. Vouchers that Lewis had signed for medicine for the Indians had been returned unpaid and he went deeper into debt by paying for the bills out of his own pocket. He raved and fumed and wrote angry letters to Washington, becoming so ill with worry that he was confined to his bed. He feared that his loyalty was being questioned and that he was being accused of treason. He wrote letters, vowing that he would not try and separate the Louisiana Territory from the United States and become a traitor.

Such a fear is not as strange as it sounds. Lewis' predecessor had been General James Wilkinson. Although barely remembered today, Wilkinson was famous in his time. Born in Maryland, he had reached the rank of commanding general during the American Revolution. After the war, he sought to make his fortune on the Ohio and Mississippi Rivers and in 1789, became the paid agent for Spain in New Orleans. Wilkinson later became involved with the treacherous Aaron Burr in a plot to make the Louisiana Territory into a separate nation. Lewis must have feared that, as Wilkinson's successor, he would be painted with the same brush.

After consulting with Clark (who advised against it), Lewis decided to journey to Washington and defend himself against charges he believed had been leveled against him. He set out down the Mississippi in 1809, planning to travel by boat from New Orleans to Washington. But on reaching Chickasaw Bluffs, now Memphis, he and his small party heard that British ships were patrolling the Gulf of Mexico. Fearing that he might fall into enemy hands, Lewis decided to make his way to Washington by land instead. He would travel along the Natchez Trace, the rough and often dangerous wilderness trail that was the main overland route of the day. By most accounts, Lewis was in no condition to travel. His companions warned him that his health would not hold for the number of days in the saddle that it would take to reach Washington. Lewis could not be dissuaded though and he purchased two pack mules for his records and borrowed three Army horses for himself and his servants. Major John Neely, the Cherokee Indian agent at the Bluffs, tried to talk Lewis out of the journey but when he failed, he decided to accompany him. They soon set out with Lewis complaining of terrible headaches and a fever.

On October 10, 1809, a torrential rainstorm fell on the party. The pack horses fled into the forest and Lewis' servants went after them. Major Neely begged Lewis to ride to the home of the nearest white settlers on the trail, promising that he would help to find the pack horses and the records they carried. Lewis agreed and the wet and sick man rode to the home of John Grinder, located about 72 miles from Nashville. The house served as an inn to other travelers along the Trace, so Mrs. Grinder graciously opened the door to him, although not before taking her children into an adjoining room. Mr. Grinder was away on business when Lewis arrived. A short time later, the servants arrived with the pack horses and Mrs. Grinder was reassured by their presence. She then prepared a meal for supper.

According to her account though, Lewis ate little. He seemed very agitated and was heard talking to himself. He lit a pipe and then smoked it, pacing back and forth on the front lawn. She said that he ranted about his enemies in Washington. Then suddenly, he would calm down and speak quite kindly to her. She wasn't sure what to think of her famous, yet quite strange, visitor. She prepared a bed for him, but he refused to sleep on it, preferring to make a pallet for himself on the floor with a buffalo robe. After that, Mrs. Grinder retired to bed with her children, but not before sending Lewis' servants to sleep in the barn.

In 1811, Dr. Alexander Wilson told Mrs. Grinder's account in detail. She stated that she was awakened several times that night by the sound of Lewis walking back and forth, once again talking to himself. In the middle of the night, she heard the sound of a gunshot and then the sound of something heavy falling to the floor. This noise was followed by the words, "Oh Lord!"

Immediately after that, she heard the sound of another gunshot and in a few moments, Lewis' voice at her door. He called out to her. "Oh, Madame, give me some water and heal my wounds." Through the chinks in the log walls, she saw him stagger and fall down between the kitchen and the room where Lewis had gone to bed. He crawled for some distance, raised himself up and then sat for a few minutes. He then staggered back to the kitchen and attempted to draw water, but was unable to. Mrs. Grinder refused to leave the room where she had been sleeping and assist him. In fact, she waited nearly two hours before even sending her children to the barn to rouse the servants. They came inside and found Lewis on his pallet again. He had been wounded in the side and once in the head. The buffalo robe that he lay on was soaked with blood and Lewis was barely hanging on to life. He whispered to them. "I am no coward. But I am strong, so hard to die." He died just as the sun was rising over the trees.

Major Neely arrived later that morning. He took charge of Lewis' papers and carried them the rest of the way to Washington. All of the protested vouchers were promptly paid. His journals were turned over to Thomas Jefferson and his records were placed in the care of the State Department. A year later, John Grinder, in whose home Lewis died, was brought before a grand jury and accused of the explorer's murder. The charges were dismissed as no evidence or motive existed for the crime.

Lewis was buried there on the property. The land now exists as the Meriwether Lewis State Park in Tennessee. According to Major Neely and the historians that have followed him, Lewis' death was clearly a suicide. The man had been deranged and drunk and took his own life in the Grinder cabin. But was this really the case? If Lewis did in fact kill himself, then why do so many questions remain? Why didn't Mrs. Grinder come to the man's assistance? Why didn't Lewis' servants hear the gunshots? Were they somehow involved in a crime.. a murder, or a robbery gone bad? Regardless, there were really no eyewitnesses to Lewis' death, as even Mrs. Grinder did not see the shots being fired.

In fact, the belief that Lewis committed suicide rests only on two accounts for his state of mind during his journey. The first account was that of Captain Gilbert Russell, the commander of Fort Pickering at Chickasaw Bluffs. He stated that Lewis was ill when he arrived there and he believed that the governor had been drinking heavily. Others refute this and say that Lewis was not drunk or deranged, but sick from a digestive ailment. However, Russell's statement also went on to say that one of Lewis' party said that he had twice attempted suicide while traveling down the river. Russell claimed to be so concerned that he confined Lewis for five days and kept both liquor and his papers away from him. Lewis seemed to recover and on September 29, he allowed him to leave the fort.

The other account that credits Lewis' death as suicide was that of Major Neely, who accompanied him but then conveniently disappeared on the night Lewis was killed. He stated that the governor was drinking while they traveled along the Natchez Trace.

While most historians accept the fact that Lewis did commit suicide, there have been many who have questioned this. They believe that his death may have been part of a far-reaching conspiracy and that this may be the reason that Lewis' ghost is still believed to walk today!

If indeed the famed adventurer's death was a murder plot, the main culprit behind it is believed to be General James Wilkinson, Lewis' predecessor. In 1804, Wilkinson had conspired with Aaron Burr to create their own "empire in the west" and had tried to extract money and weapons from both Britain and Spain. He even turned on Burr in 1806 and informed Thomas Jefferson of the plot. Burr was brought to trial but was somehow acquitted. Wilkinson too escaped punishment and in fact, even returned to the post of governor of Louisiana after Lewis' death! It has been pointed out that Frederick Bates, who did much to sabotage Lewis' career in St. Louis, was close to Wilkinson and remained in touch with him in New Orleans. It is surmised that perhaps Lewis, who was known for his honesty and integrity, may have discovered new evidence against Wilkinson and planned to use it. It is even believed that this may have been the real purpose behind his trip to Washington and even why he chose to take an overland route instead of journeying by river. Lewis may not have been afraid of British ships in the Gulf, but the fact that Wilkinson was in New Orleans!

Could agents of Wilkinson have pursued Lewis? Some believe so. In fact, Captain Russell at Fort Pickering, who imprisoned Lewis and then testified that he had been drunk and deranged, had been appointed to his position by Wilkinson, as had Major Neely. Could the two men have testified falsely against Lewis after his death? Or more shocking, could Major Neely have actually assassinated Lewis and then disappeared, only to show up at the Grinder house the next morning?

Who knows? This mystery will undoubtedly never be solved.

And perhaps this is why legends persist today that state that the ghost of Meriwether Lewis still wanders the area where he breathed his last. The stories say that on certain nights, the sound of a water dipper scrapes against an empty water bucket and whispered words of "so hard to die" can be heard on the wind near Lewis' grave site. The unsolved mystery of his death still remains and if the rumors and legends are to be believed, so does the great explorer's spirit....

GENERAL CLARK AND ST. LOUIS

Clark eventually followed his lifelong friend, Meriwether Lewis, in the office of governor of St. Louis. Clark was perceived as the best of the "Boston's" who had come to the city and his tenure as governor was seen as a great change for St. Louis. He was happy to see a group of leading citizens form the Court of Common Pleas in July 1808. Their goal was to see St. Louis incorporated as a town under a recently adopted act of the Indiana territorial legislature that provided for such incorporation at the request of just two-thirds of the local citizens. An election of the town trustees was held on July 23, although such an election was a bit premature, as the courts did not vote on the incorporation until November 9. Regardless, St. Louis was never really meticulous about observing authority and this was no different. In 1812, the Missouri Territory was organized with St. Louis as the capital.

The creation of the new territory came at a volatile time in American history. Because of the anticipated war with Britain, General Clark did not want to remain in the governor's office. He planned to serve in the military and so he managed to snag the office for a Kentucky congressman named Benjamin Howard, who would hold the post from 1809 to 1813. Unfortunately though, Clark's dreams of military service never really materialized and he returned to the governorship. He was re-appointed for three terms until Missouri became a state in 1821. His friends then urged him to make a run for the position of the new state's first governor. His heart wasn't in it though and his attempt was feeble at best. His wife was gravely ill in Virginia and his mind just wasn't on politics.

After the election, Clark stayed on in St. Louis, now working as Indian commissioner. It didn't pay as well as the governor's office did, but he was able to make a small profit from the sale of western lands and thanks to his popularity, remained one of the city's leading residents. His patience and easy manner also made him a lot of friends among the Indian tribes and he signed treaties with 29 of them. The British, during the War of 1812, worked to turn the Indians against the American settlements and in 1814, a large expedition was planned to attack St. Louis. The war parties assembled at Prairie du Chien, which is now in southwestern Wisconsin. When word reached Clark, he rode north and his troops were able to easily defeat the British and their allies, only to have them recapture Prairie du Chien while Clark was on his way back to St. Louis. Luckily, the plans to raid St. Louis were never revisited.

In 1815, General Clark, August Chouteau and Ninian Edwards all acted as United States Commissioners to sign a treaty with 19 Indian nations at Portage des Sioux, north of St. Louis on the Mississippi River. This effectively ended the Indian problems for St. Louis and created a policy that Clark would attempt to uphold in the years to come. He believed, as had Thomas Jefferson, that all of the Indian tribes should be settled west of the Mississippi. This would always be Indian territory, he believed, never realizing that in the years to come, the Native Americans would be literally wiped out by the westward movement of the nation.

Some of the Indians were already rebelling against the American policy. Although Black Hawk, the chief of the Sauk and the Fox tribes, denounced the treaties with the white man, he was persuaded to move his people across the Mississippi in 1831. However, as his people faced famine the following year, he re-crossed the river with hundreds of warriors. The Illinois militia turned out against him and Black Hawk was pursued up the Rock River Valley and into Wisconsin. In the slaughter that followed, Black Hawk was captured and was escorted to St. Louis by Lieutenant Jefferson Davis, who was then stationed at Jefferson Barracks. Black Hawk was imprisoned here but allowed a friendship with General Clark, who visited often and brought a number of distinguished visitors to meet him. He also arranged for respected western painter George Catlin to paint Black Hawk's portrait and then sent the chief off on an exhibition tour of Washington and other eastern cities.

After Black Hawk surrendered, no serious Indian fighting took place near St. Louis again. In spite of this, Clark still had to deal with Indian problems. During the period of fur trading, there were many problems between agents of the Hudson Bay Company and smaller companies, as well as with the Native Americans themselves. The biggest problem that Clark faced was with whiskey. It was illegal to trade or sell whiskey to the Indians and in 1832, it even became illegal to take it into Indian Territory at all. Clark's problems came about because the American fur trade had always been based on whiskey. Not only did the Native Americans trade pelts for it, but the traders would often get them drunk and then cheat them into better deals. Clark vowed to stop this shameful practice, but the bootlegging into the region was just too much for him to handle.

Many of Clark's friends were also unsettled by the ban on alcohol and while he hated to see his friends with problems, he was concerned for the Indians as well. He tried contacting the church to send missionaries into the Indian country, but there were none available. He also tried lecturing the chiefs who visited St. Louis on the importance of farming, but he made little progress with that. Gradually though, he did manage to move all of the local Indians westward, still managing to remain quite popular with them in the process. One Indian chief stated that: "When I go to St. Louis, I go to see Chouteau or Clark."

Clark's hospitality was famous with the city's residents as well. When Lafayette visited St. Louis, Governor Edward Bates refused to entertain the French hero because he had not been authorized to do so by the legislature. So, Clark and his friend Chouteau stepped in and organized lodging and a grand ball in his honor. Clark even presented Lafayette with a grizzly bear cub that he tried to turn into a pet. A letter from Paris later confessed failure however. As the animal grew larger, Lafayette told him, he was forced to release it into the Jardin des Plantes, which must have made a strange addition to the local wildlife population!

General Clark's wife and his young daughter, Mary, died in Virginia in 1820. In November 1821, he married Harriet Kennerly Radford, an old family friend. She passed away in 1831 and Clark spent the rest of his life alone, content with his friends and with the military exploits of his son, Meriwether Lewis Clark. The young officer left the military in 1838 and traveled to St. Louis to keep his father company. He arrived a few months before General Clark finally passed on. Clark's magnificent grave site can be visited today in Bellefountaine Cemetery.

The era of William Clark was one of the greatest in the history of St. Louis. There had been many changes in the three decades that had passed since Clark had come to the city to begin his exploration of the Louisiana Territory. He had seen the construction of many churches and buildings, including the cathedral on Walnut Street. He had seen a half a dozen newspapers begin in the city, he saw the opening of the first post office, the arrival of the first river steamer, the beginning of St. Louis University, the first water works and even the first gas lights in 1837.

And it was all just beginning.

BLOODY ISLAND

During the first half of the Nineteenth Century, it was not uncommon for men in St. Louis to settle their differences by dueling. These "affairs of honor" were violent and often to the death. They were carried out covertly, although as long as the fight was considered to be fair, the participants were usually safe from arrest. The quarrels often began in newspaper columns, in speeches, or in off-hand remarks. The duels were seen as a continuation of business or politics and often the negotiations involved in a duel could be more complicated than the quarrel that prompted the affair in the first place.

One of the earliest and strangest duels in St. Louis occurred in 1810 and involved Dr. Bernard G. Farrarr, the city's first American surgeon, and James A. Graham, a young attorney. The doctor's brother-in-law was involved in a dispute over a card game and he asked Farrarr to be his "second". Unfortunately, he failed to appear on the field of honor and left Farrarr responsible for the duel. Under the code, the doctor had to take the other man's place, even though he was not involved in the quarrel and was actually a close friend of James Graham. Both men were wounded in the battle that followed but Dr. Farrarr ignored his own injury in order to treat the wound of his friend. Sadly, Graham died a few days later.

The duel had been held at a place that Charles Dickens called "Bloody Island" in his book *American Notes* in 1844. The Farrarr-Graham affair, and many other duels, took place on an island that was located on the Mississippi River. Neither Illinois nor Missouri claimed it and because of this, it was the perfect place for activity that was considered illegal in both states.

The duel involving Dr. Farrarr would certainly not be the last duel to be fought on the island either. In 1816, Henry S. Geyer fought here against George H. Kennerly, a merchant. Both men were wounded but survived.

One of the most famous duels was fought on the island by the future Senator Thomas Hart Benton. In 1816, Benton was a fiery young attorney in St. Louis and a friend of William Clark and the Chouteau clan. During one of his cases, he argued against a lawyer named Charles Lucas. During the closing statement by Lucas, Benton took something the other man said as a personal insult and challenged Lucas to a duel. Lucas refused, stating that what he had said was simply on behalf of his client during the court case. However, Benton refused to let it rest. He challenged Lucas again and the two men met on the island. When they fired their pistols at one another, Benton shot Lucas through the neck. Although injured badly, he managed to survive.

But this was not the end of the matter. A relative of Lucas began to spread rumors about Benton around town and so Benton demanded that Lucas return to the field of honor. They met again and this time Benton was wounded, but Lucas was dead. The affair was hardly a glorious one but it did not in any way create a blemish on Benton's record. General Clark appointed him a member of the first school board and the Chouteau's made him a director of their Bank of St. Louis. He went on from there to become a Missouri Senator and one of the most important men to ever hail from St. Louis.

In the years that followed, more prominent citizens were engaged in battle on the island and in the region. In 1818, Captain Ramsay and Captain Martin of Fort Bellefountaine met on the island. Ramsay died of his wounds. In 1820, one duelist was hanged for his part in an affair. A man named William Bennett fought the last recorded duel in Illinois with Alphonse Stewart near Belleville. Unknown to the two men, their seconds had agreed to secretly remove their bullets from their guns and bring an end to the quarrel. Bennett discovered this and slipped a ball into his weapon and killed his adversary. This treachery, rather than the duel itself, managed to get him indicted and hanged for his role.

In 1823, another duel was fought between Thomas C. Rector and Joshua Barton, the brother of Judge David Barton, who penned Missouri's first constitution. Rector was the brother of William Rector, who served as the United States Surveyor-General in St. Louis. Barton, who was the U.S. Attorney for Missouri, wrote a letter to the *Missouri Enquirer* newspaper in which he charged that Rector had placed an unusual number of his relatives on the deputy surveyor payroll. Rector challenged Barton to a duel and killed him.

The most celebrated duel of the period though was the one that gave "Bloody Island" its graphic nickname. Once again, a challenge was provoked because of a letter to a newspaper. Major Thomas Biddle was the paymaster at Jefferson Barracks, the military post south of St. Louis. He wrote a letter that criticized Spencer Pettis, a member of Congress and an ally of Thomas Hart Benton and President Andrew Jackson. The President had recently closed down the Bank of the United States, of which Biddle's brother, Nicholas, had been the head. In return, Pettis, who was seeking re-election at the time, published a sharp reply to the Biddle letter. Biddle wrote an even sharper letter in response, but this was not good enough for him. A few days later, he came to Pettis' house, where the congressman was sick in bed, stormed inside and took a horsewhip to him. He continued whipping the man until members of the household pulled him away.

The code of honor called for Pettis to challenge the man to a duel, but Thomas Hart Benton pointed out to Pettis that if he were killed, there would not be enough time to find another candidate to fill the vacancy for the election. He advised Pettis to have Biddle arrested instead and then satisfy his honor after the votes were counted. On the day before the election, the two men were both taken into custody and were released after the polls were closed. Pettis, who won the sympathy vote thanks to his disgraceful beating, was re-elected by a wide margin. For a month after, both Pettis and Biddle attended to business but on August 22, Pettis challenged Biddle to a duel.

They met on the island on August 27. Because of the widespread knowledge of the affair, and the events that led up to it, thousands of people lined the levee and the riverfront housetops to watch the duel. Biddle, as the challenged party, chose the weapons and then the two men lined up with their pistols just five feet apart. Biddle was badly nearsighted and couldn't see much further than just a few feet away. It should come as no surprise that the two men killed one another. Biddle was given a military funeral and Benton paid for an elaborate service for Pettis. This gruesome event was what gave the island its "Bloody" nickname and it would be recorded that way for years to come.

There were other St. Louis duels after this one, both on the island and off. In 1845, two men named Hesterhagen and Kibbe met on Bloody Island and fought with swords. Hesterhagen wounded Kibbe in the face, but both men were able to walk away from the field with their honor satisfied.

In 1849, a duel almost took place between Frank P. Blair and Loring Pickering. Once again, the affair involved politics and Thomas Hart Benton. Blair was a supporter of Benton, while

Pickering opposed the senator. The two exchanged insults in the newspaper and Blair challenged Pickering to a duel. As the challenged party, Pickering had a choice of weapons and he decided to make a mockery out of the quarrel. He gave Blair a choice... they could shoot it out at the corner of Fourth and Pine in downtown St. Louis or they could have a running battle with knives. The two men never met on the field of honor, although they did pass one another on the street one day and starting hitting each other with their umbrellas!

What was probably the last of the Bloody Island duels took place during the Civil War between General D.M. Frost, the commander of Camp Jackson, and Edward B. Sayers, the engineer who laid out the camp. The two men quarreled and rowed out to the island to settle matters on the field of honor. Sayers fired but missed Frost and rather than kill his opponent, Frost fired into the air. By this time, with the entire nation was in the midst of war and such personal bickering must not have seemed nearly as important.

The war marked the end of dueling in St. Louis. It was not the war itself that ended it though, but rather the first effective law against such illegal activity. Laws had been passed against dueling in 1822 (and another was passed in 1835) but no one bothered with them. However, in 1865, a law was passed that stated that if anyone fought a duel, or left Missouri with the intention of fighting a duel, they could not hold public office. As so many duels were fought for political reasons among the members of the upper class in St. Louis, this finally ended the practice.

As for Bloody Island, it ceased to exist as an island just before the Civil War began. The Army Corps of Engineers, under command of an officer named Robert E. Lee, was working on ways to battle the constantly changing channels of the Mississippi River. They placed a dike in the river, causing Bloody Island to attach itself to the Illinois shore, bringing another era in St. Louis history to a close.

THE HAUNTED RIVER

Time passed and eventually eras like that of dueling and the fur trade would die out in the city. Soon though, another era would come along and bring even greater prosperity to St. Louis. It would be this time period when the city would become known as one of the greatest ports of the Mississippi River.

By the 1840's, it was generally realized that the Mississippi was making the city rich. The double-decked, tall-stacked packet boats were turning St. Louis from a wilderness settlement into a city of national importance. There was even idle talk of the city seceding from the Union in order to force the government to move the nation's capital from mosquito-infested Washington to a city that was so easily accessible by riverboat. St. Louis boomed during the 1840's and 1850's and growth was only checked for a brief time by the Civil War.

The first steamboat came to St. Louis in 1817. The *Zebulon Pike* landed at the levee but was later seen as a false start to the new era. It would be years before steamboats would begin successfully navigating the river, not because of business problems, but because of snags and the perils of the river. It flourished only after young James B. Eads of St. Louis devised a clever double-hulled boat for clearing the river of wrecks and other hazards. Still though, the people of St. Louis did not ignore the novelty of the *Zebulon Pike*. Her captain, Jacob Reed, collected one dollar from each of the curious who wanted to come aboard. And many came, although St. Louis would not really become a river port until 1825.

By this time, the westward flow of travelers, settlers and explorers began to swell and all came through St. Louis. The levee was usually tightly lined for at least one mile with packet boats, sometimes stacked two and three deep. Later came the larger boats and the "floating palaces" aboard which guests could eat, sleep, gamble and travel in comfort. Even these fine craft would only have a life expectancy of about five years though. The Mississippi was a dangerous river and in a two year period boasted 103 wrecks around a single bend in the river!

In the early days of steamboating, there were no rules or aids for navigation. Few boats had whistles and there were no signals for passing. There were also no fixed schedules, no load limits and no restrictions on boilers or engines. Steamboat races were also common, creating hazards for other vessels on the river. Even so, the captains of such ships were often urged to race any other steamers they passed. Needless to say, such races sometimes ended in disaster.

The railroad era would later bring an end to the "Golden Age of Steamboating" but not before creating many tales of legends and lore along the river. The river itself has long been considered a haunted place as well, perhaps because of the superstitions of the men who worked along it, or perhaps because the region tends to attract both the strange and the unusual. Many of the stories here concern odd events that cannot be explained, like tales of ghost lights and phantom riverboats.

One story tells of a steamship and a boiler that exploded one night and took the life of a young steersman. The captain of the ship was especially fond of the young man and spent days and nights searching for him in the river and along the banks. After the captain's own death, a ghostly light was said to appear near where the accident took place. The stories say that it is the light of the captain's lantern as he still searches for the body of the crew member.

Other stories tell of a phantom riverboat that has been known to appear all along the Mississippi River. They say that when the boat appears, and its whistle is heard, a river worker will be injured in an accident.

Such tales may be linked to stories of riverboats that literally vanished without a trace along the river. One such steamboat was the *Mississippi Queen*, which cast off from Memphis on April 17, 1873. She was last seen shortly before midnight, about twelve hours after her departure. Then, she disappeared without a trace and the ship, and her passengers, were never heard from again.

Perhaps the most famous "lost" riverboat though was the *Iron Mountain*, a large paddlewheel steamer that was famous on the Mississippi and Ohio Rivers. The steamer was in excess of 180 feet in length and in addition to carrying passengers, towed freight barges as well. The ship's calliope was well known along both rivers and could be heard long before she arrived at a port.

In June 1874, the *Iron Mountain* set off for New Orleans, carrying 57 passengers and towing a string of barges behind her. As she reached midstream and approached a bend in the river, her pilot gave a long blast on the steam whistle. The *Iron Mountain* rounded the bend.... and was never seen again. Her barges were later found, adrift on the river, with their tow ropes cut clean through. No trace of wreckage from the steamer, nor bodies of passengers and crew, were ever found. Hundreds of miles of river bottom were dragged, but without success.

Other riverboats should have seen the *Iron Mountain*, but none of them had. Except for a few deep holes that were thoroughly dragged, there was no water deep enough to have completely covered the huge riverboat. If she had been wrecked or burned, there would have been bodies and debris. Instead, there seemed to be no earthly explanation for the disappearance of the ship.

In more recent times, some researchers have come to believe that the vessel fell victim to river pirates, which were common along the Mississippi in those days. This explanation came about thanks to the stories of strange sounds that have been heard on the river at night. Many fishermen and river workers have claimed to hear screams and cries that seem to come from nowhere. These eerie noises usually include the voice of a woman, who cries out for help in French. When the witness searches for a source for these sounds, one is never found. Those with a taste for the supernatural believe the cries come from a ghostly passenger who vanished with the *Iron Mountain* many years ago. The passenger manifest of the ship recorded several French-speaking passengers on board. The other voices are those of the fellow passengers, it is thought, also calling out for help.

It is believed that pirates plundered, burned and pillaged the boat and robbing and raping the passengers. Their bodies were then buried in the forests along the river. The *Iron Mountain* herself was scrapped and dismantled, with its various sections being hidden where they would never be found. Could the ghostly voices be seeking justice, or even merely rescue, from the other side?

Even locations connected to the river have become regarded as haunted over the years. The former home of riverboat pilot Horace E. Bixby in St. Louis is said to still hold a trace of his presence behind. Bixby was the pilot who taught the young Samuel Clemens to navigate the Mississippi River and he had a townhouse constructed for him back in 1877. The house, which is located in Mississippi Avenue, was damaged by the Great Cyclone of 1896 and was not rebuilt until 1976 by its current owners. Today, the house rests across the street from Lafayette Park, restored to its former glory.

And while the owners say the house is relatively ghost-free, they do admit that the occasional smell of pipe tobacco wafts through the house. No one who lives here, at least among the living, ever smokes. Over the past three decades, the owners have occasionally been greeted by an old-aged tobacco that seems to come from nowhere and then vanishes just as mysteriously.

While no one can really say for sure that it is the ghost of Horace Bixby who makes his presence known in such a way, it's just possible that the old pilot has chosen to stick around and to watch over his old house.

THE MYSTERY OF MARK TWAIN

For those who live in St. Louis today, there is no person who embodied the glory days of the Mississippi River in the way that author and former river man Mark Twain did. Twain was a humorist, curmudgeon and gifted author who created some of the greatest American books of all time, including *Tom Sawyer* and the *Adventures of Huckleberry Finn*. It's no surprise that both of these books are closely connected to the Mississippi.

While most of us are well aware of Mark Twain's adventures, books and humor, many don't realize that the author had a mysterious side as well. Throughout his life, he made a career out of debunking pomposity and arrogance. He was willing to accept things that were "outside the norm", including telepathy, ghosts, prophetic dreams and more. He even became one of the most famous members of the widely acclaimed Society for Psychical Research.

Twain, whose real name was Samuel Langhorne Clemens, was born November 30, 1835 in what he called the "almost invisible town" of Florida, Missouri. He grew up in the small river town of Hannibal, a place that would be made famous through his books. Twain's curiosity about things unknown was awakened at about age 15, when a traveling hypnotist came to town to perform. The magician demonstrated a number of "mind reading" acts that Twain quickly figured out. This incident alerted him to fraudulent claims of the supernatural. While the hypnotist was obviously a fake to Twain, he did believe that he experienced some very real supernatural events in his early years. Just outside of town lived a farmer's wife who had a healing power to cure toothaches. She would place her hand on the victim's jaw and then shout the word "believe!". The toothache would be instantly cured. Twain was present on two different occasions when such miracles were performed. His own mother was the patient in both cases!

Such an experience would be repeated later in life with Twain's future wife, Olivia Langdon, who had become an invalid at age 16. She had become partially paralyzed after a fall on some ice and was unable to leave her bed for nearly two years. After several doctors tried to help the girl and failed, a relative suggested that the family contact an itinerant healer known as Dr. Newton. He prayed over Olivia, put his arm behind her shoulders, raised her up and after a few moments, she took several steps. Until that moment, any attempt to raise her up had brought nausea and fainting spells. Newton said that Olivia would never be totally cured, but that she would be able to walk at least several hundred yards at a time. Twain was grateful for the rest of his life and he married Olivia in 1870. Years later, he asked Newton what the secret behind his power was and the doctor told him that he didn't know. He believed that some subtle sort of electricity emanating from his body might hold the answer.

The death of Twain's father started his career. He had to leave school and he became a printer's apprentice at the Hannibal *Courier* newspaper. He then moved on to the composing rooms at several newspapers, including two in Philadelphia, and then went to become the city editor for the Virginia City *Enterprise* and a reporter for the San Francisco *Morning Cable*. In between, he traveled and worked a variety of odd jobs that enabled him to put his experiences into his work and to be hailed as one of the greatest American writers of all time.

In 1858, Twain became a steersman on the packet *Pennsylvania*, which traveled the Mississippi River between St. Louis and New Orleans. He was under the watch of Horace Bixby, who had agreed to "learn" Twain the more than 1,200 miles of river. It was at this time of his life that Twain had what he considered his more remarkable psychic experience. It was a vivid prophetic dream in which he saw his brother Henry as a corpse, lying in a metal coffin, dressed in one of Twain's own suits and with a bouquet of flowers on his chest. In the center of the flowers was a single red rose. The casket in which Henry had been placed was balanced between two wooden chairs.

When he awakened, he was still dreaming, so to speak. He stated in his book *Life on the Mississippi* that "I dressed and moved toward that door, thinking that I would go in there and look at it, but I changed my mind. I thought I could not yet bear to meet my mother.... it suddenly flashed upon me that there was nothing real about this - it was only a dream..."

Not long before, Twain had found a job for his brother on the *Pennsylvania* and the two men were very close. Usually, Henry would join Twain's watch when his own duties ended for the evening. However, this was not to be on this trip. Twain's dream took place in a room in New Orleans, where he had remained ashore. As the *Pennsylvania* had departed back upstream without him, he had advised his brother to not lose his head in the event of trouble. "Leave that to the unwisdom of the passengers," he told him. He urged him that after seeing to the safety of the women and the children, he should swim for shore himself.

Two or three days after the boat had departed from the New Orleans dock, the boiler of the *Pennsylvania* exploded. Twain managed to reach Memphis a short time later and found Henry near death, lying alongside the rest of the wounded. The details of the story are related in Twain's classic book, *Life on the Mississippi*, but in short Henry died from an accidental overdose of morphine that was given to him by an inexperienced doctor. His funeral costs were arranged thanks to the generosity of the ladies of Memphis, who had taken up a collection for the victims of the disaster. All of the deceased were laid out in coffins made from white pine, however Henry's casket had been made from metal instead. When Twain walked into the room where his brother's body was placed, he found him in an open coffin, wearing a suit of Twain's own clothing.

He immediately remembered his dream!

Just then, an elderly lady walked past him and placed a bouquet of roses on Henry's chest. The flowers were snow-white in color... except for a single red one in the center of the bundle.

Twain went on to tell of one more incident concerning this dream and its startling result. When several men took the casket to his brother-in-law's house in St. Louis and were carrying it upstairs, Twain stopped them from taking it in. He didn't want his mother to see Henry's face, as it had been badly distorted by the overdose of the drug. When Twain did go upstairs, he discovered that two chairs had been placed as a stand for the casket. Had he arrived a few minutes later, the coffin would have been in the same place as in his dream. When he stopped the men outside, he had changed the prediction of the dream.

As a result of this strange experience, Twain developed an interest in the paranormal. He was constantly intrigued by what he called "thought transference" and claimed to often speak aloud the very thoughts that his wife was having. He was also interested in the fact that he would often receive unplanned letters from friends after merely thinking of them or the subject of the letter they might write.

One example of this occurred between Twain and the Virginia City journalist William H. Wright. The Nevada silver boom was in the news and Twain's publishers felt that it was a good time for a book on the subject. Twain thought of Wright as the man to write the book and on March 2, drafted a letter to him, urging him to write the book and making several suggestions for an outline. The thought them occurred to him that if the book was written at his suggestion, then no publisher wanted it, he would be in an uncomfortable position with his friend. So, he decided not to send the letter and stuck it away in his desk.

A week later, on March 9, several letters arrived in the mail for Twain and one of them was from William Wright. Twain told a visiting relative that he could tell them the date, signature and the subject and all "without ever breaking the seal". He explained that it would be from "a Mr. Wright of Virginia City, and it is dated the second of March - seven days ago. Mr. Wright proposes to make a book about the silver mines.. and asks what I, as a friend, think of the idea".

Twain then opened the letter. He had stated the date and the contents correctly and found that it reflected the contents of his own letter, written on March 2, which had been in his desk since it had been written.

Not long after that, Twain joined the Society for Psychical Research of London in 1885. Soon, his interest in the occult deepened even further with the death of his daughter, Susy, at age 24. She had spent the last two weeks of her life in pain and delirium and eventually went blind and fell into a coma. After her death, Twain relived each terrible memory and constantly blamed himself for her suffering. His biographer, Justin Kaplan, wrote that he "searched for some sign that before she died, she had him in her thoughts, spoke of him in pride or love. 'I wonder if she left any little message for me', he wrote Livy (his wife) imploringly. "I was not deserving of it'. He wanted everything of her last days kept, even the agonizing pages she wrote in her delirium and with the light fading."

After Susy's death, Twain's wife retreated into full invalidism, staying in her room and avoiding her husband's own black despair. She lost interest in her friends and began to immerse herself in Spiritualism, a faith that believed in communication with the dead. Twain began to share her interests and while he attended a number of seances, never became convinced that he personally contacted the dead. His bleakness deepened as the years went by, until his family and friends all avoided his ranting and gloomy moods. Living in mourning and seclusion, he treated his surviving daughters like royalty and each holiday that came around was celebrated as a remembrance of Susy. He often dreamed that she was still alive and in his declining years, questioned the difference between dreams and reality, especially after his encounter with what he called "an apparition".

He was standing on his front porch one afternoon and saw a man that he wished to avoid walking up to the house. "He was a stranger," Twain said, "and I hoped that he would ring and carry his business into the house without stopping to argue with me; he would have to pass the front door to get to me, and I hoped he wouldn't take the trouble. To help, I tried to look like a stranger myself - it often works".

Twain did his best to ignore the man, but was looking straight at him when he got to within 10 feet of the door and disappeared! "I was unspeakably delighted," Twain recalled, believing that he had seen a ghost with his own eyes. He was then determined to write an account of it for the Society of Psychical Research. He examined every inch of ground around where the man had been walking and realized that there was no way the visitor could have vanished by natural means. Twain decided that "he was an apparition, without the slightest doubt". Very excited, he opened the door and went into the house, only to find the man sitting in a chair in the foyer! Somehow, he had gotten into the house and he was a flesh and blood visitor after all... not a ghost! Twain's own interests in the occult had turned the man into "an apparition". After that, Twain's belief in spirits came and went, although he never lost his interest in the psychic world.

The author's dark days of brooding did not last. His life had always run in cycles of success and despair. He began lecturing again and wrote his book on Joan of Arc. Then, in 1904, his wife Olivia passed away from heart trouble. He once again sank into grief and despair, only to revive again and begin writing and lecturing once more. He wrote a paper on a hypothetical experiment with "Mental Telegraphy" in which a man was to invent a scheme that would synchronize two minds, thousands of miles apart, enabling them to talk to one another. He was unhappy with the article and burned it, along with many other writings on the occult. He would not write such a book on the subject, he said, unless it "would write itself". He stated that he would ignore such writings but that when he was asleep, new ideas would him. However, most of these works were never completed.

In 1907, Twain received a cable from England, informing him that he was to receive an honorary degree from Oxford, which would join his other degrees from Yale and the University of Missouri. He traveled to Europe but by 1909, his health was beginning to fail. He returned to Stormfield, his house in Redding, Connecticut, where he was staying with his youngest daughter, Jean. He then traveled to Bermuda, where many of his friends and acquaintances, including Woodrow Wilson, came to visit him. He returned to America strengthened and with a new interest in astronomy. He remarked to his friend Albert Bigelow Paine that "I came in with Halley's Comet in 1835. It will be coming again next year and I expect to go out with it."

In that year of 1909, Twain suffered the last of his great losses when his daughter Jean died from heart failure caused by an epileptic seizure. In her biography, *My Father, Mark Twain*, his daughter Clara notes a strange incident that followed Jean's death. Her father wrote her that "for one who does not believe in spirits I have had a most peculiar experience". He explained that as he entered the room where Jean had died, something very odd happened. "You know how warm it always is in there, and there are no draughts. All at once I felt a cold current of air about me. I thought the door must be open; but it was closed. I said: 'Jean, is this you trying to let me know that you have found the others?' Then the cold air was gone."

A short time later, Twain's health collapsed and he became gravely ill. He never lost his sense of humor though, despite his lack of breath and the fact that he was in constant pain. Four months after Jean's death, on April 1, 1910, he died at the age of 74. His last words to Clara were "Goodbye dear, if we meet...."

And his final prediction had been correct. He came in with Halley's Comet and he did "go out" with it, just as he planned to.

FIRE, PLAGUES AND DISASTERS

While the steamboat era brought wealth and prosperity to St. Louis, it also brought darker elements to the city as well. For the first time, crime truly began to be a problem on the darkened city streets but sometimes the threat to the city came in other forms.

On the evening of May 17, 1849 a fire was discovered about the steamboat the *White Cloud*, which was tied up at the foot of Cherry Street. It was soon out of control and while the boat was cut loose from her moorings, she soon began to drift into other vessels, spreading the blaze along the riverfront. The city's volunteer firemen responded quickly to the alarms but by the time they arrived, more than 30 boats were on fire. The heat was so intense that they were forced to fall back and to try and protect the stores and warehouses along Front Street. But it wasn't enough... the fire managed to jump to a building at the corner of Front and Locust and then spread rapidly along Front Street. Strong winds pushed the fire on, sending it westward to Main Street and then to Second. The fire jumped Second Street at its intersection with Olive and then the wind turned it southward, toward the Cathedral. Sparks scattered into the air and set fire to an old barrel maker's business three blocks away and burned two city blocks.

The fire's devastation called for extraordinary measures. Blocked from access to the river water, the firemen had only primitive fire engines and little water to speak of. The captain of the Missouri Fire Brigade, Thomas B. Targee, had a desperate idea to stop the fire. He proposed that they blow up buildings to create a firebreak and not only save the Cathedral, but halt the fire in its path. The other volunteers agreed and a wagon was sent to the United States Arsenal on the south edge of the city. It returned with a load of gunpowder and delivered it to the corner of Third and Market Streets. A tarpaulin was thrown over the barrels to keep them from being ignited by sparks and volunteers were sought to carry the gunpowder into the buildings that were marked for demolition.

Targee was one of the volunteers and he successfully destroyed three of the buildings. Then, he picked up another keg of powder and entered Phillips' Music Store on Market Street. He had just passed through the door when there was a horrific explosion. It is believed that perhaps someone had already placed a barrel inside of the store and Targee was killed. His was one of three lives lost in this fire. The flames also wiped out 33 riverboats and 430 buildings, including the post office, three banks and several printing shops. A dozen city blocks were reduced to smoldering rubble and the fire of 1849 became the worst to ever occur in the United States until the Great Chicago Fire more than two decades later.

To add to the destruction, the fire took place during the worst of the city's cholera epidemics. It was not the first such epidemic though, that outbreak came in October 1832 and it raged for more than five weeks, killing hundreds. The epidemic that occurred in 1849 was even more tragic, killing an estimated 4,317 St. Louis residents. "It was proclaimed in a thousand forms of gloom, sorrow, desolation and death," reported the *Sketchbook of St. Louis* in 1857. "Funeral processions crowded every street. No vehicles could be seen except doctor's cabs and coaches passing to and from cemeteries, and hearses, often solitary, making their way towards those gloomy destinations."

While cholera had been around for centuries, the plagues of the 1800's apparently began in India in 1816 and had spread to the Near East and Russia by 1830. Over the course of the next two years, it ravaged Europe and then came to the Americas by ship, reaching New Orleans and eventually St. Louis by steamboat.

By June 1849, the city was in a state of panic. An emergency meeting at the courthouse established a Committee of Public Health and allowed them almost unlimited powers to impose rules and regulations and curfews and to impose fines for their violations. They established hospitals in each of the city's six wards and appointed doctors to serve in them. The committee also named "block inspectors" and put them in charge of cleaning out the city.

On Saturday, June 30, heaps of stone, coal, tar and sulphur were burned at every street intersection. It was hoped that the smoke from these concoctions would "dissipate the foul air which has been the cause of so much mortality." On Monday, July 2, the city held a day of prayer and fasting, but to no avail. The epidemic would continue for almost another month.

At that time, there was no clear cause for the cholera outbreak, but in later times, it has been realized that the city's water supply was likely to blame. A quarantine had been placed in effect against all steamboats from the south and while the boats may have been responsible for bringing the illness to the city, they didn't spread it to the residents. While thousands died all over St. Louis, there was not one case of cholera reported among the students at St. Louis University, then located at Ninth and Washington in one of the worst cholera areas in the city. The university drew its water from wells that were apparently uncontaminated and because of this, a source for the spread of the disease has been surmised.

A view of the destruction from the Great Cyclone of 1896 in St. Louis

While the fire and epidemic of 1849 were truly terrible events in St. Louis history, the single deadliest incident to befall the St. Louis area occurred on May 27, 1896 when a tornado tore through the south side of St. Louis, creating a ten-mile path of destruction. Within 20 minutes, 137 people died in St. Louis and 118 more were killed across the river in East St. Louis. The tornado destroyed 311 buildings, heavily damaged 7,200 others and caused harm to 1,300 more. The loss, including the destruction of riverboats, was thought to be as much as $12 million dollars at that time.

In those days, most of the city's residents lived within a few miles of the downtown river landing and the area struck by the tornado was heavily populated. The "Great Cyclone", as it has been called, arrived after three weeks of violent storms that had pummeled the country. For most of April and May, temperatures and humidity had been well above normal and earlier on the morning of the storm, newspapers had reported thunderstorms that had flattened crops in Missouri's "Boot Heel" and had swamped a riverboat near Cairo, Illinois. The forecast for the day called for "cloudy weather, favorable for local thunderstorms".

The Great Cyclone was actually part of a series of tornadoes that struck from central Missouri into southern Illinois, but it was the deadliest. The Weather Bureau office in St. Louis reported a total of 306 people who were killed, including six people about 100 miles west of St. Louis and 13 more in New Baden, Illinois. In St. Louis County, one child died when a tornado struck a farm house south of Clayton.

The St. Louis tornado touched down near the current site of the St. Louis State Hospital on Arsenal Street in the southwest part of the city. In 1896, this was the site of the city's poorhouse, women's hospital, old people's home and the insane asylum. The storm tore away roofs and porches and knocked down walls on several buildings. Miraculously, only eight people in this area were hurt.

After striking here, the tornado then turned and raced across Shaw's Garden (now the Missouri Botanical Gardens) and created more devastation just south of Tower Grove and Vandeventer Avenues, where the Liggett & Myers Tobacco Co. was erecting a large building complex. Many of the workers were still high atop the building when the tornado hit and were buried beneath steel, wood and stone.

The tornado then headed uphill toward Compton Heights. Nearly every house in the area lost its roof and in some neighborhoods, especially to the east toward Jefferson Avenue, houses were completely destroyed. Whole blocks of homes and buildings lost their upper floors and walls were ripped away and reduced to splinters.

As it reached Jefferson Avenue, the neighborhood around Lafayette Park was laid waste. The area of homes around the park was quite upscale in those days and prosperous businesses lined Jefferson Avenue, south of Chouteau. Two of the city's cable car systems, which moved cars along underground cables, had their power plants and shops here. The tornado swept in and wreaked havoc. The cable car companies were crippled, churches and homes were destroyed and all but a few of the trees in the park were snapped off at the trunk. City Hospital, just east of the park, also suffered great damage. Another miracle occurred here as well, for out of the 400 patients housed here, only one was killed outright. Two others died a few hours later, including one woman who was said to have "died of fright".

Further east, the Soulard neighborhood was the scene of greater horror. Buildings were wiped away by the tornado and one area, now a dark parking area beneath the Interstate 55 viaduct at the corner of Seventh and Rutger Streets, was called the "vortex" by newspapers of the time. This was the deadliest spot in the tornado. At this location, 14 people died as the three-story Mauchenheimer tenement collapsed into a pile of wood, stone and rubble. Among the victims were the building's owner, Fred and Kate Mauchenheimer, who ran a tavern on the ground floor and a seven year-old girl named Ida Howell. She died in the arms of her mother, Alice, and next to the body of her father, John Howell.

The storm continued on. It curved just south of downtown, although it was still strong enough to tear the roofs from downtown buildings and to break windows. It crossed the river along a line from the St. Louis approach to the current MacArthur Bridge to the East St. Louis approach of the Eads Bridge. There were 16 boats in the harbor that day and all of them were wrecked.

The tornado knocked away a portion of the Illinois approach to the Eads Bridge and then tore through the rail yards and warehouses on the Illinois side. It devastated three locomotive roundhouses, the riverfront grain elevator and four freight stations, killing 35 depot workers. The railroad hotels were also destroyed, although beneath the remains of the Martell House, a maid named Mary Mock survived for two days and was found by rescue workers.

The catastrophe of that day has never been equaled in St. Louis history and its lingering memory can still be felt in the city today. There is no doubt that the effects of the Great Cyclone of 1896 are still reverberating and it will doubtless be mentioned again in the pages ahead.

GROWTH AND COMMERCE

By the 1850's, St. Louis was meeting the expectations of its founders in terms of its growth and prosperity. The fur trade was just winding down, having made a fortune thanks to the European demand for fashionable beaver hats. The steamboat era was in full swing and other businesses were arriving in the city and providing employment and opportunities for the residents. The small frontier settlement had truly become a city and new buildings were being constructed on a steady basis to meet the demand for commercial property and housing. And as there had been no real planning since Laclede's original grid for the city, buildings were erected wherever the owners wanted them to be. St. Louis had become the prominent city of the Mississippi Valley and the structures being built needed to maintain this reputation.

The status of a city was often mirrored in that city's hotels, as first class accommodations were needed to attract businessmen and upscale travelers to the area. Several fine hotels were built in St. Louis during the first half of the Nineteenth Century, including the Southern, the Lindell, the Virginia and the Barnum. Perhaps the most extravagant though was the Planter's House.

The first hotel to bear this name opened in a wood framed building on the riverfront in 1817, where it remained until 1840, when a new hotel was planned. It was financed through the investments of private citizens like Pierre Chouteau, James Lucas and others and was started in 1837 at the corner of Fourth and Pine Streets. It was a classic and dignified building with shops and offices on the ground level and four flights of rooms. There was a large main dining room, three additional restaurants and a grand ballroom with details that were copied from the Temple of Erectheus in Greece. The Planter's House Hotel was one of the finest in the west and rooms cost an unsightly $4.25 per person, per day, which included meals. It was expensive but most agreed that it was well worth the price.

Land owners from the north and the south enjoyed the setting and brought their families to stay for the winter months. Famous visitors could often be found in the dining room and parlors. They included Abraham Lincoln, Andrew Jackson, Henry Clay, William F. Cody and even Charles Dickens. The British author was quite critical of St. Louis in his *American Notes*, but he wrote kindly about the Planter's House.

The hotel continued as the leading establishment in the city until 1887, when it was badly damaged by fire. It was closed down and the remains demolished to make room for a new, and even grander, Planter's House in 1891. The new hotel was financed in an unusual way. At that time, St. Louis was in the running for becoming the host for the Columbian Exposition and city leaders secured $5 million dollars in pledges for the fair and an additional $1 million for entertainment. When the event went to Chicago instead, the group decided to award a $1 million bonus to any person or company who would build a first class, fire-proof hotel in the city instead. Investors quickly appeared and the old site of the Planter's Hotel became the new site for its replacement.

The 400-room hotel was constructed in a Renaissance style and built into an inverted "E" shape to allow natural light in every room. The exterior of the building was granite with beige-colored bricks and trimmed stone. A magnificent front portico, made from cast iron, was added to the building and it was graced with Ionic columns.

The interior was perhaps the most elegant in the city. The lobby rotunda was huge and the walls were lined with colored marble.

The Third Planters House Hotel

(Courtesy Missouri Historical Society)

A grand staircase stood at one end, guarded by a large, bronze lion. At the base of the steps, a pair of bronze ladies held aloft glowing lamps. There was simply nothing to compare to this place in all of St. Louis.

The main restaurant was decorated with Doric columns and enhanced with Empire green and silver. There was also a Ladies Dining Room, various meeting and banquet rooms and a "Turkish Den" that was arrayed with Moorish designs, low slung furniture, tapestries and Persian rugs. It was almost like stepping into another place and time. In addition, the main saloon became a favorite meeting place for local politicians, business leaders and visitors. The huge bar was designed in a semicircle and it was here that bartender Charles Dittrich invented a lime, lemon and gin drink he called a "Tom Collins". It was named for a regular and favored customer in the saloon. Dittrich was not the first bartender here to invent a drink still enjoyed today either. One of his unnamed predecessors invented "Planter's Punch".

The new Planter's House thrived until World War I and then its popularity slowly died out. The hotel finally closed its doors in 1922 and it was converted to use as an office building until 1930. It was then named the Cotton Belt Building until it was torn down in 1976.

Another famous hotel in St. Louis, perhaps more because of its designer than the mark it left on the city, was the New St. Nicholas Hotel, which was located on North Eighth Street. It was designed by the famed architect Louis Sullivan and like the two other Sullivan buildings in St. Louis, the Union Trust Building and the Wainwright Building, it was considered a marvel of modern construction in 1893. Unlike other buildings of the time, a steel frame was used in the construction. The hotel also boasted terra cotta detailing and round-arched entrances, which were common in Sullivan designs. The hotel was considered so impressive that in 1895, it was designated at the meeting place for the American Institute of Architects.

Unfortunately though, the hotel was damaged in a 1905 fire and the owners decided to convert it into office space. They retained an architectural firm to oversee the changes and by the time they were done, little of Sullivan's original design remained. The property was re-named as the Victoria Building. The building was finally destroyed in 1973 and only a few pieces of Sullivan's terra cotta were saved.

Interestingly though, readers with an interest can find a remnant of Sullivan's wonderful work in St. Louis preserved today in an unlikely place. Located in Bellefountaine Cemetery is the tomb of the Wainwright family, for whom Sullivan also designed a building in downtown St. Louis. The tomb is located in the back part of the cemetery, along what has been dubbed "Mausoleum Row", and it is a square-shaped building with a rounded dome on the top. No name appears on the exterior of the tomb and Sullivan designed it this way for a reason. He believed that if no name were on the outside, then visitors to the cemetery would come to the door to see who was interred within. You see, the interior of the tomb is an amazing design created completely from small mosaic tiles. It is breathtaking to see and readers are encouraged to stop by for a visit. The door to the mausoleum is opened on most mornings by the cemetery staff.

Not surprisingly, many hotels gain a reputation for being haunted. The history of a hotel can boast literally thousands of visitors in a given year and occasionally, some of these visitors just may leave a piece of themselves behind. Stories of the day stated that the ghost of the Southern Hotel was almost as well known as the hotel itself. This restless spirit was apparently that of a guest who died in one of the rooms. Occasionally though, the ghosts who have appeared in St. Louis hotels have had nothing to do with events that have occurred in the building.

In 1876, a salesman from Boston was spending the night at the Pacific House Hotel in St. Louis. He was in the city on business and to visit his parents, who resided here. During the night, the ghost of his sister awakened him in his bed. She had died from cholera in St. Louis during an epidemic a few years before. The man stated that the image of the girl was so vivid that she appeared to be solid and very much alive. She materialized for a number of seconds and was so clear that the salesman was able to see a long scratch or a mark that creased the side of the young woman's face.

The salesman was so startled and shaken by the encounter that he told it in great detail to his parents at breakfast the following day. As he told of seeing his departed sister, his mother suddenly burst into tears. She confessed that she had accidentally scratched the girl's face while preparing her body for the funeral and had used makeup to cover it up. She had been the only person who knew about this, thus convincing her son that he had truly experienced a meeting with his dead sister!

Another hotel in St. Louis, and one that is very much a part of the city today, has been rumored to be inhabited by a ghost for many years. The Chase-Park Plaza Hotel on North Kingshighway was long said to be home to a red-haired ghost who haunted one of the suites. Although a spokesperson for the hotel denied the story in 1980, the tales were still being told several years later.

In 1985, a woman named Alice Dawes, who was the administrative assistant to the General Manager of the hotel, spoke about one of what may have been several ghosts at the Chase-Park Plaza. The first reported sighting of the ghost was in 1979 when a visiting businessman returned to his room one night after a dinner meeting. He was staying in Room 304 at the time. He opened the door and came inside, tired and tense from a long evening, and spotted a woman standing at the window of his room and looking outside. He described her as being attractive and red-haired but he had little patience for what he assumed was an eccentric guest. He picked up the telephone and called the front desk, demanding that security have her removed from his room. As he stood there with the telephone in his hand though, the woman abruptly vanished!

A few minutes later, a security officer and night manager arrived at the man's room to escort the woman out. The shaken businessman managed to stammer out an account of what had happened and he insisted on being moved to another room. The manager obliged him, although privately he and the other staff members surmised that the man had been caught in an embarrassing situation and had invented the story of a "ghost" in order to extricate himself from it.

At least this is what they believed until a short time later, when other guests repeated the story! A short time after the businessman's encounter, a prominent (although unnamed) film star and his wife were in town on promotional tour. They stayed at the Chase and were given Room 304, which is in a more private corner of the building. On the first night of their stay, the actor and his wife were suddenly awakened by the feeling that "someone was in the room". They looked up and at the foot of the bed saw a red-haired woman in a white gown drift past the window and vanish through the door. She never opened it either, but simply "melted right through it". Frightened by their shared encounter, they quickly dressed and went down to the front desk to report what they had seen. Suddenly, the story told by the businessman didn't seem quite so suspicious!

Another encounter occurred in Room 304 involving a writer from Los Angeles who was visiting the city for a few days. One night, he retired to his room, locking the door behind him, and went to bed. During the early morning hours, he was suddenly awakened by the strange feeling that he was not alone. He turned over and as soon as his eyes adjusted to the darkness, he saw a beautiful red-haired woman appear near the bed. She crossed the room and then vanished through the locked door. The writer was startled and thought of reporting the incident, but then decided to just dismiss it as a dream.

The next night when he returned to his room, he carefully searched it to make sure that it was empty. Then, he looked to be absolutely positive that the door and the windows were locked up tight. He turned out the lights, but this time he did not go to sleep. A little later, the apparition from the previous night appeared once again. The red-haired woman in the white gown looked just as she had the night before. She smiled faintly, crossed the room and then vanished once more through the locked door.

This time, the man knew that he had not been dreaming, so he quickly slipped into his clothes and went down to the front desk. He told the staff member on duty what had happened but the desk clerk calmly assured him that he was not the only woman to see the red-haired ghost. There had been others, although no one had any idea who she was or why she seemed to be haunting the room.

More recently though, sources that have appeared to dispute these stories, even to the point that the room number has changed from 304 to 302. According to these reports, the red-haired woman was not a ghost at all, but rather the mistress of one of the hotel's executives. Apparently, this young woman would meet her lover in Room 302, which adjoined through a kitchen in the next suite of rooms. The occupants would hear a noise and would look up to see this woman. They assumed she was a ghost because they had no idea how she could have gotten in or out of the room!

Was this really the case, or a convenient explanation to dispel the ghost stories? Who knows? While the explanation certainly makes sense, it doesn't actually reveal how the red-haired woman could "melt" through locked doors!

Progress came to St. Louis in other ways than just first rate hotels too. In 1836, a group of 25 of the city's leading merchants became unhappy with the disorganized trade practices on the levee and formed a new organization called the Chamber of Commerce. They quickly gained new members and brought about order by adopting commissions on buying and selling and by establishing rates for steamboat agents. They remained loosely organized until 1848, when they merged with the Miller's Exchange and became the Merchant's Exchange. In 1855, they bought five parcels of land, which included frontage on Main Street, and built the first Merchant's Exchange Building. A new building was later constructed at Third and Pine Streets and added a convention center to the city. In 1876, the Democratic Convention was held here in the grand hall. The convention nominated Samuel Tilden, who won more votes than his opponent, Rutherford B. Hayes, who won the presidency by one electoral vote.

The Grand Hall, inside of the Merchants Exchange

The grand hall was also the site for the first Veiled Prophet Ball in 1878, a white-tie affair that continues in a different form even today. Succeeding balls were held here until 1900. The entire building was magnificent, but the grand hall was the most admire section of the structure. The hall was 235 feet long and 98 feet wide. It was lined with 62 windows and the ceiling was decorated with three frescoes depicting the natural products of the Mississippi Valley and the four corners of the Earth. Exchange members met daily to sell grain at marble-topped tables and business was conducted from an ornate, black walnut podium.

In the 1880's, the grand hall was further enhanced by the addition of a fountain, complete with statues and water sprites. It remained in the middle of the trading floor until 1903, when it was removed for additional space. It was later taken to Fountain Park.

In 1957, the Merchant's Exchange, which was by then the oldest grain market in the United States, decided to move its headquarters and the building was sold to the Pierce Corporation. Rather than restore the building, they decided to demolish it instead. The Missouri Historical Society, and other preservationists, bemoaned the loss of the building but the company refused to be swayed. Artifacts began to disappear from the building and later ended up in St. Louis homes, restaurants and bars. In 1958, the Exchange building was finally destroyed. The site was sadly used as a parking lot until construction began on the Adam's Mark Hotel.

In 1850, the United States Congress voted its first appropriation for a new Post Office and Custom House in St. Louis. At that time, it was the largest building project west of the Mississippi River and was the site of all federal business in the Mississippi Valley during the Civil War and for many years after. The project was one of great controversy in the city. The government selected a site for the building at Second and Chestnut Streets, which was close to the business district and designed to strengthen commerce here. However, Thomas Hart Benton and other powerful men believed that a more westerly location, at Third and Olive Streets, would better. A third group of men, led by James Clemens, argued for a location at Second and Carr Streets because they believed the city would grow to the north. After intense fighting, the Third and Olive Streets site was chosen.

The Post Office and the Custom House was completed in 1859 and the building was a huge presence in the Third Street business district. The Greek Revival style building was fitted with a projecting portico that was supported by six Corinthian columns, making it an eye catching and important part of the streetscape. The building was used as a post office and a custom house and facilities for the Federal Courts. These courtrooms became famous as the site of the "Whiskey Ring" trials during the second Ulysses S. Grant administration.

The scandal began in St. Louis as a well-organized conspiracy that had been designed to fight against what was seen as a Liberal Republican threat. However, it quickly became a huge money-maker for those involved, including William McKee, the owner of the *Globe Democrat* newspaper, a number of high ranking officials in the Internal Revenue Service, the St. Louis Collector of Revenue, and even President Grant's secretary. In all, 213 indictments were handed down, bringing to trial the ring leaders, distillers, those who examined local whiskey, various politicians and those who affixed the federal revenue stamps on whiskey bottles.

The St. Louis Post Office

An investigation revealed that three times more whiskey had been distilled in St. Louis than was shown on Treasury reports and that the government had been cheated out of more than $4 million dollars between 1873 and 1875. The money had ended up in the pockets of those involved in the scandal. The trials garnered national attention and resulted in the loss of the distillery industry in St. Louis. Most of the companies either moved their business to Kentucky or went out of business altogether.

Such activity brought attention to the fact that the building was too small and almost immediately a new site was chosen on Olive Street, between Eighth and Ninth, for a larger post office. This also created problems as the new location diminished the role of the riverfront district in the business community and also pushed close to a fashionable residential area. Regardless, construction was started and completed in 1884.

From that point until after the turn of the century, the old Third Street building housed the United State's Appraisers Office, the Marine Hospital Service, the Pension Examiner's Office, the Army Recruiter's Office and the Assay Office. In later years, it also saw service as a warehouse.

In 1939 though, the building was scheduled for demolition to make way for the Jefferson National Expansion Memorial Project. Various suggestions were made, asking that the building be used as a museum or cultural site, but the National Park Service disagreed. They announced that they would renovate and save the Old Courthouse, but there was not enough room for both. Later that year, the old Post Office was torn down. Three of the large Corinthian columns, which had not only served the Post Office and Custom House, but the old St. Louis Theatre as well, were moved to the Laurel Hill Memorial Gardens. They were all that remained of one of the city's most historic sites.

The post-Civil War decades were a time of unprecedented growth, industrial expansion and urban development in America. Mark Twain and Charles Dudley Warner dubbed this era in 1873 when they published a satirical novel called *The Gilded Age - A Tale of Today.* The book mocked the material success of the time by exposing the greed and corruption at its core. People overlooked the satire behind the term however and only saw the glittering wealth and prosperity on the surface. It became a time of great growth and expansion and nowhere was this as evident as in St. Louis.

During the Civil War, trade had been restricted on the river and now city leaders viewed the postwar period as a time to promote the revival of the riverboat era and to promote St. Louis over its rival city of Chicago, which has also been impeded by the war. New buildings began to appear as monuments to commerce and government, along with religious and cultural structures as well.

St. Louis was once again on its way to greatness.

SAWBONES AND SCALPELS

St. Louis is considered today to be one of the outstanding medical training centers in the United States. Over the years, dozens of medical schools have flourished here, along with many excellent hospitals, but not since Dr. Joseph McDowell's college was closed just before the Civil War has there been another school like his. It was a place where wild rumors, lurid stories and tales of the owner's eccentricities were often told.

And unfortunately most of those stories were true.

But McDowell's Medical College was not the only one to appear in the days of Old St. Louis and he was far from the only doctor to serve the city. In the 1840's and 1850's though, medical schools and doctors were not afforded the respect they are given today. A surgeon at that time might have been jeered in the street as "old sawbones" and dissection of the dead for medical teaching was not seen as kindly, nor as understood, as it is in these more modern times.

On one occasion in 1849, the medical school at St. Louis University came under attack, thanks to malicious rumors that were being spread about abuses and cruelties being carried out in the dissection rooms. It was a prank that finally set public opinion against the school when parts of a cadaver were left out on a table in a yard adjoining the building. Someone spotted them over the high wall and soon a menacing crowd had assembled on Washington Avenue in front of the university. Some of the bolder rioters even broke into the building and furniture, books and instruments were destroyed and damaged. When word spread of the mob, Irish and German Catholics quickly gathered to defend the college. Bloody fighting broke out and was only stopped thanks to the cool head of Judge Bryan Mulanphy. He mounted his horse and rode into the street between the two factions until the violence stopped. He appealed for order and despite cries that the mob attack other medical schools instead, the crowd slowly dispersed.

The first doctor had come to St. Louis with the first settlers. Dr. Andre Auguste Conde had been posted to Fort de Chartres in Illinois but when the region was surrendered to the British, he accept Laclede's invitation to the new outpost on the other side of the Mississippi. He practiced in the city from 1766 to 1776.

He was followed by Dr. Antoine Francois Saugrain, who came to America on the suggestion of his friend, Benjamin Franklin. He settled in Ohio and then came to St. Louis in 1800 after a promise from the Spanish governor's office to build a small hospital for him here. He was not only a doctor, but a botanist as well. He planted a large herb garden and used the plants to treat many of the illnesses that plagued the early settlers. He was later instrumental in getting St. Louis residents vaccinated against smallpox. After an epidemic broke out, he rallied the newspapers and other doctors into spreading the word about vaccines. He even paid for medicine for "persons in indigent circumstances, Indians and paupers."

The first American doctor to settle in St. Louis was Bernard Farrar, who also became involved in one of the city's earliest duels. He came to the city from Virginia and he first gained his excellent reputation as a doctor from stories spread by a man named Shannon, a member of the Lewis and Clark Expedition. On another exploration trip, Shannon was shot by a Blackfoot Indian and was brought back to St. Louis. He was near death when he arrived here. Although he was considered hopeless, Dr. Farrarr amputated his leg and nursed the man back to health. Shannon recovered and went on to become a judge in Kentucky. He never forgot what the doctor had done for him and he praised the man until his dying day. Sadly, Dr. Farrar died during the terrible cholera epidemic of 1849, contracting the dreaded disease while nursing those who had been afflicted with it.

Another American doctor who died during the epidemic was William Carr Lane, the city's first mayor. The respect of his patients earned him nine successive terms in office. He was the first to organize a public health system.

The establishment of the Jefferson Barracks military post brought many army doctors to the city. Among these was William Beaumont, who after 20 years in military service set up practice in St. Louis in 1834. Beaumont became famous for his groundbreaking studies into the human digestive system. How these studies came about is the oddest part of the story. While serving in the military near the Canadian border, Beaumont treated a man named Alexis St. Martin for a gunshot wound to the abdomen. The wound refused to close, so Beaumont took advantage of the opening to study the man's digestive system. St. Martin lived with the doctor for years and Beaumont conducted a lengthy series of experiments, becoming known as the doctor who built "a window into a man's stomach." He became one of the founders of the medical school at St. Louis University and became its professor of surgery. This school went out of existence within a few years though and the present-day school can be traced back to the foundations under Dr. Charles Alexander Pope.

The city's first modern hospital was established by the Sisters of Charity in 1828 on Spruce, between Third and Fourth Streets. John Mullanphy, who provided a convent for the nuns in 1827, built a new four-story hospital in 1832, which became known as St. Louis Hospital. In 1874, the hospital was moved to Montgomery Street near Grand Avenue, and in 1930 to North Kingshighway. About 20 years after the original hospital was established, the Sisters persuaded Dr. Louis Boisinliere to come to St. Louis and help them in opening the first lying-in hospital and foundling asylum in the United States. Dr. Boisinliere became the city's first coroner in 1858.

Construction of the first city hospital was started in 1840 on a site bounded by Lafayette and Carroll Avenues and 14th and Grattan Streets. It opened in 1846 with 90 beds available for patients. It went on to become the center of a number of hospitals near the business district, including the Robert Koch Hospital for contagious diseases and the Homer G. Phillips Hospital that was originally built for only African-American patients. The hospital was later desegregated thanks to the efforts of Dr. Robert Elman, a professor of surgery at Washington University who trained many black doctors.

Today, the hospitals in St. Louis set the standard for health care in the United States and the medical schools here rank among the finest in the country. But it wasn't always this way and some of the doctors who left their mark on the city can be described as "eccentric" at best.

One unusual doctor was Ernst Schmidt, who was one of the co-founders of the Humboldt Medical College. Dr. Schmidt was a professor of anatomy and at the outbreak of the Civil War, he immediately joined one of the St. Louis regiments, the Second Missouri, with the rank of major. He was expected to provide medical care for all of his 1800 men, but was only given $66 for supplies and equipment. Frustrated, he concocted a plan to find bandages and supplies with his men and then decided to hold up a train! They went to the outskirts of the city and stopped a train that was loaded with passengers. He and a group of soldiers climbed aboard and stripped the passengers of their money and valuables, all the while explaining that it was a forced "levy for war purposes". He used the money to then purchase the much-needed supplies. In 1879, Schmidt ran for mayor of Chicago against Carter Harrison on the Socialist-Labor ticket after having refused both the Republican and Democratic nominations. He was defeated but seven of his partisans were elected to the city council.

But as unorthodox as Dr. Schmidt may have been, there was no St. Louis doctor stranger than that of Dr. Joseph N. McDowell.

The McDowell Medical College was founded in 1840 as the Medical Department of Kemper College. The head of the medical school was Dr. Joseph McDowell and it became the first to be successfully established west of the Mississippi. McDowell's school remained connected with Kemper College until 1847, when financial problems forced Kemper to drop the program. At that point, McDowell struck out on his own and constructed a building to house the school at Ninth and Gratiot Streets, overlooking Chouteau's Pond. This would become one of the most notorious buildings in the city and later would even become a Confederate prison during the Civil War.

The notoriety of the building though was often overshadowed by the notoriety of the school's founder. Joseph McDowell was considered to be one of the finest doctors of his day. His eccentricities aside (and there were many!), he was thought of as an excellent physician and a very capable surgeon in a city where medical standards were high. Many graduates of other medical schools in St. Louis would attend lectures at the McDowell school as part of a graduate course. He came from a distinguished medical family as his uncle, Ephraim McDowell, was known as the first doctor to successfully perform an ovariotomy.

In spite of this, it was McDowell's personality traits that got him talked about in the city. He was described as having "an erratic temperament that approached insanity" and he was often said to be horribly jealous and suspicious of other doctors and schools. He was also an ardent secessionist and believed strongly in the rights of the southern states and in the institution of slavery. While well known for being generous in his treatment of the poor and the sick, he was also known for his hatred of immigrants, colored people and Catholics. He would lecture on those subjects at street corners to anyone who would listen. McDowell made a habit of wearing a breastplate of armor, believing that his enemies might try and kill him at any time.. and perhaps he was right on that count!

Dr. Joseph McDowell & his notorious medical school (Courtesy Missouri Historical Society)

The building on Gratiot Street was erected to McDowell's specifications. It was designed with two large Greek Revival wings and was flanked by an octagonal tower. The tower had been fitted with an unusual deck around which six cannons had been placed to defend the school against possible attack. One of the cannons was said to have once been the bow piece on the deck of Jean Lafitte's pirate ship. He also kept the school stocked with muskets that could be handed out to the students during the possible attack. During patriotic holidays, McDowell would pass out the rifles and march the students into the field along Seventh Street. After a short speech, he would give the command to fire off the guns and to set off the cannons in the direction of Mill Creek. The staff and students at the Christian Brothers College next door always made a hasty retreat when they saw the medical students assembling on the lawn.

The building had other unusual elements as well. The central column of the tower had niches that were intended to hold the remains of the McDowell family members after their deaths. The bodies were to be placed in alcohol-filled copper tubes. The building also included a dissecting room, a chemical room, a lecture hall, a laboratory and a dispensary where the poor were treated for free. There was also a rooftop observatory and offices for the doctors on staff. It had also been fitted with an anatomical amphitheater that was 75 feet in diameter and 52 feet high. It was equipped with six large gothic windows to let in natural light.

McDowell also opened a museum that contained more than 3,000 specimens of birds and animals from North America. There were also minerals, fossils and antiquities too, all of which could be viewed for a 25 cent admission. The clergy and medical men were admitted for free.

While the building was equipped with all of the latest medical facilities, there were no living quarters at the school and students were expected to live in the boarding houses of the neighborhood. McDowell had invested $150,000 of his own money into the school and it became the largest building devoted exclusively to medicine in the United States. This attracted an eminent faculty to the school, including Dr. William Carr Lane, St. Louis' first mayor. Students were required to complete two years of study in order to graduate but when compared to modern medical study, it fell far short. In fact, it was so inadequate that it was possible for students to graduate without ever having cared for an actual patient.

McDowell was especially known for his surgical skills and he emphasized anatomy in his classes. This forced the students to take part in human dissection and it would be this practice that would bring notoriety to the school and the building. In those days, it was nearly impossible for medical colleges to get bodies for research because dissection was against the law. To obtain bodies for study, McDowell was forced to introduce the art of "body snatching" to St. Louis, although he preferred to refer to he and his student's night time forays into the city's cemeteries as "resurrectionist activities."

No matter what the good doctor called it though, local residents were horrified when they discovered just what was going on behind the walls of the college.. and where the fresh cadavers were coming from! For the most part, the school was superstitiously avoided as a haunted place, but occasionally, the more courageous citizens could be stirred into mob action. The disappearance of a German immigrant woman started a riot at the McDowell College when rumors spread that she had been killed and turned into a medical specimen. Everyone knew that McDowell hated immigrants and so it was not a big step to think that he may have killed one! The woman was later found though, wandering the streets of Alton, Illinois in a demented state.

The dispersing of mobs was another good use of McDowell's cannons and muskets. On one occasion though, he actually loosed his pet bear into the crowd. The mob scattered quickly and the bear returned unharmed to his lair in the college's basement. The animal actually lived there until its death of natural causes some years later.

But it would be an incident involving one of McDowell's stolen corpses that would change his entire attitude about the possibility of ghosts and life after death. The incident so unsettled him that he turned away from his religious upbringing as a strict Calvinist and became an ardent Spiritualist instead. At one time, McDowell was an outspoken critic of anyone who believed in ghosts or other "such frauds without foundation", but that was before the spirit of his dead mother saved his life!

Apparently, a German girl who lived in the neighborhood died of an unusual disease and McDowell and some of his students became determined to steal the body for study in the lab. They managed to make off with it and hid it away at the college. News spread of the theft and many of the local Germans became angry and vowed to break into the school and find the body.

"I received a note at my house," Dr. McDowell later wrote, "warning me that the visit was to be that night." Quickly, the doctor went down to the college to hide the body. When he arrived all was quiet and he went into the dissecting room with a light. He lifted the girl's corpse onto his shoulder, planning to carry it to the attic and conceal it in the rafters, or perhaps to hide it in a cedar chest that was out of sight in one of the closets.

"I had ascended one flight of stairs," he continued, "when out went my lamp. I laid down the corpse, and re-struck the light. I then picked up the body, when out went my light again. I felt for another match in my pocket, when I saw distinctly my dear, dead mother, standing a little distance off, beckoning to me."

McDowell said that he saw her rise up a little in front of a window and then vanish. Shaken, he walked close to the wall and climbed to the attic, where he hid the body away. He came back downstairs in the darkness and when he reached the window, he saw two Germans talking. One of them had a shotgun and the other carried a revolver. The doctor eased down the staircase and when he got to the door of the dissecting room, he looked down the stairs into the hallway below. There were another five or six men there and one of them was lighting a lamp. "I hesitated a moment as to what I should do," wrote McDowell, "as I had left my pistols in the room where I took the body. I looked in the room, as it was my only chance to get away, when I saw my spirit mother standing near the table from which I had taken the corpse. I had no light, but the halo that surrounded my mother was sufficient to enable me to see the table quite plainly."

Suddenly, footsteps sounded on the staircase below and McDowell darted into the room. He lay down on the table where the girl's body had been and pulled a sheet up over his face. The men came into the room to look for the dead girl among the other bodies that had been placed there. Sheets were lifted from the faces of the corpses and when they passed the table where McDowell lay, one of the men even remarked: "Here is a fellow who died in his boots... I guess he's a fresh one."

"I laid like marble. I thought that I would jump up and frighten them," he stated, "but I heard a voice, soft and low, close to my ear say 'be still, be still'."

The group of Germans searched the building, but they never stumbled onto the body of the girl and did not discover they were not alone in the college. Finally, McDowell heard their boots stomping down the steps and outside. He waited for a few minutes and then beat a hasty retreat himself.

After that, McDowell's newfound respect for the spirit world often affected the decisions he made and the ideas that he came up with. Of pressing concern to him were the eventual deaths of his family. He hated to think of their decay after death, so he planned to have them encased in copper tubes and installed in the niches of the medical school's tower when they died. Later though, he tried to have the bodies placed inside of Mammoth Cave in Kentucky in hopes that the cool air of the cave might preserve them. He settled on a cave closer to home though.

He purchased a cave near Hannibal, Missouri and it was here that the body of his 14 year-old daughter was taken at the time of her death. She was placed inside of one of the alcohol-filled tubes and hidden away in the cave. In his book *Life on the Mississippi*, Mark Twain mentioned the cave and its curious occupant. He stated that "there is an interesting cave a mile or two below Hannibal. In my time, the person who then owned it turned it into a mausoleum for his daughter, age 14. The body was put into a copper cylinder filled with alcohol and this was suspended in one of the dismal avenues of the cave".

Unfortunately though, his daughter did not rest here in peace for some of the locals pried the iron door off the cave and often went inside to peer at the girl as a curiosity. Perhaps because of this, McDowell purchased a mound across the river, near Cahokia, when his wife died and had a tomb for her built atop it. It was said that he would sometimes watch the tomb with his telescope from a cupola on top of his home.

At the beginning of the Civil War, McDowell's son, Drake, joined the Confederate Army under the command of General Meriwether Jeff Thompson. He took two of the school's cannons with him. McDowell had already shipped the 1,400 muskets that he had collected to the south in boxes that were labeled "polished marble". After that, he also went south to serve the Confederacy as medical director for the trans-Mississippi Department. McDowell survived the war and after traveling and lecturing in Europe, returned to St. Louis.

In November 1861, General Henry Halleck took over as a commander of the Union Army's Department of the West, headquartered in St. Louis. He converted the McDowell Medical School into a prison for captured Confederate soldiers and this will be discussed further in a later chapter.

After the war ended, the prison was closed down and McDowell returned to start up his school again. He renovated the entire building but left one room just as it had been during the prison days. He referred to it as "Hell" and in it he placed a rattlesnake, a crocodile, statues of Satan and a gallows, where an effigy of President Lincoln was left hanging.

Dr. McDowell died from pneumonia in 1868 and the college was left vacant until it was demolished in 1882. The site is now located on one of the back lots of the Ralston- Purina Company. During the years when it was abandoned though, many came to believe that the place was not empty at all, as the Civil War left its mark on the building in more ways than one...

As for McDowell, his body turned out to be safer than those that came into his grasp ended up to be. He was buried in Bellefountaine Cemetery, next to the graves of his family, including his wife from the tomb near Cahokia and his daughter, who was retrieved from the cave near Hannibal and finally laid to rest.

Whether or not the crumbling ruins of the college were haunted or not is a question to be addressed later in the book, but there is little question about the fact that many hospitals (abandoned and otherwise) do become haunted. Based on the number of people who die in these facilities each year, it is no wonder that ghostly tales are often told of patients who refuse to leave the rooms where they died. Needless to say though, there are few hospitals that will own up to such stories. Understandably, this is not exactly good advertising for a hospital and it not the type of rumor to attract new patients. Would you care to be admitted to a room from which the last occupant has not yet departed?

Many hospital stories are not quite so chilling though. In fact, some hospital ghosts can be actually kind and compassionate, like the ghost who has long haunted one of the hospitals in the St. Louis area. Unfortunately, the name of the hospital shall not be printed here, as the story was told to me in confidence. Suffice it to say that the hospital is located here in the city and it has been always been regarded as one of the finest in the city.

According to staff members and nurses at this particular hospital, the place boasts a "haunted" maternity ward. It has been reported that patients who come to the floor to give birth often have encounters with the resident ghost. Strangely though, they have no idea that the person they encountered was no longer among the living! The stories say that as women are leaving the hospital with their new babies, many of them will often stop one of the nurses on their way out and ask that they pass on a message for them. They ask that the nurses please tell the kindly nun who works the overnight shift how much they appreciated her kindness. They state that the Sister stayed by their bed at night, holding their hand and offering them blankets and ice chips. Many say that they "could not have gotten through the night without her."

In reply, the nurses always say that they will pass along the message to the nun the next time that they see her. What they don't mention though is that they never actually see this woman. In fact, the nursing staff has not seen her in nearly four decades because the nun that the patients describe died in the early 1950's!

As far as staff members here can tell, the unknowing patients are encountering the spectral presence of a nun who was a fixture at the hospital year ago. She was assigned to the maternity floor and she always worked at night. She became a favorite among the patients, and among the staff as well, and was sorely missed when she passed away. Or so it would seem... It now appears that she has stayed behind at the hospital, still bringing care and comfort to those who need her.

But not all of the presences left behind in St. Louis hospitals are so benevolent. Some of the presences might even be described as "evil", like the one that remained in a room at the old Alexian Brothers Hospital for many years. But that is a story that will be told later on in the book...

Other presences though are nearly as frightening. For years, tales of strange sounds and apparitions have circulated about the now deserted State Hospital complex on Arsenal Street. Many credit these odd happenings to the ghosts of former patients at the insane asylum that operated here.

For many years before its closing, the hospital was great overcrowded. Author Ernest Kirschten wrote that over 3,000 patients were crammed into quarters meant for just 1,500 and that the place was admittedly a "firetrap". The hospital came into existence at a time when insane asylums were less to provide treatment for the mentally ill and more to keep them away from the rest of us. Strait jackets, cages and even chains and shackles were commonly used to restrain the inmates. The overcrowded conditions, poor hygiene, lack of funds and decaying buildings often created situations where patients were sometimes inadequately cared for and even abused.

During the Great Cyclone of 1896, one of the locations that saw destruction was the State Hospital. It was said that the screaming of the inmates was even louder than the ferocious winds that rocked the building. The entire roof of one building was blown off and the tower on the main building was completely destroyed. It crashed down through the structure and carried the stone and the wood with it through three floors and into the basement.

Eight of the inmates here received wounds from flying glass and brick, but their injuries were not serious. Several of the attendants were also cut. The greatest damage occurred at what was called the "dead house". It was completely demolished from the wind and the two corpses that had been laid out here vanished into the storm.

Considering these horrific events, combined with normal daily life at the asylum, it is little wonder why some of these disturbed spirits might wander in confusion after death. More likely is the fact that hauntings that have been reported here have more to do with impressions from the past. These so-called "residual hauntings" seem to occur when traumatic events of the past somehow leave a mark on the atmosphere of a place. The events then seem to repeat themselves over and over again throughout the years. Such a haunting might explain the inexplicable sights and sounds of the old hospital.

In recent years, security guards that have been on duty at the site say that they have heard the sounds of screams coming from the abandoned wards. However, when they search the buildings, they find them empty. Some guards even claim to have seen shadowy figures prowling around in the dark corridors. When investigated though, the areas where the people have been seen are always silent and still.

Do inmates from the past still walk this place?

A CITY IN CHAINS

Although slavery was widely practiced in Missouri, and in St. Louis, there were never very many slaves in the city. Most of the slaves in the state could be found within a few miles of the Missouri River, in a section of counties that was sometimes called "Little Dixie". Here, the planters and farmers often found themselves at odds with the city workers and with those who had little use for the institution.

For the most part, St. Louis saw slavery as a "necessary evil" and, like Abraham Lincoln, believed that it would eventually die out on its own. Even in the early days of the city, the law regarded slaves as property, but the Church discouraged their sale. The first French priest even baptized the black children living in the region. The condition of many a slave was eased by allowing him to "hire his own time". This permitted him to take a job, provided that he paid a small amount of the money that he earned to his owner. Some owners allowed the slaves to purchase their freedom with these earnings. Fines and punishments were seldom regarded as cruel and slaves were entitled to a trial by jury as early as 1811. There were balls and entertainments that were given by Free People of Color and slaves were usually allowed to attend.

The largest number of slaves at any one time in St. Louis was likely around 1,500. There was little to be gained by owning slaves in the city. Slaves could sometimes be hired out as dock or warehouse workers, but with no fields to tend, they were mostly used as domestic servants. The city claimed to be an industrial and commercial community and there was little work to be done by slaves.

St. Louis accepted the Missouri Compromise of 1820, which made Missouri a slave state and Maine a free state, to avoid any further delay in being admitted to the Union. And while the city did not embrace slavery, it did not welcome the frenzy of the Abolitionists either. The city seemed content to honor the ideas of Abraham Lincoln, who in 1860 stated: "We must not interfere with the institution of slavery where it exists". Still though, in the years prior to the Civil War, the people and the politicians were not blind to the tragedy of slavery. They looked on in shame on New Year's Day, when the courts disposed of the assets in their charge, and saw slaves being auctioned off from the Courthouse steps. St. Louis was increasingly aware by this time that the question of slavery was a force that was dividing the country and Missouri was in a unique position. Although technically "neutral" during the war, it was inhabited with pro-South residents and western men for whom the Union was everything. This made for a volatile situation during the war and occasionally, before the war ever began.

Some historians would say that a man named Dred Scott was the first to legally address the question of slavery in 1846. His court case would go on to become one of the most famous cases in America and it all took place here in St. Louis.

Born in Southhampton County, Virginia, Scott was owned by a man named Peter Blow. In 1830, Blow and his family moved to St. Louis and brought Scott with them. When Blow died two years later, Scott became the property of Blow's daughter. She eventually sold him to Dr. John Emerson, an Army surgeon stationed at Jefferson Barracks, for the sum of $500.

Later, Dr. Emerson was transfered to Fort Armstrong in Rock Island, Illinois and Fort Snelling in Minnesota. In 1836, while in Minnesota, Scott met Harriet Robinson, another slave, and the two of them were married. In 1838, Dr. Emerson was sent back to St. Louis and while en route to Jefferson Barracks, the couple's daughter, Eliza, was born. Their second daughter, Lizzie, was born in St. Louis.

In 1843, Emerson died and he left the Scott family to his widow, Irene. On the advice of two sons of Peter Blow, Taylor and Henry, Dred Scott decided to sue the widow for his freedom. The Blow's believed that Scott's years in the free states of Illinois and Minnesota had earned him the legal right to his freedom. Scott entered a petition to the court in 1846 and the following year, his case was heard at the St. Louis Courthouse. Scott and his lawyer, Francis Murdoch, argued for the man's freedom, but they lost the case.

In 1850, Scott took the case to court again and this time, he won. However, his victory was short-lived for Irene Emerson appealed the court's ruling and it went to the Missouri Supreme Court. In March 1852, they reversed the lower court's ruling and Scott lost his freedom once again.

By then, Irene Emerson had re-married a Massachusetts physician and had moved to the east coast. She transferred her ownership of Scott to her brother, John Sanford. But Scott was not yet finished. He and his new attorney, Roswell Field (father of author Eugene Field), sued again in federal court, but lost once more. When they sought a second federal trial, their case was denied. In a final attempt to gain his freedom, Scott appealed to the United States Supreme Court. Montgomery Blair, a leading Washington lawyer, acted as Scott's attorney. The Court, dominated by staunch southern sympathizers, heard the case in March 1857. The nation's highest court ruled that Scott's birth as a slave negated his rights as a U.S. citizen and for that reason, he had no right to sue anyone in federal court. At the same time, the court declared that the Missouri Compromise was unconstitutional, opening the way for slavery in all of the remaining territories in the west. From that point on, public opinion both for and against slavery began to escalate into violence, eventually leading to war.

Scott's case was dismissed and shortly after the decision, John Sanford returned Scott to Taylor Blow, the son of his original owner. Taylor freed Scott on May 26, 1857. Unfortunately though, he died just over a year later in September 1858. Dred Scott was buried at the Wesleyan Cemetery at Grand and Laclede, but when it closed down, his remains were moved to Calvary Cemetery. His grave can still be seen there today and is marked with a short inscription that reads, "In memory of a simple man who wanted to be free."

As already mentioned, St. Louis had few uses for slavery, but it had even less use for the

Abolitionist movement in America. There was little severity against slaves until the owners felt compelled to protect their property against the "abolitionist slave snatchers." They had no interest in stirring up the problem and creating an issue out of something that would eventually wear itself out, as slavery undoubtedly would. In the 1830's and 1840's, St. Louis was busy building a city. The residents were not interested in a nation-rending crisis. There was simply too much to do. The problem of slavery, they believed, could be worked out gradually.

When Elijah P. Lovejoy came to St. Louis in 1827 to teach school, he was welcomed by the citizens. In the years to come however, this fiery young man would wear out his welcome with not only the slave owners in the city, but with the Catholics and the moderates in St. Louis as well. Lovejoy, they realized, was there to stir up trouble.

Elijah P. Lovejoy was born in the town of Albion, Maine on November 8, 1802. He graduated from Waterville College in 1823 and then moved west to St. Louis four years later. For a short time, he taught school and wrote for a Whig journal called *The Times* and for the *Missouri Republican*. Lovejoy began to make a name for himself as a writer and many felt that he could go far as a politician. Surprisingly though, a short time later, he converted to Presbyterianism and attended the Princeton Theological Seminary. In 1832, he was licensed to preach but instead, returned to St. Louis and began a religious newspaper called the *St. Louis Observer*. Articles with an anti-slavery bent began appearing in the newspaper in 1834 and, despite warnings from a number of prominent citizens, continued to appear into 1835.

Hard feelings against the abolitionist movement were strong in St. Louis. None of the moderates wanted trouble, but the slave owners had other concerns. Rumors began to spread throughout the city that abolitionists were plotting to encourage a slave rebellion in St. Louis. Free blacks were watched closely with both suspicion and fear. Then, in October 1835, things took a turn for the worse for Lovejoy. Reports surfaced that claimed that two Illinois men had helped several slaves from St. Louis escape across the Mississippi River. This was followed by the first threat against Lovejoy's printing press. Only a mass show of force discouraged the mob from destroying his business.

In November 1835, Lovejoy picked another target in his war of words against slavery, the Catholic Church. Not surprisingly, this led to another furor in the city but Lovejoy also found himself with a surprising number of allies. Many people in the city, who had no interest either way in the slavery question, quickly stepped up to defend the rights of Lovejoy. As far as they were concerned, the freedom of speech and the freedom of the press protected the publisher's interests in these matters. These supporters were able to curb the violence in the city, but they were not able to eliminate the opposition against Lovejoy. Editorials and speeches against him were common and some even came from his own church. Prominent Presbyterians in St. Louis claimed that he was damaging the reputation of their church in the city and stirring up trouble where none had existed before.

In February 1836, Lovejoy took his strongest position yet against slavery in a scathing editorial in the *Observer*. He wrote "Our creed is that slavery is a sin... now, heretofore, hereafter, and forever, a sin... Consequently, it follows that whoever has participate, or does now participate, in that sin, ought to repent without a moments delay."

After announcing this position, the newspaper remained quiet on the subject, and as a result, Lovejoy, his wife, Celia, and their new son, were able to enjoy a few months of peace. In April, they traveled to Pittsburgh for a meeting of the assembly of the Presbyterian Church.

When the Lovejoy's returned to St. Louis, they found the city in the midst of a racially inspired panic. Francis McIntosh, a black cook on one of the riverboats, had intervened during a fight between two of his friends and two police officers. His friends escaped but McIntosh was arrested for assaulting the two officers. As the officers were walking him to the jail, he was informed that he would be punished by 25 or 30 lashes, which didn't sit well with the cook. Rather than submit to the punishment, McIntosh decided to escape. He produced a knife and in the scuffle that followed, managed to kill one of the officers and wound the other.

The cook was quickly re-captured and taken to the jail, but soon a mob formed, looking for their own brand of justice. The crowd quickly overcame the few defenders at the jail and hauled McIntosh out into the street. He was chained to a tree and a fire was started at his feet. The mob watched and cheered as the flames roared up around him. No one responded to his pleas when he begged someone shoot him and spare him the painful death of the fire.

Lovejoy walked to the scene the next day and found the body of McIntosh still chained to the tree. Rocks had been thrown at him and his head was missing. Lovejoy was outraged and quickly returned to his office and wrote a fiery editorial about the incident. Not long after, Lovejoy and his family returned to Pittsburgh. The editor was consumed with guilt over the fact that his abolitionist stance may have played a part in causing the violence to erupt. While he was away from St. Louis, vandals broke into the offices of the newspaper several times and heavily damaged his printing press.

Lovejoy realized that he was finished in St. Louis. The city would no longer tolerate him and he could not subject his family to the violence that seemed to be coming. He sent his wife and son to her mother's home in St. Charles and made plans to move his newspaper to Alton, Illinois. His last editorial in St. Louis was aimed at the city leaders and produced a mob of over 200 people at his office. A smaller group of 20 men broke down the doors to the print shop and wrecked the place. Somehow, the printing press itself was not harmed.

He arrived in Alton in late July 1836. He sent for his family with the hopes that the free state of Illinois would provide a better environment for his abolitionist work, but that was not to be.

On Sunday, July 23, a steamboat called the *Palmyra* delivered Lovejoy's printing press to the Alton docks, even through it was contrary to Lovejoy's explicit instructions. He was unwilling to have the press moved on the Sabbath, so it was left on the Alton wharf until morning. Shortly before dawn, a group of men who were reportedly from Missouri, wrecked the press and dumped it into the river.

And this would not be the last. Lovejoy would have other presses while in Alton, but it is the story surrounding the arrival of the fourth printing press which is still told, and some say re-lived, today.

On the afternoon of November 7, 1837, a boat arrived in Alton carrying Lovejoy's fourth printing press and it was taken to a warehouse on the river, belonging to Godfrey, Gilman and Co.. Lovejoy and a number of his friends gathered at the warehouse with guns to defend the press but the day passed without incident. Later that night though, a mob gathered outside of the warehouse. Most of them were intoxicated and they called loudly for the press to be surrendered to them.

Once that demand was refused, they tried a different approach and used rocks to shatter the windows of the warehouse. Several members of the mob waved guns and Lovejoy, or someone inside the building, fired their own weapon through a broken window. One of the men outside crumpled to the ground and the mob was enraged. They stormed the warehouse, intent on revenge.

Someone placed a ladder against the building and climbed to the roof, a burning torch in his hands. Lovejoy ran outside with a pistol and ordered the man to come down. Before he could fire his own weapon though, several men in the crowd opened fire on the editor and he was hit five times. He fell to the ground, crying out, "My God, I am shot!", and died in just moments. After he fell, the defenders inside of the warehouse surrendered. The mob pushed their way inside and broke the printing press into pieces, then flung them into the Mississippi River.

Lovejoy's body was left in the warehouse overnight. The next day, on what would have been his 35th birthday, a grave was hastily dug on a high bluff and the body, without a proper ceremony, was thrown into it and haphazardly covered up. Some years later, this spot was chosen as a place for a cemetery and in 1852, when a road was set to cross over Lovejoy's grave, his body was exhumed and moved to another location. Today, a fine monument stands in tribute to fallen abolitionist and while he is highly regarded in these less troubled times, his death was never avenged.

Along the banks of the Mississippi River in Alton, Illinois is the place where the old warehouse once stood that held the printing presses of Lovejoy's abolitionist newspaper. It's hard to recognize the spot these days, as it is little more than a space between two large grain mills at the base of William Street. As the years passed, the warehouse was replaced by grain mills and all trace of it has vanished.... or has it?

According to those who live on the nearby bluffs and those who are natives of the area, the martyred Lovejoy may not rest in peace. The legends say that his spirit may still roam the waterfront in despair. Others claim that the spirits of that night in November do not walk, but the terror experienced here has left an impression on the area that still reverberates today. Many who have visited the location claim to be able to feel the madness of the crowd, the desperation of Lovejoy and his friends and the energy pulsing through the entire incident.

And Alton, Illinois is not the only location associated with the Lovejoy family, or at least their lingering spirits. The other location is a place on the other side of the river in St. Charles, Missouri. It is called Lindenwood College and it was founded as the first college for women west of the Mississippi River.

There are several ghost stories associated with the school but one in particular has long been attached to Elijah Lovejoy. In years past, residents, students and faculty members have reported the unexplained sounds of horses galloping and the sobbing sounds of a woman that seem to come from nowhere around Sibley Hall at the college. It is believed that these sobbing sounds belong to the ghost of Elijah Lovejoy's widow, Celia Lovejoy. The Sibley's were close friends of the Lovejoy family and had offered the Reverend refuge on many occasions when his enemies plotted against him. After his death, Mrs. Lovejoy came to stay with the Sibley's for short time at Lindenwood.

It is believed the impression left by her grief and outrage, both of which she undoubtedly suffered during her visit, may "echo" today and may be the eerie source for the sobbing sounds.

While it may seem that St. Louis was hardly filled with staunch abolitionists in the days before the Civil War, there were those who did actively fight against slavery. There were also a number of people involved in the Underground Railroad, a secret system of homes, farms and buildings where escaped slaves could hide while traveling to the north or to free states. The "Railroad" used these "stations" as safe houses and those who helped the slaves to escape or provided shelter for them were often referred to as "conductors".

One such St. Louis personage was Reverend Artemus Bullard, a Presbyterian and Congregational minister, who started Webster College in 1850. The centerpiece of the campus was a large stone building called the Rock House. The stories had it that the building served more than one purpose, as Reverend Bullard was closely involved with the abolitionist movement. In fact, he was even related by marriage to two of the most famous opponents to slavery, Henry Ward Beecher and Harriet Beecher Stowe, who authored the book *Uncle Tom's Cabin*. On the surface, the Rock House was nothing more than an institute of higher learning, but in the basement was rumored to be a "safe house" for slaves who had escaped via the Underground Railroad.

For many years, there was said to be an escape tunnel, several blocks long, which offered an exit from the Rock House in case the slaves were discovered. The story went on to say that the entrance to the tunnel was sealed off in the 1890's after two children from became lost in it and died before they could be rescued. This legend of a tunnel was considered to be nothing more than a story until the late 1980's, when reports claimed that the passageway had actually been uncovered.

Sadly, Reverend Bullard was killed in the same disaster that claimed the life of Henri Chouteau and many other eminent citizens of St. Louis. In 1855, he was a part of the group that plunged to their deaths in the Gasconade River disaster. The train that they were riding on caused a weakened bridge to collapse, carrying the passengers to their doom.

After Bullard's death, Webster College closed down and the Rock House became an orphanage, merging from time to time with other orphanages. During the Civil War, it was refuge for soldier's orphans with children from both the Federal and Confederate Armies sharing rooms, beds and meals. After the war, the place took in other children too, like those from refugee families and those who were orphaned by cholera and other epidemics. Later, during the Great Depression, the orphanage took in poor children whose parents could not care for them and those left homeless during the tragic economic times. In those years, it was known as the St. Louis Protestant Orphan Asylum. Finally in 1943, the name was changed to the Edgewood Children's Center and today the campus is a residential treatment center for disturbed and troubled children who have been victims of abuse and often horrific circumstances. With the addition of new dormitories, classrooms and buildings, children no longer live in the Rock House. It is still used today as administration offices for the center.

From the 1940's until the late 1980's, a number of strange occurrences were reported on the school's campus. It was said that many staff members, who happened to look outside the window of the Rock House in the early morning, were startled to see a girl playing under a huge, cottonwood tree that grew there. While this might not seem unusual in a place filled with children, this little girl was certainly different from the other children, who were still in their beds at such an hour. This child, who was perhaps nine or ten years old, was reported to hover a few inches off the ground! She would then float around the tree and then vanish!

According to Ralph Lehman, who was the director in the late 1980's and had been for more than 20 years, several different staff members independently reported seeing such an apparition. And, Lehman added, this was not the only unusual activity revolving around the Rock House.

Between 1968 and 1980, staff members at the center actually lived in the Rock House. There were a number of families, married couples and single employees who made their home on the upper level. According to these people, strange events began to take place on the east side of the second floor. Residents often became so uncomfortable that they moved out and asked to be moved to other quarters. Although too embarrassed to explain what had happened until later, the explanations were eventually revealed. The succession of tenants reported that the east side of the upper floor was inhabited by some sort of "presence" and it became especially active at night. Various items appeared and disappeared without any explanation, lights turned on and off and perhaps most disturbing were the noises that came from the attic. In the darkest hours of the morning, it would often sound as if someone were up there moving furniture around.

The reports from the second floor began to taper off though after a graduate student who was living in the building requested permission to have some psychics come to the Rock House and see what they could perceive about the haunting. According to Ralph Lehman, he visited the proceedings that night as an "interested observer." The small group spent some time in the entry hall of the building, in the attic and on the second floor, particularly on the east side. The psychics insisted that there were spirits present and identified several young children who had died in the building over the years.

One that Lehman remembered was a ghost that they claimed had been a young girl who died from extensive burns when her clothing caught on fire. Eerily, the director discovered that one of the past reports of death at the orphanage included that of a little girl whose nightgown caught on fire when she stood too close to a fireplace. She did not survive the hideous burns that she suffered. There was no way that the psychics could have had this information before visiting the Rock House.

Lehman also added that after the psychics asked the spirits in the house to move on, there were no further reports of "presences" on the second floor. However, the little girl who plays on the lawn remained behind. Who this little girl might have been, or why she still plays here, is unknown.

It should be noted that the Edgewood Center is a private facility and is not open to the public. Although the Rock House is listed on the National Register of Historic Places, it is not accessible to visitors.

MONUMENTS TO ETERNITY

There were many men and women who left their permanent marks on the city of St. Louis during its years of growth and during the so-called "Gilded Age". Some of these marks came in the form of steel and stone structures that still stand today, rare gifts to the city that hundreds continue to enjoy and even the art of the printed word.

James Buchanan Eads was born in Lawrenceburg, Indiana in May 1820 and arrived in St. Louis 1833 aboard a burning steamboat. The moment that the Eads family stepped onto the levee, the riverboat that they came on suddenly burst into flames. In just moments, they were left with nothing as all of their belongings had been destroyed in the freak accident. The family was now penniless and so to make ends meet, Eads' mother opened a boarding house and James began working in a dry goods store. He also sold apples and newspapers on the street. One of the boarders in the Eads home was a man named Barrett Williams, a partner in the store that soon employed young James. Williams was kind to the young man and often allowed the boy to look though his library of technical books, never realizing what an affect it would later have on him.

A few years later, at age 18, Eads began working on the Mississippi River. He took a position as a second clerk aboard the *Knickerbocker*, a steamboat that hauled lead from the Galena,

Illinois mines. One day, the ship became snagged on a cluster of trees that were hidden underwater near the mouth of the Ohio River. This wreck, and likely the books he had devoured as a boy, sparked an idea in Eads' mind. He would develop a ship that would salvage wrecks from the bottom of the Mississippi River. Such an idea had never been attempted before and Eads took his plans to Calvin Case and William Nelson, two St. Louis boat builders. They turned the idea into a unique, double-hulled ship that was equipped with derricks, pumps and a diving bell. They called it the *Submarine* and it became a great success.

Over the next few years, they salvaged scores of ships from the river and their business grew. Insurance companies paid them well for the cargo that was recovered and the partners were able to keep any cargo that had been underwater for more than five years. Eads himself personally made more than 500 trips to the bottom of the river in search of lost goods and ships. By the age of 25, the once penniless boy was married and living in the wealthy Compton Hill neighborhood of St. Louis.

In 1852 though, Eads lost his wife to a cholera epidemic and nearly died himself thanks to the tuberculosis that he had contracted from the hundreds of underwater trips that he made. He never understood the dangers of decompression on his lungs and his doctor urged him to retire. He did so for several years and during this time, he married a second wife, Eunice, with whom he had five daughters. Within a few years, Eads was restless however and he went back to work on the river.

In 1861, the Civil War broke out and Eads offered to use his technical expertise to build a fleet of ironclad gunboats for the Federal army. Edward Bates, a Missouri man and Lincoln's Attorney General, took the offer to the president and Lincoln agreed. Eads and William Nelson employed 4,000 men at the Union Marine Works in Carondelet to build the boats. They became crucial to the war effort on the Mississippi and were an integral part of the capture of Vicksburg and other Confederate posts.

After the war ended, Eads was again urged by his physician to retire. Instead, he took on the project of building the first steel bridge across the Mississippi River.

The Eads Bridge

He had never built a bridge and had no degree in engineering, but he refused to let this stop him. In August 1867, construction on the bridge began. The workers employed a new invention called a "caisson" (underwater support) in building the bridge, but no one had knowledge of how to use them safely. Because of this, 14 of the workers died from the "bends" during the construction due to improper decompression.

On July 4, 1874, thousands turned out for the celebration to mark the opening of the new Eads Bridge. General William T. Sherman hammered in the last spike and Eads ran 14 locomotives across the bridge to prove how strong it was. Today, the bridge is one of the city's most famous historic landmarks and an example of the genius of James Eads.

In the later years of his life, despite his age and poor health, Eads continued to develop new projects. One of them was a proposed canal that would be built across Panama. He believed this would directly assist St. Louis merchants in taking their goods by water to the Pacific coast. Eads wanted the government to grant him rights to the project but before he could pursue it further, his health began to fail and his doctors ordered him to the Bahamas to rest and recover. The government would later refuse his proposal to build a Panama Canal and the waterway would not be constructed until many years later.

Unfortunately, Eads never recovered from this last bout of illness. He caught a cold that turned into pneumonia and he died in the spring of 1887. He fought until the bitter end, insisting to his daughter that he could not die. "I have not finished my work," he told her.

His simple service took place at Christ Church and the building was filled to capacity with everyone from the Mayor to city leaders to construction workers from the Eads Bridge project. He was buried with his family in Bellefountaine Cemetery. He now rests on the same bluff that also holds the bodies of men like William Clark and other dreamers who left a mark of greatness on St. Louis.

A Vintage view of St. Louis' Union Station

One of the most famous landmarks in St. Louis today is undoubtedly the city's Union Station. Although trains have not arrived and departed from here for many years, the station itself has survived both economic crises and periods of disrepair to remain one of the most recognizable buildings in St. Louis.

Union Station was designed by an architect named Theodore Link, who was born near Heidelberg, Germany in 1850. Educated in both England and France, he studied architecture and engineering at the Ecole Centrale in Paris. In 1870, he came to America and began working as an architect in New York and Philadelphia. Three years later, he moved to St. Louis and became a technical representative for the Atlantic & Pacific Railroad. In 1875, he married Annie Fuller, with whom he had four sons and a daughter.

Link later left the railroad and took a position as an assistant chief engineer at Forest Park and later became the superintendent of public parks for St. Louis. In 1883, he went back to architecture and opened an office in the Chemical Building. He soon discovered that he was much in demand and designed a number of churches, libraries and public buildings, along with buildings for the Washington University Medical School (including Barnes Hospital) and many residences in Clayton and the Central West End. He also served as one of the architects for the 1904 World's Fair and designed the Mississippi State House and the Metallurgy buildings.

When word came that St. Louis intended to build a Union Station along Market Street in the city, Link was one of only ten architects chosen from around the country to submit designs. He won the commission in 1891 and began building his greatest architectural achievement. The main building at Union Station was 750 feet long, with a ten-acre train shed and 19 miles of tracks. The structure itself was of limestone and brick with a red-tile roof and was completed in 1894. The grand opening was held on September 1 and attended by more than 20,000 people. During its heyday, more than 100,000 people each day passed through the station.

Union Station became a St. Louis landmark, as did some of the service connected to it. Off the gigantic midway of the station was an area lined with newsstands, locker rooms and of course, the Fred Harvey restaurant. Harvey opened his first restaurant in St. Louis before the Civil War, in the days when travelers ate hurriedly at station lunch rooms on short stopovers between trains. The Harvey Restaurant was different in that it was a real place to sit down and enjoy a meal. The young ladies who worked there, dubbed the "Harvey Girls", became known all over the country thanks to the numerous passengers who came through the eatery. The restaurant in Union Station was opened in 1896 and was one of the last station facilities to close in June 1970.

After Union station had been in operation for several years, improvements were added to increase the station's capacity and efficiency. This would be tested especially in 1904 during the era of the World's Fair. The station even employed a shuttle service during this period to take visitors back and forth from the station to the fairgrounds.

In 1929, more improvements were made to increase the amount of mail that could be handled by the trains and express cars were brought in that were connected to the Post Office and the Railway Express building by way of long tunnels. In addition, the Midway of the station was finally heated. This met with great approval from train passengers, who considered the huge area the coldest place in town.

The greatest pressure ever placed on Union Station came during World War II, when the movements of troops, recruits and service personnel was all done by rail. The central location for all of the trains in the country was St. Louis and the station saw a formidable number of trains for military use, along with an increase in civilian traffic. In 1943, Fred Harvey served 2,714,570 meals to hungry travelers and also operated a cafeteria and an upstairs dining hall for military men and women only.

By the late 1950's, Union Station began to see a decline in traffic. This was in direct relation to the decline of railroad traffic all across America. The automobile had become the main method of transportation, especially in a time when everyone could afford one. This would bring about the end of many stations across the country. By 1970, many of the tracks at Union Station were removed. The last railroad tenant here was the National Railroad Passenger Corporation, a federal government agency organized to administer the passenger system. Its rail network, originally called Railpax when it was started in 1970, was later re-named Amtrak.

By June 1975, Amtrak had announced its plans to vacate Union Station and on October 31,

1978, the last train left the historic station. The station soon fell into decline and after a number of proposed (but failed) ventures, a federal grant finally restored the station into the renovated showpiece that it is today. Many of the frescoed ceilings and original architecture remain and where the Midway was once located, a visitor can find shops and restaurants. The station's Grand Hall has been refurbished to serve as the lobby for the Omni International Hotel that took over the space once used by the old Terminal Hotel.

In November 1923, Theodore Link came down with a serious cold while working in Baton Rouge, Louisiana. He was overseeing the construction of Louisiana State University at the time. Tired and weakened by his illness, he passed away on November 12. His body was returned to St. Louis and he was buried in Bellefountaine Cemetery.

And while the trains, and Theodore Link, have long since passed from view, the memories of Union Station and this eminent architect continue today.

St. Louis has also been the home of many writers, poets, playwrights and actors who have gone on to achieve national and international fame. Some of them include Sara Teasdale, Tennessee Williams, Eugene Field, T.S. Eliot and Kate Chopin, the author of *The Awakening,* who became known as one of the great writers of her day. There were also entertainers who called St. Louis home, like Josephine Baker, Betty Grable and the ghoulish and wonderfully talented actor, Vincent Price.

While all of these were creators of beauty in one way or another, there was one man who left a permanent reminder about the beauty of the natural world for all of us to enjoy. His name was Henry Shaw and he was born in England in 1800. He left Europe at age 19 and settled in St.

Louis, renting a small house on Main Street. He opened a hardware business, a profession that he had learned in England, and began amassing a fortune. He retired by the age of 40, sold his business and began traveling in Europe. During this period, he became interested in the beauty of botanical gardens and vowed to set aside a piece of his own land in St. Louis to be used for a park.

Of course, Shaw was not the only St. Louis resident who wanted to make the city beautiful. One of these was Hiram F. Leffingwell, who in 1869 persuaded the city to purchase a portion of land from Charles Chouteau, Julia Maffit and Isabella De Mun that would become Forest Park. But things had not always gone smoothly for Leffingwell's park plans for the city. In 1850, he and his real estate partner, Richard Smith Elliot, laid out Grand Avenue with a plan to create a huge street that ran from one end of the city to the other. It was to be 150 feet wide and have a park on each side of it. Henry Shaw promised a park on the north side and John O'Fallon built Fairgrounds Park on the opposite. The city refused to sanction the street though, believing that it would provide too much space for horses and the deposits those horses would leave behind!

Leffingwell was discouraged but Henry Shaw was not. He began to talk of a new project, a botanical garden for St. Louis that would be similar to London's Kew Gardens. So, in 1858 he established a 75-acre museum of plant life and opened it in 1860. He called it the Missouri Botanical Gardens, but locally, everyone knew it as Shaw's Gardens instead. In 1870, Shaw also donated a section of land from his estate that adjoined his gardens. This land, which took its name from the country estate itself, became Tower Grove Park.

Shaw continued to make real estate investments and to amass greater wealth, but his generosity matched his fortunes. In addition to his gifts of land and beauty, he also made numerous donations to orphanages, churches and hospitals. He lived to be 90 years-old, but he never married.

As Shaw grew older, he delegated his duties within the gardens, preferring to travel instead. In 1889, he spent most of the summer at Mackinac Island, Wisconsin and while the trip was a great benefit to his spirits, his health began to decline soon after returning to St. Louis.

The Henry Shaw House

He spent his last weeks reading at his garden home and slipping in an out of fevers and consciousness. On August 25, 1889, Shaw passed away with three of his trusted employees by his side, including the superintendent of his gardens, James Gurney. That morning, the gates to the garden were hung with wreathes and the flags in Tower Grove Park were flown at half-mast.

Shaw's body lay in state in the garden museum and funeral services were held for him on Saturday, August 31. There were over 50 honorary pallbearers for his coffin, including Adolphus Busch, James Yeatman and William Lemp. Offices around the city closed early and hundreds of spectators lined the streets and sidewalks near Christ Church Cathedral, where the service was held. The procession then took the body back to the botanical gardens and Shaw was placed in a mausoleum on the grounds that he had built years before. The tomb can be seen at the gardens today and is very striking, with a bas-relief carving of Henry Shaw on the lid of the vault. He appears to be asleep and fittingly, his left hand lies across his chest and clutches a rose.

According to Shaw's will, most of his estate was left to charitable organizations and institutions in St. Louis, including Washington University, the Missouri Historical Society, Good Samaritan Hospital and the Botanical Gardens. The gardens have become an attraction to people from all over the country and are known for being a leading research center for botanists studying plant life. They also boast the world's first geodesic dome greenhouse and the largest Japanese gardens in North America.

But there was a time when Henry Shaw was said to not be resting at peace in his small mausoleum tucked back in the trees of the Botanical Gardens.

Back in 1959, during the restoration of Shaw's mausoleum, one of the groundskeepers was awakened by someone knocking on his door at night. When he opened it, he found that no one was there. However, when the work on the grave site stopped, the knocking did too, leading the staff member to naturally believe that the two were connected.

And while this story is of a more recent vintage, there were actually tales of visitations from Henry Shaw's ghost that went back much further than that. In February 1890, just a few months after Shaw passed away, his former housekeeper began to report visits by her employer from beyond the grave. Some believe that these stories may have given birth to the legend (which is still told today) that the spirit of Henry Shaw still watches over the Missouri Botanical Gardens.

According to the original reports, the housekeeper, Rebecca Edom, stated that Shaw first came to her in the night. He appeared beside her bed and ordered her to get up. She said that Shaw questioned her: "Why don't you see that my wishes are carried out?" he asked her. He went on to say that his bequests were not being handled properly and that she was not visiting the gardens to insure that they were being cared for. "They are cutting down my trees!" he said.

Edom replied that she had not visited the gardens because the streets were being repaired but she promised to do so. Then, Shaw walked away, looking very angry and much younger than he had at the time of his death. And he returned two more times. Once, he demanded to know why his biography (written by David McAdam) was not finished and then he appeared to Edom from a bench at Tower Grove Park. This time, he seemed concerned that the former housekeeper was not being treated fairly by the garden's trustees. "You were my old friend," he reportedly told her.

A year later, Edom spoke out again. This time, she said that the ghost had returned because he was upset about the re-construction of his home, which had been moved from Seventh and Locust Streets to be rebuilt in the gardens. She told a newspaper writer that "Mr. Shaw often told me while walking through the grounds that he did not want the old residence within the walls of the garden, and pointed out the field between the place for students, called the Casino, and the wall on Tower Grove Avenue. It was his intention to have the house set back on this piece of ground and have a pretty lawn made in front of it."

She would later report that she had just dreamed this encounter though and that the other reports of Shaw's ghost were just as "groundless". So, what was the truth? Were the ghostly tales nothing more than a former employee's imagination at work.. or a woman embarrassed by her publicly recorded brush with the other side?

VIOLENCE AND BLOODSHED

While Chicago may be known for such tragic and violent labor riots as the Haymarket Square Riot and others, St. Louis has seen its share of spilled blood. As the city gradually turned from trade to industry, the labor unions moved in to make changes that were much needed in those days. They were not always seen as such though and in 1877, it was widely reported in national newspapers that St. Louis had fallen into the hands of "communists". This was during the national railroad strike of 1877, which began in Baltimore, but was most successful in St. Louis.

Here, it became the first general strike in American history. It was conducted not only for the restoration of railroad wage cuts, but also for fair treatment of black workers, an eight-hour day law and the end to child labor. The St. Louis strikers offered Mayor Henry Overstolz several hundred men to supplement the police and the federal troops that had been brought in to maintain order but the mayor did not seem especially disturbed by what was going on. There was no panic in St. Louis, or among members of the press, despite the "communism" headlines and even those bitterly opposed to the workers and their strike still supported their right to stop work.

In 1876, the Ohio & Mississippi Railroads had promised not to lower wages, but the following July, it joined the Pennsylvania and other railroads in doing so. Pay for brakemen, for example, was lowered $30 per month, a huge amount of money in those days. The first work stoppage in this area occurred at the East St. Louis Relay Depot and by July 22, a mass meeting was held in St. Louis. In the audience were several hundred members of the four St. Louis branches of the Worker's Party of the United States, which was made up of bakers, cigar makers, brewery workers and other labor groups. The party had over 1,000 members in St. Louis and they pledged their strength to the railroad workers. In the days that followed, other rail line workers and tradesman voted to support the railroad workers and joined the walkout. Enthusiasm for the strike was beginning to grow.

James Harrison Wilson, a Civil War cavalry commander and one of the two receivers of the bankrupt St. Louis & Southeastern Railroad, was determined not to yield to the demand for the restoration of the pay cuts. He wrote messages to banks stating "I shall certainly not permit my employees to fix their own wages and not dictate to me in any manner what my policy shall be". He also sent several telegrams to the Secretary of the Interior, asking for federal troops in St. Louis. The wires were passed on to the Secretary of War and Brigadier General John Pope was ordered to send men to the city from Fort Leavenworth. When the 300 infantrymen arrived, their commander, Colonel Jefferson C. Davis, announced that they were there merely to "protect government and public property, not to quell strikes or run trains."

But Wilson was not happy with this. He wired for more troops but officials refused to send them. The army had been reduced in numbers after the Civil War and most available troops were out west, on duty in the volatile Indian country. So Wilson urged President Hayes to call for 100,000 volunteers but advisors realized that such a call for recruits would "set off a revolution."

Other St. Louis railroad operators were not as adamant as Wilson. At the suggestion of Mayor Overstolz, the Missouri Pacific canceled the proposed wage cuts. The following day, the St. Louis, Kansas City & Northern did the same. But in each case, striking workers from other lines prevented the conceding railroads from operating. The strikers in the city and in East St. Louis were determined not to back down. Things began to get more heated with each passing day and it was beginning to grow beyond just stopping the wage cuts to the mentioned eight-hour days and the fair treatment of blacks. Meetings and parades were held and soon other trades joined the strikes. Thirty factories were closed down. Perhaps most successful of the trades who joined in the strike were the African-American roustabouts who worked on the steamboats. They marched from boat to boat on the levee and just the threat of a strike won them higher wages from every vessel.

By July 25, the strike had stopped all trains on 50,000 of the country's 75,000 miles of track. But on that day, the strike began to fall apart. In St. Louis, many of the businessmen began to fear that the growing frenzy would erupt into violence and revolution. They raised $18,000 to arm the militia and obtained 1500 rifles from the Arsenal.

Meanwhile, the strike leaders also began to grow nervous. They had continually railed against violence by the workers, but things were growing more troublesome all the time. The leaders disavowed some of the shutdowns that were not directly connected to the strike and ordered the return to work by laborers at the Belcher's sugar refinery. They obtained permission from the mayor to arrest troublemakers within their own ranks.

On the night of the 26th, a huge crowd gathered at the Lucas Market, hoping to demonstrate, however no party officials were on hand. Fearing a "failure of nerve", the crowd moved to the new party headquarters at Schuler's Hall, over a slum saloon where the party had ended up after being evicted from their last location. They stood in the street and shouted for several hours before dispersing. They returned the following day, but more as spectators than as demonstrators. The businessmen had finally galvanized their private militia into action and no one wanted to be in their way.

The militia, marching with fixed bayonets, came down the street to Schuler's Hall and charged up to the third floor. Party members scrambled out of windows and over rooftops. Seventy were arrested and no shots were fired. Soon after, Colonel Davis was persuaded to cross the river to East St. Louis and take over the railroad yards from the strikers in the name of the United States Marshal.

The revolt had been destroyed, but it was far from a failure. The strikers, most people realized, had not been without a cause. The eight-hour day was achieved and while it took longer to outlaw child labor, the labor movement began to grow in strength and become more accepted.

But there were still dark days ahead...

Further grievances from workingmen set off the East St. Louis race riots of 1919. During four days from June 30 to July 2, more than 100 people were killed and 245 houses were burned to the ground on the east side of the river. During those days, the St. Louis police were on the bridges, protecting the refugees who streamed across from the east side and keeping the rioters at a distance.

More than 1,000 refugees streamed across the river and found refuge in emergency accommodations in the old Municipal Lodging House on Twelfth Street but there were many more who came and wandered the streets. Food and other necessities were provided and the Red Cross and other groups mobilized to assist. It's not surprising that many of those who fled never returned to East St. Louis when it was all over.

In many cases of riot and bloodshed, the violence seems to be contagious and other communities seem to turn against their own. Luckily, this did not happen in 1919 and instead of becoming infected with blood lust, St. Louis was angered and appalled by what was happening. Carlos Hurd, a reporter for the *St. Louis Post-Dispatch*, witnessed the brutality first hand and wrote: "For an hour and a half last evening, I saw the massacre of helpless Negroes at Broadway and Fourth Street in downtown East St. Louis... I saw man after man, with his hands raised pleading for his life, surrounded by groups of men - men who had never seen him before and who knew nothing about him except that he was black - and saw them administer the historic sentence of intolerance, death by stoning. I saw one of these men, almost dead from a savage shower of stones, hanged with a clothes line, and when it broke, hanged with a rope which held. Within a few paces from the telephone pole from which he was suspended, four other Negroes lay dead or dying, another having been removed, dead, a short time before...."

And his report went on and on, describing small "hunting" packs of white men who shot and killed black men in the streets and white women who beat black women with stones, clubs and with their fists. To make matters worse, policemen and Illinois national guardsmen joined in the slaughter. Soldiers and policemen drove two black men from a shed and then shot them as they ran. Many of the fleeing blacks were forced back by militiamen with bayonets into the hands of the mobs they ran from. Some of the rioters were arrested but escaped from the jail by way of open cells and unlocked doors. Most of the policemen involved were described as "apathetic spectators".

City officials did nothing as black residents were killed on the lawn of city hall. Ambulances were turned back. Women and children were forced into burning buildings and bodies dumped into Cahokia Creek. Several black women were actually scalped and black passengers were pulled from interurban cars and killed in the street. One African-American woman was nearly raped but as her dress was being torn from her body, a white storekeeper attacked the mob and pulled them off of her. He was beaten for it, but the woman was left alone. Tragically, she, her husband and her son had been pulled from a streetcar just moments before. She was the only person in her family to survive the night.

Eventually, things began to cool down. The fires burned themselves out and the blood in the streets dried and was washed away. Those responsible for the depravity and death began to slink away, perhaps wondering what had come over them.

An investigating committee was appointed by the governor to find a cause for the riots. Crime, corruption and labor unrest had created a mix that eventually boiled over. But this was no excuse for what occurred, even though the local political machine tried everything they could to pass the buck onto others. One politician, Thomas Canavan, stated: "The prime cause of the trouble was the avarice of the manufacturers. They wanted to get rid of the white workers because they could not handle them. Negroes came in by the hundreds, and there were many bad Negroes among them".

Although Canavan was obviously blaming the victims of the riot for "bringing the whole things on themselves", there was truth to at least some of what he said. Despite the war boom, the absentee-owned East St. Louis industries were having labor problems. Pay was lower in East St. Louis than in surrounding communities and it was common knowledge that many of the workers were forced to "kick back" a portion of their day's wages for the privilege of being allowed to come back to work the next day. Union organizers had a tough time in the city, but there were strikes, including a long and bitter one in progress at the Aluminum Ore Co.. The company had armed its guards and an officer in the employ of the company had access to the "East St. Louis Rifle Club", from which he borrowed 30 rifles and 10,000 rounds of ammunition, which he turned over to the company. There was also a threat of a streetcar strike. In fact, National Guardsmen were even housed on the property of the streetcar company and refused to act when the riot started, saying that they were only charged with the defense of property.

The labor unrest was aggravated by the importation of black workers by the company. Most of them had been recruited by railroad agents in the south to be replacement workers and to take lower paying jobs from workers who were already in place. They were offered free transportation and offered pay that never materialized. They still arrived in droves however and white workers began to lose their jobs to them. And while these new arrivals cannot be blamed for the violence that befell so many of them, their mere presence in the city made the problems even worse.

Another contributing factor to the violence was the vice situation in East St. Louis at the time. In the evening, workers at the nearby plants would cross the Whiskey Chute (St. Clair Avenue) that separated East St. Louis from National City, a town incorporated to keep the packers off the East St. Louis tax books. This notorious "Valley" was home to places like Aunt Kate's Honky-Tonk, Something Doin' Every Minute and other disreputable dives. The area was filled with saloons, bordellos and gambling houses and spilled over into nearby Brooklyn, a town so corrupt that even the police chief owned one of the "wine rooms".

Which brings us to perhaps the greatest cause behind the viciousness in East St. Louis, the incredible political corruption of the time. The city was largely in the hands of a boss named Locke Tarlton, his partners and his underlings, like Mayor Mollman. Huge amounts of money were made, bribery was commonplace and investigations into illegal practices in the city were quickly hushed up.

East St. Louis was ready to boil over and by the end of June 1919, the heat had been turned up even more. On June 25, a meeting was held by workers at the Aluminum Ore Co. and began to speak about how disadvantaged they had become after the importation of more than 8,000 black workers. They called on Mayor Mollman to put a stop to it and he promised to try, despite the fact that he had been directly responsible for recruiting the black workers in the first place. Threats were made and speakers were said to have stopped just short of inciting the workers to riot.

Trouble began just hours after a report on June 30 that two white men had been attacked by African-Americans and that the black men had been talking of a "Fourth of July Massacre". It is unlikely that any such incident occurred at all, but it was enough to finally put the match the powder keg that had been smoldering for some time. East St. Louis finally exploded.

It came to an end on July 2. Shortly after midnight, two policemen were shot by a group of black men, allegedly called into action by the ringing of their church bell. That night, white men in two cars had shot up a black neighborhood, but this time, the victims returned fire. The cars, full of bullet holes, were later found but the police asked no questions. By that afternoon, the fighting had come to an end.

Despite the attempts by local officials to cover up the rioting, or to place blame everywhere but on those responsible, the state's Attorney General appointed several prosecutors and put a grand jury into place to look into the affair. In less than six months, the St. Clair County grand jury indicted more than 100 persons, both white and black. In the months that followed, 17 men were sent to the penitentiary in Chester, 10 were jailed elsewhere, 11 were fined and 4 were acquitted. East St. Louis, at least for a time, had been cleaned up.

A different kind of labor problem led to years of violence within the city of St. Louis. To understand where it all began, we have to look back to the days before the Great Fire of 1849. These times were glory days of the volunteer firefighters in America. These ordinary men gave up their everyday jobs at the sound of an alarm and put themselves into peril to make their homes and cities safe. They used primitive equipment to battle what were often ferocious blazes and became both heroes and sometimes victims in the process. The volunteer fire companies became important social and political forces as the men organized by profession, neighborhood or ethnic groups. Often, their place in a fire company assured them business and political careers for, to the community, these men were heroes.

The annual firemen's parade was held each year in May in St. Louis. It was an important civic event and a great show. The companies marched along with their polished pumps and machines and a good portion of the city turned out to watch. Just a few days after the annual parade in 1849, the Great Fire began aboard a steamer and devastated the levee and much of the downtown business district. It was the worst fire in the history of America at that point. Three were killed, hundreds were left homeless and thousands were put out of work. In the end though, the fire cleared ground and hastened the growth of St. Louis. The wharf area was expanded, streets were widened and new buildings were constructed.

The Volunteer Fire Companies did not fare so well though. For a short period, they basked in their heroic efforts during the fire and were covered in glory by the death of Thomas Targee. The days after the Great Fire represented a high point in the Volunteer Fire Companies' history, but it wouldn't last for long.

In 1850, city officials decided to modernize the firefighting capabilities of the companies. An officer was appointed to supervise them, regulations were drafted for them to follow and they were granted a stipend from the city of $1,000 per year. The money had a terrible effect on the companies. They could no longer be seen as volunteers and yet they were not really city employees either. The men were demoralized and many drifted away. Their places were soon taken over by another sort of man, one drawn by the money and by the chance to loaf around the firehouse waiting for calls to come in. These less than desirable sorts began to turn firefighting into something more than just a civic duty. It had become a competition between companies as to who could put out a fire first.

In many situations, more than one company might answer an alarm. Engines would frequently meet at an intersection and then try to position themselves closest to the fire. In this way, they might have the best opportunity to reach the water at the fireplug. Sometimes though, when an engine company would not reach the plug first, they might cut a gap in the other company's hose so that they could put out the fire instead. Such a trick would often lead to an altercation between the companies with fists, clubs and stones... leaving the fire completely unattended.

In 1851, a bizarre incident took place when William H. Carroll, Captain of Laclede Company, began pumping water with the engine of Liberty Company when the hose for his own engine burst. At that, his own men mutinied and leaving their equipment at the scene, left for home. Two of his other men got into a fist fight over the incident. Amazingly, Carroll was brought before a disciplinary committee for using the other company's engine.

The fights and skirmishes at the fire scenes led to grudges and outright warfare between individual companies. The groups often went back and forth between firehouses and exchanged taunts with one another, or pulled false alarms to draw out the enemy companies. Shouting matches often turned into brawls and stone-throwing and often escalated into sabotage. Pieces of equipment like hose reels and even engines were stolen and hidden from their owners. Often, equipment would be thrown into the river and the company would have to try and recover it.

Perhaps the two most bitter rivals were Franklin and Liberty Companies. One night in 1853, a group of Franklin men stole into the Liberty firehouse and made off with their hose reel. They removed the hose from the reel and dumped it in the street in front of the house of the Liberty's captain and then broke the reel itself into pieces and tossed it into a pond. There was no way for the Liberty men to recover the reel and they vowed revenge.

On May 21, a small building near a foundry on Carr Street caught fire. Both Liberty and Franklin Companies responded to the alarm. The fire was easily handled but a few minutes after, the two companies came together in the street. According to newspaper accounts of the time, two Liberty men climbed to the roof of a house on the east side of Broadway and began pitching bricks down to their comrades below. Threats and insults were thrown back and forth and then bricks, clubs, rocks and fists began to fly. The bloody firefighters battled it out in the street for a few minutes and then someone drew a pistol. Shots were fired on both sides and men began to fall. A horrified spectator summoned the police just as the Franklin men routed the Liberty crew and sent them running. Many of the men were wounded but only nine of them had serious injuries. However, one man, Owen Foy of the Liberty Company, was dead. One account stated that he had been shot, while others claimed that he had been pummeled to death with rocks. Either way, a firefighter had been killed and not in the course of doing his job, but by other firefighters.

Unfortunately, this was not the end to the battles either. Riots and brawls were often common finishes to a fire. Alarms bells would waken the entire city in the night, only to turn out to be false alarms set off by rival fire companies. But a change was coming...

Just one month after the battle between the Liberty and Franklin Companies, the city of Cincinnati began the first paid fire department in America. The first time the professionals went out, they had to fight a mob of disgruntled volunteer firefighters to even get to the burning building. But the paid department had an advantage over the volunteers in Cincinnati, a steam fire engine that had been designed just the year before. The new engine used steam pressure and could fire a stream of water much further than the old manually-pumped engines could.

Other cities followed Cincinnati's lead, including St. Louis, which inaugurated the first professional department in 1858. It came at a perfect time too for in February of that year, the battles between the volunteers reached their lowest point. The firehouse belonging to Liberty Company had been burned down. The fire had clearly been set and the arsonists had taken the time to remove a wheel from each Liberty engine so that they could not be rolled out to safety. The house and the equipment were lost and it was plain to see that whoever had set the fire had known what they were doing. Any guesses as to who the culprits might have been?

Some of the volunteer companies went gracefully in the wake of the new professional department. Many of them joined the paid force and served with pride and honor. Others, who were likely the cause of the volunteer companies' downfall in the first place, continued to harass the paid firefighters, sabotaging their equipment, stabbing their horses and more for some time to come. Some of the volunteer groups who owned their own station houses refused to sell them to the city, as they were required to do by law. These worthless ruffians often tried to prevent fires from being extinguished and to keep alarms from being sounded.

Eventually though, it all died down and within a few years, the professional firefighters were allowed to serve with distinction and continue to do so today.

Vintage Stereoscopic View of the 1904 Worlds Fair in St. Louis

THE WORLD CAME TO ST. LOUIS

"Open ye gates! Swing wide ye portals! Enter herein ye sons of man. Learn the lessons here taught and

gather from it inspiration for still greater accomplishments!"

DAVID FRANCIS at the Opening of the Louisiana Purchase Exposition, 1904

In 1893, the Columbian Exposition was to be held in St. Louis, but of course, it was held in Chicago instead. Despite pleas and campaigning on the part of the city, St. Louis lost out on the chance to host this phenomenal event. This instilled a great desire on the part of the eminent citizens of St. Louis, especially on the part of David R. Francis, who would soon be elected Governor of Missouri, to snag the next great event to come along. A few years later, people began to talk of a fair to celebrate the 100th anniversary of the Louisiana Purchase in 1904. What better place to have such a fair than in St. Louis, the "gateway to the west"? Civil leaders pledged to raise $15 million to hold the event, the same amount Jefferson paid for the Louisiana Purchase, and the 1904 World's Fair was to become a part of the city's history.

After terrific debate, the western side of Forest Park was chosen for the site of the fair. Businessmen of the south side were very disturbed, stating it was a more attractive and viable location, but their complaints fell on deaf ears. Enthusiasm began to run high in the city as the Jefferson Hotel was erected on Twelfth Boulevard and the city began to improve its streetcars and other services. The west end of the city began to feel the effect of the coming fair as 94 new hotels were established in 1903 and 15 more were completed before April 1904.

The area of the park chosen for the event covered about 650 acres but it was soon evident that more land would be needed. Additional tracts were leased from the new, but unoccupied, Washington University campus and this nearly doubled the size of the fairgrounds. Preparations ran at a feverish pitch for several years and as the centennial date approached, it was obvious that the fair was not going to open on time. A dedication was held anyway on April 30, 1903 with thousands of troops parading through the grounds and President Theodore Roosevelt on hand to deliver the opening address. Right after that, everything was shut down again when Congress granted the request for a postponement of one year to 1904. This gave the organizers more time to obtain foreign exhibits and to get more companies to plan displays.

A view of the Fairgrounds - now Forest Park (Courtesy Missouri Historical Society)

By the cold spring of 1904, the Exposition was ready to open. Organizers began to panic though on April 20 when a late snowstorm slowed all of the operations. Luckily, things cleared off and on April 30, the fair opened. The Opening Day ceremony (the second one!) was held in the Plaza of St. Louis and included prayer, music and an assortment of speeches. John Phillip Sousa led his band and 400 voices sang a rendition of "Hymn of the West" that had been written for the occasion. William Howard Taft, the United States Secretary of War, made the principal address and David Francis touched a telegraph key that alerted President Roosevelt that the fair had officially opened. At that same moment, 10,000 flags were unfurled, fountains began to spray geysers into the air and the fairgrounds opened to almost 20 million visitors from around the world over the course of the next seven months.

The architecture and design that went into the fair was amazing and breathtaking. A few years before, Peninsular Lake in the park had been re-shaped and re-designed. The lake acquired a new name, the Grand Basin, and it was connected throughout the park with other lagoons to provide waterways and boating during the festivities. Above the lake, on the natural semi-circular hill now known as Art Hill, was the Festival Hall, one of the grand attractions. On each side of it were smaller pavilions from which cascades of water descended to the lake. Along the cascades were large staircases that were adorned with statues, benches and landscaped gardens.

The Colonnade of States, linking Festival Hall and the many fair pavilions, was graced with giant seated figures, seven on each side, each representing a state or territory that had been part of the Louisiana Purchase. Eight ornate exhibition palaces surrounded the Great Basin. These included Mines and Metallurgy, Liberal Arts, Education and Social Economy, Manufactures, Electricity, Varied Industries, Transportation and Machinery. Each of them was different in design but was massive in size, each covering several acres.

Although the buildings were detailed and highly decorated (and look in photographs as if they would last forever!), they were all made from temporary materials and were not substantial at all. The material used to construct them was "staff", a mixture of fibers soaked in plaster-of-paris. The hardened material was very adaptable and could be used just like wood. By pouring "staff" into glue molds, many ornamental pieces, which appeared to be hand made, could be achieved in a short time. The structure under the "staff" was always steel or wood so that the buildings didn't simply collapse.

A few of the structure from the fair were meant to be permanent though. One of these was the Art Palace, a building that would be used by more than 20 nations to house priceless works of art during the Exposition. Two temporary buildings flanked the center one and a smaller sculpture building was located on the south, creating a beautiful courtyard between them. The temporary buildings were removed after the fair and the Art Palace was donated to the city and today holds the St. Louis Art Museum.

The area of the park occupied today by the St. Louis Zoo was the Plateau of States, where many states erected large houses to greet visitors and to show off the attractions of their individual states. Some of the buildings were replicas of important historic sites like the Cabildo of New Orleans (where the Louisiana Purchase had been signed), Tennessee's Hermitage and Virginia's Monticello. Missouri, the host state, constructed a building entirely of native materials. It was designed as a permanent building, with a large dome and a heating and cooling system, which no other building on the fairgrounds could boast at the time. Unfortunately, on November 19, just two weeks before the end of the fair, the building and all of its contents were destroyed by fire. No attempt was ever made to replace the structure.

A permanent contribution to the fair was left nearby though. After the fair ended, a pavilion was constructed and was given to the city of St. Louis by the Exposition Company that organized the event. This pavilion was erected as a historic marker for the fair and because it has been known over the years as the World's Fair Pavilion, most assume incorrectly that it is a remnant of the fair itself.

Not far from the present-day site of this pavilion was the U.S. Fisheries building during the Exposition. This site was a constant attraction with 40 glass-fronted tanks and a center pool for seals. On this hill today, a colored fountain and landscaped gardens can be seen.

Also located nearby was the Bird Cage, a unique structure and the largest of its kind ever built. It was an exhibition created by the Smithsonian Institution that allowed sightseers to actually walk through the cage and interact with the numerous species of birds inside. After the fair, the cage was donated to the city and it became a part of the St. Louis Zoo. Visitors can still experience it today.

As mentioned already, the Grand Basin was the focal point of the fair's activities. Boat parades were held here almost daily and the lagoons and waterways that led away from the Basin flowed between the exhibition buildings. North of the Basin was the Plaza of St. Louis, where the official proceedings were always held. The Plaza was graced with a tall monument for the Louisiana Purchase and the statue of St. Louis. Stretching away from the Plaza was Louisiana Way, the main thoroughfare of the grounds. On one side of it was the United States building and on the other was the French Palace, honoring the two countries involved in the Louisiana Purchase.

The amazing Agriculture Palace that was erected for the Exposition

The long gentle hill to the west of Forest Park provided a space large enough for the agricultural exhibits and the largest building on the fairgrounds, the Agriculture Palace. It had an eastern facade that was one-third of a mile long. The area was covered with displays showing various types of grass, pools with water plants, windmills and livestock shows and judging that occurred each day. Near the north entrance to the Agriculture Palace was a giant floral clock that was 112 feet in diameter. It was made from trimmed flowers and foliage and had giant hands that were operated by compressed air. They were controlled by a master clock that was located in a small pavilion at the number "12". Gardens surrounded the clock and they were illuminated with thousands of lights at night, hidden in the foliage, so that visitors could visit here even in the dark. The booming bells that sounded at the hour and half-hour could be heard all over the fairgrounds.

Washington University's new campus not only provided much of the space needed for the fair, but it also served as the model for the ideal university. The Administrations Building (Brookings Hall) was the place of all the official meetings and the reception of important guests. Other buildings furnished space for exhibits, offices and meeting rooms. At the western end of the campus, the athletic fields and gymnasium were used for an elaborate physical culture program and also for the Olympic Games of 1904.

At the eastern end of the campus were the halls set up by foreign states, including China, Sweden, Brazil and others. The British Building was a copy of Queen Anne's Orangery at Kensington Gardens. After the fair, it was purchased by the University and for years was the home of the School of Fine Arts. The college abandoned the building in 1926 and moved into the new Bixby Hall. Many of the decorations from the original building were retained in the new one.

Perhaps the most fascinating of the exhibits at the fair to turn-of-the-century visitors was the Philippines' Stockade. This was the largest and most expensive of the foreign displays and brought 1,100 Filipinos to live in St. Louis for almost seven months. Arrowhead Lake provided a 47-acre setting and around the lake was set up various communities of "primitive" people. Each tribe constructed its own village of thatched huts and houses on stilts along the water. The tribe's customs and homes fascinated visitors and in turn, these primitive people were enthralled by the trappings of modern society. One tribal chief created a problem when he refused to let his tribe be viewed until a telephone was installed in his hut! Another tribe caused a scandal with their demand for dogs, the main staple of their diet. Following the fair, the natives returned home and Arrowhead Lake was drained and the land was used for park development.

The section that most people remembered when they later recalled the 1904 World's Fair was the Pike, an inviting one-mile section along the northern edge of the fairgrounds. This area was like a giant amusement park with concessions and attractions that lured in people from all over the fair. It was here that the ice cream cone was invented and first sampled. The forerunner of the popsickle also appeared here. Known as the "fruit icicle", these summer treats were made of fruit juice that was frozen in a narrow tin tube. Another welcome "first' from the Pike was iced tea. It was first served almost as a fluke. A tea house was having a hard time selling hot tea on summer days and one of the employees suggested that they try serving it over crushed ice. It's also been said that the first hot dog was served on the Pike during the fair as well, but the jury's still out on that one.

The attractions of the Pike undoubtedly influenced the design of future fairs and amusement parks. At the eastern end of the area were massive reproductions of the Alps, hovering over a storybook Swiss village. Here, visitors could take a train ride into the mountains and then dine in the great hall below, where many official gatherings were held. President Roosevelt was honored in this room at a banquet promoted by St. Louis brewers.

Next to the Alps was an Irish village with medieval buildings and Celtic designs. It featured a restaurant, along with Blarney Castle, a theater where visitors could enjoy a show. Also on the Pike was Hagenbeck's Animal Paradise, which attracted large crowds in these days before the modern zoo. Here, visitors could see bears and an assortment of exotic animals. All types of foreign cultures and concessions were also represented, as was a display about the deadly Galveston flood, the North Pole and the Siberian wastes. There was also entertainment and rides. Fair goers might watch a little-known comedian named Will Rogers or hear "ragtime" musicians, which got their its in St. Louis. Scott Joplin, an entertainer still remembered today, was here and wrote "Cascade Rag" in honor of the fair. Other rags at the time were "On the Pike" and "Strolling Down the Pike". In addition to hearing the strains of "Meet Me in St. Louie", visitors might experience the Magic Whirlpool, the Water Chutes or the Scenic Railway.

But there was no greater ride at the fair than the immense Observation Wheel. The 250 feet-high wheel was created by George Ferris, an engineer who first used it at the 1893 Columbian Exposition in Chicago. The "Ferris Wheel" was so successful that it was brought to St. Louis. Sadly, the wheel never left the city at the end of the fair. It was scheduled to be taken to Coney Island next but the demolition contractor for the fair found it to be too much trouble. So, he dynamited it and sold the scrap for $1800. In later years, workers in Forest Park have dug up pieces of the wheel under the golf course near the Forsyth entrance to the park. The original wheel became the model for all such attractions to follow, but there has never been another of such gigantic proportions ever built.

The visitors came throughout the summer and into the fall of 1904. But as December approached, sadness filled the air. The Exposition closed down at midnight on December 1. From early morning and right up until the time the clock struck midnight, thousands gathered to celebrate and to pay homage to David Francis, the man responsible for bringing the fair to the city. Schools and businesses closed for the day and it was like a carnival that was tinged with grief. It became one of the wildest nights ever witnessed in St. Louis with the authorities on high alert, should the celebration turn overly buoyant.

As the midnight hour approached, Francis made one final speech from the Plaza of St. Louis and then he threw a switch that plunged the entire fairgrounds into darkness. The band played "Auld Lang Syne" and then suddenly the air was filled with blinding fireworks as "Farewell" was spelled out along one wall and "Good Night" along another.

The Louisiana Purchase Exposition of 1904 had come to an end.

The devastation of the fairgrounds began on December 2. Demolition was started by the Chicago Housewrecking Co., who had been awarded the $450,000 contract to remove the fair buildings. Even through the fair was officially closed, visitors were able to view the demolition for a 25-cent admission. The demolition process produced mountains of "staff", which nearly all of the pavilions had been made of. Useful only for landfill, it was hauled away over miles of railroad tracks that had been laid down before the fair for the construction and removal of the buildings on the grounds. The tracks were then covered with asphalt during the fair and then opened again to remove the debris when the fair ended.

The exhibition buildings were removed quickly, as the contract specified that the demolition be completed within six months, but many of the concessions on the Pike remained for months, as no one wanted to buy them. Oddities were just as difficult to have removed. One of them, a cabin that once belonged to General Ulysses S. Grant was moved to the fairgrounds to be used by the Blanke Coffee Co. No one wanted it at the end of the fair but it was finally purchased by Adolphus Busch and moved to Gravois Road. It is now a part of the Anheuser-Busch company attraction, Grant's Farm.

The American State's buildings were the easiest to get rid of. Many of them, made from permanent materials were purchased and hauled away to nearby sites as homes. The New Jersey House was moved to Kirkwood and served as an apartment building for a time. The New Hampshire House, although altered, became a home on Litzinger Road.

The Oklahoma structure was taken to El Reno, Oklahoma, where it became an Elk's Lodge. The Michigan and Minnesota Houses became permanent fair buildings in their home states. New Mexico became a public library in Santa Fe. Iowa was moved to become an asylum for alcoholics.

Belgium's palace was purchased by Anheuser-Busch and was used for many years as their glass works. The Swedish Building was taken to Lindsborg, Kansas and became the Art Department for Bethany College. The 50-foot statue of Vulcan, a donation from the city of Birmingham, Alabama, was removed back to its home city on seven freights cars and while it rusted in storage for years, was later restored on a hill overlooking the city. Many other statues were given to the city of St. Louis and were assigned to parks and public places but their locations have been lost and forgotten over the years.

An attempt was made to preserve the Pike as a permanent attraction in St. Louis, with the reproduction of the Alps being the major benefit of the plan. However, the officials at Washington University viewed an amusement center of this sort being too big a distraction for their students and lobbied against the idea. Then Adolphus Busch purchased the Alps, planning to install them as an attraction in Forest Park, along with a summer theater. This plan never came about either and eventually the mountain range was destroyed.

Although little remains from the fair in the city today, save for a few impressive mementoes to that bygone era, the Louisiana Exposition has never been really forgotten. Never again would a World's Fair be held that had the magnitude of the St. Louis Fair and while others would follow, the magnificence of that brief season in 1904 would leave a lasting mark on the country, and perhaps the world.

THE MYSTERY OF PATIENCE WORTH

Over the years, St. Louis has been plagued with what some supernatural enthusiasts might consider to be two of the greatest unsolved mysteries of all time. One of these mysteries dates back to the year 1913. It was a time when St. Louis had reached the end of its "Gilded Age" and had entered a time when a Great War was on the horizon. The city was a different place than it had been just a few years before and the glitter of the World's Fair was beginning to tarnish in St. Louis. And during these darkening times, many residents started to look for something brighter and embraced a movement that was again becoming popular all over America.

The movement was called Spiritualism and it was based on the idea that the dead could communicate with the living. It got its start in 1848 in Hydesville, New York with two sisters from a family named Fox who claimed to be able to speak to the ghost of a murdered man who haunted their home. The communications between Kate and Margaret Fox and the unseen spirit caught the attention of the entire nation and within a year the girls were giving public demonstrations of their psychic powers. Seemingly overnight, what became known as Spiritualism grew into a full-blown movement, complete with scores of followers, its own brand of phenomena and codes of conduct for speaking with the dead.

Spiritualists believed that ghosts could communicate through "mediums", or sensitive persons who were in tune with the next world. Those persons passed along messages that were relayed while the mediums were in a trance state. This could be done in a variety of ways, including through speech, through automatic writing (when the spirit allegedly controlled the writing hand of the medium) or through devices like Ouija boards, which spelled out the spirit messages.

While most professional mediums contacted the spirit world during seances, dark room sessions where the ghosts supposedly manifested in various ways, many people all over the country began arranging what were called "home circles". These were really just small gatherings of family and friends who attempted to communicate with the spirits on an amateur level. Such sessions usually involved table tipping, where the ghosts would knock or cause a table to tilt in reply to a question, or the Ouija board, which was the most popular.

Ouija, or "talking boards", were wooden trays that had been painted with the letters of the alphabet that were arranged in two long lines across the board. Below these letters were the numbers 1-10 and the words "yes" and "no". According to those who used them, the boards allowed ordinary people to communicate with the spirits as the ghosts were allowed to cause the pointer (planchette) on the board to move about. This occurred when sitters placed their fingertips very lightly on top of it. Allegedly, the ghosts who were present would then work through the sitters to spell out messages.

Controversy has raged since the inception of the Ouija board as to whether or not the messages that come from them are real, clever hoaxes, or simply hidden thoughts that are dredged up from the unconscious mind of the sitter. No real consensus on how the Ouija board actually works has ever been reached and like the Spiritualist movement itself, remains a mystery even to this day.

Which is why what happened to a St. Louis housewife in 1913 remains an enigma, even after all of these years.

Pearl Curran had little interest in the occult prior to 1913. She was born Pearl Leonore Pollard in Mound City, Illinois in February 1883. She grew up in Texas, playing outdoors and exploring the countryside. Her parents, George and Mary, were easy-going and never really demanded much from Pearl, which probably made her an indifferent student. She left school after the eighth grade and began to study music in Chicago, where her uncle lived. She also played the piano at her uncle's Spiritualist church, where he was a medium. But Pearl and her parents were not Spiritualists and in fact, had no interest in the movement at all. Pearl had attended Sunday School as a child but few of the teachings ever stuck with her. She did not attend church as a child and never read the bible.

In fact, she rarely ever read anything at all. She had enjoyed books like *Black Beauty* and *Little Women* as a child and was always entertained by fairy tales but, probably thanks to her education, she had little interest in books or writing. Her only creative desires were to learn the piano and to perhaps act on stage, but she gave up that idea at age 24 when she married John Curran.

Her marriage was an uneventful as her childhood had been. The Curran's were not rich, but they did make a comfortable living. Pearl had a maid to take care of the household chores and she and her husband enjoyed going to restaurants and to the theater. They were a social couple and enjoyed meeting friends and playing cards with neighbors in the evening. They seldom read anything, outside of the daily newspaper and some of the periodicals of the day and never really had an opportunity to associate with well-educated writers or poets. They were happy though and content in their middle-class home with their close friends and acquaintances.

Never could they have imagined the changes that were coming to their lives.

In the afternoons, while their husbands were at work, Pearl would often have tea with her mother and with a friend who lived nearby, a neighbor named Mrs. Hutchings. It's likely that the Ouija board that was in the house on the afternoon of July 8, 1913 actually belonged to Mrs. Hutchings, who was curious about the contraption. It's likely that Pearl had seen one of the boards before, and had even experimented with it at her uncle's home, but she professed to have no interest in it at all. In fact, she believed that Ouija boards were a boring and silly pastime having seen the pointer spell out nothing but gibberish.

Then, to the ladies surprise, the message on the board seemed to make sense. "Many moons ago I lived. Again I come. Patience Worth is my name," it spelled out.

The three women were startled. They certainly knew no one by that name. Who could Patience Worth have been? Pearl was the most skeptical of the three, doubting that the dead could make contact by way of a wooden board. However, at her friend's urging, she asked the sender of the message to tell them something about herself. Replies to her queries began to come through the message board and were recorded by Pearl's mother. According to the spirit who called herself Patience Worth, she had lived in Dorsetshire, England in either 1649 or 1694 (the pointer included both dates) but even that information was difficult to obtain. Patience spoke in an archaic fashion, using words like "thee" and "thou" and sometimes refusing to answer their questions directly. When Mrs. Hutchings pushed for more information, the spirit first replied by saying "About me ye would know much. Yesterday is dead. Let thy mind rest as to the past."

Eventually though, the ladies would learn that Patience claimed to come to America, where she was murdered by Indians.

The initial contact with Patience Worth came through the Ouija board when Pearl and Mrs. Hutchings controlled it. But it was soon evident that Pearl was mainly responsible for the contact, for no matter who sat with her, the messages from Patience would come. The messages continued to be very strange in that whoever was speaking had an extensive knowledge of not only 17th century vernacular but of clothing, mechanical items, musical instruments and household articles of the period. "A good wife keepeth the floor well sanded and rushes in plenty to burn. The pewter should reflect the fire's bright glow," said one message from the Ouija board, "but in thy day housewifery is a sorry trade."

Pearl was fascinated with the messages that they were receiving and began devoting more and more time to the Ouija board. Eventually though, the messages began coming so fast that no one could write them down and Pearl suddenly realized that she didn't need the board anymore. The sentences were forming in her mind at the same time they were being spelled out on the board. She began to "dictate" the replies and messages from Patience to anyone who would write them. She would first employ a secretary, but later Pearl would record the words herself, using first a pencil and then a typewriter.

For the next 25 years, Patience Worth dictated a total of about 400,000 words. Her works were vast and consisted of not only her personal messages, but creative writings as well. She passed along nearly 5,000 poems, a play, many short works and several novels that were published to critical acclaim.

Shortly after Patience made her presence known, the Curran house in south St. Louis began to overflow with friends, neighbors and curiosity-seekers. When word reached the press, Casper Yost, the Sunday editor of the *St. Louis Post-Dispatch*, began publishing articles about Pearl Curran and the mysterious spirit who seemed to be dictating to her. In 1915, he even published a book called *Patience Worth, A Psychic Mystery* and the housewife from St. Louis became a national celebrity.

People came from all over and the Curran's, always gracious and unpretentious, welcomed visitors who wanted to witness the automatic writings sessions where Pearl received information from Patience Worth. Authorities in the field of psychic investigation came, as well as people from all over the country who had begun to read and admire the writings attributed to Patience. The Curran's never charged any admission to the house and all of the writing sessions were conducted with openness and candor. There were no trappings of Spiritualism here with darkened rooms and candles. Pearl would usually just sit in a brightly lit room with her notebook or typewriter and when the messages began to come to her, she would begin to write.

In addition to the stories and novels, Patience produced thousands of poems through Pearl Curran. One of her unusual abilities was to present poems that would suit any topics suggested by the company present. On January 12, 1926, at Straus's Studio in St. Louis, during a meeting of the Current Topics Club, suggestions were made by some of the members and Patience composed two poems called *Lavender and Lace* and *Gibraltar*. Each poem was presented with no noticeable delay and without change of word. Neither of them had ever been produced before. The famous poet, Edgar Lee Masters, was asked if anyone could actually write poetry that way, instantly and to topics suggested by a group, and he replied, "There is only one answer to that... it simply can't be done!"

Not surprisingly, many questioned the reality of the spectral Patience Worth and while she had her critics, she had her defenders as well. Witnesses were hard put to get Patience to offer much detail about her past. She seemed to think that her origins were unimportant, however she did mention landmarks and scenery around her former home in England. The newspaperman Casper Yost, who was one of the spirit's greatest defenders, took a trip abroad during the height of the phenomenon and when he reached Patience's alleged home in Dorset he did find the cliffs, old buildings, a monastery and scenery just as Patience had described it. And while this is interesting, it is hardly proof.

Perhaps the most convincing evidence that Patience Worth was not the conscious or unconscious creation of Pearl Curran is the material that she dictated for her books and stories. Patience seemed to be able to pass between old English dialects at will or could write in a semblance of modern English, as she did with most of her poetry.

The *Story of Telka* was one of her novels and it is a poetic drama of medieval life in rural England, written mostly in Anglo-Saxon words. It was composed during a series of sittings and as with other Patience Worth dictations, there were no revisions and no breaks where sentences left off and began again. The only comparable work to this novel is the Wickcliffe's Bible of the 14th Century, which is also composed of almost pure Anglo-Saxon. However, the language in *The Story of Telka* does not resemble the language in this particular bible. In the novel, there are few words that the modern reader cannot understand, as if the desire by the writer was to create something that seemed old but could still be comprehended. Many argued that it would be impossible for a person living in turn-of-the-century St. Louis to create such a dramatic work and then limit the vocabulary in the work to only easily understood words in an ancient form of their own language. It simply could not be done, they believed.

And this was far from Patience's only book. *The Sorry Tale* was a lengthy novel that was set in the time of Christ and in it, the author brought to life the Jews, Romans, Greeks and Arabians of the period. The book was also filled with an accurate knowledge of the political, social and religious conditions of the time. Critics hailed it as a masterpiece. It had been started on July 14, 1915 and two or three evenings a week were given over to the story until it was completed. The tale proceeded as fast as John Curran could take it down in abbreviated longhand and continued each night for as long as Pearl was physically able to receive it.

Professor W.T. Allison of the English Department of the University of Manitoba stated that "No book outside of the Bible gives such and intimate picture of the earthly life of Jesus and no book has ever thrown such a clear light upon the manner of life of Jews and Romans in the Palestine of the day of our Lord."

At the same time that *The Sorry Tale* was being produced, *The Merry Tale* was started as a relief from the sadness of the previous book. For a time, work was done on both novels during a single evening.

When the first words of the next book, *Hope Trueblood*, appeared, the sitters gathered at the Curran home were astonished. For the first time since Patience Worth's arrival, then four years before, the material was in plain English. Her previous stories had dealt with ancient Rome, Palestine and Medieval England. This book told the story of a young girl's effort to find her family in Victorian England. When the book appeared in Great Britain, no clues were given as to its mysterious origins and reviewers accepted it as the work of a new and promising British author. Once critic stated that "the story is marked by strong individuality, and we should look with interest for further products of this author's pen."

While critics were impressed with the works she produced, those who witnessed Pearl taking dictation from the spirit were even more astounded. For instance, *The Story of Telka,* which came in at over 70,000 words, was written over several sessions but was completed in just 35 hours. This type of speed was fairly typical too. Once, in a single evening, 32 poems were delivered, along with several short stories. Sometimes in the course in one evening, Patience dictated portions of four novels, always resuming the work on each one at the same place she left off. Pearl took down all of the words, usually in the presence of a number of witnesses, and never made any revisions.

Those who came to investigate the strange events often made requests of Patience in order to test her. She never hesitated to respond to questions or tasks they put to her. When asked to compose a poem on a certain subject, she would deliver the stanzas so quickly that they had to be taken down in shorthand. Weeks later, when asked to reproduce the poem, she could do so without any changes or errors. One night, author and psychic investigator Walter Franklin Prince, who was a regular visitor to the Curran house, posed an unusual task for Patience. Could she deliver a poem about the "folly of being an atheist" while simultaneously producing a dialogue that might take place between a wench and a jester at a medieval-era fair? He asked that she alternate the dialogue every two or three lines. Not only could Patience accomplish this, but she did it so quickly that dictation was given to Pearl within eight seconds after the request was made. When she finished, Pearl stated that she felt as if her head had been placed in a steel vise.

It should come as no surprise to learn that Pearl Curran's life was permanently changed by the arrival of Patience Worth. While the alliance was undoubtedly a wondrous affair, as Pearl often stated, it also demanded a lot from her, both physically and mentally. She never allowed herself to become obsessed with Patience either and the Curran's never attempted to exploit the "partnership" for material gain. Pearl continued, with the help of her maid, to do all her own shopping, cooking and housework and she continued to visit with friends as she had always done. Two or three nights each week were set aside for writing sessions and Patience always dictated to Pearl, no matter how many people were in the house. She only stopped when frightened by loud or sudden noises or when Pearl halted to converse with the guests.

Pearl explained that as the words flowed into her head, she would feel a pressure and then scenes and images would appear to her. She would see the details of each scene. If two characters were talking along a road, she would see the roadway, the grass on either side of it and perhaps the landscape in the distance. If they spoke a foreign language, she would hear them speaking but above them, she would hear the voice of Patience as she interpreted the speech and indicated what part of the dialogue she wanted in the story. She would sometimes even see herself in the scenes, standing as an onlooker or moving between the characters. The experience was so sharp and so vivid that she became familiar with things that she could have never known about living in St. Louis. These items included lamps, jugs and cooking utensils used long ago in distant countries, types of clothing and jewelry word by people in other times and the sounds and smells of places that she had never even heard of before.

On once occasion, Pearl was shown a small yellow bird sitting on a hedge. Patience wished to include it in a poem, but Pearl had no idea what type of bird it was. Finally, Patience became frustrated and said, "He who knoweth the hedgerows knoweth the yellow-hammer." Pearl and her husband later consulted an old encyclopedia and saw that the yellow-hammer in her vision was not a type seen in America, but only in England.

In spite of the visions and odd experiences though, Pearl never went into a trance during the writing sessions, as a Spiritualist medium would have done. She understood the writing as it came and yet while calling out the words to the stenographer, she would smoke cigarettes, drink coffee and eat. She seemed always to be aware of her surroundings, no matter what else might be going on with her.

As time passed, Pearl was not completely satisfied with the literary reputation that was being achieved by Patience Worth. She became determined to take up writing herself, even though she had never written anything before and had never had the urge to do so. Unfortunately though, her writings reflected her lack of education and talent. She wound up selling two of her stories to the *Saturday Evening Post*, but likely more for her fame as a conduit for Patience than for her own literary ability.

Patience was tolerant but condescending of her host's abilities, which may have been what prompted the love-hate relationship between them. Patience often scorned Pearl, but never failed to show her kindness. She simply seemed to think that her human counterpart was slightly stupid and that only by perseverance was she able to make herself known, especially when Pearl failed to grasp the spellings and meanings of certain words. But they plodded on together, continuing to amass a great body of work until about 1922.

In this year, the connection between the two of them began to deteriorate, possibly due to changes in Pearl's life and the fact that she had become pregnant for the first time at age 39. After her husband and her mother both died, the contact between Patience and Pearl became less and less often and eventually it died away.

By this time too, public interest in the mystery had faded, especially as no solution had ever been posed as to how the St. Louis housewife was accomplishing such remarkable feats. After the publication of several books and hundreds of poems, interest in Patience Worth vanished and cynicism replaced it. Debunkers accused Pearl of hiding her literary talent in order to exploit it in such a bizarre way and become famous. However, exhaustive studies have shown this to be highly unlikely, if not impossible. Scholars have analyzed Patience's works and have found them to accurate in historical detail and written in such a way that only someone with an intimate knowledge of the time could have created them.

Pearl Curran died in California on December 4, 1937. The *St. Louis Globe-Democrat* headlined her obituary with the words: "Patience Worth is Dead." And whatever the secret of the mysterious "ghost writer", it went to the grave with her.

So, what really happened in this case and why does it remain today as one of our great unsolved mysteries? Was there actually an entity speaking to Pearl from beyond the grave? Or could the writings have simply come from her unconscious mind?

No verification was ever made that Patience Worth actually lived in the 1600's and yet experts who studied Pearl Curran doubted that she could have produced the works attributed to the ghost on her own. She was a woman of limited education with no knowledge of the language used or the history and subject matter that was written of by the alleged Patience Worth. Pearl simply could not have created the works of literary quality that have become known as the works of her spiritual counterpart.

Could the writings have come from her unconscious mind though? Was Patience Worth a secondary personality of Pearl Curran? This too seems unlikely because on the rare occasions when secondary (or split) personalities have been documented, they have always been shown to supplant the main personality for a time. This was not true in Pearl's case. Her own personality co-existed with that of Patience Worth and Pearl was well aware of this fact.

So, what was it? What did happen here? Was it a true case of afterlife communication or the greatest hoax ever perpetrated on both the literary and paranormal communities? It's unlikely that we will ever know for sure, but in the absence of any other explanation, this one will have to be filed under "unexplained".

Washington Avenue - Early 1900's (Courtesy Missouri Historical Society)

II. MILITARY SPIRITS & PATRIOTIC GHOSTS

History & Hauntings of Military Life in St. Louis

Military officers and soldiers have been with St. Louis since the very beginnings of the city. Soldiers traveled with Laclede to the region, many of them abandoning Fort de Chartres to British rule and following their French comrades to the new settlement of St. Louis. In the early days though, St. Louis was no military post. The residents defended the town against Indian attack by constructing their own barricades. These fortifications ran westward from the river roughly along what is now Biddle Street, turned south along Third to Chouteau Avenue and then back to the river. In 1780, a watch tower was added at approximately Fourth and Walnut Streets to warn the settlers of approaching problems.

When St. Louis fell under Spanish rule, the authorities established a token garrison in the city. It consisted of two sergeants, five corporals, one drummer and 25 soldiers. Because it was obvious that these men could not defend the city against any sort of major attack, the townsfolk established their own militia of about 150 infantrymen and a few officers. Three other officers formed a cavalry of 47 men.

The first real fort would not come to St. Louis until the Americans arrived following the signing of the Louisiana Purchase agreement. Fort Bellefountaine was established in 1805 to protect the pioneers and settlers who were heading west to the frontier. At that time, the fort was the most remote of any posts built by the Army and it was located just north of St. Louis, near the confluence of the Mississippi and Missouri Rivers. It would provide crucial military protection to St. Louis and the region's fur trade for the next 20 years.

By 1826 though, Fort Bellefountaine had fallen into deplorable condition. The buildings were dilapidated and the whole place was considered "unhealthy", thanks to frequent flooding. It was finally decided that the site was to be abandoned. On March 4, 1826, Colonel Henry Atkinson was assigned to find a more suitable location for a new military post in St. Louis.

HAUNTED JEFFERSON BARRACKS

One could reasonably argue that per square acre, Jefferson Barracks is the most haunted location in the St. Louis metropolitan area. The post is comprised of 135 acres, containing buildings of various shapes and sizes... of those "occupied" buildings, 13 or more have stories of paranormal activity associated with them that I am aware of. I am sure that if truth were told, there are more ghost stories out there that are waiting to be unearthed.

DAVID GOODWIN from GHOSTS OF JEFFERSON BARRACKS

The site that Atkinson selected was south of the city. He discovered that the spot was in a fine natural position and there was an abundance of natural building supplies, as well as a nearby civilian population for which both supplies and labor could be obtained. The new post was dubbed Jefferson Barracks and it was officially established on October 23, 1826. The fort was named in honor of former president Thomas Jefferson, who had died earlier that same year.

The earliest role for Jefferson Barracks was to house the soldiers protecting the settlers from Indian attacks. In April 1832, a steamer of troops were sent north to participate in the Black Hawk War. A young lieutenant named Jefferson Davis, who would later go on to serve as the president of the Confederacy during the Civil War, was assigned to escort the captured Indian leader back to Jefferson Barracks. In 1836, other troops from the post would be sent to Florida to take part in battles against the Seminole Indians.

Life at the frontier post was difficult in the early days. Lieutenant Phillip St. George Cook, who graduated West Point in 1827 and came to Jefferson Barracks on his first assignment in a long and distinguished military career, had little good to say about the conditions of the fort. He recalled the infantrymen being crowded several to a room in stone barracks that were half-finished and uncomfortable. During the summer, heat in the region was oppressive and the flooded marshes along the Mississippi River bred insects and diseases, including cholera, yellow fever and smallpox.

A soldier's military training at that time consisted mostly of small arms practice on the parade field, marching and guard duty. For the most part, life in the garrison was boring and monotonous and when left to their own devices, the men usually turned to drinking, fighting and visiting the local prostitutes. The boredom also led many of the officers to get involving in duels, which as we learned in an earlier section of the book could sometimes have deadly consequences.

The early soldiers here were also subject to strict and unflinching discipline in those days. The most common offenses perpetrated by enlisted men were drunkenness and desertion. In most case, soldiers found guilty of drinking were reduced in rank and fined. Other punishments included being abused, threatened and even beaten. This, as well as the other drawbacks to life on the post like poor food and lack of medical care, led to literally hundreds of desertions. Some of the men who fled hid on the trains that stopped at the Jefferson Barracks railroad depot, stole boats or even swam across the Mississippi River. The army paid $30 for each deserter who was captured and returned to the post.

Deserters who had been captured were then incarcerated in the post's stockade. Here, they experienced harsh and sadistic punishments, in addition to living in cramped and foul cells that were infested with bed bugs. They were sometimes punished by being hanged by their thumbs or shackled to the floor with chains. It's not surprising that at least one of the old stockades is still allegedly inhabited by soldiers still seeking their release!

The post's "reservoir building" was refurbished into a guardhouse and jail in 1883. The rooms on the second floor were used to house the guards and the duty officer and the first floor served as the stockade. The floor was separated into two rooms. One side was the "garrison", which housed soldiers who had committed general offenses and the other was "general side", which was made up of an iron cage that was used to hold men who had committed more serious offenses. The men on this side slept on the floor or on bed slats with no mattresses. Those in the "garrison" were given bunks or hammocks if they were available. However, both sides were prone to flooding and were infested with lice and vermin. Eventually, it was torn down but memories of the past apparently lingered.

In 1897, a new building was constructed on the same spot and also served as the guard house and jail. In the 1990's, the building was remodeled and today, the first floor serves as the post's dining facility and the ground level is used by the Air National Guard. Over the past few years, unsettling incidents have shaken residents of the building, including the sighting of a ghost one morning in 1992. A female Air Guard soldier was walking down a hallway when a smoky human form appeared, floating a few feet off the floor. It appeared to move ahead of her, leaving a hazy trail behind it, until it finally disappeared.

Changes came to the conditions of the base in 1889. In June of that year, a man named Frank Woodward enlisted in the United States Army and was assigned to Jefferson Barracks for his training. What no one knew was that Woodward was an undercover reporter for the *St. Louis Post-Dispatch*. He had enlisted to investigate why so many men were deserting from the post and he soon discovered the horrible conditions, the inedible food, the bed bug infestations and mess sergeants who were stealing government food and the re-selling it off post. Woodward learned that this had caused a number of unexplained food shortages at the fort. Woodward also told of the violence on the post, such as the beatings of the enlisted men and an incident involving a black soldier who was beaten to death by an NCO for sitting in an area that was off limits to blacks.

Woodward's graphic reports made front-page news in St. Louis and were an embarrassment to high-ranking officers at Jefferson Barracks. Thanks to the reports, and the public outcry that followed, an investigation was launched into the disciplinary practices and the conditions at the post. The findings of the military inquiry caused many of the officers here to be reassigned and demoted.

Jefferson Barracks was first used as staging area for troops and equipment in 1846 during the Mexican War. When the fighting ended, the post was also used as a "mustering out" point for men returning to civilian life. This would take place again during many wars to follow, including the Civil War. The post would play an important role in St. Louis during the Civil War. As for the state of Missouri, it was sharply divided between North and South, however Jefferson Barracks and the Federal Arsenal in St. Louis remained loyal to the Federal government.

When war was declared in April 1861, Jefferson Barracks became a training post for Missouri's Union volunteers. Men and equipment poured into the post, arriving and departing by land, rail and river steamer. The roads to Jefferson Barracks were inundated with militia, horses, artillery and regular Army units. To make matters worse, thousands of volunteers for the Union flooded the post as well.

As the war entered its second year, Jefferson Barracks changed from an armed camp to a Federal medical facility. In the fall of 1862, the Army Medical Department built nine, temporary medical buildings on the post. Injured troops were transported to the barracks by train and boat from all over the country. Most hospitals during the war were terrifying and unsanitary places, Jefferson Barracks included. The facilities were overcrowded and dirty and ignorance and disease killed more men than battle wounds did.

After the war, medical procedures began to improve and while the facilities at Jefferson Barracks were reportedly better than most, there were cases of men who were injured or permanently crippled by the carelessness of post physicians. Not surprisingly, the hospitals of Jefferson Barracks have their own ghostly stories to tell.

The Jefferson Barracks "Station" Hospital was built around 1905 and served the soldiers of the post until the base was closed down in 1946. The third floor of the brick building served as a surgical center, while the basement housed the morgue. When Jefferson Barracks was closed in 1946, many of the outer buildings of the post were considered "surplus" by the military and were sold off to companies and individuals. The hospital became the property of the Mehlville School District in 1946.

The hospital was converted into a high school for a number of years but today, it is used as the school district's Facility Department. It is mainly used for storage and while few people spend much time in the building anymore, there have been a number of employees here over the years. Those who have been in the building after hours report the sounds of ghostly footsteps roaming the hallways and incidents where lights have turned on and off by themselves. There has also been the ghost of a child who has been seen walking through the basement. She always vanishes without explanation.

Author Dave Goodwin, who penned the complete story of the post's spirits, *Ghosts of Jefferson Barracks*, recalled an afternoon when he went into the old hospital's morgue. It is now used as a storage area and the basement is broken up into three rooms. A heavy metal door separates each room from the morgue's hallway. He noted that when he entered the morgue itself, he felt a sudden and extreme temperature drop. "This sudden change caused goose bumps to break out on my arms and for a split second, I felt like I just wanted to leave the area immediately," he said. And while he wouldn't attribute the explained cold chill to anything supernatural, one has to wonder if, based on the other paranormal reports from the building, he didn't come face to face with a ghostly soldier on that afternoon?

In January 1922, President Warren G. Harding ordered a section of Jefferson Barracks to become the home of a Veteran's Hospital, which opened in March 1923. The physicians here were given the task of caring for wounded and invalid soldiers and the hospital began providing continuous treatment for veterans until the base closed down. During the years of its operation, the building became known for hosting a ghost.

According to a story, there was once a private Halloween party that was held at the hospital. Security officers who worked the gate later commented to one of the party organizers about the "excellent" Civil War officer's uniform that one of the guests had worn to the party. The official was taken aback and replied that there had been no one wearing such a costume. The security officer was just as surprised because he distinctly remembered a man in a Civil War-era uniform who had entered the hospital grounds, presumably to attend the party that was going on.

Another similar version of the story involves the same Halloween party at the hospital. The host of the party, who was one of the officials at the hospital, noticed a man in a Civil War officer's uniform sitting on a stone wall at the edge of the throng of guests. The host walked over to the man and asked him how he liked the party. The soldier whispered a hoarse reply "Like it good", he said. The host, apparently miffed at the guest's crude reply, turned around and started to walk away. However, he looked back over his shoulder a few moments later and saw that the man in the Civil War costume was gone. He later discovered that no one invited to the party, or in attendance that night, wore such a costume to the event.

JEFFERSON BARRACKS NATIONAL CEMETERY

Soldiers who did not survive their stay at the Jefferson Barracks hospital of the time, were buried in the National Cemetery, which was established south of the post in 1863. The cemetery here did not have such an auspicious beginning though. It was originally started as a small piece of land set aside for soldiers and their families who died while stationed at Jefferson Barracks. The first person buried in the cemetery was Elizabeth Ann Lash, the 18 month-old daughter of an officer who was posted here, and her death was followed by other victims of disease, duels and violence on the frontier.

The small burial ground grew and a wooden fence was erected around it in a foolhardy attempt to keep out wild animals. But time was not kind to the post cemetery and thanks to the fact that most of the soldiers who buried friends or loved ones here were usually reassigned or moved on, there was no one to take care of the graves. Soon, the cemetery fell into a state of disrepair. As the cemetery expanded years later, the old memorials were forgotten and in many cases the identities of those buried beneath them were lost. The remains of these poor souls were reinterred with only a number or the word "unknown" carved on their headstone.

By 1862, it was obvious that more space than was currently available was going to be needed to bury the men killed during the Civil War. Major General Henry Halleck, commander of the Department of Missouri, recognized that the post cemetery at Jefferson Barracks could easily be expanded and would make an excellent choice for a national cemetery, as it was easily accessible from both land and riverboat. Based on his observations, President Abraham Lincoln expanded the "Old Post Cemetery" in 1863 and formally designated the burial ground as Jefferson Barracks National Cemetery.

A 1910's postcard of the Jefferson Barracks National Cemetery (Courtesy David Goodwin)

The grave sites began to fill quickly as the remains of soldiers from both the North and the South began to arrive at the post for burial. In addition, men who died at the post hospitals were also buried in the cemetery. Before the war ended, more than 1,140 Confederate soldiers were buried at Jefferson Barracks and were joined by over 12,000 men who fought for the Union.

In 1867, Sylvanus Beeman was appointed as the first superintendent of the cemetery with Martin Burke installed as his assistant the following year. Under their care, the cemetery was enlarged and improved and divided into sections for the ease of identification. A short time later, other military cemeteries from the region began to turn over their dead to Jefferson Barracks.

In 1876, the first graves were moved. The remains of 470 people were taken from a place called Arsenal Island and were reburied at Jefferson Barracks. The island, which was also known as Quarantine Island, was little more than a glorified sandbar that had been created by the currents of the Mississippi River. Located just north of Arsenal Street in St. Louis, it was only a half-mile wide and three-quarters of a mile long. Arsenal Island served the city for many years as a quarantine camp, where soldiers and civilian river passengers were taken when they were suspected of carrying some sort of contagious diseases. During its years of operation, it saw cases of cholera, smallpox, yellow fever and more. Steamboats were often directed to the island if suspicious illnesses were on board and the passengers could be held in quarantine for weeks. Medical surgeons on the island inspected the passengers before allowing them into St. Louis and if they were found to be sick, forced them to live on the island until they recovered or died from their illness. Those who died were buried on the north end of the island.

The bodies from the island graveyard were moved because of the threat to the island caused by the changing channels of the river. By 1880, surveyors discovered that the island had moved nearly 4,800 feet downriver, a half mile from its position in 1862. Frequent spring flooding had already washed away many of the graves of the diseased and it was not uncommon to find human remains in the river. For that reason, the bodies were moved and their graves marked with tombstones bearing the legend "unknown".

In April 1904, the remains of 33 officers, soldiers and civilians who had been buried at Fort Bellefountaine were moved to the National Cemetery as well. These "unknown" burials, which did include the two year-old daughter of former officer and explorer Zebulon Pike, were buried on the same bluff, near the grave of Elizabeth Lash... a young child who may not rest in peace.

As with many great graveyards, the Jefferson Barracks National Cemetery has its share of ghostly stories. One of these involves a spectral child who has been seen on a bluff in the cemetery. As she has often been spotted near the grave of little Elizabeth Lash, legend holds that it is her ghost who walks here. Unfortunately, little is known about the Lash family or how the young girl actually died. She was buried in the Old Post Cemetery on August 5, 1827 and its likely that she passed away from one of the many diseases that were prevalent in the Mississippi Valley in those days. But what might make her ghost become restless?

That part of the story remains a mystery but what we do know is that employees of the cemetery and at least one soldier assigned to Jefferson Barracks have seen the ghost of a very small girl walking between the marble tombstone near Elizabeth's grave. But is it really Elizabeth Lash?

Author Dave Goodwin isn't so sure. He believes there may be another explanation for a toddler spirit to be wandering the cemetery. In 1900, shortly after the death of Martin Burke, who was by then the superintendent of the graveyard, a new caretaker took his place named Edward Past. Not long after filling this position, he discovered the remains of several unidentified children in the Old Post section of the cemetery. Their graves had long been hidden beneath bushes and undergrowth. While their identities and the reasons for their deaths could not be discovered, it's likely that they were the victims of some epidemic, like cholera.

It's possible that one of these young spirits may be the little girl who roams the cemetery, perhaps in an attempt to somehow not be forgotten after all.

And there is another legend that has long been told of this cemetery, involving two ghosts. One of them is a Federal "Buffalo Soldier" and the other is a Confederate soldier. It has been told that the graves of these two men are located close to one another and that at certain times this black man from the north and this white man from the south both appear near their grave sites to acknowledge one another.

It is said that this ghostly greeting occurs around sunset or occasionally in the morning, around dawn. The two shadowy forms rise from their graves and have been seen moving across the cemetery toward one another. When they meet, witnesses claims that they extend a hand to one another in friendship and some have surmised that they are doomed to continuously try and make peace with one another, not only for themselves but also for the fallen soldiers who are buried around them.

After the Civil War, Jefferson Barracks continued providing troops and support for the Indian wars in the west. The post would see action again in 1898 when America became embroiled in the Spanish-American War in Cuba. Once again, Jefferson Barracks served as an induction point and training center for volunteers and National Guardsmen who were called up to serve. Men from all walks of life heard President McKinley's call to join up, even a large contingent of African-American men. Four units made up almost entirely of black soldiers were formed at Jefferson Barracks to fight in Cuba. The special units were formed because it was thought at that time that black soldiers were immune to the yellow fever and typhoid that were ravaging white troops in the war zone. Up until this time, white officers always led black units but during the Spanish-American War, black soldiers were allowed to obtain the rank of lieutenant and lead colored troops. While this was some progress, the segregation of military units would last until after World War II.

The war ended in August 1898 and victorious troops from Cuba, Puerto Rico and Manila arrived at Jefferson Barracks to be mustered out of the service. In 1899, the post was presented with a cannon that was recovered from the Spanish battleship *Oquenda*, which was sunk in Santiago Bay. The cannon is still displayed on the bluff behind the post headquarters today.

In 1915, Jefferson Barracks also took part in a military campaign that is largely forgotten today. This operation was under the command of General John "Black Jack" Pershing and it was organized to capture the Mexican bandit leader Pancho Villa, who had been conducting raids into American territory.

But it was another conflict that officers at Jefferson Barracks were watching more closely, a conflict that was threatening to become the "war to end all wars". Battles were raging across Europe, while America waited and watched. Beginning in 1914, German planes and airships starting bombing England and France and their submarines were sending ships to the bottom of the ocean. Finally, attacks on merchant vessels sailing to and from the United States drew American into the war and a formal declaration against Germany was made on April 6, 1917.

Jefferson Barracks was again to serve as the country's leading induction site and thousands of soldiers passed through the post on their way to the battlefields of Europe. By 1919, it was all over and the soldiers returned to St. Louis and then on to civilian life.

Jefferson Barracks was back in the action again at the start of World War II. In fact, on the morning following the attack on Pearl Harbor, shots were even fired on the post! After a declaration of war was announced, all furloughs were cancelled and sentries were posted at key points all over the base with orders to fire on any intruders. In the cool, early morning hours of December 8, 1941, an unknown vehicle attempted to run past through the front gate, failing to stop when ordered to by the soldiers on duty. Following orders, they opened fire on the truck and finally brought it to a halt. Yanking the doors of the vehicle open, they found a shaken milkman who was making his morning deliveries and hadn't realized that the post had been closed!

In the days and weeks to follow, thousands of soldiers passed through Jefferson Barracks on their way to military service. During the course of the war, it is estimated that more than 400,000 soldiers were processed and trained here. And the outbreak of the war caused the population on the post to multiply by ten. Men overflowed the barracks and on the weekend were always looking for something to do. Not surprisingly, medical personnel on the post began to see a sharp rise in cases of venereal disease. A crackdown on local vice and prostitution by the St. Louis police brought about a large drop in the number of cases treated, but the trend continued throughout the war.

During World War II, Jefferson Barracks was also used as a prisoner of war camp. Over 400 German and Italian soldiers were confined to the base during the fighting but during the Flood of 1943, the prisoners helped to fill sandbags and worked side by side with their captors to hold back the river. The men were used as laborers on the base, but not for a short time in 1945, when they participated in a work strike to protest the treatment of a prisoner. They laid down their tools and refused to work but eventually, a diet of only bread and water brought them peacefully back to their labors. Before the war ended, seven of these prisoners died and were laid to rest in the Jefferson Barracks cemetery.

With the end of the war came the end of Jefferson Barracks. On June 30, 1946, the flag was lowered here for the final time. Of the original 1700 acres, the Missouri Air National Guard acquired 135 acres and the rest was deemed to be "surplus". In the years that followed, the property fell into a state of decay and vandals and souvenir hunters managed to damage the old and unattended buildings. In 1950 though, the St. Louis County Parks and Recreation Department acquired 500 acres of the land to create the Jefferson Barracks Historical Park. Today, it holds athletic fields, picnic shelters, an amphitheater and several museums.

The military has not altogether abandoned the site either. These days, it is home to units of the Missouri Air National Guard, the Missouri Army National Guard and the U.S. Army Reserve. There are 41 buildings remaining on the post and both military and civilian employees occupy 35 of them at different times. The buildings serve as administrative offices, classrooms and maintenance facilities for the national guard and reserve units on the base, while others serve as storage areas and warehouse.

And out of these historic old buildings.. a great many of them are haunted!

HISTORIC GHOSTS

Many of the ghost stories told at Jefferson Barracks have been a part of the local lore for years. Some of them even date back as far as the Civil War. One such tale is that of the specter who has been reported on the grounds near the post headquarters.

During the Civil War, and for years after, soldiers guarded the train depot and the railroad tracks located along the Mississippi River. They also guarded the headquarters building that was located on the bluff above the depot. One night during the Civil War, a sentry was walking his post near the building. As he rounded the corner, he reportedly observed a solitary figure walking up the grassy hill from the train yard. As the soldier stood watching, he realized that the man was not a person at all, but what was described as a blurry "spook".

There is also a long-running legend about a ghost who haunts the post's old powder magazine as well. The massive limestone building was built in 1857 as a secure location to store rifles, cannons and gunpowder for the troops at the post. In 1871, the Federal Arsenal in St. Louis was closed and its contents were also moved to Jefferson Barracks. The powder magazine remained in constant use until the post closed in 1946. In more recent times, it has become a historical museum that is run by the St. Louis County Parks and Recreation Department.

The story of the ghost here has its beginnings around the start of World War II. In the dark days at the start of the war, sentries were posted all around the fort to protect it from possible incursion. One of the most important guard positions was the powder magazine. Armed sentries were often seen patrolling around the building or walking across the top of the stone wall that surrounded the magazine.

Several of the soldiers who stood guard here reported seeing a ghostly sentry who would occasionally appear and challenge the confused guard who was standing his post. The threatening spirit was said to have "a bullet hole in his head, running red with blood" and was said to be so frightening that several guards allegedly threw down their guns and deserted their posts after encountering him. One story had it that a certain soldier was so frightened that he not only left his post one night, but that he also left the army! According to the story, the spectral sentry was a guard who had been killed years before when a raiding party attempted to steal munitions from the powder magazine. He was believed to have confronted his living counterparts because he thought they were trespassers. Even after all of these years, he was still on duty, even in death.

Another old story tells of a ghost who long haunted the grounds around the post's old north gate. He was believed to be the spirit of Second Lieutenant Thomas May, who was killed in a duel near the north gate in 1830. Legends also tell of a ghostly woman who has been spotted at the Laborer's House, a historic structure that was built in 1851. It was once used a residence by civilians who worked at the ordnance depot and today is operated as a gift shop by the Parks Department.

But not all of the ghosts of Jefferson Barracks are old stories and legends from years ago. First hand encounters with the unknown still continue to take place on the post today! There are many haunted buildings here, where strange and unusual things have happened for years, but in these pages, we'll take a look at what might consider the "most haunted" sites of Jefferson Barracks.

The Old Post Headquarters (Courtesy of David Goodwin)

POST HEADQUARTERS

The Post Headquarters, or Building 1, was constructed in 1900. Built on the edge of the parade field and on a bluff overlooking the river, the three-story brick building has seen many occupants over the years. History seems to stand still here. Evidence remains that one large room was used as a ballroom and many of the ornamental wood fixtures still remain as remnants of days gone by. The Missouri Air National Guard has recently refurbished it and perhaps these renovations have "stirred up" the spirits of the past. The most famous ghost to haunt this building is believed to be the spirit of a Civil War general who has been seen in the post commander's office.

A number of employees have reported seeing a shadowy figure, seated at a desk near a window on the second floor of the building. The apparition appears to be writing dispatches by candlelight and has the hazy outlines of a man in uniform. When employees enter the building and attempt to investigate the second floor office though, the figure has always vanished. Strangely, they have discovered that when they approach the doorway to the room, they often hear the sound of footsteps walking away from them. However, there is no other way out of the room and no one inside of it!

And while this has happened many times in years past, the most detailed encounter was experienced by Sergeant William McWilliams, who is currently assigned to the Funeral Honors Program at Jefferson Barracks. One evening in 1998, while he was residing in one of the nearby buildings, McWilliams decided to go for a run around the post. After a short time, he decided to stop and rest near the Spanish battleship cannon that is located behind Building 1. As he rested for a moment, he happened to look up and see what appeared to be candlelight coming from one of the windows of the building. The light flickered against the glass of an office on the first floor, near the north end of the headquarters. The rest of the building was dark and so the odd light made McWilliams curious as to its source.

He walked up to the window and was startled to see an older man, wearing what McWilliams believed to be a Confederate military uniform, seated at a desk in the office. The man appeared to be writing something on paper, using an old-fashioned pen. He sat quietly working for what McWilliams estimated was three or four minutes and then stood and walked toward to door of the room with the candle in one hand and the pen in the other. The officer neared the doorway and then simply faded away into nothing. McWilliams recalled that he did not stick around to see if the general came back!

Another person with first hand experience with the ghosts of the Headquarters building is Security Officer Richard Dickson, who is employed by the Missouri Department of Public Safety. Dickson was working by himself one evening and he came into Building 1 to get a soda from the vending machine in the basement. As he started to walk back out, he neared the first floor landing and heard the unmistakable sound of a typewriter hammering away on the second floor. This was strange as no one was working in the building that evening and all of the lights had already been turned off.

Dickson put down his soda and started upstairs to investigate the sound. As he neared the second floor though, the typewriter abruptly stopped! The officer shook his head and considered that perhaps he had been mistaken about the sound. Perhaps it had been something outside that sounded like a typewriter? He turned and started back down the stairs and then suddenly, the clacking of the typewriter keys began again! This time though, the officer chose not to investigate and he quickly left the building.

And these men are not alone when it comes to ghostly experiences in Building 1. Many Air National Guard employees who have worked after hours in the Headquarters building have their own stories to tell. They claim to hear phantom footsteps when no one else is in the building, hear furniture being moved about and see lights go on and off without assistance.

Master Sergeant Judy Jarvis, an Information Manager for the Missouri Air National Guard, was working in the building one night in the fall of 1992 when she heard what seemed to be several desks moving about on the second floor of the building. The noises were so loud that she could hear them plainly from her office near the first floor foyer. Jarvis thought nothing about this though. Several other employees had mentioned moving some furniture around and she thought that perhaps this was simply the evening that they had decided to do it.

A little later on, Jarvis finished her work for the night and decided to leave. As she left, she called loudly up the stairs "I'm leaving now!" and then turned out the lights and locked the exterior door of the building, guessing that the others could let themselves out when then left. When she got to the parking lot though, she realized that her car was the only one parked there. The rest of the lot was empty! Where were the cars belonging to the employees upstairs? Jarvis quickly went back inside. She unlocked the door and stepped in, only to discover that one of the hallway lights was on. She distinctly remembered turning it off just moments before. Jarvis then proceeded to check the entire building and found it empty. There was no one else there and no reason that any noises should have been coming from the upper floor that evening!

BUILDING 28

This former barracks was built back in 1897 as a double barracks with a three-story tower in the center. It had been designed to hold up to four companies of cavalry soldiers and their non-commissioned officers. Today it is the home of the 218th Engineer Squadron.

Throughout the 1970's, men working inside of the building reported hearing ghostly footsteps pacing the corridors of the building. One night, a man was working on some training records for an upcoming inspection when he heard someone walking around on the second floor above his office. He didn't think that anyone else was in the building, but as it simply sounded like another soldier working upstairs, he never bothered to check on it. Later though, more footsteps joined the first set and the noise became very distracting as he tried to finish his reports. Finally, he tossed aside his papers and went upstairs but when he got to the area where he believed the sounds had been coming from, he find nobody there! He looked around for a few moments and then decided to write the whole thing off to his imagination. However, as soon as he got back downstairs to his desk, the footsteps started again. This time, he decided to just wrap up his reports and call it a night.

One evening in the fall of 1980, Chief Master Sergeant Eugene Anacker and several other Air National Guard NCO's were working late in the building. When they decided to leave for the night, the group turned out the lights, locked the doors and then walked out into the parking lot in front of the building, where they stood talking for a few minutes. As they started to leave, Anacker happened to look up and notice that one of the lights on the third floor of the building had been accidentally left on. He dispatched the lowest ranking of the small group to go back into the building and turn it off.

The young NCO unlocked the main doors, climbed the stairs to the third floor and turned the light off. A few moments later, he re-appeared downstairs and he locked the door behind him as he left the building again. As the young man walked toward him, Chief Anacker looked up and noticed that the same light was on once again, even though they had just seen the other soldier turn it off. Thinking that the wiring in the old building was going bad, he sent the same NCO back into the building again to turn it off.

When the NCO returned to the parking lot once more, Anacker was stunned to see that the same third floor light was once again shining. Again, he sent the same NCO back inside to turn the light off once more. This time when he came out though, none of them looked to see if the light had turned itself back on.

This time, they simply got into their cars and went home!

Atkinson Hall or Building 78 (Courtesy of David Goodwin)

ATKINSON HALL

Building 78, which is also known as Atkinson Hall, was erected in 1912 to serve as the post's main dining facility. The structure, with its distinctive whitewashed exterior was planned to replace the old dining hall, which had been dubbed the "Cockroach Bogey". The building was always extremely busing during "chow time" and served as a focal point of activity for the soldier's here until the post closed down in 1946.

Years after the post closed, the building was renovated for the new occupants of the place, the Army Reserve and the National Guard. During these renovations, one of the greatest mysteries of the building was uncovered. While work was being done, a secret room was discovered on the third floor, near the main staircase. The room was not shown on any of the building plans and had obviously been added without anyone's knowledge. Inside of the room, workers found a collection of military personnel files, books and photographs from the early part of the century. The mystery of this room was compounded by the story that the contractor who had designed the building also committed suicide inside of it a few years later. Could his ghost be one of the phantoms who have been reported wandering the hallways?

Today, Building 78 is used by several units from the Missouri National Guard and apparently plays host to a variety of spirits. Several military and civilian employees have reported that the ghost of a World War I era soldier walks through the building, apparently looking around and insuring that everything is secure.

And there are others. Major William Smith had his own encounter in Atkinson Hall while he was the Battalion Logistics Officer assigned to the 1138th Engineer Battalion in this building before they moved to Building 27 in the early 1990's. Smith was working in the basement by himself one night after hours. As he was waking down a hallway on his way to the restroom, he suddenly had the overwhelming feeling that someone was watching him as he walked down the corridor. The feeling passed and he dismissed it, sure that it was just the "creepy atmosphere" of the building that had gotten to him. He shrugged and went on towards the restroom, which was just around the corner.

Then suddenly, what he described as a "shadowy transparent form" crossed the hallway in front of him! "It was like catching a quick glimpse of something," Smith later recalled. He stepped up his pace and reached the spot where he had seen the shape. Just as he was about to walk into the intersecting hallway, Smith saw the "shadowy form" peer around the corner at him! It lingered there for just a few moments and then disappeared. Instead of curious, this time Smith was scared. "I turned on all of the lights," he said, "to see if anyone else was in the basement. It was different, it was like someone was really there."

Sergeant McWilliams, the same man who encountered the ghostly soldier in the post headquarters, actually lived in Building 78 for a time when he first started with the Funeral Honors Program. He and another man who also resided here often claimed to share Smith's feeling of being watched. They also reported waking up at night and hearing someone going up and down the stairs inside of the building. A quick search would always find the building empty. One night, he woke up and said that the room in which he was sleeping had inexplicably turned very cold. In fact, "icy cold, so cold you could see your breath," he added. McWilliams said that the room then turned warm again a few moments later. He could never find an explanation for how, or why, this could have happened.

BUILDING 27 & 27A

Located at the far end of the post from the Headquarters Building is Building 27. It was constructed in 1896 as quarters for enlisted soldiers and is a large rectangular building with a three-story center and two wings jutting out from each end. It was designed to hold up to four companies of soldiers and their NCO's. The original mess hall was located in the basement but in the 1940's, a smaller, one-story building was built directly behind Building 27. It was designated as Building 27A and it was used as the mess hall

Building 27 (Courtesy of David Goodwin)

Today, Building 27 is the home of the 1138th Engineer Battalion and the smaller attached building serves as the battalion's Headquarters Detachment. Both buildings are also home to more of Jefferson Barracks' ghosts!

The eerie atmosphere of the place seems to "infect" those who work here. One veteran battalion supply sergeant has stated that he is always looking for a light switch to turn on when he is in the building alone because he often feels like someone is watching him. A battalion staff officer who often spends the night in the building has said that on at least one occasion, he thought he heard "muffled footsteps" on the stairs and doors opening and closing when he was alone in the building.

In September 2000, Specialist Nicole Howell had an encounter that went beyond footsteps and doors when she actually saw a phantom soldier in the main foyer of Building 27. She described the apparition is that of a "cavalry scout" from the Civil War period. He was dressed in uniform pants with a stripe down the side, had shoulder-length hair and was wearing a sword. When she first spied the chilling figure, she saw only boots and pants walking across the foyer! Then, his upper torso and his head appeared. As the specter moved about, he seemed to "phase in and out", fading and appearing again as he moved from place to place.

She later observed this same scout on the landing of the stairs leading up to the second floor of the building and again in the mail room. Each time that she saw him, she again stressed the fact that the ghost seemed to fade in an out.

Specialist Howell's husband, Sergeant Charles Howell, Administrative NCO for the 203rd Engineer Company, had a similar encounter with a phantom soldier, although apparently one of another era. He was working late one evening in March 2001, going through administration files in the Orderly Room. As he was bent over some papers, he got the distinct impression that someone was behind him. When he looked up, he saw a man that he didn't recognize standing in the office. The unknown visitor was solidly-built and was wearing a blue uniform shirt from the Spanish-American war period, khaki colored pants and a dirty, cowboy style hat.

Not really realizing what he was seeing for a moment, Howell looked back down at his papers and then quickly jerked his head up again. Just as he did so, the man faded away.

After this sighting, Howell was convinced that the ghost was the same mysterious "prankster" who had been playing tricks on him in recent months, flipping lights on and off and moving things about. On one occasion, he had even seen a boot pass by his desk out of the corner of his eye. When he turned to look, there was no one there.

About a month after his sighting of the "visitor", Howell was again working late in the Orderly Room. He had locked the hallway door after turning off the lights in the corridor outside. He had left the door to the Orderly Room open and was working quietly when he heard the hallway door (which had been locked!) slam open! The slamming sound was followed by footsteps marching down the hall towards the office.

Sergeant Howell jumped up to see who was there, still hearing the heavy footsteps as they approached his location. As he neared the door, he expected to see someone either pass by or turn into his office. Instead, he heard the footsteps continue past the door and proceed to the end of the hall. He never saw whoever was making the sounds of the marching boots!

After gathering his courage, Howell went out into the darkened corridor and looked around. There was no one else there. He also checked the hallways door that he had heard open up. It was closed now and inexplicably, it was also locked. Sergeant Howell then turned on his heels and went back to the Orderly Room. He closed the door behind him and switched on the radio, turning the volume up quite loud.

That way, he wouldn't hear any more strange noises in the hallway!

David Goodwin is a Captain in the Missouri National Guard and is also the Commander of the Headquarters Detachment of the 1138th Engineer Battalion, assigned to Building 27. In addition, he is a good friend of mine and the already mentioned author of the book *Ghosts of Jefferson Barracks*. When he began collecting stories for his book about ghostly sightings on the post, he was merely taking other soldier's tales and committing them to paper. He never expected to have an unexplained experience of his own, but as I have often told people who have asked about my own experiences as a writer... sometimes the author becomes a part of the story!

In the summer of 2001, Dave was working late one evening on some paperwork in Building 27A. His unit was preparing to go to annual training and a small group of soldiers were planning to leave early the next morning. One of the men who would be leaving the following morning lived some distance away and for this reason, planned to bunk down in the building rather than drive in during the pre-dawn hours.

As Dave was working that night, he heard the soldier moving around upstairs, likely getting ready to bed down for the evening. He heard someone moving back and forth, footsteps and the occasional bump and thud of a man packing gear and turning down his bed. This continued for as long as Dave finished his work and made plans to leave the building. As he got his things together, he paged the soldier upstairs and asked him to come downstairs to the foyer so that Dave could find out what doors needed to be locked on the way out. Almost as soon as he put down the telephone, he heard the soldier come running down the stairs from the second floor. He then heard him come through the main foyer, enter the Annex and come to a stop outside of his office door.

"I was packing my suitcase," Dave explained, "and thinking that the person standing outside of my office was the soldier that I had paged, I commented out loud that he did not have to wait outside of the office while I finished packing."

Dave called out to the soldier several times and asked him to come into the office. After three or four times, and no one came in, he started to wonder what was going on. He had certainly heard someone come into the hallway from the foyer and no one had left. After a few more seconds, he went to the door and looked out.

No one was there.

Dave paged the soldier again over the intercom and asked that he come down to the lobby. With his suitcase in hand, Dave waited in the foyer for nearly five minutes but no one came downstairs. "I knew that someone was in the building," he said, "but I didn't know where."

He put down his suitcase and went down to the basement, thinking that perhaps the soldier had gone there to pack equipment for his trip. The basement was deserted and so he began to search the rest of the place, covering the entire building floor by floor. The reader will not likely be surprised to find that Dave was in the building alone!

But even after all of the research that he had done and all of the ghostly tales that he had collected, Dave was determined not to let his imagination run away with him. He was sure that there was a logical explanation for what had happened and so the next morning, he set out to track down the soldier he had believed was upstairs the night before. He met with the other man and Dave was informed that after the soldier had been dismissed for the day, he had changed clothes and had gone to his sister-in-law's house. The soldier had at no time returned to the building and at about the time that Dave had heard someone running down the stairs, the soldier had been having dinner with his family at a local restaurant.

"On this particular night, I know for a fact that someone was moving around the building and that someone, or something, responded to my page," Dave stated without a doubt. "For me, that experience in Building 27A proved without a shadow of a doubt that there had to be some truth to the ghost stories I had collected from the civilians and soldiers working at Jefferson Barracks."

SPIRITS OF THE CIVIL WAR

In 1821, Missouri was admitted to the Union as a state, but only on the condition that it was admitted as a "slave state", meaning that it was permissible for slaves to be owned and kept within its borders. This was a result of Henry Clay's "Missouri Compromise", which maintained the balance between free and slave states and still prohibited slavery within the Louisiana Purchase territory outside of Missouri and north of Missouri's southern boundary. But as mentioned earlier, Missouri was never a typical slave state. In 1860, only three slave states had fewer slaves than Missouri and of those, only Delaware had a smaller percentage of slaves in its total population. Slave ownership was simply uncommon in Missouri as only one in eight families owned slaves and most owned less than five.

And if slavery was uncommon in the state of Missouri, it was downright rare in St. Louis. As discussed earlier, there simply wasn't much for a slave to do in the city, outside of domestic work. St. Louis had also become a haven for the state's free blacks.

Because of the "boom time" that St. Louis experienced in the decade before the Civil War, there was almost always work to be found, further negating the need for slavery. The commercial and industrial markets both grew dramatically in this period, especially after the arrival of the railroad in 1853. The riverboat era was still in its heyday and thanks to this, St. Louis was really the only urban area in Missouri that was even worthy of being called a city. This tended to put the region at odds with the rest of the state, which was primarily made up of farmers and small merchants and who owned the vast majority of the slaves.

St. Louis also differed from the rest of the state politically. In November 1860, white male Missourians went to the polls to vote for a successor to President James Buchanan. Four candidates appeared on the ballots. Stephen Douglas, the famous Democrat from Illinois, received nearly 36 percent of Missouri's votes. John Bell, who ran on the Constitutional ticket, drew 35 percent of the vote. Another candidate, John C. Breckenridge, was the "Southern Rights" democrat on the ticket and he garnered about 19 percent of the vote. And finally, Abraham Lincoln, the candidate from the young Republican Party, received the votes of only 10 percent of Missouri voters.

Those were the votes in the state of Missouri, but again, things were different in St. Louis. The city became only one of two counties in the entire state in which Abraham Lincoln carried the election. Breckenridge, the "slavery candidate", only received barely over two percent of the vote. In all of the slave states combined, Lincoln only received 27,000 votes, but more than 17,000 of these votes came from the German-Americans of Missouri and more than half of those came from St. Louis alone.

A few months before the national election, the state of Missouri had elected Claiborne Fox Jackson, from the planter class of central Missouri, as governor. While Jackson claimed to be a "Douglas Democrat", which put him more on the moderate side, his views were more in line with "slavery candidate" Breckenridge. Jackson would soon find himself at odds with the political force in St. Louis, which was beginning to challenge the dominance that the slave-holding elite of Central Missouri had long held over politics in the state. A civil war was coming to America and the state of Missouri was ready to erupt.

WAR COMES TO ST. LOUIS

By the early part of 1861, many believed that St. Louis was feeling the electric tension that comes as the calm before the storm. The merchants and the planters had been friends for years, believing in moderation and compromise. No one in the city wanted war, or so they professed, but even the most optimistic among them began to feel that trouble was coming.

In January 1861, Claiborne Jackson had taken the oath of the governor's office of Missouri. His inaugural address left no doubt that he intended to align the state with the rapidly forming Confederacy in the south. State conventions were suddenly being held to discuss secession from the Union. They met for the first time on February 28. In return, moderates began to call for meetings of a Constitutional Union party, hoping to preserve not only the Union, but also peace in the nation and in the state of Missouri. Other pro-Union men were not so moderate. Men like Frank Blair, Jr., the political heir of Thomas Hart Benton, had given up all hope for compromise and supported President Lincoln in ending the threat of secession once and for all. Many St. Louis men were allied with Blair, including James O. Broadhead, who would go on to become the first president of the American Bar Association. At that time, he was the District Attorney in St. Louis and he pushed for not only toppling Governor Jackson, but for war if needed.

The Constitutional Unionists and the Black Republicans, like Blair and Broadhead, watched closely the maneuverings of the Jackson men in St. Louis. Armed militiamen were stationed at the Berthold Mansion, where the Missouri secessionist banner with its single bar and crescent waved proudly. Meanwhile, Union men drilled openly and operated a headquarters at Turner Hall. Governor Yates of Illinois sent them 2,000 muskets in a load of beer barrels with which to prepare for trouble. Both groups had their eyes on the well-stocked St. Louis Arsenal near the river. Here, either side could easily capture more than 60,000 guns, along with 200 barrels of powder and other munitions.

The Berthold Mansion
(Courtesy of Missouri Historical Society)

Governor Jackson constantly warned that the secessionist men should take the Arsenal, but to no avail. However, he was reassured by General D.M Frost, who reported that Major Bell at the Arsenal was loyal to the state of Missouri and would not allow the facility to fall into Unionist hands.

Meanwhile, Isaac Sturgeon, federal assistant treasurer in St. Louis, was also concerned and not only about the Arsenal, but the funds in his charge as well. With very few United States regulars west of the Mississippi, he contacted Washington with his concerns. A short time later, a detachment was sent to strengthen the forces at Jefferson Barracks. Then, on the urgings of Mayor Oliver Filley, a loyal Union man, a group of soldiers marched into the city, took over the Customs House and removed the government's money.

The chief military commander in Missouri at that time was General William Selby Harney, a close friend of Jefferson Davis. He was living in St. Louis at the time and saw no cause for alarm over the events that were being set into motion. However, Major David Hunter, who had conferred in the city with Isaac Sturgeon, was not so confident. Soon, Harney received a telegram from the War Department, asking whether or not it might be wise to bring soldiers from

Jefferson Barracks to guard over the Arsenal. A few days later, Captain Nathaniel Lyon was sent from Fort Riley to St. Louis with a detachment of troops. Within a short time, he was placed in charge of the Arsenal and General Harney was called to Washington.

A View of the St. Louis Arsenal in the 1930's

In the midst of all of this, the delegates, both pro and anti-Union, began meeting in Jefferson City to discuss whether or not Missouri should secede from the Union. The convention opened and on the first day, former Governor Sterling Price (who would later command Confederate troops in the state) was elected chairman. On the second day, the delegates voted to adjourn and then re-convene at the Mercantile Library Hall in St. Louis. The delegates from the city had voted in unison for the state to remain in the Union.

While their statements were loyal, they were also conciliatory in an attempt to keep Missouri from being ripped apart. They remained hopeful until April 12... and the firing on Fort Sumter. After that, all bets were off.

The first acts of aggression from the Confederacy sent ripples through the cautious peace in St. Louis. But when President Lincoln called for four regiments of volunteers from Missouri, Governor Jackson denounced the call as "illegal, unconstitutional and revolutionary". Meanwhile, a Committee of Public Safety was formed in St. Louis, headed by Oliver Filley, Francis Blair, Jr., James Broadhead and other pro-Union Republicans and Democrats. They pledged "unalterable fidelity to the Union under all circumstances" and they met daily at Turner Hall.

Four days after Jackson refused to obey the President's orders, Captain Nathaniel Lyon was ordered to muster four regiments into public service. Before nightfall, he had them at the Arsenal, supplied with both arms and ammunition. On April 30, Lyon was informed that if he and the Committee of Public Safety deemed it necessary, he could proclaim martial law in the city of St. Louis.

On May 2, the secessionists in Jefferson City held a special legislative session to organize their own militia. The state troops were ordered into camp to support Missouri's ties to the Confederacy and two St. Louis units obeyed this order on May 6. They marched to Camp Jackson, formerly Lindell Grove, on the east side of Grand Avenue between Olive Street and Laclede Avenue. One regiment, under the command of Lieutenant Colonel Sam Bowen was made up of mostly Confederate sympathizers, while the other was made up of mostly men loyal to the Union. It is doubtful whether most of the soldiers had any idea of Governor Jackson's plans, but the plans were all too obvious to the Committee of Public Safety. They became even plainer after the Committee learned that the governor had asked Jefferson Davis to send cannons for a siege of the Arsenal. Davis returned a message that stated that the South was looking "anxiously and hopefully for the day when the Star of Missouri shall be added to the constellation of the Confederate States of America" and he also sent along several 12-pound howitzers and some 32-pound guns to make sure that the day would come sooner rather than later. On May 8, the *J.C. Swon*, flying a Confederate flag, reached the St. Louis levee. It carried the requested guns in crates marked as "Tamaroa Marble". Major James A. Shaler escorted the crates to Camp Jackson, unaware that he was under surveillance at the time.

In my personal opinion, Captain Nathaniel Lyon may be one of the unsung heroes of the Civil War, at least as far as St. Louis is concerned! On May 9, Lyon disguised himself in women's clothing and drove through Camp Jackson to look things over. Not liking what he found, he called a meeting of the Committee of Public Safety as soon as he returned to the Arsenal. The American flag was still flying over Camp Jackson, he reported, but General Daniel Frost (a West Point classmate of Lyon's) was preparing to attack the Arsenal anyway. Lyon decided that, even though he had no official orders, he would make the first move and would capture the camp and disarm the militia.

Early the next morning, six volunteer regiments marched toward Camp Jackson. They surrounded the camp and brought about a half-dozen artillery pieces to a ridge along Grand Avenue and to a hill near Olive Street and Garrison Avenue. Lyon then demanded Frost's surrender, stating that the troops of mostly secessionists and men loyal to the Confederacy were engaging in acts hostile to the United States government.

Frost protested and declared Lyon's demand as "unconstitutional", which seems to have been the standard reply by any of the secessionists when they were accused of thwarting the interests of the government. Still though, Frost admitted that he was in no position to defend the camp against Lyon's superior force and that he had no choice but to surrender. Lyon offered immediate parole to all of those who would take an oath of allegiance but only eight or nine of the 800 men in the camp agreed. The others refused and said that they had already taken the oath and to repeat it would be a confession that they had violated it and had become enemies of the nation. Lyon and his men gathered up all of the weapons in the camp and the militiamen were formed into lines to be marched downtown between Union soldiers.

The activity in the camp had drawn a large crowd and many of the spectators began shouting taunts and threats at the soldiers who had captured the camp. The crowd began milling into the camp and between the lines of soldiers, creating confusion and chaos. Finally, the column began to move, marching north on Grand and then east on Olive. Then, a pistol shot rang out and stones and bricks began to be thrown toward the soldiers. Who fired that first shot is unknown, but the Union soldiers reacted as though in a combat situation and they fired into the mob. Several soldiers fell and orders came to wheel, load and fire. Those who had been throwing rocks and insults just moments before were now running for their lives. Many of them went down in the street, blood pooling around their prone bodies. At almost the same time, a less serious skirmish took place near the head of the column at Olive Street and Garrison Avenue.

Major John Schofield, who was in charge of General Frost and his officers and still in the middle of the camp, immediately spurred his horse to the gate. He discovered that 90 people had been shot in the fighting. Later, 28 of them perished from their wounds. Despite the fact that it might seem to many readers that the soldiers who fired on the crowd did so without thought and without provocation, reports from the time said otherwise. Colonel James Peckham stated that "Not until one of his men was shot dead, several severely wounded, and himself shot in the leg, did Captain Blandowski feel it his duty to retaliate. As he fell, he commanded his men to fire."

The hours following the assault were tense to say the least. Anger spread among the southern sympathizers in the city. Speeches were made from the steps of the Planter's House Hotel and from the Berthold Mansion. The streets became increasingly unsafe and the police force had trouble keeping the crowds in line. At one point, officers had to line up shoulder to shoulder to keep a mob from attacking the *Anzeiger* newspaper and then had to repeat their show of force to keep a crowd from the offices of the *Democrat*. More rioting followed the next day. A German volunteer regiment marched from the Arsenal up Third Street, turning west on Walnut. As the first recruits reached Seventh Street, shots rang out from the steps of a church on the corner and a soldier fell dead. Panicked, the untrained troops stopped and fired down the street, killing not only their attackers, but some of their fellow soldiers as well! Six men were killed in this "skirmish" and four of them were recruits.

On June 17, more shots were exchanged between soldiers and civilians. A detachment of home guards, which had been patrolling railroad tracks beyond the city, marched downtown from the railroad station and turned onto Seventh Street. This time, the crowds who saw them coming cheered the men but between Olive and Pine Streets, shots rang out and bullets tore into the center of the column. The soldiers halted and began to return fire, aiming at the balcony of the recorder's court on the second floor of the Missouri Engine House. Four people were killed and two were seriously wounded. Captain J. W. Bissell was accused of being too severe in his retaliation, but experienced officers stated that he had to defend his men. The killers had mingled with the crowd with the idea that they could fire at the soldiers and the mass of people would protect them against the soldier's firing back. As soon as it was made clear that the soldiers would return fire, there were no more attacks on columns of troops.

A few days after the attack on Camp Jackson, General Harney returned from Washington. He refused to comment on the handling of the affair by Captain Lyon and within a few days had held a conference with General Sterling Price. The two men reached a truce of sorts that said that Harney would do nothing to interfere with Price's sanction by the governor of the state. In other words, he pledged to let Price and Jackson do what they wanted and he promised to stay out of it! It seemed a bit odd for a United States general to reach any sort of truce with the military representative of a governor who had defied President Lincoln and who had essentially raised the banner of rebellion in Missouri, but Harney did it anyway.

In spite of how questionable such a truce actually was, several representatives of the moderate and still hopeful in St. Louis went to Washington to try and persuade President Lincoln to accept Harney's policy. The men of the Committee of Public Safety were of a different mind though. To them, an acceptance of Harney's truce could mean the loss of Missouri from the Union. On May 16, Francis Blair, Jr. obtained an order that called for Harney's removal and President Lincoln authorized him to serve it if he deemed it necessary. Blair delivered the order on May 31 and Nathaniel Lyon, who had been made a brigadier general, took over command in Missouri until the arrival of John Charles Fremont in early July. Lyon soon had the opportunity to show that his earlier attack on Camp Jackson had not been mere bluster or a fool's luck.

Early in June, Governor Jackson and General Price called on Lyon at the Planter's House and ordered that he disband all his regiments and that strict neutrality be maintained throughout the state. Lyon was enraged! "Rather than concede to the state of Missouri for one moment the right to dictate to my government in any matter, however unimportant," he shouted, pointing directly at the governor's face, "I would see you and every man, woman and child dead and buried."

He leaned forward until his eyes met directly with Governor Jackson. "This means war," he said to the highest official in the state of Missouri. "In an hour, one of my officers will call for you and conduct you out of my lines."

Jackson was insulted and angry. He countered Lyon's words with a call for 50,000 troops from Missouri to "repel this invasion". On June 14, hearing that troops were on their way to Jefferson City, he left the capital and his office was declared vacant. A provisional governor was appointed in his place and Jackson's senators were expelled from the U.S. Congress and loyal Unionists were put in their places. On June 17, Jackson's forces were defeated at Boonville but managed to rally at Carthage and escape the state. Jackson attempted to bring Missouri into the Confederacy, establishing a makeshift capital at Neosho, in the southwestern corner of the state. This region became a hotbed of battles and skirmishes.

Nathaniel Lyon took command in the area and hearing that a southern army was moving up from Arkansas to take Springfield, he met them with an inadequate force in the battle at Wilson's Creek. This time, Lyon's bravery got the better of him. Already twice wounded, he rallied an Iowa regiment and led them back to attack again. A bullet struck him in the heart and he was killed. He left $30,000, almost his entire estate, to the government to use in continuing the war effort. Lyon had given his life to save St. Louis and Missouri for the Union.

Things were not going well in St. Louis under Fremont's command. Despite the defenses he was erecting around the city, President Lincoln was being deluged by demanding messages from him and was growing concerned over reports of favoritism and corruption. Francis Blair, whose brother Montgomery was the Postmaster General in Lincoln's cabinet and was himself an ardent supporter of the president, was sent by Lincoln to call on Fremont. With him was General John Schofield, a West Point man who had returned to the military from the Washington University faculty. Both were angry with Fremont after the meeting.

Schofield later wrote that "to my great surprise, no questions were asked, nor mention made of the bloody field from which I had just come, where Lyon had been killed." Instead, Fremont only lectured the two men on how gloriously he would win the war. Schofield stated that what he and Blair had to say about the general after the meeting were "rather too strong to print."

President Lincoln read their report with great interest and soon was even more outraged by Fremont. On August 30, Fremont declared martial law throughout Missouri and threatened to shoot suspected southern sympathizers caught carrying arms. He also ordered the confiscation of their property and he freed their slaves. Lincoln immediately demanded that Fremont countermand the order. If he started shooting secessionists, "the Confederates would very certainly shoot our best man in their hands for retaliation," he said. He also told him that taking property and freeing slaves was sure to turn what few southern Union friends they had against them and ruin their prospects for Kentucky.

Lincoln wrote to Fremont on September 2 and on September 8, Fremont's wife, Jessie (the daughter of Thomas Hart Benton) left for Washington with Fremont's reply. And while the president received her politely, it was all that he could do to not take out his frustrations with the husband on the wife! The President told her that Fremont had exceeded his authority that that the Negro should have never been brought into the war. She protested that the emancipation had been merely a military device (as Lincoln himself would use it in 1863) and that wars were won with ideas as well as guns. She said that Fremont could make the plan effective, despite Lincoln's order that it be repealed. The army, Lincoln replied, had no independent generals!

Jessie left, filled with anger against Lincoln and Francis Blair. She and her husband had known that the abolitionist press would praise their efforts in Missouri and that emancipation would be applauded in the north, in spite of the anger with which it would be received in the south. Fremont had his eye on the presidency more than on the war. He had made one bid for the White House before the war and would make another before war's end. Taking his anger out on Blair, Fremont accused him of soliciting a crooked contract for a friend and twice had him jailed at Jefferson Barracks. Needless to say, the false charges failed to stick.

Blair and his allies went on the offensive against Fremont. Not only had there been charges made already that Fremont has failed to support Nathaniel Lyon with men and supplies, but soon other charges were being made as well. According to a report that was sent to Washington, Fremont had again failed to support the fighting men in Missouri. On September 20, Colonel James A. Mulligan and 1,600 men from Chicago's Irish Brigade had been forced to surrender Lexington on the Missouri River, after defending it for eight days against 20,000 Confederates. Fremont had done nothing to assist them.

Fremont eventually did take the field against Price though. Jessie, at the headquarters in St. Louis, intercepted a message from Washington that said that her husband was to be replaced as the Commander of Union forces in Missouri unless he was actually engaged in battle or was on the verge of battle. Jessie frantically traveled across the state to Fremont's headquarters outside of Springfield with the stolen order. After commanding that no messenger was to approach him, he prepared to attack. Before he could though, President Lincoln's message was officially delivered and Fremont lost his position. He had been in command of Missouri for exactly 100 days.

Although Fremont was later exonerated of corruption charges, he had done plenty of damage while in command. Most importantly, he had weakened northern support of Lincoln, especially among the abolitionists. They had praised Fremont's emancipation orders and had condemned Lincoln when he revoked it. St. Louis Germans, who were strongly opposed to slavery, were loyal to Fremont, as were the Radical Republicans. When John Schofield took over command in St. Louis, he had his hands full. And not only did he have political problems, but military ones as well. Thanks to Fremont's failure to maintain order in the state, Missouri was now filled with bushwhackers and guerillas who were raiding and burning half the state. When he tried to organize ten regiments to combat the guerillas, he ran into more bickering between the pro and anti-slavery factions in the state.

One group, organized by Charles Daniel Drake, called itself the "Committee of Seventy" and boasted one man from each county in the state. The group, which was actually more like 80 men, called on President Lincoln and demanded the immediate and unconditional emancipation of slaves in all of the border states. They also protested Schofield's suspension of the writ of habeas corpus, his measures against the press and more. Lincoln supported Schofield though. He carried out the president's orders and supported the war effort. In addition, Lincoln did not want the problems that would come from freeing the slaves. He feared losing any Union men who happened to be proslavery and feared desertions by soldiers who had enlisted to save the country, not to free the slaves.

Another commander of the Department of Missouri was General Henry Halleck, who has been described as a "bookish man" and one of agonizing slowness and petty jealousies. He would be directly involved with famous general William T. Sherman, a St. Louis legend that we will hear more of later in this chapter. Sherman lost most of his respect for Halleck over time but he did concede that the man understood the importance of preserving St. Louis and the Mississippi

River valley.

St. Louis had become important in the war effort and news of victories from local heroes like Sherman thrilled the residents of the city. On hearing of the fall of Fort Donelson, the men of the Merchant's Exchange stopped what they were doing to sing a rendition of the "Star-Spangled Banner" and then marched to Halleck's headquarters to cheer on the soldiers. The only real threat to St. Louis came in 1864 with Price's foray into Missouri but as it had long been the base of exploration of the west, the city also became the base of the war in the west too. Troops, munitions and supplies went out by rail, river and road and the wounded, the refugees and the prisoners came into St. Louis the same way.

Thanks to all of this, a great many changes came to the city during this period. Jefferson Barracks was the heart of the army in the west. It had long been a place through which soldiers passed on their way to battle, but the Civil War made the post a much busier place. More troops came in and out and the construction of hospitals and a new National Cemetery made Jefferson Barracks more of a destination point than it had ever been before. Fremont had also built Benton Barracks, a training camp on 150 acres of farmland provided by John O' Fallon. The number of wounded men who came into the city forced the building of new hospitals and the re-organizing of old ones. The immense task of supplying and staffing these facilities led to the formation of the Western Sanitary Commission in 1861. The volunteer organization assumed almost total responsibility for military hospitals throughout the western states and also was in charge of assisting war refugees who were displaced by the fighting. An asylum was also opened for the orphans of soldiers and accommodations were provided for wounded and discharged troops and for wives and relatives visiting, or seeking the fate of, loved ones. There was also the wartime work of sending aid to the front in the form of food, blankets, socks, rolled bandages and more.

And while these changes were positive for the city, there was still danger, death and bloodshed in Civil War St. Louis. There was also profiteering going on. For instance, the military commanders of the city had a simple way for raising funds, they simply fined those who were suspected of sympathizing with the south. Even pro-Union men like Francis Blair frowned on this and when President Lincoln heard about it, he sent a telegraph to Halleck that ordered him to "stop the thing at once." But at least this money, while questionably raised, was going toward the war effort. A lot of other money that was made from the war was not!

Bitterness from the war lasted for decades after it ended but St. Louis could never be accused of not supporting the Union. The city sent more men into Lincoln's armies that any other city of its size. Nearly 200,000 men from Missouri fought under the American banner and only four other states (New York, Pennsylvania, Ohio and Illinois) had more men in Federal uniform. In addition, St. Louis had no draft riots, which other large cities could not claim.

By the time the war ended though, St. Louis was glad to see it done with. As soon as news of the surrender of Richmond came, the city decorated itself with flags. And when word came that Johnston has surrendered to Sherman and Lee to Grant, Mayor Thomas C. Fletcher proclaimed April 15 a day of thanksgiving.

The most violent, and most soul-shattering, years in St. Louis history had come to an end.

THE MARCH TO THE SEA

Without a doubt, the most famous of St. Louis' Civil War heroes was William Tecumseh Sherman. Born as the sixth child of eleven to Charles and Mary Sherman of Lancaster, Ohio, he came into the world on February 8, 1820. Sherman's father was a judge on the Ohio Supreme

Court, but when he died in 1829, Mary Sherman found herself in dire financial straits. In order to alleviate her burden, William was taken into the home of the Sherman's neighbor, Thomas Ewing, a family friend and prominent U.S. Senator.

General William T. Sherman

Ewing raised the boy as his own and insured that he was able to attend West Point. Sherman stood high in his graduating class of 1840, but his military career was largely unsuccessful after leaving West Point. He served in Florida, South Carolina and at Jefferson Barracks, where he learned to love St. Louis so much that he vowed to make it his home. At the outbreak of the Mexican War, when so many other young officers were achieving fame and glory on the battlefield, Sherman was assigned to a desk job as adjutant to the commander of the Pacific division in California. The highlights of his assignment were meeting Kit Carson and investigating the claims that gold had been discovered at Sutter's mill, an event that started the 1849 California Gold Rush. In 1850, Sherman was at Jefferson Barracks and he leased a home on Chouteau Street.

Sherman returned east and he married Ellen Ewing, the daughter of his foster father, Thomas Ewing, who was now the Secretary of the Interior for President Zachary Taylor. The wedding was attended by guests like Thomas Hart Benton, Daniel Webster and Henry Clay.

Sherman pursued several professions after leaving his inglorious life in the military. He had resigned from the army in 1853 and through his friend, Major Turner, he became the manager of Lucas, Turner & Co., the San Francisco branch of the St. Louis banking house of James H. Lucas & Co. When it closed down during the depression in 1857, he was sent to New York. But the parent bank also failed and Sherman practiced law briefly. Then in October 1859, he accepted the presidency of a new military school in Alexandria, Louisiana. Sherman soon became a respected teacher and administrator and made many friends. He was contented with his new life, but this would not last. As talk of secession became louder, Sherman became more and more uncomfortable in the south. He would never approve of the dissolution of the Union and in January 1861, he left Louisiana and returned to St. Louis.

As the early months of 1861 became more and more unsettled, Sherman decided to visit Washington and to see his brother, John, who was a Senator from Ohio. With what seemed to be prophetic foresight, Sherman told his brother how terrible a civil war could be. He was sure that Louisiana was going to secede and he wanted to make sure that his brother understood what could happen if they did. John immediately took him to see President Lincoln, who to Sherman still did not seem sufficiently concerned. John urged Sherman to go back to Ohio and to raise a company of volunteers but Sherman wasn't comfortable with his former home anymore. Even when Governor Dennison offered him the command of Ohio's troops, Sherman turned it down and the command went to Cincinnati railroad president George B. McClellan instead. Sherman also rejected an appointment that would have made him Secretary of War within a few months too. Back in St. Louis, he turned down Francis Blair's offer that he take charge of the Missouri volunteers. He could not afford even a few months as a volunteer. He had a wife and children to support and he was nearly broke. He shunned military command and took a position as president of the Lucas horse car line.

When things began to come apart in St. Louis and tensions developed between the pro-Union factions in St. Louis and Governor Jackson's office, Sherman watched the events unravel with growing dread. He feared what would happen to the city should the secessionists take over. None of the politicians, even the good ones like Blair, were soldiers. He knew that the Confederacy would field good officers and commanders, many of whom had remained in active service. Many of the northern officers, like Sherman himself, had put away the uniform and had taken jobs in the private sector. One such man was Ulysses S. Grant, who Sherman knew from West Point. Grant had also been assigned to Jefferson Barracks as a young officer and while in St. Louis had met and become engaged to a young woman named Julia Dent. Her father owned a Missouri plantation and the two of them had married after Grant had returned from the Mexican War.

In 1852 though, Grant was assigned to the Oregon frontier and his beloved Julia had to stay behind in the Midwest. Like Sherman, he learned that army life on the west coast was grim and for Grant, was made even more so by an unfair commanding officer. Poorly paid, depressed and lonely, Grant took to the whisky bottle, which was not uncommon in that era's hard-drinking army. He got into a scrape and although it wasn't serious, his commander, Colonel Robert C. Buchanan, told him that he had to either resign his commission or face court martial. Although a court would have likely cleared him, Grant quit the army in disgust. He arrived in New York in 1854, completely broke. A West Point friend, Simon B. Buckner, lent him some money, which Grant repaid after a draft from his father arrived. Grant would remember this favor years later. When Buckner surrendered Fort Donelson to him during the war, Grant handed him his billfold and said "you'll need this now."

General Ulysses S. Grant

Beaten down and discouraged, Grant returned to St. Louis. Here, Colonel Dent turned over 60 acres of woodland south of the city to him. If he could clear the land, it would make a good farm and so Grant set to work cutting down trees and selling the firewood in order to survive. He and Julia called the place "Hardscrabble Farm". The land lived up to its name, as Grant was no farmer. His first crop failed and he lost the second to the depression of 1857. He gave up farming and went into the real estate business in St. Louis. That soon ended though, and defeated he moved back to his home in Galena, Illinois. He had always vowed that he would never work in his father's tannery but by 1860, he was so broke that he swallowed his pride and asked for a job. Luckily, Galena was in the midst of lead mining boom at the time and Jesse Grant had opened a leather store in town. He gave Grant the chance to work it with his two brothers.

But Grant had been born to be a soldier, proving this by failing at everything else. When war came, he eagerly took the opportunity to drill the Illinois volunteers for Governor Yates.

Meanwhile, in St. Louis, Sherman was becoming more and more disillusioned with the politicians and the volunteer soldiers. He knew that war was coming and he also knew that a war could only be won with a regular army. The problem was that the army would have to be completely re-organized as many of the best officers had put on Confederate uniforms. Robert E. Lee, Albert Sidney Johnson, John Bell Hood, James Longstreet and so many others had turned to the south. In Washington, Secretary of War Cameron was railing about the fact that West Point was a "breeding ground for traitors" and this certainly seemed to be the case. Almost 300 graduates of the academy had defected to the southern states but Sherman knew there were many good officers still loyal to the Union. He also knew that the Federal government would need every one of them. As for himself though, he vowed to Ellen that he was not going to war until the politicians realized that it was a war for trained soldiers.

However, the war in St. Louis was not waiting for Sherman.

In early May, the affair at Camp Jackson took place and blood was spilled in the streets of St. Louis when an unruly crowd fired upon Union soldiers. Their deadly response left dozens of men dead.

Expecting a parade that day, rather than a battle, Sherman walked out onto Grand Avenue with his son, Willy, and his young brother-in-law Charles Ewing. As bullets sprayed the crowd and tore through the trees over their head, Ewing fell on Willy to protect him. When Sherman saw the soldiers preparing to fire again, he grabbed Willy and Ewing and pulled them into a ditch. Also in the crowd that day was Ulysses Grant. Governor Yates had sent him to Belleville, Illinois to raise more men and he happened to be on the scene after the capture of Camp Jackson. It is unknown just how close the stray bullets came to Grant, but imagine what might have been if he and Sherman had been accidentally killed that day? We might be living in an entirely different type of country today if they had!

A few days after the Camp Jackson affair, Sherman received a telegram offering him a commission in the regular Army. His old St. Louis friend, Major Turner, had gone to Washington and he lobbied for Sherman to be given the rank of brigadier general. However, when Sherman reported to President Lincoln, he asked for no rank higher than that of colonel. He was given the command of the new 13th Infantry.

And while Sherman was offered a higher rank, his failure to accept it did not bode well to many observers. His mood had been dark since he had returned from Louisiana. He was loyal to the Union, but he also had a deep affection for the south. He had been offered a Confederate general's stars, but he had turned them down. He was torn and confused but his love for the Union won out. In one of his last letters to Louisiana, he wrote to a friend that "there are good, fine people everywhere... if the present politicians break up our country, let us resolve to re-establish it."

Sherman received his baptism of fire at Manassas in July. In that first confusing clash between untrained armies, he managed to skillfully cover the Federal retreat. On August 3, he was promoted to a brigadier general of volunteers but he had seen that day what he had feared all along... the Union troops were untrained and ill prepared for a war. He was now so cautious that when he was sent to free loyal West Virginia, a Cincinnati newspaper called him "insane".

He asked that he be relieved of his duties and his conduct aroused such concern that Ellen Sherman went so far as to contact President Lincoln and tell him that her husband was "sick". He had suffered a nervous breakdown and was sent back to St. Louis. He was quickly himself again and he returned to the Planter's House, where he outlined to General Halleck a plan to divide the south by conquering the Mississippi River.

The Confederacy had attempted to cut the river by erecting fortifications at Vicksburg, but they had neglected the Tennessee and the Cumberland Rivers, except for the hasty additions of Fort Henry and Fort Donelson. If this land could be taken, the Federal forces would have a road straight into the heart of the Confederacy. The war could be won in the west, Sherman assured Halleck. Grant would command the advance and Sherman would keep him supplied. Unfortunately, this was not an easy plan, thanks to the difficult ways of General Halleck. Over time, Sherman lost respect for the man while Grant had little to start with. They would succeed in spite of their commanding officer.

Even with the hesitations in St. Louis, Fort Henry was taken and then Fort Donelson. Sherman yielded the command of the armies to Grant and yet managed to save the field for him at Shiloh. There, Sherman was twice wounded, in the hand and shoulder and his hat was filled with bullet holes. Neither of the wounds was serious and neither kept him down for long. Corinth was taken and then Vicksburg fell on the day after Lee abandoned Gettysburg to Meade. Even though the eastern generals were fighting inconclusively, Grant and Sherman moved into Tennessee. From there, Grant began his campaign against Lee and Richmond and Sherman began his legendary "March to the Sea".

Sherman's men besieged Atlanta and then, abandoning their communications lines, disappeared for 32 days to cut a swath across the south. Sherman had only to fight two major battles along his march, at Kennesaw Mountain and at Peachtree Creek and he ruined the career of Confederate General Joe Johnston. Johnston's men had been dug in at Kennesaw Mountain, on the way to Atlanta. Sherman decided to attack them and destroy the southern resistance in one fierce battle. They stormed the Confederate position but were driven by the superior positions of the southerners. Sherman's men were mowed down like standing targets. One Confederate soldier later wrote that "all that was necessary was to load and shoot." Three days later though, Sherman was on the move again, flanking Johnston over and over again until the Union army was in easy reach of Atlanta. A short time later, Jefferson Davis, frustrated with Johnston's failure, relieved the general of his command.

Johnston was replaced by John Bell Hood, who attacked Sherman at Peachtree Creek, north of the city. The attack was driven back while Sherman's most trusted officer, James B. McPherson, marched on Atlanta from the east. Hood maneuvered to block McPherson and the fighting raged all afternoon with lines forming, attacking and then falling back. McPherson himself went to inspect a Federal line and rode right into a company of Confederate troops. He was ordered to surrender, but he raised his hat in a taunting salute and rode off. He was shot from his horse and died! Sherman, stunned with grief over the death of his friend, covered his body with an American flag and wept. He replaced McPherson with Illinois General John "Black Jack" Logan, who reformed the men and led a counter assault on the city. He rode hard along the lines crying out "McPherson and revenge, boys!" Hood's army was driven from the field.

After the siege and surrender of Atlanta, Sherman vowed to "make Georgia howl" and living off the land, his troops began to move across the state. Atlanta was a smoldering ruin as the column departed, intent on defeating the southern army by crushing the will of the civilians who sustained it. The Federal troops looted homes and burned mansions, raiding and stealing everything in their path. "We cannot change the hearts of the people of the South," Sherman said, "but we can make war so terrible and make them so sick of war that generations will pass away before they again appeal to it."

Sherman's army marched west, raiding town after town. At Milledgeville, the Georgia capital, they built bonfires of Confederate currency and ransacked the state's records and library. Before it was over, the army crossed 425 miles of hostile territory and did over $100 million dollars in damage. All along the route they left behind "Sherman's Hairpins", iron railroad tracks that were torn from their ties, heated and wrapped around trees. The march was, as Lincoln said, a matter of Grant holding the bear by the hind foot while Sherman skinned it.

On December 22, 1864, Sherman sent a telegram to President Lincoln. "I beg to present you, as a Christmas gift, the city of Savannah..." The march was over and the feats accomplished by Sherman have never been equaled in American history. Never before, or since, has one man's army been able to bring an entire state to its knees. "There has been no such army," said General Joe Johnston, "since the days of Julius Caesar."

Because of this, Sherman is hated more than any other Union General is by the people of Georgia and the south, even today. This was a fact that he was well aware of in the years following the war. "I doubt if history provides a parallel to the deep and utter enmity of the women of the south," he later admitted. "No one sees them or hears them, but must feel the intensity of their hate."

But while the people of the south may have been calling for the blood of Sherman and Grant, the people of St. Louis thrilled to hear of their victories. Residents marched in the streets, cheered their names and waved flags in their honor. By the spring of 1865, the war was over and Sherman joined Grant and Lincoln to present the President's terms for peace. Sherman liked and respected both Lincoln and Grant and he and the President spoke for several hours about the future and their hopes for peace. Lincoln later stated that he was surprised to find that Sherman, his most ruthless general, had the most generous sentiments about peace and rebuilding the country.

But Lincoln and Sherman's "generous" sentiments were not meant to be. After Lincoln's assassination, the Black Republicans came into power and were against Lincoln's plans of "charity for all and malice toward none". Sherman was once again amongst the politicians and after his foster brother, Tom Ewing, was attacked for his defense of three men who had been accused in Lincoln's murder, he was thoroughly sickened by Washington and was ready to return to St. Louis.

St. Louis was glad to have him back. Having celebrated his victories, it was simple to organize a committee that would arrange a celebration for his return. A large dinner was held at the Lindell Hotel on his behalf and a collection was taken up that amounted to $30,000 with which he bought a fine house at Garrison and Franklin avenues. Sherman thanked the committee and wrote "I deem it a most fortunate accident that events have led me back to the very point whence I sallied at the beginning of the tremendous struggle now happily ended. And if the good citizens of St. Louis account me one of them, I accept the title with honor and satisfaction."

Sherman was now the commander of the Army's new Division of the Mississippi and he made St. Louis his headquarters. The military's work was now in the west and the General felt that the city would provide the perfect center point between the eastern government and the western frontier. He also loved St. Louis itself and the river and had many friends here. It was a also place where he and his family could live well on a soldier's pay. His wife and children were contented because, as devout Catholics, they find respect and tolerance in St. Louis. And perhaps most of all, Sherman found the city to be far away from the politics of Washington, which he detested.

Sherman urged all of his soldier friends to stay out of politics. Francis Blair, with whom Sherman had become close, was pressured to remain in the military after the war. Sherman pleaded with him to make a career in the Army. Blair died on July 8, 1875 a frustrated man after being defeated for the vice-presidency in 1868 and for re-election to the Senate in 1874. Sherman dedicated a monument to him in Forest Park and privately remarked that Blair "was a noble and intelligent soldier, but as a politician he was erratic and unstable."

Another friend that he tried to persuade to stay out of politics was U.S. Grant. Prior to the war, the two men had never been close. They knew one another from West Point, but their classes had been too far apart for them to become acquainted. The war had changed all of that though and with the fighting now over, Sherman told Grant to avoid the politicians who were now coming into power. Sherman saw nothing but carpet bagging and revenge on the horizon, but Grant was too naive to listen. Sherman respected his friend's honesty and integrity, but he also knew his limitations. "I have been with General Grant in the midst of death and slaughter," Sherman mourned, "and yet I have never seen him more troubled than since he had been in Washington."

Perhaps it was Julia Grant's entrancement with the White House that kept Grant in Washington for as long as he stayed. She urged her husband to seek a third term in office and then the two of them would return to St. Louis to live out the rest of their lives. But the scandals that took shape around President Grant made this impossible. Grant was called a "complacent accomplice" to the corruption in his administration, although congressional investigations cleared him of any wrongdoing. In St. Louis, many saw the results of the Whiskey Ring scandal, which took root from Grant's office. Distillers avoided paying taxes with the help of corrupt collectors and by blackmailing honest distillers into silence. Treasury agents acted as spies for the crooked "ring" and newspapers were bought off to keep them from reporting the crimes. The money poured into the Republican coffers and all the while, Grant was kept in the dark from what was going on. Still though, after the news of the scandal broke, he realized that he would be held responsible for what happened. "My name will carry it long after I am dead," he later wrote.

With so much trouble swirling around St. Louis, Grant moved to New York instead of returning to White Haven, the old Dent estate on the edge of the city. There, Grant became involved in another unknowing scandal. A fast-talking investor made him a partner in a firm called Grant & Ward. The company promised "high interest and no risk" and it was, unfortunately, a swindle from the very beginning. Grant's credulity and indifference kept him from discovering that anything was wrong until it was too late. When the crash came, Grant & Ward was forced to pay up for huge amounts of money that they owed to clients.. and Ward had naturally disappeared. It was a harsh lesson for Grant but he did make a gallant, if hopeless, effort to assume the debt and repay it. The farm in St. Louis and the fine house in New York were sold. Contributions from friends saved the Grant's from abject poverty, but there was little left.

In the final days of Grant's life, Sherman visited his friend and remained loyal to him, even after the scandals and rumors that had plagued the former general and president. And he wasn't alone in his loyalty. As Grant grew sicker and sicker, he began writing articles of his Civil War recollections for *Century* magazine to pay the bills. It was all that he could do to make ends meet but then his long-time friend Mark Twain proposed an idea for a book that would be published through his own company, Charles L. Webster & Co., which was managed by Twain's nephew. He offered Grant 70 percent of the net profits for a two-volume edition of *Memoirs*. Even though Grant had been plagued by political problems, the general public still adored the man and before Grant could even finish the book, the publisher's salesmen had pre-sold over 100,000 sets.

The writing of the book became a crusade for Grant. He knew that he was dying from throat cancer and yet he continued to write until his hands gave out. At that point, he sent for a stenographer and dictated 9,000 words in a single sitting. He continued to work every two or three days with intervals of exhaustion and recovery. Then, he lost his voice but Grant carefully continued, writing all that he could with a notebook and a pencil. Finally, he put aside the paper and announced that he was finished.

Ulysses S. Grant died three days later.

Grant's *Memoirs* turned out to be a huge success and Twain's publishing company sent a first royalty check to Julia Grant for $200,000 in February 1886. Eight months later, she received a second check for $150,000. It was the largest royalty ever paid to an author up to that time.

Sherman would publish his own book of Civil War experiences, but the book would never sell as well as Grant's. Sherman seemed to go out of his way to make sure that he was never as famous as his comrade in arms was. Sherman's term as the commander of the United States Army was filled with problems. The politicians resented him because he opposed the employment of soldiers as police officers in the Reconstruction regimes of the south. Like Lincoln, he had favored a "kindler and gentler" peace with the southern states and believed that such behavior toward the former Confederacy was both wrong and counterproductive. Because of this, presidential advisors accordingly bypassed him in issuing orders.

When scandals in Washington forced Grant's Secretary of War to resign in 1876, the President asked Sherman to come to Washington to help clean things up. Sherman also served there after his brother's friend, Rutherford B. Hayes, became president in 1877. Sherman was happy to help, but he always returned to St. Louis. He simply hated politics and he missed no opportunity to declare that he did not plan to seek public office. The "Sherman for President" calls started almost as soon as the war was over, but the general was not interested. In fact, he killed the first one with a letter that stated "If forced to choose between the penitentiary and the White House... I would say the penitentiary, thank you."

Sherman was happy in St. Louis and although he was one of the nation's most popular speakers, he was content to remain out of the limelight, especially politically. He once told Philemon Ewing that "I lead a peaceful life here and if I ran for President I'd wake up one morning and find all over the newspapers that I'd poisoned my grandmother."

In 1886 though, Sherman moved to New York. His daughter, son-in-law and their children had moved east the year before and Sherman had written to his brother that "I confess the move of Minnie and her children will change the aspect of St. Louis." He settled in the city, enjoying the theater and its people, but he lost his wife in November 1888. She passed away from heart disease and her body was sent back to St. Louis, where she was buried in Calvary Cemetery. For weeks after, family and friends could barely communicate with Sherman. He lost weight, his health declined and he was never the same after that. Two years later, on Valentine's Day 1891, Sherman died.

President Benjamin Harrison, who served under Sherman during the March to the Sea, sent a message to his family. "I loved and venerated General Sherman, and would stand very near to the more deeply afflicted members of the family in this hour of bereavement. It will be as if there were one dead in every loyal household in the land."

Sherman's body was displayed in the front parlor of his home, dressed in full military uniform. The coffin was draped with an American flag and three military guards stood at attention. Hundreds of people, both military and civilian, filed through the room. All of the flags in New York were lowered to half-mast and the New York Stock Exchange closed at noon. Thousands turned out for the funeral procession and the private service before it included Benjamin Harrison, Julia Grant and former presidents Grover Cleveland and Rutherford Hayes. Among the honorary pallbearers was Confederate General Joseph Johnston, who fought against Sherman and surrendered to him at the war's end. The two of them had become friends after the war. Ironically, Johnston died of pneumonia one month later because of the cold weather during the funeral march. The casket passed through the streets lined with people and then Sherman came back to St. Louis.

On February 21, the funeral train was met by Missouri Governor David Francis and hundreds of St. Louis residents. People lined the streets as the general's coffin passed by. It took nearly three hours to travel to Calvary Cemetery, where Sherman was laid to rest. The words "Faithful and Honorable" remain on his tombstone today, a simple and fitting tribute to one of America's, and St. Louis', greatest heroes.

THE GRATIOT STREET PRISON

The McDowell Medical College was founded in St. Louis by one of the city's most colorful characters. As noted in an earlier chapter, Dr. Joseph McDowell was held in high regard by those in the medical community although he was also known for his erratic temperament and his loyalties to the south. To make his volatile political positions quite clear, he often placed a loaded revolver on the table in front of him when discussing issues of slavery, state's rights or secession.

On May 10, 1861, around the time of the events at Camp Jackson, a small detachment of home guards arrived at the medical college to search it for the arms and ammunition that were rumored to be kept there for the doctor's personal use. He had already shipped over 1,400 muskets to the southern forces in Memphis but he still had his two cannons. Threatened by the actions of the Unionists, McDowell's son, Drake, left St. Louis to join the Confederate army. The surgeon followed soon after. In early August, they arrived in the camp of General Meriwether Thompson in southeast Missouri and somehow managed to bring the two cannons with them.

After it was abandoned, Provost Marshall George E. Leighton seized the McDowell Medical College and it was taken over by the Union Army. It was first used as a recruiting office for St. Louis and then, since General Fremont's headquarters was nearby, it was converted into barracks. The arrival of Confederate prisoners of war turned the place into the Gratiot Street Prison to help relieve the overcrowding of a smaller prison at Fifth and Myrtle Streets.

That prison, which had once been called Lynch's Slave Pen, was a brick building that had been taken over by Federal authorities on September 3. It had been used as a slave auction house but with the outbreak of the war, the owner, Bernard Lynch, had fled from St. Louis. In early September, the first 27 prisoners were moved into the building. Ironically, one of them was Dr. McDowell's son, Max, who had stayed behind in St. Louis to recruit southern sympathizers for the Missouri state guard. The maximum number of men to be incarcerated at Myrtle Street was 100 but 150 were already housed there when word came that 2,000 more were coming from the battlefields of southwest Missouri.

The job of converting the medical college to a prison was given to a Major Butterworth. In December 1861, 50 men, including 15 former slaves, were put to work renovating the college and cleaning out what the medical students had left behind. The former slaves were given the distasteful task of removing the three wagon loads of human bones and the assorted medical specimens that were found in the basement. Cooking stoves and sleeping bunks were constructed and McDowell's dissecting room was converted into a dining hall. General Halleck, who was the commander of the Department of the West by this time, placed Colonel James M. Tuttle in charge of the prison's operations.

The first prisoners arrived on December 22. A large crowd of curious spectators gathered at the train depot to watch them come in but before the train arrived, the crowd became unruly and two regiments of soldiers from Iowa and Indiana had to be dispatched to the station to maintain order. As the train stopped, the Indiana regiment formed two lines from the cars to the prison. A military band, which had assembled at the scene, began to play "Yankee Doodle" as the men climbed from the train and "Hail Columbia" as they were forced to march off to the prison. The Confederates were in sorry shape when they arrived, having no uniforms and with their clothing tattered and torn. Some had rags instead of shoes on their feet and their outer wear consisted of nothing more than blankets, quilts and buffalo robes. The officer's clothing was in better shape, but not by much.

The highest-ranking officer in the group was Colonel Ebenezer Magoffin, the brother of the governor of Kentucky. He and the 1300 Confederates that arrived on the first train had been captured by General John Pope at Blackwater, Missouri.

The soldiers were taken to the Gratiot Street Prison and it was soon obvious that the prison had been poorly planned and prepared. The building's capacity was about one-third of the number that arrived on the first day. The holding areas were badly ventilated and not suited for large numbers of people and the latrine procedures that were planned quickly became useless. The waste buckets that had been placed in the rooms were insufficient for the number of men who had to use them, as was the trench latrine in the fenced-in yard area. In an effort to keep the prison as clean as possible, Colonel Tuttle issued an edict that would make the prisoners responsible for the cleanliness of their quarters. They were to sweep the rooms each morning and scrub them every two weeks. Unfortunately though, the overcrowded conditions made this impossible. When the scrubbing details were enforced, water sloshed around on the floor and seeped into the lower rooms, making the situation even worse.

Conditions here were chaotic because of the lack of organization of prisoners. Prisoners of all types could be housed in the same rooms. Held within the walls were not only Confederate prisoners of war, but suspected southern sympathizers, bush whackers, spies, Union deserters, Union soldiers arrested for criminal activity and, separated from the rest of the population but often confined in the next room, women accused of harboring fugitives or sympathizing with the south.

Discipline in the prison was harsh, especially in the beginning when St. Louis was still embroiled in the incidents, murders and shootings that marked the early days of the war. Guards were ordered to shoot anyone who not only tried to escape, but even who simply stuck a head or body part out of a window! And the guards were often accused of showing no hesitancy to shoot. It was said that they often took potshots at the prisoners just to practice their aim.

One prisoner, Captain Griffin Frost of Missouri State Guard, who was captured in Arkansas, noted in his journal that "the officers of the regiment now guarding us are perfect devils - there is nothing too low, mean or insulting for them to say and do... we are surrounded by bayonets and artillery, guarded by soldiers who curse, swear and fire among us when they please, and resort to balls, chains and dungeons for the slightest offense". Another prisoner, Henry M. Cheavens, who was captured after the battle at Wilson's Creek, wrote "one night, the guards shot at one [prisoner] because he refused to put out the light."

Perhaps fearing more of the problems that plagued St. Louis in recent times, the approaches to the prison were heavily guarded. For the first three years of its existence, no visitors or parcels of any kind were allowed inside. Soon after it opened, even the provost-marshal general was sternly turned away and prohibited from entering the building until Colonel Tuttle came to his aid.

And if the fortress-like appearance and security of the prison were not enough, the forbidding interior had a medieval and dungeon-like look about it. Two of the largest areas where prisoners were kept were in the "round room" and the "square room". The round room, which was described as a "very dark and gloomy place, and very filthy besides", was the middle level of the octagonal tower section of the building, the same tower atop where Dr. McDowell had mounted his cannons and where the vaults had been constructed to hold the dead members of his family. The room was about 60 feet in diameter and usually had about 250 men crammed inside of it. Although crowded, it was at least better ventilated than the "square room". This chamber was about 70 by 15 feet and held another 250 or so prisoners. It was described as being in "utter disregard to the rules of hygiene." Sickness and disease ran rampant in both rooms, but especially in the square room. Captain Griffin Frost wrote that "all through the night can be heard coughing, swearing, singing and praying, sometimes drowned out by almost unearthly noises, issuing from uproarious gangs, laughing, shouting, stamping and howling, making night hideous with their unnatural clang. It is surely a hell on earth."

The officer's quarters, which were cleaner and not so crowded, were 16 feet square and had eight men confined to each room. Here, the prisoners slept on bunks rather than on the floor and were allowed to walk in the halls and look out the windows into the street. These chambers were reconditioned classrooms and were located on the upper story of the building.

Federal officers and attendants occupied one wing of the prison, with the Confederate officers on the top floor. The north wing contained the divided basement, where McDowell's pet bear had once lived. It now had a large room to hold prisoners. The middle floor was also divided, with one room for prisoners. An upper amphitheater, which had once been the pride of the medical school with its large area to view the dissection of cadavers and its six gothic windows, was later converted into two stories. One of them was a convalescent hospital and the other, a dungeon.

All of the large rooms were fitted with three-tier double bunks with one and two rows to a room. As the prison continued to get more crowded, men with no bunks slept on the floor. The rooms were extremely cold in the winter and impossible to heat. There were only two stoves in each room to warm more than 200 men.

The dining room, where human bodies had once been cut open and studied, was located on the middle floor of the north wing. The cook room was located in the basement and was fitted with brick furnaces for baking and grilling food. The cooks and staff were chosen from among the prisoners. As might be expected, the food was terrible. In fact, it was noted that "the fare is so rough, it seems an excellent place to starve."

Above the dining room and extending the length of the entire north wing was the prison hospital. When the medical college had been in operation, this had been Dr. McDowell's wonderful museum of curiosities. There is no mention of what happened to the exhibits and artifacts once the Federal soldiers moved in to renovate the building. The attic room of this area, where McDowell had hidden away the body of the young German girl and subsequently saw his mother's ghost, was used as a room to store the bodies of those who died under hospital care. The convalescent hospital was located in the upper floor of the old amphitheater. The hospital contained 76 bunks arranged into four wards. Most of the sick were cared for by Confederate surgeons who had been taken prisoner and who had volunteered for sick duty under the direction of a Federal medical officer. Hospital attendants were detailed from among the prisoners. During the prison's operation, smallpox occurred here in almost epidemic proportions, along with outbreaks of measles, pneumonia, vermin infestations and the war's most accomplished killer, chronic diarrhea. The *St. Louis Republican* newspaper called the hospital "filthy and unhealthy".

The prison itself continued to be a horrifying place. The population soared and sanitary conditions and food rations further declined. Many of the prisoners were transferred out to another prison in Alton, Illinois, where a smallpox epidemic also broke out. Illness also wreaked havoc at Gratiot Street and with the hospital always filled, the sick and dying were left lying on the floor. The dawn of each new day would reveal from one to four dead men stretched out on the cold stone.

Griffin Frost wrote: "The prisoners were poorly fed, worse bedded and nearly suffocated in the impure air. It has been said there have been as many as 1,700 men at one time in the lower quarters. The number could scarcely find standing room; sleeping would be out of the question; of course, they must suffer, sicken and die."

By 1863, the lack of space, food and medical supplies was continuing to plague the facility. In March, a smallpox epidemic raged through the close quarters and the polluted conditions in the lower rooms declined further. Lice and bed bugs invaded the prisoners, their clothing and everything else.

In April, the Western Sanitary Commission appointed two physicians to look into the situation at the prison. Among other things, they found that the bunks for the men were spaced so tightly together that a man could scarcely pass between them and that the prisoner's bedding had been reduced to scraps of blanket and pieces of carpet. The floors were so encrusted with filth that the stone had started to resembled dirt flooring. They concluded their report with "it is difficult to conceive how human beings can continue to live in such an atmosphere."

Not surprisingly, many of them couldn't continue to live. Prisoners were dying at an alarming rate, sometimes as many as four a day. Between August 1863 and April 1864, the monthly death rate averaged more than 10 percent of the sick men in the prison hospital and in some months went up to 15 percent. The mortality rate even rose to over 50 percent between October 1864 and January 1865, thanks to outbreaks of smallpox and typhoid.

Constant new inmates for the prison, many of which were dead on arrival or died soon after, propelled the population at Gratiot Street to new highs in 1864. Horrified at the rate of death and illness within the prison walls, Union surgeon general George Rex reported that despite the attention that has been called to the problem of overcrowding, the "evil still continues unabated." The authorities were using the Myrtle Street Prison and the prison in Alton as an overflow to prevent overcrowding, but these facilities were above capacity as well. Prisoners were placed in the barracks at the Schofield and Benton training camps and at the state penitentiary in Jefferson City, but the Gratiot Street prison remained packed into 1865. By this time, the conditions inside had collapsed beyond imagination.

In June and early July 1865, the last prisoners who remained in Alton, Illinois were moved to the Gratiot Street prison to await release. After that was accomplished, Gratiot Street closed down and soon after, Dr. McDowell returned to re-establish the medical school. He cleaned and renovated all of the rooms, except for one, which was left just as it had been when the prison was open. He called that room "Hell" and most likely, the description was a fitting one.

McDowell died in 1868 and the medical school was left vacant for years. In June 1878, the south wing was condemned as being unsafe and was demolished by order of the fire department. The octagonal tower and the north wing remained until 1882, when they were torn down. Nothing remains of the building today and it is merely a forgotten spot on the Ralston-Purina lot.

But for years after the building closed down for good, it was anything but a forgotten place for the people who lived in the neighborhood around the old college. To them it was a "haunted" and forbidding place and not only because of the horrific experiments they believed had once been conducted by Dr. McDowell and his ghoulish students. The people in the area were convinced that the ghosts of men who died at the Gratiot Street Prison remained behind at the site.

According to the stories, including one told to me by the descendant of a German man who once lived in this neighborhood, the college really was a haunted place and ghosts were often seen peering out of its dark and usually broken windows. They saw faces and wisps of clothing passing by and then vanishing into the shadows. Most feared to approach the structure, but those who dared to go inside hear cries, wails, mournful screams and the sounds of men weeping in otherwise empty rooms. The noises that came from the confines of the walls were often so loud that they could be heard outside.

The great-grandson of a man who once lived nearby passed on one story of the former college and prison to me. As a boy, his elder relative played inside of the building with his friends on several occasions. In spite of the fact that another boy claimed to see the apparition of a man in one of the rooms one day and refused to go back inside, the group of friends boldly entered the college on a summer afternoon. They soon found that the bright sunshine outside was not enough to penetrate the darkness in the old school. The atmosphere was gloomy and thick and they must have then realized that they had made a mistake by going in. The boys wandered about through the corridors for a time though and then they heard a strange sound that seemed to be coming from the direction of the octagonal tower. The sound, which was described to several generations of my storyteller's family as being a "loud, screeching, banging and yelling that made the blood curdle", could be heard echoing through what seemed to be the whole structure. The boys had no idea where the sound was coming from for sure, or even what it was, but they turned and ran immediately from the building. The man's great-grandfather told his family that he had never ventured inside of the prison again. A few years later, it was torn down.

What could the boys have heard in the building that day? Was it really ghosts, or perhaps some strange echo from the past? When I first heard this story, I couldn't help but remember something that I had read about the Gratiot Street Prison when I was doing research for this book. I searched back through my notes and I found a quote that was taken from Captain Griffin Frost, the Confederate prisoner who had written extensively about his experiences in "surely a hell on earth." He wrote that on many nights, it was impossible to sleep because of the sounds that came from the lower levels of the prison. The natural sounds of incarcerated men were "sometimes drowned out by almost unearthly noises... laughing, shouting, stamping and howling, making night hideous with their unnatural clang."

Could an eerie replay of such a cacophony of noise have been what the group of friends heard that day? I wish there was a way that the German boy and Captain Frost could have compared notes about their experiences in that hellish place but unfortunately, they have both long since departed this world for one that is hopefully a better one.

SPIRITS OF INJUSTICE

There are perhaps no greater blots on the history of the Civil War in St. Louis than the "revenge" executions that were carried out by Federal officers against the Confederate military. While many would feel that the executions were warranted, and perhaps even justified, at least one of them has had lasting repercussions. According to legends that have been told in the area around Lafayette Park, the spirits of six men who were executed here may still not rest in peace.

In October 1864, six Confederate soldiers were executed by Special Orders No. 279. Their deaths shocked many but they were condemned in retaliation for the murders of Union soldiers, creating a confusing and violent series of events. To understand what occurred on October 29 at the edge of Lafayette Park, we first have to look into the events that caused the executions to be carried out.

James Wilson enlisted in the Federal Army in May 1861 and his leadership skills and bravery caused him to rise rapidly in rank. By December of that year, he was first sergeant of Company G, 10th Cavalry, Missouri State Militia. Not long after the regiment became designated as the 3d Cavalry, Wilson was promoted to captain. By May 1863, he was commissioned a major. Wilson received promotions during a time when his regiment was actively battling Confederate regular and guerilla forces. In most of these bloody struggles, quarter was seldom asked for or given to either side. This was brutal fighting and ambushes and civilian casualties were not uncommon.

On September 26, 1864, the first day of the battle at Pilot Knob, Missouri, Wilson led a force that drove the Confederates out of the Arcadia Valley. The following day, during a Confederate attack on Fort Davidson, he and a number of other Union soldiers were cut off and captured. The prisoners, both military and civilian, began an 80-mile march the next morning to a point about ten miles west of Union, Missouri. They arrived there on October 2 and Major Wilson and six enlisted men were singled out and were turned over to Confederate guerilla leader Timothy Reeves.

Reeves and Wilson were bitter enemies who had clashed often in the region and Reeves had special reason to hate the Union officer. A week before the battle at Pilot Knob, Federal cavalry troops burned Doniphan, Missouri, Reeve's hometown. There are also accounts that say that on Christmas Day, 1863, Wilson and the 3d Missouri Cavalry surprised Reeve's men in their camp.

Unknown to Wilson at the time, the guerilla's families had come there for a holiday gathering. The attack was said to have resulted in as many as 30 civilian casualties, including three of the Confederate's wives.

When Wilson was brought before the guerilla leader, two witnesses later reported that Reeves said to Wilson, "Major, you are a brave man - but you never showed my men quarter, neither will I give you quarter." Wilson and the six enlisted men were then executed. The remainder of the prisoners taken were paroled and sent home.

News of the deaths reached General William Rosecrans in St. Louis a few days later. On October 6, he issued Special Orders No. 277 calling for a Confederate major and six enlisted men to be held in solitary confinement until they could find out for sure what had happened to Major Wilson. News traveling from the battlefield was not always reliable and Rosecrans was advised not to act without assurances. A search was conducted and the bodies of Wilson and his men were discovered on October 23. By this time, the badly decomposed corpses had been partially eaten by wild hogs, which roamed the woods where the bodies were hastily buried.

On October 25, Rosecrans' provost general in St. Louis directed that the first Confederate major that was captured from General Sterling Prices' troops be sent to him without delay for execution. However, there were no majors in custody at that time. On October 28, Special Orders No. 279 extended the Federal retaliation to six Confederate enlisted men as well, so they were selected at random from the prisoners at Gratiot Street. Only one of the six who were luckless enough to be chosen had been in the same battle with the murdered Union soldiers.

After the men were pulled aside, it was learned that one of the prisoners, John Ferguson, was a teamster and had never carried arms. He was sent back and George Bunch was chosen to take his place. The other men were James W. Gates, Asa V. Ladd, Charles W. Minnekin and John A. Nichols. The oldest of the men was Harvey Blackburn, who hailed from the St. Louis area. Before the war, he had lived in the community known as Possum Hollow near Florissant. In 1861, he had left St. Louis for Arkansas and had joined the Confederate cavalry.

Around 2:00 in the afternoon on October 29, the six soldiers were taken out of the Gratiot Street Prison and led to a waiting covered wagon. They were escorted without music and in somber silence to Fort No. 4, one of a string of forts along Jefferson Avenue in the city. It was located just south of Lafayette Park. Six posts had been erected along the west side of the fort and in the presence of about 3,000 spectators, the prisoners were tied to the posts with their hands behind them.

After the sentence was read, Charles Minnekin, who was only 21 years-old at the time and one of the youngest of the six prisoners, asked for permission to speak. According to the *Missouri Democrat,* he cried out to the crowd:

Soldiers, and all of you who hear me, take warning from me. I have been a Confederate soldier four years and have served my country faithfully. I am now to be shot for what other men have done, that I had no hand in, and know nothing about. I never was a guerilla, and I am sorry to be shot for what I had nothing to do with, and what I am not guilty of. When I took a prisoner I always treated him kindly and never harmed a man after he surrendered. I hope God will take me to his Bosom when I am dead. Oh Lord, be with me.

The firing squad of 54 soldiers, including men from the 10th Kansas and the 41st Missouri infantry regiments, stood about ten paces away from the condemned men. There were 18 men from the party who stood in reserve in case a second volley from the executioners would be needed. Some of the Kansas men were reportedly uneasy about the prospect of firing on the prisoners. An officer harshly reminded them of their duties and that they should remember that Confederates had taken the lives of many Union men who were as innocent as these men were. Blindfolds were then tied over the prisoner's eyes and on command, 36 soldiers opened fire at the same time. After that first volley of shots, two of the victims groaned and one cried out, but they were left there, tied to the posts. Within a few minutes, all of them were dead. The six Confederates were buried in adjacent graves at Jefferson Barracks National Cemetery.

But the orders had still not completely carried out. There was still a Confederate major to contend with and on November 7, Major Enoch O. Wolf was captured during Prices' defeat in western Missouri. His death sentence was read to him on the morning after his capture and he was scheduled to die. When it was learned that Wolf was a Freemason, a local minister and the members of the local Masonic Lodge interceded to repeatedly delay Wolf's execution. Finally, in February 1865, Wolf was transferred to Johnson's Island prison in Ohio and was exchanged. In this way, he managed to elude the bitter bite of a random death.

And what of the ghosts? Could these tragic events from October 1864 explain the sightings of ghostly soldiers who have been seen in and around Lafayette Park over the years? The stories say that spectral men in soldier's clothing have been seen walking through darkened yards and across open spaces in the park since the late 1800's. It certainly seems possible that men who died such violent, and some would say unjust, deaths might stay behind in this world. Perhaps they are still seeking the justice that was denied to them during the war.

According to author Robbi Courtaway, a young woman whose bedroom window overlooked Lafayette Park was unable to sleep one winter's night and as she got out of bed, she happened to glance outside. Her gaze happened to catch a flicker of movement and a light and she peered closer to see three men in military uniforms huddled around a campfire. She was startled to see the men disappear into thin air! Could they have been three of the six who were executed, or another set of ghosts altogether?

Other neighborhood residents have reported similar sightings. One man told me of coming home from work late one night and parking his car on the street in front of the house. "It was an unusually quiet night, I remember," the man later told me, "but it was very late as I had been kept at work with a number of reports that needed to be finished by the end of the month." This statement reminded him to tell me that it was late October when the strange incident occurred.

As he closed the car door and started walking up to the house, he noticed someone standing in the shadows near the edge of the building. A little unsettled, he picked up his pace toward the front door, thinking that he would undoubtedly reach it before the person that was standing in the dark could reach him. Just as he was nearing the front steps, the unknown person moved just slightly and the witness got the distinct impression that it was a man wearing a military uniform.

He slowed his pace for a moment and watched as the man turned and then started walking away down the street. "He was wearing a uniform of some sort," the witness recalled, "and while I'm no expert, it certainly looked like it was from the Civil War era. He had on boots and a leather belt and sort of a beat up looking old hat. I wish that I could have seen him closer but by the time he reached the front of my neighbor's house, he just disappeared!"

The man that the witness believed to be a soldier simply faded from sight and was gone. Although this incident occurred several years ago, it's unlikely that the man has never forgotten it. After he told me about it, I told him about the execution of the Confederate soldiers at Fort No. 4 in 1864. He had never heard about it before.

The story seemed especially important to him, as he happens to live just south of Lafayette Park!

Guard at Jefferson Barracks (Courtesy of David Goodwin)

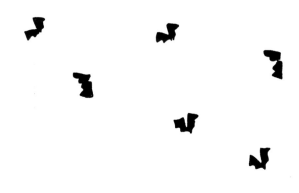

III. SPIRITS OF ANOTHER KIND

History & Hauntings of the St. Louis Breweries

In 1929, Gerald Holland wrote in the *American Mercury* magazine that "whatever odium may be attached to beer in other parts of the Republic, its status in St. Louis is as firmly grounded as James Eads' span across the Mississippi... beer made St. Louis."

And he was right. Even today, when there are fewer and fewer independent breweries around, the greatest in America still operates in the city. It seems that it has always been this way too. Even from the very beginning, there was beer in St. Louis.

Prior to 1830, and before the greatest influx of Germans settlers, beer was hard to find in this region. It's not that it wasn't here, there just wasn't as much of it as there would be a few decades down the road. The St. Vrain Brewery was in operation in 1810, offering barrels of beer for $10 each. St. Vrain was a French settler who lived in Bellefontaine. He was a farmer but found the work tedious and began a brewery instead. Ahead of his time, he launched an advertising campaign in the town newspaper that stated that he was now taking orders for his table beer. Unfortunately, there was little interest and he went out of business. He died soon after.

Despite his failures though, others came along who tried to bring beer to St. Louis. Jacob Phillipson was a competitor of St. Vrain and offered his beer by the quart in stores. He sold out to John Mullanphy in 1821 but he didn't last long in the business. His brewery was destroyed by arson in 1829.

Ezra English opened a brewery on the south side and became one of the first to utilize the natural caves underneath the city for the storage of beer. The cave that he used, known as "English Cave", was a place of ghostly legend that was said to have carried a curse on those who used it. In the next chapter, we'll take a closer look at the mysterious caverns beneath St. Louis and at the unlucky Ezra English and the others who followed in his path.

It was the huge tide of German immigration to St. Louis that created the beer brewing industry that we know today. Soon, breweries and beer-gardens began to appear all over town and none of them suffered for lack of patronage. A number of smaller breweries began to appear as the residents of the city began to join the Germans in their appreciation for beer. In 1831, Ellis Wainwright opened the Fulton Brewery and was followed in 1834 by James and William Finney, who opened the City Brewery on Cherry Street. By 1840, the breweries could barely keep up with local demand.

The first brewery of any size was that of Adam Lemp, who came to St. Louis in 1838. Here, he established a small mercantile store and marketed items that he manufactured himself, including vinegar and beer. In 1840, he officially began producing the first lager beer in St. Louis. Lager beer was different than the thick ales that were common at the time and the term "lager" came from the German word "lagern", meaning to store. Early German brewers stored their product in cooling caves during the summer and this aging process would allow the yeast to settle, improve the flavor of the beer and allow it to be stored for a longer period of time. The end result is a crisp, clean, sparkling beer and not only did it taste better, but it created a product that did not have to be consumed as quickly before it went bad. Lemp helped to start a revolution in the industry and he is rightly considered the "father of modern brewing in St. Louis". The history, the tragic story of the family and the haunting of their family home will be detailed later on in the chapter.

Another successful brewery of the middle 1800's was the Green Tree Brewery on Second Street. It was founded by Joseph Schnaider, who came to St. Louis from Germany in 1854. He had mastered the brewer's art after a three-year apprenticeship at a large brewery near Strasburg. On arriving in St. Louis, he became the foreman of the Philadelphia Brewery and then two years later, opened the Green Tree Brewery. They remained at the same location for seven years and then opened a new facility on Sidney Street. In 1865, he sold out to his partner and built a new brewery on Chouteau Avenue that included a beer garden. He enjoyed much success with this new establishment and was known for good food, fine music and a family atmosphere. After the Civil War, Schnaider also formed a light opera company to compete with the St. Louis Browns, as the team's success attracted many of his customers away from the beer garden. The St. Louis Grand Orchestra and the Musical Union Symphony also played at Schnaider's beer gardens, as did other popular bands, and it is believed that the site was the basis for the founding of the St. Louis Symphony Orchestra. Schnaider died at the young age of only 49 in 1881 but the Chouteau Avenue Brewery buildings and lagering cellars were not destroyed until 1960.

Other breweries also came along like the Julius Winkelmeyer Brewery, Phoenix Brewery, Lafayette, Home, Excelsior and many others. Another well-known company was the Griesedieck Bros. Brewing Company, which was started by Joseph Griesedieck in 1912. Five years later, Griesedieck left the company that he had started with his brother and opened a company that made beer and soft drinks. In 1921, the changed the name to the Falstaff Brewing Company, having purchased the "Falstaff" trademark from William Lemp.

In 1860, there were 40 breweries operating in St. Louis, producing about 23,000 barrels of beer each year. That would all soon change though, thanks to the energies of the founder of what is considered the greatest of the St. Louis breweries. It was a legend that came about by accident but would go on to create brewing history.

ANHEUSER-BUSCH BREWERY

During the heyday of the German breweries, a man named Eberhard Anheuser came to St. Louis. He didn't come here to make beer though, but rather soap. He did well at this and began to prosper. In 1852, a man named Schneider opened a brewery that began producing 3,000 barrels of beer during its first year of operation. Schneider was a poor businessman and within three years, sold out to a competitor, Urban & Hammer. In order to buy the brewery, the firm borrowed $90,000 from Eberhard Anheuser. The name was changed to the Bavarian Brewery and production was increased. Unfortunately though, Urban & Hammer weren't much better businessmen than Schneider and by 1857 were out of business. They defaulted on their loans with Anheuser being their largest creditor. He bought out the other debts and managed the brewery along with his soap factory for the next eight years.

It was in 1860 that everything began to change. In was in that year that a young German man named Adolphus Busch came to St. Louis. Busch was the well-educated son of a successful businessman and had been born in 1842. He attended school at the Gymnasium of Mainz, the Academy of Darmstadt and the Collegiate Institute of Brussels. He spoke, in addition to German, fluent French and English and was proficient in Italian and Spanish as well. Having once been a rafts man on the Rhine, he went to work on Mississippi steamers for a time after coming to America and then took a job as a salesman for Anheuser's brewery.

Adolphus Busch

(Courtesy Missouri Historical Society)

In 1861, he married Anheuser's daughter, Lilly. The ceremony was a double one as his brother, Ulrich, was also married to Lilly's sister, Anna, at the same time. Busch then went off to serve the Union Army in the Civil War for 14 months. He joined up with one of the regiments from the south side of the city and was sent to fight in southern and western Missouri. After the war, Eberhard Anheuser decided to turn his attentions back to his soap business and put the management of the brewery into the hands of his capable son-in-law. In five years, Busch had increased the production of beer from 8,000 barrels each year to 18,000.

In 1875, Busch was made a full partner in the company and the works were incorporated with the new name of Anheuser-Busch. Eberhard died in 1880 and Busch began working to conquer the local beer market, as at that time it was expected to be the extent of the company's operations.

Brewing was then a local industry as there was no bottled beer and beer in kegs was sure to spoil if shipped to some distant market. But there was a huge amount of money to be made in St. Louis and Busch set out to make it.

Unfortunately though, Busch could not make claim to having the best brew in town. That honor was held by the Lemp family, however even bad beer, if marketed correctly, could make an exorbitant amount of money. In those days, the sales strategy for beer centered around the "beer collector", who bought beer but did not sell it. All brewers had such spending agents, but Busch gathered together an accomplished group and soon his beer was selling as well as the

Lemp's. Every saloon that sold Busch beer was favored by a visit from the collector once each month and in it he would spend an amount that was proportionate to its monthly buy. This made the collector an important person and his social position was high. He was treated with great respect and he spent time with men from all walks of life. And he made no complaint for as long as it was Busch beer that was being consumed, it didn't matter who was consuming it. He would buy a man a beer as long as that man turned around and bought two more for himself and his friends.

The collector had other duties besides just buying drinks. He was expected to attend the funerals of the families of saloon keepers and to exhibit the right amount of grief. That way, there would be plenty of Busch beer buying after the rites were over. He also attended weddings and purchased handsome Christmas gifts for the saloon keeper's wife and children. The collectors were in positions to wield considerable influence in local politics and as long as they kept customers buying Busch beer, they were treated well by the company and by Adolphus himself.

Busch was well known for his advertising, in the early days and later on as well. He gave away pocketknives, watch fobs, chinaware, trays and other novelties. One of the early trays was especially popular. It was embellished with a picture of the Anheuser-Busch Brewery with flags flying from every cupola and tower. Sitting in a prominent spot was a large-breasted and lovely young lady with a wisp of a veil over her lap, obviously promoting the virtues of Busch beer. She was apparently the first of the now-famous Budweiser girls!

And there were many of these young ladies depicted in Busch artwork and they sold a lot of beer, but not nearly as much as General Custer did. That was the day of elegant artwork in saloons and every brewery issued a complimentary series of paintings. One of the most inspiring was Cassilly Adams' detailed picture of the Battle of Little Bighorn, which Busch bought the rights to for $35,000. The painting, which was turned into an Anheuser-Busch advertisement, became so popular that the brewery still receives requests for copies of it today. The original was sent to Custer's regiment, the Seventh Cavalry, for its mess hall at Fort Riley, Kansas. The painting became one of the most popular pieces of artwork in the world and was widely displayed as posters and smaller reproductions. The star-crowned "A" and the eagle of Anheuser-Busch has appeared on hundreds of different kinds of advertising, but to this day, there has never been another ad like "Custer's Last Fight".

During the years that the breweries were running at full stream, there was probably more beer consumed in St. Louis than in any other city of its size in the world. With beer sold at only a nickel a glass (which also included the customary free lunch), it was a luxury that was within the reach of almost everyone. And for a time, St. Louis beer was even cheaper than that.

In the late 1890's, an English syndicate came to St. Louis and attempted to corner the local beer market. They succeeded in buying up many of the smaller breweries but William Lemp and Adolphus Busch refused to sell. A beer war ensued and the price for a barrel of beer dropped from $6 to $3. The saloon keepers cut their prices to two glasses for just 5 cents. The silliest point in the entire affair came when one quick-thinking tavern owner offered two glasses of beer and a boat ride on the lake adjoining his establishment for just 5 cents! Lemp and Busch weathered the battle and the Englishmen were beaten by the Germans and withdrew.

Because of the constant fighting within the local market, the process of obtaining a saloon to operate became a simple task for any aspiring barkeep with a 100 dollars or so in his pocket. He only needed to hint to some of the brewery collectors of his intentions and then wait for the offers to come in. Busch was usually the first to appear with a generous proposal. The candidate first had to get the approval of the majority of the residents of the neighborhood in which he planned to set up shop. Once he had that, he bought a government license for $25. After that, he had to obtain fixtures, glassware and a city license, which cost around $600. However, if the saloon keeper agreed to become a Busch beer establishment, Busch would take care of all of these costs for him. He would arrange for the rental of the shop, would install fixtures and a few choice murals and advertisement and then instruct the man on how to begin his operation. He charged the new customer $9 for a keg of $6 beer and applied the additional $3 to the amount the man owed him.

Despite of all these ingenious plans and clever marketing schemes though, Busch was still trailing the Lemp's in popularity and sales when the great beer revolution began. That turning point in brewing history came in 1873, when bottled beer became available. Its importance lay in the fact that bottled beer could be brought into the home or shipped to distant places and would remain unspoiled. Busch didn't have the first bottled beer in town, but he was the first to bottle it for shipping. And he accomplished this under unusual circumstances.

A close friend, Carl Conrad, who was wine merchant and owned a restaurant, has been called the "father of Budweiser", which remains today the Anheuser-Busch company's most popular beer. Conrad was traveling in Europe in the early 1870's and the story goes that he dined in a small monastery and was served a wonderful beer that he declared to be the best that he had ever had. He offered the monks who made it a good price for the recipe and they gladly handed it over. Returning to America, he asked his friend Adolphus to make the beer for him and he called it "Budweiser" after the town of Budweis, where he had found it. He bottled the drink in his own small shop. Not long after, he began to run into financial trouble and he borrowed money from Busch to stay afloat. At the same time Conrad was running deeper into debt, the new "pasteurization" process came along and made it possible to bottle beer in a way that it would make it impossible to spoil. Busch then approached Conrad with an offer to wipe out his debt in exchange for the Budweiser recipe. He agreed and even joined the brewery as a technician.

Budweiser was different than the other beers being produced because it was brewed with rice rather than corn grits for natural carbonation. It was then subjected to a second fermentation process and aged, as a true lager must be. Despite the beer's higher price, it was soon in such demand that Busch was scarcely able to get enough bottles to its suppliers. So, the brewery invested in glass factories. Busch founded the Adolphus Busch Glass Factory of St. Louis and Belleville, Illinois and the Streator Glass Company of Streator, Illinois and remained chief stockholder in both to keep the cost advantage for the brewery.

Now, Busch not only had bottled beer to sell, but he had the best bottled beer in the country. His innovations were disastrous to the small breweries that were left in the city and by 1900, only 19 of them remained in St. Louis. Brewing had changed from a local, neighborhood business to one with potential to reach markets everywhere, which is just what Busch began to do. While his competitors in St. Louis were struggling, he invested deeply and became a "traveling ambassador of beer".

Word of Budweiser beer began to spread and Busch began marketing and advertising in every state in the country. The plant in St. Louis began to expand, employing as many as 7,500 men and covering 142 acres of ground. Each year, Anheuser-Busch produced 1,600,000 barrels of beer. All but a small amount of that was consumed in the United States, but even the small amount sent aboard exceeded the entire sales, domestic and foreign, of most of the company's rivals.

Busch continued to expand and bought railroads, a coal mine and several hotels, all to further the cause of his beer. With Budweiser now the chief product of the brewery, he reduced his 16 brands to just four, Budweiser, Michelob, Faust and the standard pale beer. At that time, Michelob was the finest beer being made in America and was also the most expensive at 25 cents per glass. Like Budweiser, it originated in Bohemia, but it was Adolphus himself who discovered it. He bought a glass of beer one day for a few cents and it struck him as being even better than Budweiser. He returned home and ordered his staff to duplicate it. Michelob was the result, but it cost so much that sales were always low. This brand would not be bottled for many years. The Faust brand was named in honor of Tony Faust, a St. Louis restaurant proprietor.

As for Busch's competition, there was only the Lemp family to contend with. They had desperately followed Busch's lead in national distribution and refrigerated railroad cars with their Falstaff brand but they were unable to keep with the meteoric rise of Anheuser-Busch. The company now had no true rivals.

A Vintage View of the Anheuser-Busch Brewery in the 1930's

As Busch made more and more money, he began to spend it quite freely. He maintained his family in luxury and constructed a mansion known as No. 1 Busch Place. It was located on a park-like section of the brewery grounds and it was enlarged in time to be more suitable to their entertainment needs. The spacious rooms were known for their color schemes (as in the Rose Room, the Green Room, the Blue Room and others) and the inlaid floors were covered in expensive rugs. Stained glass windows emitted filtered light and walls, table and shelves were jammed with art objects, as was the fashion of the time. Expensive and imported furniture filled every inch of space and along with frescoed ceilings, tapestries and paintings added to the overall decor. In the main salon, the ceiling was filled with scantily clad and plump young ladies who floated across it and the walls were covered by paintings from some of the great artists of the day. Busch was one of the first to recognize the talents of American landscape artist William Keith and he was also an admirer of John Singer Sargent and James Abbott McNeill Whistler.

Everyone of note who visited St. Louis also visited with the Busch family, including Enrico Caruso, Theodore Roosevelt, Edward, Prince of Wales and many others. They entertained local friends quite often and held grand parties at the house. Busch also loved children and holidays. Every year, during the first week of December, a brewery watchman dressed as St. Nicholas visited the children, filling their stockings with fruit and treats to start the holiday season. On Christmas Eve, a huge tree on a revolving stand was the center of activity for everyone. Easter brought even more festivity when Busch decided to have an egg hunt for his and his neighbor's children. It turned out to be a huge success and each year brought even larger numbers of "neighbor" children that the event was finally moved to Forest Park.

Busch also loved animals, especially horses, as is evidenced by the brewery's modern reputation for its outstanding Clydesdales. Busch worried so much about the care of the horses that were used to transport his guests to parties that he could not stand to think of them outside in bad weather, shivering under a blanket. So, after discharging passengers, the horses and carriages were driven into a large rotunda in the carriage house. The horses were stabled and the coachmen could relax in a recreation room, where both food and Budweiser were kept on hand.

Busch also maintained one of the finest stables of riding and carriage horses in the United States. The stable building, located just across the drive from the mansion, would house up to 30 horses at one time. He also kept a large collection of carriages, coaches, barouches, landaus, shooting wagons and more. Sets of gold and silver mounted harnesses were kept in glass cases along the walls. Much of this can still be seen today at Anheuser-Busch's Grant's Farm location.

In the early 1900's, Busch also became interested in the "horseless carriage" as well. He commissioned an ornate Pope-Toledo automobile with a specially built wicker body and brass fittings. It was one of the first automobiles seen in St. Louis.

But while the Busch family lived in luxury, Adolphus was generous with his money to others as well. He always made it clear though that he gave because he wanted to and not because he thought that he owed the world anything. His gift included handsome donations to Washington University and to Harvard and every Ground Hog Day, he gave $5,000 to a convent in St. Louis. He also gave large amounts of money to charities in Germany, a habit that would come back to haunt the family with the advent of World War I.

His employees also fared well. Every man in the brewery was entitled to a generous portion of free beer each day and not only that, he was expected to drink it. The trips to the keg were seen as an important part of the day's routine. It was thought that a man needed a certain amount of beer each day to maintain good work habits and good health.

Busch was well-liked by the people of St. Louis, especially the common people. In spite of his vast wealth, he encountered a social coolness from the upper crust of St. Louis though, but he didn't care. He gathered his own circle of friends about him and managed to stay in the good graces of those who were spending the money and buying the beer. Thousands of these same people turned out for a grand celebration of Adolphus and Lilly Busch's 50th wedding anniversary in 1911.

Prior to that, most of the daily operations of the brewery had been turned over to Busch's son, August. He had become so skilled at the business affairs of the company that Adolphus and Lilly had the time to indulge their love of travel. They traveled to Europe and all over the country, including to their two houses in Pasadena, California and to the house in Cooperstown, New York.

When the time came for the special anniversary in 1911, Adolphus and Lilly wanted to make sure that each of their children had their own home. August and his wife received a grand home that had been built at Grant's Farm; Edmee Reisinger and her husband Hugo, received a mansion on Fifth Avenue in New York; Clara von Gotard was given a mansion in Berlin, Germany; Mrs. J.W. Loeb received a home near Lincoln Park in Chicago; and Mrs. Edward A. Scharrer was given a house in Stuttgart, Germany.

There was also a huge celebration in St. Louis to mark the event, although Adolphus and Lilly were unable to attend. They were in Pasadena at the time, where Busch was seriously ill. Some 13,000 employees and friends celebrated in their place though. The party took place at the Coliseum, where a 50-piece band played and employees paraded, sang, danced and waved flags. Lights gleamed on a center fountain that fired off a 30-foot jet of water and the crowd danced, drank and ate into the night. It was reported that 40,000 bottles of beer were consumed, along with 100,000 sandwiches!

Unfortunately, Busch's health did not improve and in 1913, he visited Villa Lilly, his home that overlooked the Rhine River in Germany. He hoped that the brisk autumn weather would improve his health but it seemed to have the opposite effect. On October 10, at the age of 76, Busch had a heart attack while sitting at his desk. He died peacefully a few hours later. His body was returned to St. Louis and a viewing was held at No. 1 Busch Place.

The house that had welcomed dignitaries, friends and common men alike bade its owner a final farewell. After Busch's death, Lilly divided her time between Europe and California, with only occasional stops in St. Louis. The house was seldom used and after her death in 1928, the Busch children divided the furniture, art and paintings and it was closed up for good. It was finally demolished to make more room for the brewery in 1929.

The funeral procession left No. 1 Busch Place and departed for Bellefontaine Cemetery. St. Louis residents solidly lined the 20-mile route. Mayor Henry Kiel asked that all business in the city be halted for five minutes during the burial. The Jefferson Hotel and the Planter's House turned off all of their lights for that same interval and all of the streetcars in the city were stopped. A committee of Busch employees asked permission to carry the casket through the brewery and along the same route that Adolphus had once walked each day. Busch was laid to rest and a grand mausoleum now stands at his burial place. I encourage the readers of this book to visit Bellefontaine Cemetery and especially to see the Busch tomb, which was constructed in the design of a miniature cathedral, complete with gargoyles and even its own watering system for plants and bushes.

Charles Nagel, one of the leading citizens of St. Louis, spoke the eulogy that day. He was joined by a number of other honored guests, including congressmen, the presidents of Harvard and the University of Missouri and Baron von Lesner, the personal representative of the German Kaiser Wilhelm II, a longtime friend of Busch. Nagel called Busch "a giant among men. Like a descendant of one of the great and vigorous ancient gods, he rested among us and with his optimism, his far seeing vision, his undaunted courage and his energy, shaped the affairs of men."

Without doubt, Adolphus Busch changed the shape, history and commerce of St. Louis for all time. He was a legend in his day and has left a permanent mark on the city that can be felt in hundreds of ways today.

August A. Busch took over the entire management of the company and continued the growth and the expansion until the outbreak of World War I. By 1917, the United States had entered the conflict, which brought dark times to the family. The two countries that the Busch's were devoted to were now at war. Lilly Busch was actually in Germany when America entered the war and it took former senator Harry Hawes seven and a half months to get her home. The brewery was directly handicapped by the talk that the Busch family was pro-German. Malicious tongues in St. Louis were not silenced by the purchase of Liberty bonds by the family and the brewery either. The Busch family, and the Germans population of St. Louis, were kept under close watch during these troubled times but they managed to passively weather the storm... until something even worse came along.

By 1910's, Anheuser-Busch was confronted with the impending Volstead Act, or Prohibition, which prohibited the sale and manufacture of alcohol in America. In an effort to combat the growing threat against beer, Busch filled with newspapers with ads in favor of personal liberty. But all the while, the company prepared for the inevitable and began working on a non-alcoholic, or "near-beer", called Bevo. They began production in 1916 and the popularity of it steadily grew. By 1919, it was sold all over the world so there was little cause for concern when the brewing of beer was stopped in October 1918. No one realized at the time that the disappearance of real beer would largely destroy the demand for the near-beer. Prohibition brought about the hip flask, the speakeasy, bathtub gin and rum runners and it also brought about the creation of sweet mixed drinks. The flavor of the illegal alcohol was usually so bad that it had to be disguised. People who became accustomed to the taste of these new drinks also lost their taste for the tart flavor of beer, or in this case, near-beer. By 1923, the sale of Bevo fell off to almost nothing and the grave situation was being felt at Anheuser-Busch.

And they were grim years all over the south side of St. Louis. The Lemp Brewery, the neighbor and chief competitor of Anheuser-Busch, closed down for good and shuttered its doors during this period. They sold off their huge plant for a fraction of what it was worth. But August Busch refused to give up. He told the members of the family that they had to think of something to keep the company afloat. So, Anheuser-Busch began to produce truck bodies and refrigerator cabinets and they went into the yeast business. Their superior product soon gained control of the entire market and money began trickling back into the coffers again. They also began bottling all kinds of soft drinks, including Busch Extra-Dry Ginger Ale and canned malt syrup, which was often used illegally to make home brew by eager customers.

But Busch was not happy just holding the company together. He wanted to make beer and he loathed Prohibition. On his own, he began investigating corruption and hypocrisy of the law and making his findings public. He discovered that liquor was sold aboard American flag ships and discovered the failures of law enforcement and outright graft within the ranks of the Anti-Saloon League. He pressed for a uniform and effective enforcement of the law as long as it was on the books. On the other hand though, he used his attorneys to appeal to President Coolidge, President Hoover and to Congress to repeal the law. Law-abiding businessmen were suffering while lawbreakers flourished, as long as Prohibition was the law of the land. Busch supported just about any politician who stood against Prohibition and finally President Franklin D. Roosevelt was elected in 1932 by stating that he "wants repeal, and I am confident that the United States of America wants repeal." Prohibition finally came to an end on April 7, 1933.

Under a permit to brew beer in advance of the date for its legal sale, Anheuser-Busch had 250,000 barrels ready and while they planned to resume business quietly, April 7 arrived in St. Louis like the New Year! A jubilant crowd surrounded the brewery! The gates were opened and a fleet of trucks rolled out to deliver the first Budweiser to the city's packed taverns. It was a great night in south St. Louis as August Busch had brought the old brewery from "doom to boom".

Sadly though, August A. Busch would not be around to enjoy it for long. As the company began to enter a new period of growth, Busch's life came to an end. He had suffered from several heart attacks during the hard years and was pained by gout and dropsy. On the night of February 13, 1934, in tremendous agony, he wrote a note to his family that read "Goodbye, precious Mommie and adorable children", turned up his radio and shot himself. He was succeeded by Adolphus Busch III, known around the brewery simply as "The Third". He was retiring man who had to handle the problems the company faced during the Depression and World War II. He died after a short illness on August 29, 1946.

August A. Busch Jr., or "Gussie" became the fourth Busch to become president of Anheuser-Busch and is remembered today as one of the most popular and outgoing members of the family. He carefully protected the reputation of the company and further expanded its image to make it one of the best known (or perhaps *the* best known) brewery in the world today. In 1953, when it was thought that the St. Louis Cardinals might be sold away from St. Louis, Gussie wrote the check that bought the baseball team and turned Sportsman's Park into Busch Stadium.

And while the Busch family, and the brewery, continue to thrive in St. Louis today, the family has not been without its scandals and troubles over the years, from brushes with the law, death and even kidnappings. Through it all though, they have managed to prosper and to build a great legacy in St. Louis.

For no matter what scandal may have afflicted them, they have managed to avoid the reputation that has become attached to the other great brewing family of St. Louis, the infamous Lemp family.

SUICIDE & SPIRITS
The Haunted History of the Lemp Family
The Lemp's came to prominence in the middle 1800's as one of the premier brewing families of St. Louis. For years, they were seen as the fiercest rival of Anheuser-Busch and the first makers of lager beer in middle America but today, they are largely forgotten and remembered more for the house they once built than for the beer they once brewed. That house stands now as a fitting memorial to decadence, wealth, tragedy and suicide. Perhaps for this reason, there is a sadness that hangs over the place and an eerie feeling that has remained from its days of disrepair and abandonment. It has since been restored into a restaurant and inn, but yet the sorrow seems to remain. By day, the mansion is a bustling restaurant, filled with people and activity, but at night,

after everyone is gone and the doors have been locked tight...

Something still walks the halls of the Lemp Mansion.

Are the ghosts here the restless spirits of the Lemp family, still unable to find rest? Quite possibly, for this unusual family was as haunted as their house is purported to be today. They were once one of the leading families in St. Louis but all that would change and the eccentricities of the family would eventually be their ruin.

The story of the Lemp brewing empire began with the birth of Johann Adam Lemp on May 25, 1793 in Gruningen, a small town in central Germany. His father, Wilhelm Christoph Lemp, was a barrel maker and a church caretaker and he instructed his son on learning a craft. Adam Lemp began to learn the brewer's trade as a young man and he became a master brewer in the towns of Gruningen and Eschwege.

In 1836, Lemp came to America and moved to Cincinnati. He spent nearly two years there before coming further west to St. Louis. In 1838, he opened a small mercantile store at what is now Delmar and Sixth Streets and in addition to common household items, he also sold vinegar and beer that he made himself. Apparently, Lemp began to see that he did better business with these items than with anything else and he soon established a small factory to make them at 112 South Second Street, between Walnut and Elm. This would be approximately where the Gateway Arch now stands along the St. Louis riverfront.

The new plant produced both vinegar and beer and for the first few years, Lemp sold his beer in a pub that was attached to the brewery. It is believed that during this period, Lemp introduced St. Louis to the first lager beer. This new beer was a great change from the English-type ales that had previously been popular and the lighter beer soon became a regional favorite. Business prospered and by 1845, the popularity of the beer was enough to allow him to discontinue vinegar production and concentrate on beer alone.

The company expanded rapidly, thanks to a demand for the beer, but Lemp soon found that the brewery was too small to handle the production of the beer and the storage needed for the lagering process as well. He found a solution to his problem in a limestone cave that had been discovered just south of the city limits of the time. The cave, which was located at the present-day corner of Cherokee and De Menil Place, could be kept cool by chopping ice from the nearby Mississippi River and depositing it inside. This would keep the cavern cool enough for the lagering process to run its course.

Lemp purchased a lot over the entrance to the cave and then began excavating and enlarging it to make room for the wooden casks needed to store the beer. The remodeling was completed in 1845 and caused a stir in the city. Other brewers were looking for ways to model their brews after the Lemp lager beer and soon these companies also began using the natural caves under the city to store beer and to open drinking establishments. The Lemp's own saloon added greatly to the early growth of the company. It was one of the largest around and served only Lemp beer and no hard liquor. This policy served two purposes in that it added to beer sales and also created a wholesome atmosphere for families as beer was considered a very healthy drink, especially to the growing numbers of German immigrants in the city.

The Lemp's Western Brewing Co. continued to grow during the 1840's and by the 1850's was one of the largest in the city. Demand for the beer continued to increase too, as it was highly regarded by almost everyone. In 1858, the beer even captured first place at the annual St. Louis fair.

Adam Lemp died on August 25, 1862, a very wealthy and distinguished man. He had created the leading brewery in St. Louis, the country's most competitive beer market, and had lived the American dream, discovering riches and happiness in the new world.

In his will, Adam left the Western Brewery to his son William and to his grandson, Charles Brauneck. Some believe that there may have been friction between these two men as the will added the condition that if either man contested it, the other would receive the entire property. Brauneck and Lemp formed a partnership in 1862 and agreed to run the company under the name of William J. Lemp & Co. The partnership was a short one and was dissolved in February 1864 when William bought out Brauneck's share of the company for $3,000.

Adam Lemp had left a thriving business in the hands of his son and under this new leadership, it began to grow in ways that its founder could have never conceived of. Many companies fall apart after the death of a strong leader, but the Western Brewery actually began to blossom after William took control.

William Lemp had been born in Germany in 1836, just before his parents came to America. He spent his childhood there and was brought to St. Louis by his father at age 12. He was educated at St. Louis University and after graduation, he joined his father at Western Brewery. After a short time, he struck out on his own and partnered in a brewery that had been started by William Stumpf in 1852. At the outbreak of the Civil War, he enlisted in the Union Army but was mustered out within a year. Some say that it was because of his height, which was only five feet, one inch. If this is true though, Lemp never let it stand in his way and he would quickly become known as a "giant" in the brewing industry. Soon after leaving the military, he married Julia Feickert and the couple would have nine children together.

After the death of Adam Lemp, William returned to the Western Brewery and began a major expansion. He purchased a five-block area around the storage house on Cherokee, which was located above the lagering caves.

William J. Lemp, Sr.
(Encyclopedia of the History of St. Louis)

Here, he began the construction of a new brewery so that moving the kegs by wagon from the Second Street brewery to the cave would no longer be necessary. By the 1870's, the Lemp factory was regarded as the largest in the entire city and by 1876 was producing 61,000 barrels of beer each year. A bottling plant was added the following year and artificial refrigeration was added to the plant in 1878. This would be the first year that the brewery's production would reach over 100,000 barrels.

A portion of the Lemp Brewery, shown here many years after it was abandoned

By the middle 1890's, the Lemp brewery was becoming known all over America. They had already introduced the popular "Falstaff" beer, which is still brewed by another company today although the familiar logo once had the name "Lemp" emblazoned across it. This beer became a favorite across the country, something that had never really been done by a regional brewer before. Lemp was also the first brewery to establish coast-to-coast distribution of its beer. It was transported in about 500 refrigerated railroad cars, averaging about 10,000 shipments per year. They operated their own railroad, the Western Cable Railway Company, which connected all of the brewery's main buildings with the shipping yards along the Mississippi. From here, they connected to major railroads and then spread out around the country.

Then, having expanded throughout the United States, Lemp also spread to overseas markets and by the late 1890's, the beer could be found in Canada, Mexico, Britain, Germany, Central and South America, the West Indies, the Hawaiian Islands, Australia, Japan and beyond.

The brewery had also grown to the point that it employed over 700 men and as many as 100 horses were needed to pull the delivery wagons in St. Louis alone. The brewery was now producing up to 500,000 barrels of beer each year and was ranked as the eight largest in the country. Construction of new buildings, and renovations of the current ones, continued on a daily basis at the Lemp brewery. The entire complex was designed in an Italian Renaissance style with arched windows, brick cornices and added Lemp shields and eventually grew to cover a five city blocks.

In addition to William Lemp's financial success, he was also well-liked and popular among the citizens of St. Louis. He was on the board of several organizations, including a planning committee for the 1904 World's Fair and many others. His family life was happy and his sons were very involved in the business. In November 1892, when the Western Brewery was incorporated as the William J. Lemp Brewing Co., William Jr. was named as vice-president and his brother, Louis, was made superintendent. William Jr., or Will as he was commonly known, was born in St. Louis on August 13, 1867. He attended Washington University and the United States Brewer's Academy in New York. He was well-known in St. Louis for his flamboyant lifestyle and in 1899, married Lillian Handlan.

His brother, Louis, was born on January 11, 1870. He learned the brewer's trade from some of the best master brewers in Germany and assisted his brother in the management of the company. He became involved with several political and civic organizations in St. Louis and as a young man explored his passion for sports. He would turn this passion into horses and became a successful breeder. In 1906, he sold his interest in the brewery and moved to New York to work with horses permanently. He and his wife, Agnes, had one daughter, Louise, and he died in New York in October 1931.

William's other sons were Frederick, Charles and Edwin and he had three daughters, Anna, Elsa and Hilda. In 1897, Hilda married the son of one of William's best friends, Milwaukee brewer Frederick Pabst. William and Julia also had one other child, an infant that died that was not carried to term.

The famous Lemp Mansion, shown here after extensive renovations started in the 1970's

During the time of the Lemp Brewery's greatest success, William Lemp also purchased a home for his family a short distance away from the brewery complex. The house was built by Jacob Feickert, Julia Lemp's father, in 1868 and was likely financed by William. In 1876, Lemp purchased it outright for use as a residence and as an auxiliary brewery office. Although already an impressive house before, Lemp immediately began renovating and expanding it and turning it into a showplace of the period. The mansion boasted 33 rooms, elegant artwork, handcrafted wood decor, ornately painted ceilings, large beautiful bathrooms and even an elevator that replaced the main staircase in 1904. The house was also installed with three room-sized, walk-in vaults where paintings, jewelry and other valuables were stored. It was a unique and wondrous place and one fitting of the first family of St. Louis brewing.

And the mansion was as impressive underground as it was above. A tunnel exited the basement of the house and entered into a portion of the cave that Adam Lemp had discovered for his beer lagering years before. Traveling along a quarried shaft, the Lemp's could journey beneath the street, all the way to the brewery. The advent of mechanical refrigeration also made it possible to use parts of the cave for things other than business. One large chamber was converted into a natural auditorium and a theater with constructed scenery of plaster and wire. Crude floodlights were used to illuminate the scene and the Lemp's were believed to have hired actors on the theater and vaudeville circuits of the day to come into the cave for private performances. This section of the cave was accessible by way of a spiral staircase that once ascended to Cherokee Street. This entrance is sealed today and the spiral stairs were cut away to prevent anyone from entering the cave.

About 22 feet east of the theater was another innovation of the Lemp family. Just below the intersection of Cherokee and De Menil was a large, concrete-lined pool that had been a reservoir back in the days of underground lagering. In the years that followed, the Lemp's converted it into a swimming pool by using hot water that was piped in from the brewery's boiler house, which was located only a short distance away.

After Prohibition, the caves were abandoned and the entrances sealed shut. In the 1940's, portions of the caves would be re-opened and turned into Cherokee Cave for several years.

Ironically, in the midst of all of this happiness and success, the Lemp family's troubles truly began.

The first death in the family was that of Frederick Lemp, William Sr.'s favorite son and the heir apparent to the Lemp empire. He had been groomed for years to take over the family business and was known as the most ambitious and hard working of the Lemp children. Frederick had been born on November 20, 1873 and attended both Washington University, where he received a degree in mechanical engineering, and the United States Brewers Academy. In 1898, Frederick married Irene Verdin and the couple was reportedly very happy. Frederick was well-known in social circles and was regarded as a friendly and popular fellow. In spite of this, he also spent countless hours at the brewery, working hard to improve the company's future. It is possible that he may have literally worked himself to death.

In 1901, Frederick's health began to fail and so he decided to take some time off in October of that year and temporarily move to Pasadena, California. He hoped that a change of climate might be beneficial to him. By December, he was greatly improved and after his parents visited with him after Thanksgiving, William returned to St. Louis with hopes that his son would be returned to him soon. Unfortunately, that never happened. On December 12, Frederick suffered a sudden relapse and he died at the age of only 28. His death was brought about by heart failure, due to a complication of other diseases.

Frederick's death was devastating to his parents, especially to his father. Brewery secretary

Henry Vahlkamp later wrote that when news came of the young man's death, William Lemp "broke down utterly and cried like a child... He took it so seriously that we feared it would completely shatter his health and looked for the worst to happen."

Lemp's friends and co-workers said that he was never the same again after Frederick's death. It was obvious to all of them that he was not coping well and he began to slowly withdraw from the world. He was rarely seen in public and chose to walk to the brewery each day by using the cave system beneath the house. Before his son's death, Lemp had taken pleasure in paying the men each week. He also would join the workers in any department and work alongside them in their daily activities or go personally among them and discuss any problems or any questions they had. After Frederick died though, these practices ceased almost completely.

In 1902, in tribute to his son, Lemp erected a magnificent mausoleum in Bellefontaine Cemetery. At a cost of $60,000 it stands today as the largest such structure in the cemetery and little did William know when he had it built, just how many of the Lemp's would need it in the short years to come....

On January 1, 1904, William Lemp suffered another crushing blow with the death of his closest friend, Frederick Pabst. This tragedy changed Lemp even more and soon he became indifferent to the details of running the brewery. Although he still came to the office each day, he paid little attention to the work and those who knew him said that he now seemed nervous and unsettled and his physical and mental health were both beginning to decline. On February 13, 1904, his suffering became unbearable.

When Lemp awoke that morning, he ate breakfast and mentioned to one of the servants that he was not feeling well. He finished eating, excused himself and went back upstairs to his bedroom. Around 9:30, he took a .38 caliber Smith & Wesson revolver and shot himself in the head with it. There was no one else in the house at the time of the shooting except for the servants. A servant girl, upon hearing the sound of the gunshot, ran to the door but she found it locked. She immediately ran to the brewery office, about a half block away, and summoned William Jr. and Edwin. They hurried back to the house and broke down the bedroom door. Inside, they found their father lying on the bed in a pool of blood. The revolver was still gripped in his right hand and there was a gaping and bloody wound at his right temple. At that point, Lemp was still breathing but unconscious.

One of the boys called the family physician, Dr. Henry J. Harnisch, by telephone and he came at once. He and three other doctors examined William but there was nothing they could do. William died just as his wife returned home from a shopping trip downtown. No suicide note was ever found.

Immediately after the shooting, the house was closed to everyone but relatives and brewery employees were posted to intercept callers and newspapermen at the front gate. Funeral arrangements were immediately made and the funeral took place the next day in the mansion's south parlor. The brewery was closed for the day and employees came to pay their respects before the private service was held. Everyone in the family was present except for Louis and Anna, who were unable to arrive in time.

After the service, a cortege of 40 carriages traveled to Bellefontaine Cemetery, although Julia, Elsa and Hilda were too grief-stricken to go to the burial ground. Eight men who had worked for Lemp for more than 30 years served as pallbearers and honorary pallbearers included many notable St. Louis residents, including Adolphus Busch, who had liked and respected his principal competitor. William was placed inside the mausoleum next to his beloved son, Frederick, although the crypt was not sealed so that Anna and Louis would be able to look on their father one last time.

Lemp's terrible and tragic death came at a terrible time as far as the company was concerned. In the wake of his burial, all of St. Louis was preparing for the opening of the Louisiana Purchase Exposition, perhaps the greatest event to ever come to St. Louis. Not only had William been elected to the fair's Board of Directors, but the brewery was also involved in beer sales and displays for the event. William Jr. took his father's place and became active with the Agriculture Committee and with supervising the William J. Lemp Brewing Company's display in Agriculture Hall, where brewers and distillers from around the world assembled to show off their products. The St. Louis brewers also combined for the restaurant and pavilion at the Alps section of the Pike, one of the fair's most popular attractions.

William Lemp, Jr. (St. Louis Post-Dispatch)

Finally, in November 1904, William Lemp Jr. took over as the new president of the William J. Lemp Brewing Company. He inherited the family business and with it, a great fortune. He filled the house with servants, built country houses and spent huge sums on carriages, clothing and art.

In 1899, Will had married Lillian Handlan, the daughter of a wealthy manufacturer. Together, the two of them had one child, William J. Lemp III. Lillian was nicknamed the "Lavender Lady" because of her fondness for dressing in that color. She was soon spending the Lemp fortune as quickly as her husband was. While Will enjoyed showing off his trophy wife, he eventually grew tired of her and decided to divorce her. Their divorce, and the court proceedings around it, created a scandal that all of St. Louis talked about. When it was all over, the "Lavender Lady" went into seclusion and retired from the public eye.

But Will's troubles were just beginning that year. The Lemp brewery was also facing a much-altered St. Louis beer market in 1906 when nine of the large area breweries combined to form the Independent Breweries Company. This was the second large merger in the local market. The first had been controlled by the English syndicate and had absorbed a number of the smaller companies. The formation of these two combines left only Lemp, Anheuser-Busch, the Louis Obert Brewing Co. and a handful of small neighborhood breweries as the only independent beer makers in St. Louis.

Of even more concern was the expanding temperance movement in America. The growing clamor of those speaking out against alcohol was beginning to be heard in all corners of the country. It looked as though the heyday of brewing was coming to an end.

The year 1906 also marked the death of Will's mother. It was discovered that she had cancer in 1905 and by March 1906, her condition had deteriorated to the point that she was in constant pain and suffering. She died in her home a short time later. Her funeral was held in the mansion and she was laid to rest in the mausoleum at Bellefontaine Cemetery.

Despite the fact that Julia was the richest woman in St. Louis at the time of her death, little is known about her personal life. She was rarely involved in social circles and preferred to remain at home with her family. William Jr. was the closest of the children to his mother and because of this, her death seemed to affect him the most. Combined with his scandalous divorce and the problems at the brewery, his mother's death surely made 1906 one of the worst years of his life.

After the divorce, Lillian and Will sought a more peaceful life. Lillian moved in with her parents for a time and later to New York. Will moved outside of the city to an area that was then mostly rough and secluded wilderness near Webster Groves, Missouri. On a bluff overlooking the Meramec River, he built a country estate that soon became his permanent home.

In 1911, the last major improvements were made to the Lemp brewery when giant grain elevators were erected on the south side of the complex. With the shadow of Prohibition beginning to fall across the land, Lemp, like many other breweries, began producing a near-beer malt beverage called Cerva. While Cerva did sell moderately well at first, revenues were nowhere near enough to cover the operating expenses used to make it. Eventually, it would be abandoned.

It was also in 1911 that the Lemp mansion was converted and remodeled into the new offices of the brewing company. A number of changes were made to the structure, including the addition of the immense bay window directly atop the atrium on the south side of the house. Inside, the front part of the house was converted into private offices, lobbies and rooms for clerks. Even with these changes though, the park-like settings of the grounds and the carriage houses were retained.

In 1915, Will married again, this time to Ellie Limberg, the widow of St. Louis brewer Rudolph Limberg. She was the daughter of Caspar Koehler, president of the Columbia Brewery. It was known that the two had been seeing one another for some time, but their wedding came as a surprise to everyone.

Like most of its competitors, the Lemp brewery limped along through the years of World War I. According to numerous accounts though, Lemp was in far worse shape that many of the other companies. Will had allowed the company's equipment to deteriorate and by not keeping abreast of industry innovations, much of the brewing facilities had become outmoded.

And to make matters worse, Prohibition was coming.

When William Lemp took over the Lemp brewing company after the death of his father, Adam, the company actually grew and expanded in the years that followed. It should be obvious to the reader though that the brewery did not prosper under the control of William's son. The combination of poor management and the passing of the 18th Amendment, which made Prohibition the law of the land, had a devastating effect on the Lemp Brewery.

Brewers were stunned by the passing of the amendment and by the Volstead Act, which made prohibition enforceable by law. The more resourceful companies had attempted to market their near-beers, but as alcohol actually became illegal, sales for these inferior brews began to dwindle and then disappear. Lemp's Cerva was officially dropped in June 1919.

This seemed to signal the real death of the company. As the individual family members were quite wealthy aside from the profits from the company, there was little incentive to keep the brewery afloat. Will gave up on the idea that Congress would suddenly repeal Prohibition and he closed the Lemp plant down without notice. The workers learned of the closing when they came to work one day and found the doors shut and the gates locked.

Will decided to simply liquidate the assets of the plant and auction off the buildings. He sold the famous Lemp "Falstaff" logo to brewer Joseph Griesedieck for the sum of $25,000. He purchased the recognizable Falstaff name and shield with the idea that eventually the government would see Prohibition for the folly that it was and that beer would be back. Lemp no longer shared the other man's enthusiasm though and in 1922, he saw the brewery sold off to the International Shoe Co. for just $588,000, a small fraction of its estimated worth of $7 million in the years before Prohibition. Sadly, virtually all of the Lemp company records were pitched when the shoe company moved into the complex. International Shoe Co. would use the larger buildings, and portions of the cave, as warehouse space.

With Prohibition finally destroying the brewery, the 1920's looked to be a dismal decade for the Lemp family. As bad as it first seemed though, things almost immediately became worse with the suicide of Elsa Lemp Wright in 1920. She became the second member of the family to take her own life.

Elsa was born in 1883 and was the youngest child in the Lemp family. With the death of her mother in 1906, she became the wealthiest unmarried woman in the city after inheriting her portion of her father's estate. In 1910, she became even richer when she married Thomas Wright, the president of the More-Jones Brass and Metal Co. They moved into a home at 13 Hortense Place in St. Louis' Central West End. During the years between 1910 and 1918, their marriage was reportedly an unhappy and stormy one. They separated in December 1918 and in February 1919, Elsa filed for divorce. In her petition, Elsa maintained that her husband had taken away her peace and happiness by his conduct and that he had long since ceased to love her. She also alleged that Wright treated her with indifference and that he stayed away from their home so that he could avoid her. All of these things had put her into a state of great mental anguish and had impaired her physical health as well.

Unlike the sensational divorce of her brother, Elsa's legal battle was kept quiet and the details of the divorce were not revealed. It was granted however in less than an hour and the reasons were cited as "general indignities".

By March 8, 1920 though, Elsa and Wright had reconciled and the two were remarried in New York City. They returned home to St. Louis and found their house filled with flowers and cards from friends and well-wishers.

The night of March 19 was a restless one for Elsa. Apparently, she suffered with frequent bouts of indigestion and nausea and this would cause periods of severe depression. She was awake for most of this night and slept very little. When her husband awoke the next morning, Elsa told him that she was feeling better but wanted to remain in bed. Wright agreed that this was the best thing for her and he went into the bathroom and turned on the water in the tub. He then returned to the bedroom for a change of underwear, retrieved them from the closet and went back into the bathroom. Moments after he closed the door, he heard a sharp cracking sound that he sensed over the sound of the running water.

Thinking that it was Elsa trying to get his attention, Wright opened the door and called to his wife. When she didn't answer, he walked into the bedroom and found her on the bed. Her eyes were open and she seemed to be looking at him. When Wright got closer, he saw a revolver on the bed next to her.

Elsa tried to speak but couldn't and a few moments later, she was dead. No note or letter was ever found and Wright could give no reason as to why she would have killed herself. He was not even aware that she owned a gun.

The only other persons present that morning were members of the household staff. None of them heard the shot, not did they see any sign that Elsa intended to end her life. They quickly summoned Dr. M.B. Clopton and Samuel Fordyce, a family friend. Strangely, the police were not notified of Elsa's death for more than two hours and even then, the news came indirectly through Samuel Fordyce. Wright became "highly agitated" under the scrutiny of the police investigation that followed and his only excuse for not contacting the authorities was that he was bewildered and did not know what to do.

And while the mysterious circumstances around Elsa's death have had some suggesting there was more to the story than was told, her brothers seemed to find little out of the ordinary about her demise. Will and Edwin rushed to the house as soon as they heard about the shooting. When Will arrived and was told what had happened, he only had one comment to make.

"That's the Lemp family for you", he said.

Will was soon to face depression and death himself. He had already slipped into a dark state of mind following the end of the Lemp's brewing dynasty, but he took an even sharper turn for the worse after the sale of the plant to the International Shoe Co. He was downcast and bitter and had always believed that the brewery could have been turned into something great, even after Prohibition, and now it was nothing more than a warehouse. His family's hopes, dreams and legacies had turned to dust.

The months that followed the auction were difficult ones for him as not only had the family business died, but Will himself had been responsible for selling off the last pieces of Adam and William Lemp's life's work. It was likely this indignity that bothered Lemp the most. He never really recovered from his role in the company's dissolution and his state of mind began to deteriorate. Perhaps it was a "curse" that ran in the Lemp bloodline, or perhaps they were all simply sad products of their time, but mental instability and depression seemed to be a common factor among members of the family. Will soon began to follow in the footsteps of his father and he became increasingly nervous and erratic. He shunned public life and kept to himself, complaining often of ill health and headaches.

By December 29, 1922, he had reached the limit of his madness.

On that morning, Lemp secretary Henry Vahlkamp arrived at the Lemp brewery offices around 9:00. When he came in the front door, he found Will already in his office. The two of them were joined shortly after by Olivia Bercheck, a stenographer for the brewery and Lemp's personal secretary.

Vahlkamp later recalled that Lemp's face was flushed that morning and that when he entered his employer's office, he had an elbow on the desk and he was resting his forehead on his hand. He asked Lemp how he was feeling and Will replied that he felt quite bad.

"I think you are looking better today that you did yesterday," Vahlkamp noted in an effort to cheer up the other man.

"You may think so," Will replied, "but I am feeling worse."

Vahlkamp then left and went to his own office on the second floor of the converted mansion.

Moments after this exchange, Miss Bercheck telephoned Will's wife, Ellie, about instructions for the day's mail and as she was speaking to her, Lemp picked up the other line and spoke to his wife himself. The secretary recalled that he spoke very quietly and she did not hear what turned out to be his last words to his wife. After Lemp finished the conversation, Bercheck asked him a question about some copying that she was doing from a blueprint. He first told her that what she had was fine and then he changed his mind and suggested that she go down to the basement and speak to the brewery's architect, Mr. Norton.

While she was on her way downstairs, she heard a loud noise. Because there were men working in the basement, she thought nothing of it, assuming that someone had dropped something. When she came back upstairs though, she found that a porter had Lemp lying on a pillow. He had been working downstairs and had come running when he heard the noise, realizing that it had been a gunshot. He had come into the office and had found Lemp lying on the floor with his feet under the desk. He called for help and men from the office across the hall came over and laid Will out on a pillow.

Apparently, just after speaking to Miss Bercheck, Lemp had shot himself in the heart with a .38 caliber revolver. He had unbuttoned his vest and then fired the gun through his shirt. When discovered, Lemp was still breathing, but he had expired by the time a doctor could arrive.

Captain William Doyle, the lead police investigator on the scene, searched Lemp's pockets and desk for a suicide note, but as with his father and his sister before him, Will left no indication as to why he believed suicide was the answer to his problems.

His wife collapsed upon being given the news of her husband's death and his son, William III, ran into his father's office and knelt beside the body on the floor. "You knew I knew it," he cried, "I was afraid this was coming." He declined to explain his remarks to the police.

Staff members in the office volunteered their own thoughts on the situation and discussed his increasingly strange behavior, nervousness and depression. Will had always been the friendly and flamboyant member of the family but since the end of the brewing business, he was constantly ill, tired and unlike himself.

Oddly, Lemp seemed to have no intention of suicide, even a short time before. Apparently, the final turn in his downward spiral had come on quite suddenly. After the sale of the brewery, he had discussed selling off the rest of the assets, like land parcels and saloon locations, and planned to then just "take it easy". Not long after that announcement, he had even put his estate in Webster Groves up for sale, stating that he planned to travel to Europe for awhile. Even a week before his death, he had dined with his friend August A. Busch, who said that Lemp seemed "cheerful" at the time and that he gave no indication that he was worrying about business or anything else. "He was a fine fellow," Busch added, "and it is hard to believe that he has taken his own life."

Interestingly, a new term came into use by the St. Louis police department around this time. It was coined because of the number of suicides among prominent St. Louis German-Americans, which included a number of brewers. These suicides became so notorious that police officers that investigated the untimely deaths began referring to them as the "Dutch Act". The term was a slang word that was used for German, or "deutsch". Several members of the Lemp family followed their father to the grave by killing themselves, but they were not the only ones.

Patrick Henry Nolan was the vice-president and general manager of the Mutual Brewing Co. in St. Louis. The company had erected a brewery in 1912 but within two years was hard hit with financial problems. Nolan committed suicide at the brewery office on the night before a scheduled appearance in bankruptcy court.

Otto Stifel of the Union Brewery also took his own life. Distraught about the passage of Prohibition and stuck with large gambling and business debts, he shot himself in the mouth at his Valley Park farm in August 1920. He left several rambling suicide notes, blaming his death on Prohibition and dishonest family members and business associates.

Readers will also remember the tragic death of August A. Busch, who committed suicide after keeping the family business running through the Prohibition years. Plagued with failing health, he chose to commit suicide rather than live with the pain that he had been enduring.

The funeral of William Lemp Jr. was held on December 31 at the Lemp mansion. The offices were used as the setting for the services for sentimental reasons, staff members said. He was interred in the family mausoleum at Bellefontaine Cemetery, in the crypt just above his sister Elsa.

With William Jr. gone and his brothers involved with their own endeavors, it seemed that the days of the Lemp empire had come to an end at last. The two brothers still in St. Louis had left the family enterprise long before it had closed down. Charles worked in banking and finance and Edwin had entered a life in seclusion at his estate in Kirkwood in 1911. The great fortune they had amassed was more than enough to keep the surviving members of the family comfortable through the Great Depression and beyond.

But the days of Lemp tragedy were not yet over.

In 1933, Prohibition was officially repealed and almost immediately, the Falstaff Brewing Corporation (the company that Griesedieck had built around the former Lemp label) had beer ready to distribute in St. Louis. Falstaff received Federal Permit Number 1 when Prohibition ended as they had been one of the few companies that had continued to produce near-beer. All that they had to do to be ready for the real thing was to drop the dealcoholization process. After Falstaff took over the old Union Brewery, they started a vast expansion program that took them first to Omaha, then New Orleans and other American cities. They proved for the first time that identical beer could be brewed in different locations, which was thought to be impossible at that time. Falstaff is still brewed today, although it no longer is brewed in St. Louis. In this way, the Lemp legacy lives on... even if it is in name and label only!

While the future seemed bright for Falstaff, the cycle of disaster continued for the Lemp family. In 1934, trouble had reared its head for William Lemp III. He and his wife, Agnes, were having trouble holding onto the estate in Webster Groves that his father had once owned. They occupied the house but the Board of Finance of the Methodist Episcopal Church actually held the mortgage for the property. They eventually sued the Lemp's and foreclosed on the estate, then valued at $200,000. The land was later subdivided into a residential area known as Lemp Estates.

Meanwhile, William's misfortunes affected his marriage as well. He and Agnes separated in March 1936 and within a year, Agnes had filed for a decree of separation maintenance, alleging that her husband had refused to give her any money and that she had been forced to pawn some of her jewelry and to take a position in a downtown department store to survive. The Lemp's divorced officially a short time later.

In 1939, William took the Lemp name back into the brewing business. He entered into an agreement with Central Breweries, Incorporated of East St. Louis, Illinois and licensed them to use the Lemp name in connection with their beer. In return, the brewery would pay him royalties on all beer sold with the name of Lemp. In October 1939, Central changed its name to the William J. Lemp Brewing Company and launched a massive advertising campaign to announce the rebirth of the famous Lemp name. Lemp beer began to officially be brewed again on November 1 and initial sales exceeded all expectations. The new endeavor seemed destined for success.

In the end, it barely lasted a year. By September 1940, the William J. Lemp Brewing Company was in serious trouble. They had accumulated a mountain of liabilities and owed back taxes, payrolls, accounts and interest on second mortgage bonds that added up to more than $260,000. The total assets of the company were listed at $150,000, which included 13,000 barrels of beer that they had on hand. Trading on the company's common stock was suspended on December 19 because the company was deemed insolvent and wiped out. Early the following year, it was officially bankrupt.

The once strong name of Lemp was now unable to dominate the market as it once had. Ems Brewing Co. took over the brewery in December and they immediately terminated the contract with William Lemp III. Starting on March 1, 1945, they discontinued the name "Lemp" in connection with beer. The plan to bring the Lemp label back to life had failed miserably and the Lemp empire had now breathed its last.

Perhaps it was for the best that William never lived to see the final days. He passed away in 1943 and was interred in the family tomb with the innovative brewers that he had tried so hard to honor.

By the late 1920's, only Charles and Edwin Lemp remained from the immediate family. Throughout his life, Charles was never much involved with the Lemp Brewery, although he was named as treasurer around 1900 and was second vice-president in 1911. His interests had been elsewhere, but when the family home was renovated into offices, he made his residence at the Racquet Club in St. Louis.

He ended his connections with the family business that same year and took the first of what would be many positions in the banking and financial industries. In 1917, he became vice-president of the German Savings Institution and then on to Liberty Central Trust in 1921. He stayed on here for several years and eventually got into the automobile casualty business as president of the Indemnity Company of America. In 1929, Charles also moved back to the Lemp mansion and the house became a private residence once more.

He continued to look after his real estate holdings and investments and among them was the East St. Louis, Columbia and Waterloo electric railroad line, which went out of business in 1932. Lemp also enjoyed traveling, which he did extensively until World War II interfered. He was also involved with politics and was a powerful member of the Democratic Party in St. Louis.

Despite his very visible business and political life though, Charles remained a mysterious figure who became even odder and more reclusive with age. He remained a bachelor his entire life and lived alone in his old rambling house with only his two servants, Albert and Lena Bittner for company. By the age of 77, he was arthritic and quite ill. Legend has it that he was deathly afraid of germs and wore gloves to avoid any contact with bacteria. He had grown quite bitter and eccentric and had developed a morbid attachment to the Lemp family home. Thanks to the history of the place, his brother Edwin often encouraged him to move out, but Charles refused. Finally, when he could stand no more of life, he became the fourth member of the Lemp family to commit suicide.

On May 10, 1949, Alfred Bittner, one of Charles' staff, went to the kitchen and prepared breakfast for Lemp as he normally did. He then placed the breakfast tray on the desk in the office next to Lemp's bedroom, as he had been doing for years. Bittner later recalled that the door to the bedroom was closed and he did not look inside. At about 8:00, Bittner returned to the office to remove the tray and found it to be untouched. Concerned, he opened the bedroom door to see if Charles was awake and discovered that he was dead from a bullet wound to the head. Bittner hurried to inform his wife of what had happened and she contacted Richard Hawes, Lemp's nephew, who then summoned the police to the mansion.

When the police arrived, they found Lemp still in bed and lightly holding a .38 caliber Army Colt revolver in his right hand. He was the only one of the family who had left a suicide note behind. He had dated the letter May 9 and had written "In case I am found dead blame it on no one but me" and had signed it at the bottom.

Oddly, Charles had made detailed funeral arrangements for himself long before his death. He would be the only member of the family not interred at the mausoleum at Bellefontaine Cemetery and while this might be unusual, it was nearly as strange as the rest of the instructions that he left behind. In a letter that was received at a south St. Louis funeral home in 1941, Lemp ordered that upon his death his body should be immediately taken to the Missouri Crematory. His ashes were then to be placed in a wicker box and buried on his farm.

He also ordered that his body not be bathed, changed or clothed and that no services were to be held for him and no death notice published, no matter what any surviving members of his family might want.

On May 11, 1949, Edwin Lemp picked up his brother's remains at the funeral home and took them to the farm to be buried. And while these instructions were certainly odd, they were not the most enduring mystery to the situation. You see, even after all of these years, there is no indication as to where Charles Lemp's farm was located!

The Lemp family, which had once been so large and prosperous, had now been almost utterly destroyed in a span of less than a century. Only Edwin Lemp remained and he had long avoided the life that had turned so tragic for the rest of his family. He was known as a quiet, reclusive man who had walked away from the Lemp Brewery in 1913 to live a peaceful life on his secluded estate in Kirkwood. Here, he communed with nature and became an excellent cook, gourmet and animal lover. He collected fine art and entertained his intimate friends.

Edwin managed to escape from the family "curse" but as he grew older, he did become more eccentric and developed a terrible fear of being alone. He never spoke about his family or their tragic lives, but it must have preyed on him all the same. His fears caused him to simply entertain more and to keep a companion with him at his estate almost all the time.

His most loyal friend and companion was John Bopp, the caretaker of the estate for the last 30 years of Edwin's life. His loyalty to his employer was absolute and it is believed that Bopp was never away from the estate for more than five days at a time during his entire time there. He never discussed any of Lemp's personal thoughts or habits but would sometimes speak of the famous parties held at the estate and the well-known guests who attended them. He remained faithful to Edwin even after his friend's death.

Edwin passed away quietly of natural causes at age 90 in 1970. The last order that John Bopp carried out for him must have been the worst. According to Edwin's wishes, he burned all of the paintings that Lemp had collected throughout his life, as well as priceless Lemp family papers and artifacts. These irreplaceable pieces of history vanished in the smoke of a blazing bonfire.

And like the Lemp empire... lost forever.

The Lemp family line died out with him and the family's resting place can now be found in beautiful Bellefontaine Cemetery. But while no one remains in the Lemp family today, it certainly doesn't mean that some of them are not still around.

After the death of Charles Lemp, the mansion was sold and turned into a boarding house. Shortly after that, it fell on hard times and began to deteriorate, along with the nearby neighborhood. In later years, stories began to emerge that residents of the boarding house often complained of ghostly knocks and phantom footsteps in the house. As these tales spread, it became increasingly hard to find tenants to occupy the rooms and because of this, the old Lemp Mansion was rarely filled. These stories seem to contradict the skeptics who claim that the ghosts are a more recent addition to the house!

According to author Stephen Walker, who wrote an excellent book about the Lemp family and their brewing company called *Lemp - The Haunting History*, there are other stories to confirm that the house was haunted in the boarding house days as well. After his own book was written, he was told about a young girl and her friends who decided to sneak into the house one day around 1949, shortly after Charles died. The house was still vacant at the time but they managed to get into the front door and they started up the main staircase to the second floor. They climbed the steps to the first landing and then prepared to go up the last set of stairs to the upper level. Just as they reached the landing, they looked up and saw a filmy apparition coming down the steps toward them! The young girl much later described it as an almost human-shaped puff of smoke. The group took one look at it and ran! She told Walker in the late 1990's that she had never been in the house since and had no desire to ever go back.

The decline of the house continued until 1975, when Dick Pointer and his family purchased it. The Pointer's began remodeling and renovating the place, working for many years to turn it into a restaurant and an inn. But the Pointer's were soon to find out that they were not alone in the house...

The bulk of the remodeling was done in the 1970's and during this time, workers reported strange things happening in the house, leading many to believe the place was haunted. Reports often varied between feelings of being watched, vanishing tools and strange sounds. Many of the workers actually left the job site and never came back.

At one point in the renovations, a painter was brought in to work on the ceilings and he stayed overnight in the house while he completed the job. One day, he was in his room and ran downstairs to tell one of the Pointer's that he had heard the sound of horse's hooves on the cobblestones outside of his window. The other man convinced the painter that he was mistaken. There were no horses and no cobblestones outside! In time, the man finished the ceilings and left, but the story stayed on Pointer's mind. Later that year, he noticed that some of the grass in the yard had turned brown. He dug underneath it and found that beneath the top level of the soil was a layer of cobblestones! During the Lemp's residency in the house, that portion of the yard had been a drive to the carriage house! Pointer had the cobblestones removed and then used them as floor stones in one area of the mansion's basement.

Later in the restoration, an artist was brought in to restore the painted ceiling in one of the front dining rooms. It had been covered over with paper years before. While he was lying on his back on the scaffolding, he felt a sensation of what he believed was a "spirit moving past him". It frightened him so badly that he left the house without his brushes and tools and refused to return and get them. Some time after this event, an elderly man came into the restaurant and told one of the staff members that he had once been a driver for the Lemp family. He explained that the ceiling in the dining room had been papered over because William Lemp hated the design that had been printed on it. The staff members, upon hearing this story, noted that the artist had gotten the distinct impression that the "spirit" he encountered had been angry. Perhaps because he was restoring the unwanted ceiling?

During the restorations, Mr. Pointer's son, Richard "Dick" Pointer, lived alone in the house and became quite an expert on the ghostly manifestations that have been reported here. One night, he was lying in bed reading and he heard a door slam loudly in another part of the house. No one else was supposed to be in the house and he was sure that he had locked all of the doors. Fearing that someone might have broken in, he and his dog, a large Doberman named Shadow, decided to take a look around. The dog was spooked by this time, having also heard the sound, and she had her ears turned up, listening for anything else. They searched the entire house and found no one there. Every door had been locked, just as Pointer had left them! He reported that the same thing happened again about a month later, but again, nothing was found.

Since the restaurant has opened, staff members also have had their own odd experiences. Glasses have been seen to lift off the bar and fly through the air, sounds are often heard that do not have explanation and some have even glimpsed actual apparitions who appear and vanish at will. In addition, many customers and visitors to the house report some pretty weird incidents. It is said that doors lock and unlock on their own, the piano in the bar plays by itself, voices and sounds come from nowhere and even the spirit of the "Lavender Lady" has been spotted on occasion.

Late one evening, Dick Jr. was bartending after most of the customers had departed and the water in a pitcher began swirling around of its own volition. Pointer was sure that he was just seeing things but all of the customers who remained that night swore they all saw the same thing. Then one night in August 1981, Dick and an employee were startled to hear the piano start playing a few notes by itself. There was no one around it at the time and in fact, no one else in the entire building.

And while the ghostly atmosphere of the place has admittedly attracted a number of patrons, it has also caused the owners to lose a number of valuable employees of the house. One of them was a former waitress named Bonnie Strayhorn, who encountered an unusual customer while working one day. The restaurant had not yet opened for business and yet she saw a dark-haired man seated at one of the tables in the rear dining room. She was surprised that someone had come so early, but she went over to ask if he would like a cup of coffee. He simply sat there are did not answer. Bonnie frowned and looked away for a moment. When she looked back, just moments later, the man was gone! She has continued to maintain that the man could not have left the room in the brief seconds when she was not looking at him. After that incident, she left the Lemp Mansion and went to work in a non-haunted location!

In addition to customers, the house has also attracted ghost hunters from around the country, who have come partly due to the November 1980 *LIFE* magazine article, which named the Lemp Mansion as "one of the most haunted houses in America". It remains a popular place for dinner and spirits today.

The hauntings at the house first gained attention due to investigations conducted there in the late 1970's by the "Haunt Hunters", two St. Louis men named Phil Goodwilling and Gordon Hoener. They actively researched ghost stories and sightings in the area and during that period, even conducted a class on ghosts for St. Louis University. They promised their students that they would take them to a real haunted place and decided that the Lemp Mansion fit the bill. In October 1979, they brought the class to the house and brought along a local television crew to film the event.

Goodwilling and Hoener divided the students up into small groups and gave them all writing "planchettes" to try and contact the spirits with. The devices, like Ouija boards, were used to spell out messages from the ghosts. Each of the groups of students was divided into groups of four.

One of the groups asked: "Is there an unseen presence that wishes to communicate?"

"Yes", came the answer. It scrawled out on a large piece of paper as the planchette, with its pencil tip, moved across the surface.

The students asked another question: "Will you identify yourself?"

The planchette scratched out a reply: "Charles Lemp"

Goodwilling later noted that the students who received this message were the most skeptical in the class. He also noted that no one in the room that night, with the exception of Dick Pointer, had any idea that Charles had committed suicide. At that time, the history of the house had not been widely publicized.

After the name was revealed, the spirit added that he had taken his own life. When asked why he did this, the spirit replied in three words: "Help, death, rest"

It might also be added that by the time this seance was over, the four students were no longer the most skeptical in the class!

In November, the Haunt Hunters returned to the house and this time brought along a camera crew from the show *Real People*. Goodwilling and Hoener participated in a seance with two other participants, neither of who had any idea about the past history of the mansion. They once again made contact with the spirit who identified himself as "Charles Lemp" and he was asked again why he had committed suicide. The spirit reportedly used a derogatory term and then added "... damn Roosevelt". Apparently, the Lemp's had not been fond of the politics practiced by Franklin D. Roosevelt during their time.

But the seance continued with the next question from the group: "Is there a message for someone in this house?"

The answer came: "Yes, yes, Edwin, money"

The group then asked if there was anything they could do to free the spirit from being trapped in the house? "Yes, yes," the ghost replied. Unfortunately though, they were unsuccessful in finding out what they could do to help.

Goodwilling felt that if the spirit was actually Charles Lemp, then he might have stayed behind in the house because of his suicide. He probably became active because of the remodeling in the 1970's or perhaps because he still had a message for his brother, Edwin Lemp, who he tried to contact during the seance. He may have believed that Edwin was still alive and based on the conversation, was trying to pass along a message about money. Could this be what caused Charles Lemp's ghost to remain behind? Could there be a secret treasure hidden somewhere in the house? If so, it has yet to be found!

Most importantly perhaps to the reader is the question of whether the Lemp Mansion still remains haunted today? Most can tell you that it does although the current owners of the house accept this as just part of the house's unusual ambience. One of the owners, Paul Pointer, helps to maintain the place as a wonderful eating and lodging establishment. He takes the ghosts as just another part of the strange mansion. "People come here expecting to experience weird things," he said, " and fortunately for us, they are rarely disappointed."

One of the Lemp Trains (Courtesy Missouri Historical Society)

IV. BENEATH ST. LOUIS

The Mysterious History of the City's Lost Caves

While not necessarily haunted, the caves of St. Louis represent one of the most strange and mysterious elements of this fascinating city. The entire city of St. Louis is built upon a huge and complex system of natural caves. In fact, no other city on earth has as many caves beneath its streets, sidewalks and buildings. While most of them have been abandoned and closed off, they have not been forgotten and many tales, stories, legends and accounts of their unusual history are still told today.

Caves were used as man's earliest storage cellars. Thanks to the natural coolness of them, food and other items could be stored in them and kept from spoiling. This was perfect for the lagering that was done to beer by St. Louis brewers. Adam Lemp, who first brought lager beer to thirsty St. Louisans, was the first of the German brewers to put the caves to work for him, but he was far from the only one. These brewers altered the caves beneath the city to suit their purposes. They constructed stone arches and brick ceilings to prevent water from seeping in and paved the uneven cave floors. They also constructed staircases and walkways and installed massive wooden kegs where the beer could be aged. While the brewers did save money by having the cave as a starting point, the caverns were expensive to open and renovate. For this reason, many of them did double duty as not only a place for beer storage, but for sales as well. A number of beer gardens and taverns were once located in St. Louis caves and became popular drinking establishments and night spots.

Many of the caves would also boast a rich history. In some cases, breweries might not have been built at all but for the existence of the cave beneath the earth. The Anheuser-Busch brewery cave was first discovered in 1852 by a German brewer named George Schneider. He built a small brewery on the land above it and operated for three years before going out of business. The company was taken over by a competitor, Urban & Hammer, who renamed the property the Bavarian Brewery. As noted in the last chapter, they launched an expansion program that was funded by Eberhard Anheuser, who later ended up owning the company.

In addition to beer lagering, the cave was also used by the military. During the Civil War, it was located close to the Arsenal and the tunnels here were used to hide arms and ammunition. The guns were concealed in beer wagons and were taken to the cave for safekeeping when a raid on the Arsenal was feared.

Later, when Anheuser-Busch began using artificial refrigeration in its plant, the cave beneath the brewery were abandoned and forgotten. It was rediscovered in the 1930's though when excavations were being done for underground storehouses. Although no longer used today, the cave is a piece of Anheuser-Busch and St. Louis history.

Take a trip back through the long and strange history of the caves of St. Louis. Most of them have been forgotten now, but it cannot be denied that they have left quite a mark on city and on those who discover their legacy today. For I have no doubt that you will be left wondering what lies beneath your feet the next time you walk along a downtown St. Louis street!

CHEROKEE CAVE

There is no question that the most famous of St. Louis' caves was a place that would become known in later years as Cherokee Cave. Originally, this was part of the same cave that was discovered by Adam Lemp and used for his brewery. Thanks to the unusual additions made by the Lemp family to the cave in later years, it remains as perhaps the most enigmatic in the city.

A reporter for the *Missouri Republican* newspaper wrote that Lemp's cave had three separate chambers and that each one of them contained large casks that were capable of holding 20-30 barrels of beer. The lagering cellars were opened for use in 1845, but Lemp soon expanded them to store more than 3,000 barrels of beer at a time. The beer cellars had been created by simply clearing out the natural underground river channels that had been carved from the limestone. They were divided off by the construction of masonry and brick walls into artificial rooms. During the early period of the brewery's history, Lemp was still brewing the beer on Second Street and taking it by wagon to the cave for the lagering period. After the death of Adam Lemp, his son, William, would construct a new brewery above the cave.

Around 1850, and around the time that the Lemp Brewery was just beginning to grow, fur trader Henri Chatillon built a home on a piece of property that adjoined Lemp's property at the crest of Arsenal Hill on Thirteenth Street. In 1856, Dr. Nicholas DeMenil purchased the house and land and he began enlarging and expanding the farm house a few years later.

DeMenil added several rooms to the house and a magnificent portico that faced eastward and looked out over his large garden and the Mississippi River. The Greek Revival mansion became a favorite landmark for river pilots rounding Chatillon's Bend.

In 1865, DeMenil leased the southwest corner of the property to the Minnehaha Brewery and they built a small, two-story frame brewery on the site. For several years, DeMenil had been using a cave that was located beneath his house as a place to store perishable goods and he also leased a portion of this to cave to Charles Fritschle and Louis Zepp, the owners of the brewery. Like Adam Lemp, they planned to use the caverns as a place to lager beer and over the course of the next year, they made a number of improvements to the cave. Unfortunately though, the brewery went out of business in 1867 and DeMenil acquired the buildings.

During the years of operations though, both the Lemp's and the Minnehaha Brewery were using different parts of the same cave. A wall had been constructed between the two businesses but the Lemp's had little to fear from this short-lived competition. It is also believed that they must have been on good terms with Dr. DeMenil. When the Lemp family built their home just down the street from the DeMenil mansion, an arrangement was made to run three pipelines through DeMenil's cave, furnishing the Lemp mansion with hot water, cold water and beer from the brewery complex down the street.

The Lemp's continued to use the cave until the time when artificial refrigeration was installed at the factory. After that, the cave no longer played in role in beer production, so it was turned into a private playground for the Lemp family. During the heyday of the Lemp empire, they constructed a swimming pool, a ballroom and a vaudeville theater in the cave and all of those are still intact today. Their portion of the cave, which connected from entrances in the Lemp mansion and along Cherokee Street, was closed off after Prohibition and was no longer used. Today, it is still a curiosity to many and occasionally is seen by the public.

However, this was not the end for the Minnehaha portion of the cave. In November 1946, a pharmaceutical manufacturer named Lee Hess bought not only the Minnehaha portion of the cave but the old DeMenil Mansion and grounds as well. He set to work developing the cave as a tourist attraction after first tearing down the deserted brewery buildings and a row of ten buildings that Dr. DeMenil had constructed as stores and homes between Cave and Cherokee Streets. In their place, he erected a museum building and parking lot to serve what he dubbed "Cherokee Cave". The cave became a popular tourist attraction but staff members at the DeMenil House talk about Hess and his strange obsession with the cave. He nearly lost his entire fortune trying to develop it and only two rooms of the sprawling DeMenil house were used during his time there. He and his wife shared one room and Albert Hoffman, who managed the cave for Hess, lived in the other. Staff members say that he moved all of the house's antiques and furniture into the attic while he was living here.

Before the cave was opened, Hess hired workmen to tear open an entrance into the Lemp part of the cave and in the process found that the passageway between the two cellars had been filled to the ceiling with clay. In the course of digging it out, workers found a number of bones that were linked to extinct animals and rare creatures that had no scientists had thought had lived in this area. Scientific research was conducted and Hess later got back to re-opening the cave. In April 1950, Cherokee Cave was opened to the public and it was a popular attraction for more than ten years. Visitors to the cave were able to stroll along on a tour that took them to Cherokee Lake and the Petrified Falls and of course to the famed Spaghetti Room, where slender cave formations hung down from the ceiling like strands of pasta.

The cave remained open until 1960 and in 1961, it was purchased by the Missouri Highway department to clear the way for Interstate 55. Hess battled to the end of his life to keep the state from destroying the DeMenil mansion and he eventually succeeded, although the cave museum and entrance could not be saved. The building and the entrance that Hess had created were demolished in 1964. Today, the only reminder of this unique place is a short street near Broadway and Cherokee in St. Louis called "Cave Street". The De Menil Mansion was also scheduled to be destroyed but that plan was later changed and the house became a historic site and museum.

For years after the Interstate tore though this historic portion of the city, it was believed that Cherokee Cave had been filled in and completely destroyed. However, those with an interest in that sort of thing can tell you that portions of the cave do still exist today. While not in any way accessible to the public, the mystery of the place still remains alive.

Many can tell you though that the Lemp caverns are still accessible and have been toured in recent years. Past visits to the labyrinth of rooms that were constructed by the Lemp's would even reveal the remains of broken and rotted wooden casks where beer was once aged in the cellars. Visitors would also pass through oversized doorways and into rooms lined with brick and stone. The swimming pool remains as well, now filthy and covered with mud. The theater still exists, although today it is hard to imagine audiences who might have assembled here to watch a performance. When the theater was built, the Lemp's tore out the natural formations of the cave and replaced with them with formations made from plaster and wood. Tinted in odd colors, this formed the backdrop for the stage.

And while many can attest to the haunting that occurs in the Lemp mansion, once accessible from the cave, there are others who insist that the cave is haunted too. Stories have been told (and none that I can verify, mind you) about strange sounds and shapes that have been seen and heard down here and cannot be explained away as the weird, but natural, happenings in a cave. In recent times, the cave has occasionally been the site of a "haunted house" attraction that has been put on by the current owners of the Lemp Mansion Restaurant. They feel that visitors will likely be more frightened by artificial "hauntings" in a genuine haunted place. In some cases though, the customers may get a little more than they bargained for. On at least one occasion, the attraction was reportedly closed down after a staff member spotted someone in an off-limits area that leads into the abandoned section of Cherokee Cave. The customers were stopped at the door while employees tracked down this wandering visitor and escorted them out. However, after a thorough search, there was no one found! The trespasser had completely vanished!

I have also been told that when the heavy iron door, installed by the International Shoe Co. in 1944 between their warehouses and the cave, was locked after the attraction closed for the night, it was always locked from the outside. The latch was thrown so that anyone entering the cave would have easy access... but whatever was inside would be unable to get out!

UHRIG'S CAVE

In 1852, Dr. William Beaumont, a famous St. Louis surgeon and the post doctor at Jefferson Barracks for many years, decided to sell of a portion of his land. He owned a large wooded tract that was bounded to the north by Locust Street and to the south by Washington Avenue. The land was notable for the fact that it had a large natural cave beneath it and it was this part of the land that Beaumont offered for sale.

Around this same period, there were German brothers, Franz and Andrew Uhrig, who owned a brewery on Market Street, just southeast of the Beaumont property. Franz had come to America in 1836 and after arriving in St. Louis two years later, purchased a flat boat and began ferrying cordwood to the city from the Illinois River where his brother, Andrew, had a farm. In 1839, they went into the beer business and started the Camp Springs Brewery, near the present-day site of Union Station. It would later be re-named the Uhrig Brewery and it operated until 1884.

In the 1850's though, the Uhrig's were keeping their beer cold enough for the lagering process at their brewery buildings. They chopped ice from the Mississippi during the winter months and then packed it with sawdust to keep the beer cold throughout the rest of the year. It was an inefficient and time-consuming process and it forced them to keep their company small. So when they heard about the land being offering by Dr. Beaumont, they quickly bought it. The cave, with its natural spring and cool temperature, would save them time and money and would help them to expand.

The Uhrig's soon began expanding the existing cave's length to 170 feet. They also built brick walls and high arched ceilings to prevent water seepage and spent an estimated $100,000 to connect their cave with a series of other caverns and to install a narrow gauge railroad that could transport their beer from the brewery to the cave.

The area around the cave was an attractive grove of trees and only a short buggy ride from the downtown area. For these reasons, Uhrig's became a popular St. Louis spot for customers to enjoy a glass of beer and listen to music. Tables were moved into one of the larger chambers and band concerts were often held, along with dining and dancing. Tours were also conducted through the cave as well. It was not the first to do so, but it would be this cave that would give rise to the use of other caverns as places to entertain guests and Uhrig's became known as the "original" St. Louis beer garden.

During the Civil War, entertaining here was suspended and the cave became a headquarters for the militia. A home guard regiment was stationed here and they often used the larger tunnels to hold their drills. After the war, operations were started up again and the cave soon regained its customers. In the late 1860's, the Uhrig's sold the cave to Chris Nuntz, who added a small theater and tried to turn the place into an opera house. He was successful but leased the cave out in 1881.

In 1884, he sold the site to Thomas McNeary, a saloon keeper. He further expanded on the idea of the theater and turned the cave into a full-blown vaudeville house. McNeary and his brothers ushered in the period of the cave's greatest glory, attracting popular entertainers like John Drew, Julia Marlow and other stars to their stage. They also installed the first electric lights used in any St. Louis entertainment spot. During its peak, the cave boasted an audience of up to 3,000 per night and they came to drink and enjoy music, plays and comic operas.

These glory days would not last long though. In 1888, the McNeary's lost their liquor license and the cave was abandoned until 1900, when they failed in an effort to revive the site as a legitimate theater. From 1903 to 1908, the cave was used at different times as a roller rink, a bowling alley and a mushroom farm. Finally, the McNeary's gave up and offered a 90-year lease to a syndicate called the Business Men's League, who built a large auditorium that covered the cave, the beer garden and much of the surrounding area. They planned to create a facility to host sporting events, theatrical performances and more. They broke ground in 1908 and planned to call the location the St. Louis Coliseum.

The Coliseum had a grand opening in 1909 when famed evangelist Gypsy Smith began a series of revival meetings here. Smith attracted more than 10,000 per night and paved the way for horses show and circuses and for many of the Veiled Prophet Balls. Many popular performers played here including Enrico Caruso and John McCormack. Bill Tilden played tennis here and Johnny Weismuller swam in what was called "the world's largest indoor swimming pool". It was installed in 1925 and could be covered by a removable floor when arena space was needed. One of the most popular events to be held here was a championship wrestling match in 1927 between Joe Stecker and Ed "Strangler" Lewis. The Coliseum was completely sold out and the brutal match lasted until the wee hours of the morning, with the "Strangler" finally emerging as the winner.

Despite all of this, the Coliseum was never a financial success. As early as 1914, it was cited for back taxes and for being behind in rent. Ownership reverted back to the McNeary estate (Tom McNeary died in 1893), which held it until 1925, when it was purchased by a New York syndicate with plans to renovate it. They tried to stimulate new interest in the place by installing the immense swimming pool and by varying the use of the building but by then it was almost too late. The construction of the St. Louis Arena in 1929 and the Kiel Auditorium in 1934 drew most of the large events away from the Coliseum. To make matters worse, the building had no real parking available, which was another problem in the days when more Americans were buying automobiles. The last event held at the Coliseum was a wrestling match in 1939 and during World War II, it was used as a storage spot for new automobiles that had been "frozen" by government regulations at the start of the war.

From 1950 on, the building remained empty and by 1953 was condemned as unsafe by the city. City Building Commissioner A.H. Baum Jr. stated that "the building will have to be torn down or cleaned up and repaired. If it remains standing, it will have to be made safe, which it isn't now." Later that year, the St. Louis Coliseum was demolished.

Cave explorers and historians got one last look at the old cave in 1954 when the Jefferson Bank & Trust Company building was being constructed on the site. Many of the passageways still remained, along with the man-made arched brickwork and the natural features like the small spring. Some of the smaller tunnels had been closed off during Prohibition when an illegal liquor still was discovered in a connecting cavern at Jefferson and Delmar. One tunnel had served as a secret entrance for bootleggers, while another part of the cave had hidden a vat for whiskey mash. The walls of the one of the chambers beneath Eighteenth Street had been decorated with Egyptian figures and artwork and was believed to have been a speakeasy at one time.

One has to wonder if the Uhrig's brothers had any idea, when they purchased the site in the middle 1800's, of the history their small brewery cave would see in the years to come.

OTHER BREWERY CAVES

There were a number of other breweries that also used the natural cave systems of the city during the heyday of beer brewing in St. Louis. Ironically, many of them used different portions of the same caves, never realizing that they were actually connected. One such cavern was once part of Uhrig's Cave and was generally known as the "Winkelmeyer and Excelsior Cave". It was used by four separate breweries during the middle to late 1800's.

In 1847, it was used by Julius Winkelmeyer and his brother -in-law, Frederick Stiffel, who started the Winkelmeyer Brewery along the western bank of Chouteau's Pond. They chose the site because of the underlying natural cave and because of the fact that the lake was a popular recreation site for a time. Sadly, Stiffel and his wife both died during one of the epidemics that was blamed on the polluted conditions of Chouteau's Pond. Winkelmeyer himself passed away in 1867 but his wife carried on the business and changed the name to the Union Brewery in 1873. It ceased operations in 1892.

In 1880, another brewer set up operations in a portion of the same cave and became known as the Excelsior Brewery. They shared the cave with another brewery, Franklin Brewery, which had been started in 1855 and was located just south of Market Street. The area was cleared to make way for Union Station in 1894, but by then, all of the companies had long gone out of business and the cave they had used for lagering had been forgotten.

But it would not stay forgotten for long. In 1933, the city made plans to widen Market Street and as city engineers started their excavations, they broke into the abandoned cave. Surveyors entered the cave and found the remains of the old Winkelmeyer plant, as well as a second level of the cave that contained wooden fermenting tanks. They discovered masonry walls and brick columns and at one end of a tunnel, found an abandoned mushroom bed. Beneath this level, they entered a deep cellar that was now only accessible by a shaky ladder. The large sub-cellar had vaulted arches and huge wooden chambers and vats for beer that were still intact. The cave was sealed up and remained that way for only a few years. At that time, the new Post Office was built and the cave was surveyed again.

In 1955, re-development work was started on the Plaza, which led to a collapse of a part of the cave in 1959. Engineers had tried to fill in the cave a few years before, but a depression developed that was almost 25 feet deep. They added 4,000 cubic yards of fill to the cavern, but in 1960, a sidewalk collapsed in front of the Post Office. Government engineers had to drive steel beams into the cave beneath the sidewalk in order to support the pavement. It had become another St. Louis cave that simply refused to be forgotten!

In 1833, a German immigrant named Christian Staehlin came to St. Louis and was followed four years later by his father. Together, the two of them opened the Staehlin Brewery at the corner of Eighteenth and Lafayette Streets, choosing the site because of the access to the natural cave and spring beneath the area. The company later became known as the Phoenix Brewery and they began a plan to expand the natural caves by adding brick and mason work and moving lagering equipment into what visitors called a "labyrinth" of tunnels.

Christian Staehlin remained in charge of the Phoenix Brewery until 1877, when he sold out to Anton Griesedieck, who changed the name to the A. Griesedieck Brewing Company. He in turn sold the plant in 1889 to the St. Louis Brewing Association. The brewery closed for good in 1920.

In 1964, the old brewery buildings were destroyed to make way for the expansion of Interstate 55. Today, a tangle of highways crosses the area above the cave and it is no longer accessible.

In 1839, another German immigrant named Carl Klausmann came to American and settled in Louisville, Kentucky. During his brief stay there, he met a young woman named M.A. Uhrig, the sister of the Uhrig brewing brothers of St. Louis. A short time later, she moved to St. Louis with the rest of her family and Klausmann followed. The two of them married in 1841 and the couple opened a restaurant at the corner of Walnut and Third Streets called "Our House". The establishment did quite well and so they decided to follow the family tradition and open their own brewery along South Broadway. Here, they used a large cave in which to lager their beer.

Unfortunately, just two years after the brewery was opened, Klausmann died and left his widow to run the business. Even though she had been left with six children to raise on her own, the company prospered and she amassed a considerable fortune. The beer garden that she had added on the property, known as "Klausmann's Cave", became very popular and drew large crowds. In 1877, she even expanded it and added regular concerts. In addition, the brewery was doing quite well too. In 1881, a malting department was built and in 1883, they began bottling the beer and selling it outside of the city. Mrs. Klausmann died in 1898, but even after her death, the brewery and the cave continued to do well as a branch of the St. Louis Brewing Association, which had acquired the business at the time of her death.

Even after the turn of the century, the cave continued to be popular. In 1902, the Carondelet Business Men's Association sponsored a week-long carnival at the cave and beer gardens. The crowds who attended were so large that special arrangements had to be made to have all of the streetcars on Broadway running to Klausmann's Cave. They also convinced the ferry companies on the Mississippi to bring over visitors from Illinois.

Like so many other breweries though, Prohibition killed the Klausmann operation. They were just too small to survive the years of forced inactivity and the company was shut down.

Eventually, the buildings here were demolished. The entrance to the cave was later filled in for the safety of the children who lived in the neighborhood and as far as I know, it remains silent and empty today... forgotten by time.

In the late 1850's, a large natural cave that was located near Sidney Street, from the Mississippi River to Eleventh Street, was used by a total of 14 different breweries. As mentioned earlier, in many cases the companies had no idea that they were using the cave and believed that clay falls and rock slides were the ends of the cave. They didn't realize that these were simply natural occurrences that blocked off passageways leading from one portion of the cave to another. Some of the breweries that used the Sidney Street Cave were also companies who came along after others had gone out of business or which had sold out to other breweries.

One of the companies who used the cave was the Whitteman and Rost Weis Beer Brewery, who had a small factory just east of the river on Anna. There was also another early brewery called the Suesert and Berger Brewery that was located on the south side of Sidney Street. It was also in this area that the Green Tree Brewery was located, which was discussed already.

The Theo. Schwer and Co. Brewery was located on Lynch Street, which is one block south of Sidney Street and near Carondelet, now South Broadway. This brewery operated for only a single year, in 1891, and bottled a short-lived label called "Our Favorite".

The Excelsior Brewery was located at Seventh and Lynch Streets and closed down in 1880. At that time, all of its operations were moved to the Uhrig Brewery.

On the north side of Sidney and east of today's Broadway was the Pittsburg Brewery. It was started in 1857 and within a year was producing more than 3,000 barrels of beer each year. By 1859, that number had increased to 8,000 and so they opened a new branch called the Cave, located at Rosatti and Lynch Street.

The Jackson Brewery, also started in 1857, stood on the same block as the Pittsburg Brewery. The company, owned by Jacob Stagner, got off to a good start, producing about 1,000 barrels of lager beer the first year but production soon dropped off and the brewery went out of business.

The year 1857 also saw the opening of the Arsenal Brewery, which was built by F.F. Heinscher just south of Sidney and west of Broadway. The company began producing about 8,000 barrels of beer with about half that number being lagered in the cave. They opened a second branch some time about 1875 at the corner of Rosatti Street and Lynch.

On the north side of Sidney at Buel, the Schlop Brewery was opened by Louis Koch in 1860. This company only produced about 500 barrels of beer during its first year and a few years later, Koch built another brewery called Koch & Feldkamp's and it operated under that name until 1875. It was later known as Schilling and Schneider.

One block west on Sidney at Tenth Street was the Gambrinus Brewery, which was started in 1856 by Anton Yager. Named for St. Gambrinus, the patron saint of brewers, the brewery produced 4,000 barrels of beer during its initial year of operation. By 1860 though, production had fallen by half and apparently being named for a saint wasn't enough as the brewery went out of business.

Also located in the Sidney Street area was a brewery with a rather unusual look and an unusual story behind it. The Anthony & Kuhn's Brewery was the largest and best known factory in this district and legend had it that it was built in cooperation with the Catholic Church. It was understood that if the brewery was not successful, then it would be converted into a church. The building was constructed with a gothic appearance, just in case the church ever had to take over the site. The company prospered however and the church never had to step in!

This was not the first brewery on the site though. The original company was founded by a Colonel Jaeger, who opened the Jaeger Brewery before the Civil War. Jaeger was active in the military and during the war, the brewery was used as the armory for the First Regiment of the U.S. Reserve Corps of Missouri Volunteers. Jaeger was later killed in the fighting at Lexington, Missouri.

In 1870, Henry Anthony and Francis Kuhn purchased the site. Beneath the brewery, they had access to what we have called the Sidney Street Cave. Their portion of it was described as extending from all directions from an elevator shaft. It was dry, cool and well-ventilated with stone floors and walls and ceilings of brick. Above the earth, the site consisted of the brewery buildings, a "mammoth" beer garden and a grand pavilion where performances by military bands were common.

The Anthony & Kuhn's Brewery grew quickly and their section of the cavern was expanded to increase productions. In 1875, they required thirty men and six beer wagons to deliver their product throughout the city. It continued to operate until the owners sold out to the St. Louis Brewing Association conglomerate in 1899. The syndicate promptly closed it down. In 1922, the building was sold to a laundry company and was later torn down.

Most of the cave was destroyed but rumors persist that a portion of it still remains under the south side of Menard Street. It is really quite sad to think that the Sidney Street Cave, like so many others in St. Louis, is no longer accessible. Based on the sheer number of breweries that used it in days gone by, this was surely one of the most productive caves in the city!

THE OTHER ST. LOUIS CAVES

While a good many of the forgotten caves of St. Louis were used by the brewing industry for lagering beer, there were many others that were not. As mentioned already, the city is literally honeycombed with caves and there were probably a large number of them that were never found. It's possible that some of these caves still exist today, still untouched by human hands. In addition, there are also a large number of caves that were known to our ancestors but have been forgotten over time. These caves are seldom seen or mentioned today and are kept secret by small bands of spelunkers who still roams the world under the city streets.

One such cave is located beneath the exclusive neighborhood known as Compton Heights in south St. Louis. While the cave is still believed to exist in its natural state today, there is no record of anyone having entered it, save for an architect, a few sewer workers and a newspaper reporter. If anyone else has ever walked here, he had kept his journey a closely guarded secret.

The cave was mentioned in a newspaper article in 1888 when an architect, who lived in the wealthy, mostly German, neighborhood discovered the entrance to a "tunnel" on his property. He entered it and walked for some distance, finding that he could walk upright in some areas of the passage but had to crawl on his hands and knees in others. The architect reported that the tunnel seemed to head towards the Mississippi River and that all of the water that he saw seemed to move rapidly in that direction. The architect's identity was never disclosed in the article, perhaps to keep the location of the cave a secret, but it did quote a neighbor named Julius Pitzman, a well-known surveyor and city planner, who confirmed the existence of the cave. He added that there was an opening in his own yard, also in the Compton Heights neighborhood, where the sound of rushing water could be heard.

The cave was not mentioned again until 1924, when another opening was discovered under

Nebraska Avenue, near Lafayette Avenue. While workers were tunneling for a relief sewer, a reporter decided to explore the cave. He crawled through the sewer tunnel and then entered a muddy opening that was about five feet in length. He then came upon a large room that was filled with hundreds of cave formations. He was able to walk about and noted a stream of water flowed across the floor and that the place was muddy and wet. He discovered a natural bridge and after crossing a small stream, he found walking easier and less muddy. He traveled about 300 feet, finding a number of bridges and other cave formation, before finally turning back. There seemed to be no end to the passageway and it eventually just vanished into the shadows.

In 1925, the cave was discovered again. A separate group of workmen were constructing a relief sewer and they accidentally broke into the cave just north of California Avenue and Sidney Street. Several workmen were lowered into the cavern below them, but they were overwhelmed with gas and had to be pulled back out. Fresh air was pumped into the cave and (in these days before worker's compensation claims!) they went back in again. Their comrades lowered them down and they spent a brief time exploring the cavern. They found a number of large rooms and cave formations and noticed that a steady stream of water followed the route of the cave as it disappeared into the darkness.

The cave meant great difficulties for the men constructing the sewer line and despite the fact that rock existed between the streets and the ceiling of the cave, the workmen had to use in shoring in several places to keep the tunnels from collapsing. The United Construction Company, which was in charge of the project, saw their budget skyrocket because of the problems caused by the cave. When they finished though, they had extended a 7,000-foot sewer line from California and Sidney to a point near Lafayette and Nebraska. When the work was completed, the cave entrance was sealed off and a reporter of the day predicted that the cavern would soon be forgotten.

And perhaps he was right.

Other caves of St. Louis, or at least portions of them, could not boast the industrious uses that were given to similar caverns by the brewing industry. Many of these caves were used by criminals, adventurous boys and tramps as hideouts and camps. Those caverns not in use by the breweries provided excellent locations for those who needed secret hiding places in the city and the history of St. Louis provides colorful tales of these sorts of caves.

In 1876, the police department became suspicious about tramps they believed were hiding out in caves near the river. Records say that they decided to investigate and near the south wall of the Arsenal, they found a narrow passage that opened into a large cave. The walls and ceiling had been blackened by smoke and a bench seat had been carved from the side wall. Holes that were opened up appeared to serve as sleeping compartments. The cave was also fitted with doors and padlocks at various turns in the passageway. The mysterious cavern was kept under watch for several nights and then a raid on the location snared the men responsible for it. There were about 20 men arrested in all, mainly dock workers, who had been using the cave to run a gambling operation. After the men were hauled away, the police officers sealed the entrance to the cave by blowing it up with gunpowder. While this apparently sealed off the entrance near the river, it did not damage the rest of the cave itself. In 1966, a small pond in Lyon Park kept being drained of all of its water as it emptied into an underground cavern beneath the park. It is believed that this was the same cave that was once used as a gambling parlor and that part of it may still exist intact beneath the park.

Interestingly, another cave (or part of the same one?) was discovered a few years later in this same area near Lyon Park, west of the Arsenal. This time, the police entered a passage that opened from the side of a sinkhole and found themselves in a cave. Apparently, it had been used by some of the neighborhood boys, who had been ditching school, as a makeshift gambling den. The police officers reportedly found a complete keno set-up in a hole inside of the cave.

Around 1880, a "den of thieves" was discovered by workers hauling driftwood up from the river at the foot of Lesperance Street. The opening to the cave had been disguised as well with water drawing equipment installed over it. A shaft had been dug down and about one-third of it had been cleverly filled with water. Just above the water line though, a tunnel ran off to the side and entered the cave. The floor of the cave was found to be covered with cotton and straw mattresses and authorities believed that it was a headquarters for thieves operating along the riverfront. The police had been investigating the increasing number of thefts in the city at this time and suspected that the perpetrators were living in various caves.

One account tells of a police officer who was walking the beat on Washington Avenue in the middle of the winter. He happened to notice the lack of ice and snow around one of the iron grates near a sewer inlet and as he got closer, he saw steam rising out of it. Thinking this odd, as there were no houses nearby, he called for some help to investigate it. Officers kept watch over the grate and observed several bootblacks and newsboys entering an area nearby. One by one, they would crawl under a large pile of brick and stone and then vanish. They would occasionally leave during the night and would return with small amounts of food and coal that had been stolen from wagons and stands near Union Street. The following day, police raided the lair.

The cave had been floored and walled with wooden boards and around the sides of it were three tiers of bunks. In one corner was a small cook stove with a pipe that led into the sewer. It had been the heat from the stove that had caught the police officer's attention and had led to the raid on the cave. Eleven boys were taken into custody and police confiscated stolen merchandise, cigar stumps, racy song lyrics, erotic pictures and "sensational novels". The boys were returned to their respective homes, which they had run away from in order to live an independent life with extra money to go to the theater and gamble. The group had been living in the cave for about three months.

HAUNTED ENGLISH CAVE

Perhaps the most famous St. Louis cave is one that few living people have ever seen. Now filled with water and inaccessible, English Cave has long been a place of legend in the city. It is the one such cave that has been regarded as "haunted" since it was first discovered and the stories have it that it brought bad luck and misfortune to every person who owned it!

The original entrance to English Cave, as it came to be known, was located just east of Benton Park, between Arsenal and Wyoming Streets in south St. Louis. The only entrance was by way of a natural shaft that extended about 60 feet below ground. At the bottom of the shaft, a visitor would then enter a chamber that was close to 400 feet long.

In the early days of the city, the cave was known only to the Native Americans of the region. There came to be a legend associated with the cave that not only may account for the alleged curse attached to the place, but also for the reports of hauntings that followed in the years to come. According to the story, there was a young Indian woman who fell in love with one of the men from her village. The young man reciprocated her feelings but was unable to marry the girl as she had already been promised to the tribe's war chief, a violent and disagreeable man. Rather than see her in the arms of another, the man convinced his lover to run away with him. They managed to find refuge in the cave and hid there, waiting for the danger to pass. The chief somehow tracked them to the cave though and he and his warriors stationed themselves outside, determined to take back his intended bride. Rather than surrender to the chief, the couple stayed in the cave until they starved to death.

Many years later, this tale was repeated to the white explorers who entered the cave and seemed to have a ring of truth after the bones of two people were discovered inside. If there is any truth to the story, it might explain the accounts that were passed on about the cave, including the ghostly sounds of crying and weeping reported here and the eerie voices that speak in an unknown dialect. Could the spirits of the two Indians have lingered behind in the cave and if so, could they account for the curse that was believed to plague the owners?

Ezra O. English was the first of the luckless proprietors of the place. In 1826, English built a small ale brewery next to the cave and east of the commons. He later set up the brewery inside of the cave and became the first person in St. Louis to use a cave as a commercial property. Unlike those who followed his example, English did little to improve the cave's interior, although he did wall up the mouth, removed some of the stone and earth from the floors and carve out 50 stone steps into the first chamber. Beyond this was the second chamber, which was ten feet lower than the first. Here, a small spring emerged from the ceiling and created a small waterfall. The first chamber was the principal part of the early business though. He used it as a place to store ale and he also provided accommodations for customers who wanted to sample cool drinks.

In 1839, English took on a partner named Isaac McHose, a local businessman, and they began calling the place the St. Louis Brewery. The business grew and by 1842, they had developed the first subterranean beer garden and resort in the city. While the men were expanding the business, they gained a new neighbor. The city was also converting the commons next door to the brewery into a public burial ground. Cholera epidemics had been striking the city and the graveyard began to grow.

By 1849, the renovations to the cave had been completed and English and McHose re-named their project Mammoth Cave and Park, perhaps borrowing the name from the cave of the same name in Kentucky, which was just then starting to attract visitors from all over the country. English and McHose also did their bit to attract visitors to their cave. They built gardens and arbors around the property and hired a family of vocalists to entertain in the cave on Sundays. Later, they constructed a sail swing, arranged hot air balloon rides and hired a military band to play full-time.

Unfortunately, they saw little success. The year 1849 is remembered by most in the city as the "year of misfortune", thanks to the terrible cholera epidemic that swept through the city and the great fire that devastated the riverfront. No one seemed to have much interest in the attractions that the cave offered and by 1851, English was the sole proprietor of the cave again. Within a few years, he faded from public records.

Several years later, the city passed an ordnance for the removal of all bodies from the cemetery that adjoined the site. They were to be taken to the "Quarantine Burying Grounds" that were located some distance south of Jefferson Barracks. When all of the bodies were removed from the St. Louis Cemetery, another ordnance established it as a public park in 1866. It was named after Thomas Hart Benton and the cave was largely forgotten.

However in 1887, two businessmen named F.K. Binz and George Schaper attempted to resurrect English Cave as a commercial mushroom farm. They hoped to fare better than their predecessors had and were constantly reminded of the cave's failures. Even a newspaper article that was released at the time wished the men well "in spite of the history of failure that has hung around the place." The operation was soon in full swing and the men tended their crop by light of kerosene lanterns. For a time, the business was moderately successful and regular customers reportedly came and paid 75 cents for a pound of mushrooms. It didn't last though and in less than two years, the cave was abandoned once again.

The next unlucky occupant was Paul-Wack Wine Co., which became widely acclaimed for the fine wines they offered. Great wines or not though, they didn't stay around much longer than the mushroom farm. In 1897, the company used the cave for storage for their nearby winery but soon closed down. The winery was the last company to use the cave for business purposes, but its history had not yet ended.

Shortly after the turn of the century, a St. Louis park commissioner suggested opening a portion of the cave as a part of Benton Park. He recommended that an ornamental entrance be constructed from the park for he believed the cave would draw visitors from all over, as there was no other park with such a unique attraction connected with it. The plans were never realized though and eventually the cave really was forgotten.

During the 1960's though, interest in the cave was revived thanks to Hubert and Charlotte Rother, the authors of the excellent and indispensable book, *Lost Caves of St. Louis*. They proposed a plan for re-opening the cave with the help of the Hondo Grotto, a local chapter of the Missouri Speological Society, a group of cave explorers. The society surveyed Benton Park and used sounding equipment to try and detect an approximate depth of the cave. They discovered that the ground under Benton Park was catacombed with large rooms and ten passageways that left the park and travel in all directions. They tried to interest two different St. Louis mayors and the City Park Department in their plans, but no one was interested.

Instead of giving up though, their interest in the cave grew. They began digging through old records and searching for information. They discovered that although the cave had been closed in 1897, it created a myriad of problems for the park years later. It seemed that periodically, the lake in Benton Park would suddenly lose all of its water. Apparently, the water was flooding down into the cave below. The Park Department constructed a concrete bottom for the lake and sealed off the leak but it would later be discovered that this would not be enough to keep water out of the cave.

The problem faced by the Rother's back in the 1960's though was how to get into the cave again. The original entrance had been closed off, but thanks to newspaper accounts that were written about their plans for the cave, many older people in the area came forward with their memories of the cave. One woman told them that she recalled entering the cave in 1889 and had gone in through the backyard of a confectionary, just east of Benton Park. The owner of the confectionary charged his customers 25 cents to see the cave. Another man claimed to have visited the cave in 1911 by way of a staircase in the back of an old shed. Another remembered a spiral staircase and yet another told of an entrance through an abandoned frame building off an alley. He and some friends had pried two wooden cellar doors away from the entrance and had gone down a flight of steps.

They continued to pick up promising clues and bits of information and tried to follow as many leads as possible. They learned of an entrance that had once been located in a boarded-up shed that stood near the intersection of the alley behind Provenger Place. There was also an alleged entrance from a basement of a house near Benton Park. The Rother's check out the address, but there was no building there so they asked about the basement entrance at houses up and down the block. "All we received," Charlotte Rother later wrote," were suspicious looks and blank faces." They followed every story and every possible lead, but ran into a blank wall. There was seemingly no way into the cave.

Unfortunately, it turns out that all of their searching may have been for nothing. At the time of this writing, I have learned that the cave is completely underwater and inaccessible today. I have been told that there are some grates in Benton Park that would look down into the cave, if they were not filled with water! A few years ago, in the middle 1990's, a group of amateur cave explorers were able to get into the cavern during a time when the water levels were very low. Even then, the water was more than waist-deep in spots. The group managed to come out with some priceless video footage of the cave, showing brick walls and arched ceilings that had been installed during the expansion done by English and McHose. Since that time, as far as I am aware, no one has been back into the cave.

Is the curse of English Cave finally ended then? Will curious visitors and unlucky brewery owners no longer disturb the rest of the Indian girl and her lover? Perhaps now the two can live out their eternity within the damp and murky darkness of English Cave and be no longer bothered by trespassers from the world above.

V. GHOSTLY GREETINGS FROM THE GRAVEYARD

History & Hauntings of St. Louis Cemeteries

There is not a single person among us who has not contemplated the mystery of death at one time or another. We all wonder, no matter what we believe in, what will happen to us after we pass on from this world. Some believe that everything comes to an end, that life in this world is our only existence. Others feel that we are born again, as an old soul in a new body, while others believe that our spirits pass on to another place... or perhaps even remain behind as ghosts.

We all wonder about such things... and perhaps this is the reason that we have dreamed up so many rituals and practices dealing with death. Death has been celebrated and feared since the beginning of time itself. We have immortalized it with cemeteries, grave markers and of course, with our darkest and most frightening legends and lore.

It is a common belief among experts of the occult that cemeteries are not usually the best places to find ghosts. While most would fancy a misty, abandoned graveyard to be the perfect setting for a ghost story, such stories are not as common as you might believe. A cemetery is meant to be the final stop in our journey from this world to the next, but is it always that way?

Nearly every ghost enthusiast would agree that a place becomes haunted after a traumatic event or unexpected death occurs at that location. History is filled with stories of houses that have become haunted after a murder has taken place there, or after some horrible event occurs that echoes over the decades as a haunting.

But what of a haunted cemetery? Do such places really exist? Most assuredly they do, but ghosts who haunt cemeteries seem to be a different sort than those you might find lingering in a haunted house. Most of these ghosts seem to be connected to the cemetery in some way that excludes events that occurred during their lifetime. As most spirits reportedly remain in this world because of some sort of unfinished business in life, this seems to leave out a cemetery as a place where such business might remain undone.

Graveyard ghosts seem to have a few things in common. These spirits seems to be connected to the burial ground because of events that occurred after their deaths, rather than before. In other cases, the ghosts seem to be seeking eternal rest that eludes them at the spot where their physical bodies are currently found. Cemeteries gain a reputation for being haunted for reasons that include the desecration of the dead and grave robbery, unmarked or forgotten burials, natural disasters that disturb resting places, or sometimes event because the deceased was not properly buried at all!

With that said, St. Louis *should* have its share of haunted graveyards! If for no other reason than the fact that two of the cities largest and most opulent burial grounds were literally created by removing bodies from smaller cemeteries and transferring the remains to another location. Unmarked graves abound and buildings and city streets have covered small burial grounds. All of these are, according to cemetery lore, just the sorts of things that can occur and that cause graveyards to become haunted.

And yet the cemeteries of St. Louis are strangely quiet....

Now that's not to say that we have no ghosts in the boneyards of this fair city, but they are certainly hard to find. Earlier we encountered the ghosts of the National Cemetery at Jefferson Barracks, so there is no need to revisit those stories here. However, there are a handful of others that may have you watching your rearview mirror as you travel down the street or perhaps wondering what might be buried just beneath your feet!

AMERICA'S GARDEN CEMETERIES

The city of St. Louis can boast two of the largest and most beautiful cemeteries in the Midwest, and perhaps America. Those readers who have been fortunate enough to visit either Bellefontaine or Calvary Cemetery can attest to the glory of the rolling hills, the shaded walkways and the incredible artwork that went into creating the monuments to the dead that cover the grounds. But it wasn't always this way for years ago, cemeteries were a hellish and often frightening place.

Death, as they say, is the final darkness at the end of life. It has been both feared and worshipped since the beginnings of history. For this reason, our civilization has dreamed up countless practices and rituals to deal with and perhaps understand it. We have even personified this great unknown with a semi-human figure, the "Grim Reaper", and have given him a menacing scythe to harvest human souls with. Yet, death remains a mystery.

Maybe because of this mystery, we have chosen to immortalize death with stones and markers that tell about the people who are buried beneath them. We take the bodies of those whose spirits have departed and place them in the ground, or in the enclosure of the tomb, and place a monument over these remains that speaks of the life once lived. This is not only out of respect for the dead because it also serves as a reminder for the living. It reminds us of the person who has died... and it also reminds us that someday, it will be our bodies that lie moldering below the earth.

The stone monuments became cemeteries, or repositories of the dead, where the living could come and feel some small connection with the one that passed on. The earliest of the modern cemeteries, or what is referred to as a "garden" cemetery, began in Europe in the 1800's.

Before the beginning of the Garden cemetery, the dead were buried strictly in the churchyards of Europe. For the rich, burial within the church itself was preferred. For those who could not be buried inside of the church, the churchyard became the next best thing. Even here, one's social status depended on the section of the ground where you were buried. The most favored sites were those to the east, as close as possible to the church. In such a location, the dead would be assured the best view of the rising sun on the Day of Judgment. People of lesser distinction were buried on the south side, while the north corner of the graveyard was considered the Devil's domain. It was reserved for stillborns, bastards and strangers unfortunate enough to die while passing through the local parish.

Suicides, if they were buried in consecrated ground at all, were usually deposited in the north end, although their corpses were not allowed to pass through the cemetery gates to enter. They had to be passed over the top of the stone wall. During the late Middle Ages, the pressure of space finally "exorcized" the Devil from the north end of the churchyard to make way for more burials.

As expected, it soon became nearly impossible for the churchyards to hold the bodies of the dead. As towns and cities swelled in population during the 1700's, a chronic shortage of space began to develop. The first solution to the problem was simply to pack the coffins more closely together. Later on, coffins were stacked atop one another and the earth rose to the extent that some churchyards rose twenty feet or more above that of the church floor. Another solution was to grant only limited occupation of a grave site. However, it actually got to the point that occupancy of a plot was measured in only days, or even hours, before the coffin was removed and another was put in its place.

It became impossible for the churchyards to hold the dead and by the middle 1700's, the situation had reached crisis proportions in France. Dirt and stone walls had been added around the graveyards in an attempt to hold back the bodies but they often collapsed, leaving human remains scattered about the streets of Paris. The government was finally forced into taking action. In 1786, it was decided to move all of the bodies from the Cemetery of the Innocents and transport them to catacombs that had been carved beneath the southern part of the city. It was a massive undertaking. There was no way to identify the individual remains, so it was decided to arrange the bones into rows of skulls, femurs and so on. It has been estimated that the Paris catacombs contain the bodies of between 3 and 6 million people.

In addition to the catacombs, four cemeteries were built within the confines of the city. One of them Pere-Lachaise has become known as the first of the "garden" cemeteries. It was named after the confessor priest of Louis XIV and is probably the most celebrated burial ground in the world. Today, the walls of this graveyard hold the bodies of the most illustrious people in France and a number of other celebrities as well. The dead include Balzac, Victor Hugo, Colette, Marcel Proust, Chopin, Oscar Wilde, Sarah Bernhardt and Jim Morrison of the Doors (if you believe he's dead, that is).

Pere-Lachaise became known around the world for its size and beauty. It covered hundreds of acres and was landscaped and fashioned with pathways for carriages. It reflected the new creative age where art and nature could combine to celebrate the lives of those buried there.

Paris set the standard and America slowly followed. In this country, the churchyard remained the most common burial place through the end of the 1800's. While these spots are regarded as picturesque today, years ago, they varied little from their European counterparts.

After the founding of the Pere-Lachaise Cemetery in Paris, the movement toward creating "garden" cemeteries spread to America. The first of these was Mount Auburn Cemetery in Cambridge, Massachusetts, which was consecrated in 1831. Proposed by Dr. Jacob Bigelow in 1825 and laid out by Henry A.S. Dearborn, it featured an Egyptian style gate and fence, a Norman tower and a granite chapel. It was planned as an "oasis" on the outskirts of the city and defined a new romantic kind of cemetery with winding paths and a forested setting. It was the opposite of the crowded churchyard and it became an immediate success, giving rise to many other similar burial grounds in cities across the country. In fact, they became so popular as not only burial grounds, but as public recreation areas as well. Here, people could enjoy the shaded walkways and even picnic on weekend afternoons. The Garden cemetery would go on to inspire the American Park movement and virtually create the field of landscape architecture.

The idea of the Garden cemetery spread across America and by the early 1900's was the perfect answer to the old, overcrowded burial grounds. Many of these early cemeteries had been established close to the center of town and were soon in the way of urban growth. Small towns and large ones across the country were soon hurrying to move the graves of those buried in years past to the new cemeteries, which were always located outside of town.

In Chicago, Illinois, one burial ground actually created several Garden Cemeteries, although the most spectacular of them is undoubtedly Graceland Cemetery. Graceland and several others came about thanks to the closure of the old Chicago City Cemetery around 1870.

The City Cemetery was located exactly where Chicago's Lincoln Park is located today. Before its establishment, most of the early pioneers simply buried their dead out in the back yard, leading to many gruesome discoveries as the downtown was developed years later. Two cemeteries were later set aside for both Protestants and Catholics, but both of them were located along the lake shore, leading to the frequent unearthing of caskets whenever the water was high. Finally, the city set aside land at Clark Street and North Avenue for the Chicago City Cemetery. Soon, many of the bodies were moved from the other sites.

Within ten years of the opening of the cemetery, it became the subject of much criticism. Not only was it severely overcrowded from both population growth and cholera epidemics, but many also felt that poorly carried out burials here were creating health problems and contaminating the water supply. To make matters worse, both the city morgue and the local Pest House, a quarantine building for epidemic victims, were located on the cemetery grounds. Soon, local families and churches were moving their loved ones to burial grounds considered to be safer and the City Cemetery was closed down.

One cemetery that benefited from the closure of the graveyard was Graceland Cemetery, located on North Clark Street. When it was started in 1860 by real estate developer Thomas B. Bryan, it was located far away from the city and over the years, a number of different architects have worked to preserve the natural setting of its 120 acres. It is regarded as one of the most beautiful burial grounds in all of Chicago today,

And there are many other examples of wonderful Garden cemeteries scattered across America, including Bellefontaine and Calvary Cemeteries in St. Louis. Both of them were created because of overcrowded conditions and have come to be regarded as showplaces of American cemetery artwork and design.

ST. LOUIS GRAVEYARDS

People were dying in St. Louis in 1849. The numbers of dead from cholera epidemics were slowly climbing but little was being done to curb the spread of the disease. The graveyards of St. Louis were beginning to fill with the victims of this dreaded illness.

In March 1849, a banker and church leader named William McPherson and a lawyer and St. Louis Mayor named John Darby, incorporated a new burial ground outside of the city. Together, they gathered a group of men, regardless of religious affiliation, and purchased 138 acres of land (which later grew to 327 acres) that became the "Rural Cemetery Association". That spring, the state of Missouri issued a charter to the men for the land along Bellefontaine Road and the graveyard later changed its name from "Rural" to "Bellefontaine".

The cemetery today is largely the work of its first superintendent, Almerin Hotchkiss, a landscape architect and the former caretaker of famed Greenwood Cemetery in Brooklyn, New York. He remained at Bellefontaine for more than 46 years, creating a forested burial ground with over fourteen miles of roads.

The cemetery grew rapidly, thanks mostly to the epidemic that was raging though the region. The people of St. Louis turned to Bellefontaine as a place to bury their dead. At the height of the epidemic, there were more than thirty burials each day. Thanks to a law that went into effect forcing all burial grounds to be located outside of the city for health reasons, Bellefontaine began to receive internments from most of the churches in St. Louis. Graves were later unearthed all over the city and they gave up their dead to Bellefontaine.

Today, the cemetery has become the resting place of governors, war heroes, writers and adventurers and noted residents include Thomas Hart Benton, General William Clark, Sara Teasdale, William S. Burroughs, the infamous Lemp Family and others.

Located on the other side of the roadway from Bellefontaine is Calvary Cemetery, another beautiful example of the classic Garden burial ground. Calvary was started in 1857 and also came about because of the epidemic of 1849. After the death of so many St. Louis citizens from cholera, most of the city's cemeteries, including all of the Catholic cemeteries were filled. In addition, many of these burial grounds stood in the way of new development. There was no question that St. Louis Catholics were in need of a larger burial ground, and thanks to the new law, one located outside of the city limits.

Located about six miles outside of the city was a piece of land that was owned by Henry Clay of Kentucky. The Whig politician and statesman was a popular figure in St. Louis, having helped Missouri acquire statehood and having been a Whig candidate for president in 1844. A few years later, in 1847, Clay made a lengthy visit to St. Louis and was warmly welcomed by the local politicians, business and social leaders. His main purpose for visiting the city though was to sell off that large piece of property. It was called Old Orchard Farm and it overlooked the confluence of the Missouri and Mississippi Rivers. Clay speculated in Missouri land and hoped to make a large profit on the farm.

When Old Orchard Farm was offered for sale at the courthouse, a huge crowd turned out to watch the bidding. Unfortunately though, none of them came to bid on the land, they simply wanted a glimpse of the famous owner. When it became clear to Clay that the farm was not going to bring a good price, he bought it back for $128 an acre. He was not particularly upset about this as he liked St. Louis and knew the city would someday grow and the land would be worth much more that he had paid for it.

Around 1849, Clay built a brick country house on the farm for his son, James Clay, and his daughter-in-law, Susanna. The young Clay's moved into the mansion in 1851 and lived in grand style. The house was of Italianate design and constructed of red brick. A broad veranda crossed the front, supported by brick pillars, and a square tower rose above the roof to take in the commanding view of the countryside and the rivers. Two of the most impressive features of the house were the heating plant and the indoor bathroom, both rare conveniences in those days.

Henry Clay House at Calvary Cemetery
(Courtesy of Missouri Historical Society)

Despite the luxuries the house offered, the Clay's only lived here for less than a year. Susanna found the mansion and farm to be too isolated and remote and St. Louis society not to her taste. She had been a popular belle back in Louisville and she desired to move back to more a more hospitable climate.

When the land came up for sale again, it seemed that the Catholic archdiocese of St. Louis finally had the answer for their cemetery problem. In 1853, Archbishop Peter Richard Kenrick purchased the 323-acre piece of land. Kenrick established his own farm on half of the property and gave the other half for use as a cemetery. The ground had already been used for burials in the past, as a portion of the land had once been an ancient Indian burial site. In addition, Native Americans and soldiers from nearby Fort Bellefontaine had also buried the dead here. After Kenrick purchased the ground, all of these remains were exhumed and moved to a mass grave. A large crucifix was placed on top of the site and it is located at one of the highest points in the cemetery today.

Kenrick lived in a mansion on the western edge of the grounds for many years, even after the Calvary Cemetery Association was incorporated in 1867. Archbishop Kenrick became its first president. Around this same time, many of the smaller Catholic cemeteries in the area were moved to Calvary, which now contains over 315,000 graves on 477 acres of ground.

Like Bellefontaine Cemetery, Calvary also takes advantage of the natural wooded setting and rolling hills. It also features amazing displays of cemetery artwork and the final resting places of many notable people like Dred Scott, William Tecumseh Sherman, Dr. Thomas A. Dooley, Tennessee Williams, Kate Chopin, and many others.

The Carmelite Sisters were the next residents of the Clay mansion, after Kenrick, but they stayed only as long as it took to find more suitable quarters in the city. Caretakers and staff members for the cemetery came next and then through the 1930's, it was used as a Catholic Outing Home, which allowed underprivileged children the chance to have a summer vacation in the country. Electricity and real plumbing were installed, as well as a swimming pool, and caretakers maintained the place in the winter months. In the 1940's though, the house was demolished, as the second half of the Old Orchard Farm was needed for cemetery expansion.

Several notable monuments in both of these cemeteries have already been mentioned in the course of this book, like the mausoleum of the Adolphus Busch family, which has been designed to resemble a French cathedral, right down to the gargoyles. Another famous tomb belongs to the Wainwright family. It was designed by architect Louis Sullivan, who refused to put the family name on the exterior of the crypt. He wanted cemetery visitors to look inside out of curiosity. When they do, they discover a domed ceiling and walls that are completely covered with intricate mosaic tile designs. There is also the stunning monument to General William Clark, the mausoleum of the Lemp family and the fascinating Egyptian-themed tombs that can be found in both cemeteries.

A stroll through either cemetery can leave the visitor amazed by the stunning artwork that can be viewed. There are mourners draped in ghostly shrouds, weeping and victorious angels, scantily clad women in veils and gowns, life-size figures of the dead and much more. Believe it or not, I actually have my favorite monuments in both graveyards and friends and relatives who visit from out of town are often taken on a short tour of the cemeteries during outings to see famous St. Louis sites.

The Girl in the Shadow Box

In Bellefontaine Cemetery, my favorite stone is not only stunning, but the story behind it is fascinating as well. Located in the far corner of the cemetery, near "Mausoleum Row" (where the Lemp tomb is located) is an immense "shadow box" that contains the massive, 12-foot marble statue of a young woman. The statue marks the grave of a St. Louis drug store owner named Herman Luyties. It seems that in the early 1900's, Luyties was on a tour of Italy and he met and fell in love with a sculptor's model. Luyties was so enraptured with her that he proposed marriage. The beautiful young woman declined and the man returned to St. Louis brokenhearted. Before leaving Italy though, he commissioned the sculptor to produce a huge marble statue based on his beloved model. The sculptor then created a duplicate of a statue for which the woman had already posed. It decorated a cemetery grave and the model had been given angel's wings. For Luyties' statue, the wings were removed.

The statue was then crated and shipped to St. Louis, where Luyties had it installed in the foyer of his home. In this way, he could see it each day as he came and went from the house. Luyties died at the age of 50 and after his death, his relatives pondered what to do with the several ton statue. Finally, they decided to move it to Bellefontaine Cemetery and to place it over the grave of the man who had never really stopped loving the woman the statue had been based on.

My choice for often-visited monument in Calvary has a much different story to tell. This monument is a somber, if not tragic one, and unlike the "girl in the shadow box", it is not protected from the weather and the elements. The years that have passed since the statues were erected have caused the features on them to become downright eerie. Located in a rather out of the way corner of Calvary Cemetery is a memorial to the Morrison brothers. The two monuments here recall the short lives the boys had as invalids. One of the statues is confined to a wheelchair and the other to a crib. The wheels of the chair are broken, but the symbolism of that is not really clear. It may represent the child's freedom from an earthly prison of illness and pain. Regardless, the deteriorating memorial is sad and a little frightening too. The eyes of the boys, especially the older boy in the wheelchair, are guaranteed to send a chill down the spine of the even the most hardened cemetery visitor.

And these are just two of the amazing monuments in St. Louis' most astounding graveyards. I urge the reader to come and visit these places some afternoon. I can promise that you won't be disappointed!

But if you do come to Bellefontaine or Calvary Cemeteries, don't come with the idea of looking for ghosts. Strangely, neither one of these graveyards boasts a single ghost story, however there is a spirited tale connected to Calvary Drive, the road that runs between the two burial grounds, connecting Broadway and West Florissant Road.

There are actually three different versions of the story, but each concerns a phantom that appears along this gloomy stretch of road. The first is a classic "Vanishing Hitchhiker" story about a girl who is sometimes picked up along the road but who then vanishes from the car. A writer named Mike Schrader, who tried to track down the story, said that it started back in the 1940's when she was referred to as "Hitchhike Annie". He also wrote that she limits her appearances to the time of day when the sun is setting and that she also sometimes appears on different roads in the same general vicinity.

There are tales of "vanishing hitchhikers" all over the country, so it's really no surprise that St. Louis seems to have one of its own. There are perhaps a dozen variations of the general theme of such a story, but basically it goes something like this:

A young man was on his way to a dance one night. He picked up an attractive blonde girl who was standing on a corner in a cocktail dress and took her along with him. Everyone at the party found her to be very charming and after the dance was over, the boy offered to drive her home as the night had turned quite chilly. She accepted and because it was so cold out, he gave her his coat to wear.

The young man asked for her address and she gave it to him and they left together. A short time later, they pulled into the driveway of the house where the girl said that she lived and the driver turned to tell her that they had arrived. To his astonishment, she was gone! The passenger's seat of the car was empty, although the door had never opened. The blond had simply vanished!

Not knowing what else to do, the boy went up to the door and knocked. An elderly woman answered the door and he explained to her what had happened. Right away, she seemed to know exactly what he was talking about. The young girl he had taken to the dance was her daughter... but she had died ten years before in an auto accident!

The horrified boy didn't believe her, even though the name of the girl he had taken to the dance and the woman's daughter were the same. In order to convince him, the old woman even told him where to find the grave of the dead girl in the local cemetery. The young man quickly drove there and following the directions he had been given, found the stone with the girl's name on it. Folded neatly over the top of the marker was the coat that the girl had borrowed to ward off the night chill!

Of course, that's a typical version of the story, although most of them are not that complicated. St. Louis' own "Hitchhike Annie" for instance is simply the tale of a young woman who is picked up in cars and then disappears. According to the accounts, motorists who passed along Calvary Drive (and sometimes other streets in the area) would be flagged down by a young girl in a white dress. She was usually described as being quite attractive with long brown hair and pale skin. After climbing into the car, she would sometimes claim that she had been stranded or that her car had broken down. Either way, she would ask for a ride and direct the driver to take her down the street. In every case though, just as the automobile would near the entrance to Bellefontaine Cemetery, the girl would mysteriously vanish from the vehicle! The door would never open and no warning would come to say that she was getting out. Annie would simply be gone.

The story of Annie persisted for many years, but by the early 1980's seemed to die out. If the girl has been seen in recent times, I have been unable to find anyone who has encountered her. This was the same problem that Mike Schrader ran into as well. While writing about this story, he found many second-hand accounts, but no one who had actually picked up the girl. However, he did meet a Sixth District police officer that introduced him to the second version of the "hitchhiker" story.

In this version, the phantom is a boy who is dressed in old-fashioned clothing from the late 1800's. He is said to appear in the middle of Calvary Drive when there are cars coming, causing the vehicles to swerve and slam on their brakes to avoid hitting what they think is a flesh and blood child. When the drivers try to look for him, they always discover that he has simply vanished.

And that's not the only ghost who allegedly haunts this stretch of roadway either. Stories were also told for many years of a woman in a black mourning dress who would also cross this roadway. According to the man who passed the story on to me, who remembered it being a current tale when he was a child about two decades ago, the woman would suddenly appear in the street, much like the little boy. She looked like a real person, clad in a long, rather old-fashioned dress and wearing a hat and a veil over her face. From the description, she was apparently an almost stereotypical mourner from the Victorian era. The woman walked out into the street, or appeared suddenly in the middle of the roadway, and drivers were forced to come to sudden stops so that they wouldn't strike her. Each time though, she would vanish before their eyes.

Once again, this story made the rounds for a number of years and then seemed to fade away. What was it that made this stretch of road one of the most haunted highways in St. Louis, at least for a time? Could it have been the close proximity of the city's two most hallowed burial grounds, or something else? And what caused the stories to stop being told? Could the haunting here have ended... or could it be waiting to simply start back up again someday?

Who knows? My advice though, is that if you happen to be traveling along Calvary Drive someday and you happen to see a girl in a white dress trying to flag you down for a ride... you may not want to stop and pick her up!

Earlier in this chapter, I briefly mentioned man's fear of death. One has to wonder if perhaps the fear of what may be waiting for us on the other side may also extend to our fear of ghosts? Our fear of death has its roots in the not so distant past. In centuries gone by, life was short and death came far too soon. A mother during the Victorian era might give birth to six children in order that three might survive to adulthood. People simply didn't live very long in those days, creating a fear of death that was both primal and deep-seated.

Today, things have changed. We live much longer and death has become remote and sanitized. In these modern times, few adults under forty have even seen a corpse. When death finally comes for us, it does so in the clinical setting of a hospital. We are protected and shielded from our dark dreams of death.... or are we?

In spite of all of these changes, death is just as mysterious now as it was two hundred years ago. Our cause of death may differ, but the result is still the same. What happens when we die? Is there a life beyond this mortal one?

And thus, our fear of ghosts is born.

What rational person wishes to return from the grave to wander the earth for eternity? Who would wish to spend their postmortem days and nights aimlessly pacing the corridors of the house where they once lived, doomed to loneliness, isolation and despair? Most importantly, what creature would desire to be trapped for all time among the crypts, monuments and tombs of a forgotten graveyard?

Earlier, I also asked the question... do haunted graveyards really exist? And if so, what causes the spirits to linger in them? The ghosts who haunt these spots seem to stay behind because of events that take place after their deaths. An indignity carried out on our body after we die is a fear that has remained with us since the days of the "body snatchers". Society endows on a lifeless corpse the capacity for feeling hurt and the expectation of respect. All forms of the defilement of the dead, especially thefts and the desecration of corpses, are regarded as not only distasteful but almost unholy.

And perhaps society is right about that, for the majority of graveyard ghost tales stem from terrible events that occur within the bounds of the cemetery, long after the hapless victims have died. And of all of the reasons why cemeteries become haunted, the desecration of graves remains probably the highest cause on the list. There are many graveyards that have been disturbed (in one way or another) and currently boast ghosts and hauntings. There are also many different ways that a cemetery can become disturbed. In some cases, nature plays a hand in the desecration as natural disasters take place that may unearth bodies or destroy grave sites.

In most cases though, it is the hand of man that does the most damage. The expansion of cities and homes can often be the culprit as new building sites are laid out without much thought as to what may have been present on the location before. Construction crews often uncover some gruesome surprises in the course of a day's work.

St. Louis boasts a handful of such sites. These are locations that are not cemeteries today, but they used to be and some believe this may be why they have gained a reputation for being haunted.

Author Robbi Courtaway dug up (so to speak!) just such a story when she spoke to a man named Sayeed Fareed, who lived in a haunted bungalow from 1966 to 1974. The house was located on Fyler Avenue and was built at the edge of the St. Louis State Hospital complex shortly after World War II. The site that the house was built on had apparently been part of the old potter's field, where indigent persons and unclaimed bodies were buried. It had been established by the city around 1855 but was later moved. All of the bodies were disinterred and taken to other cemeteries. Fareed's bungalow was also said to rest on a portion of the burial ground where cremated remains from the State Hospital were buried. Neighborhood stories had it that this remains were not moved before the houses on the block were built!

Fareed and his family frequently encountered the ghost of an old woman who would walk through the kitchen toward the back of the house. He described her as wearing a skirt and a white blouse and she seemed oblivious to her surroundings and to the living people who were present. Fareed saw the woman on many occasions, as did his wife, children and his sister. On at least one occasion, Fareed came home late one evening and found his wife standing outside of the front door. When he asked her what she was doing, she replied that someone had rang the front door bell and even though she had opened the door in a matter or moments, no one was there!

Another former burial ground that now boasts ghostly tales is Roosevelt High School, located along Hartford Street on the city's south side. In the 1840's, this site was located next to English Cave, a brewery and beer garden in the city. Readers may recall that the only thing that adjoined the cave was the St. Louis Commons, which was converted into a cemetery after the devastating epidemics that swept through the region. The section of the commons that was located directly where the high school now stands was taken over by the German Evangelical Protestant Congregation and they began calling it Picker Cemetery. The last burials that took place here were in 1901 and after that, the cemetery was closed. A few years later, graves began to be unearthed because of demands for the property. The last remains were removed in either 1916 or in 1922, depending on the records.

Not long after the last of the bodies were thought to have been removed, excavations and construction began on the new Southside High School, which was later re-named Roosevelt High School. Almost as soon as they began to dig, workmen began to uncover lost skeletons, the remains of caskets and buried tombstones. Apparently, no one really had any idea just how many people had actually been buried in the cemetery, thanks to poor records, unmarked graves and lost markers and stones. And while this would be the first grisly discovery on the site, it would certainly not be the last. As time has passed, more of the odd discoveries have been unearthed.

It's no surprise that the disturbance of the bodies, and the remnants left behind here, have given birth to stories of ghosts and hauntings at the high school. According to some staff members, people who are alone in the building will sometimes hear voices in the hallways when no one else is present. The sounds are never clear enough for anyone to understand what they are saying, but they can be easily heard. No explanation has been given that adequately explains where the voices come from.

In addition, staff members and custodians have also reported the erratic behavior of lights on the fourth floor of the building. On many occasions, they have been positive that the lights have been turned off and yet when someone goes back up there, or happens to notice from outside, the lights are burning once again. A few times, custodians claim to have gone upstairs to turn off the lights and have found them on again moments later... with the light switches physically tripped!

The South Main Street antique district in nearby St. Charles, Missouri is a quaint, historic area with a number of old, original buildings and a distinguished past. This small town, alongside the Missouri River, dates back more than two centuries and the footsteps of history have certainly left their mark on the brick streets and cobblestone walks. This may be one of the reasons why the town is considered so haunted and why South Main Street has so many ghosts. But it's not only the passage of time that has left spirits behind here... some believe an old cemetery may have something to do with it as well!

The first settlers came to St. Charles in 1769 when a French Canadian trapper named Louis Blanchette arrived in the area. He started a small settlement and called the region "Les Petites Cote" or "The Little Hills". Blanchette became the first commander of St. Charles, under Spanish rule, but the area was soon filled with French settlers. In 1800, Spain gave the Louisiana Territory to France and then in 1804, it was sold to the United States under Thomas Jefferson. The president then established an expedition to explore the new region and to chart the course of the Missouri River. Jefferson put the command of the expedition into the hands of Meriwether Lewis and William Clark. In May 1804, the two men outfitted their journey in St. Charles and then departed for the western frontier. Another famous explorer was Daniel Boone, who came to St. Charles from Kentucky in 1795. He joined his sons, who had a homestead south of town. Boone continued to explore the region and a trail that he created here, Boone's Lick Road, became the starting point for both the Oregon and Santa Fe Trails.

As St. Charles began to grow, it saw an influx of German settlers, thanks to reports that the area resembled the Rhine Valley back in Germany. German businesses began to spring up all over town, including a tobacco factory and a brewery. In 1821, when Missouri became a state, the first capitol was located in St. Charles. It was located here for five years while a permanent building was constructed in Jefferson City.

Despite all of this, it is the old cemetery that is blamed for many of the hauntings on South Main Street. In 1789, the St. Borromeo Cemetery was established in the 400 block of this district. Although the bodies were exhumed and moved to a newer graveyard on Randolph Street in the 1800's, many people believe that a number of bodies were left behind. One of those people is John Dengler, the owner of the reportedly haunted Farmer's Home Building. Dengler is a past president and board member of the South Main Preservation Society and a member of the St. Charles Historical Preservation Society. He is sure that many of the bodies buried in the old cemetery were never found.

"Evidently, that cemetery was pretty good-sized and went all the way up to Third or Fourth Street," Dengler stated. "There were bodies there, and in fact, they are still there."

He distinctly recalled some work that was being done behind a corner building that is sometimes called the Armory or the French Armory. A construction crew was excavating to enlarge a nearby structure and when they dug into the hillside, they found a large number of bodies that had not been removed. At another site, a cluster of forgotten bones was encased in concrete when the floor of the building was laid.

"Almost every building on South Main Street has a story to tell," Dengler once wrote in an article for *St. Charles Living Magazine*, "and sometimes these ghostly happenings are more apparent."

One such building with a story to tell is Dengler's own place, the Farmer's Home Building, where he owns a tobacco shop. This building was constructed directly on top of where the old cemetery once stood. I have had several opportunities to visit with this charming and delightful man and he never shies away from recounting the hauntings of the shop, even though he maintains a healthy skepticism about the supernatural.

The building was constructed around 1815 and up until 1856, it was the Farmer's Tavern, a popular hotel and restaurant. John Dengler's Tobacco Shop, which has been in operation since 1917, is located in what was once the ladies' dining room of the inn and sometimes the smell of ham and green beans wafts through the air, even though no one is cooking.

Dengler and his wife, Tru, use the second floor of the building as living quarters, while he rents out the other shops on the first floor. The other staff members in the building have also had some rather strange encounters that they have trouble explaining away. Peggy Behm of "Country Stichin'" once accused John of playing a prank on her. She was walking down a staircase in the back part of the building and distinctly felt a hand fall on her shoulder. Then, a voice whispered eerily in her ear. "Peggy, Peggy", it said. Startled, she hurried down the steps to find Dengler just walking in the door from a meeting that had kept him out of the building all morning. Even though she first assumed that he had played a trick on her, she quickly realized that she had no explanation for what had just happened.

They have also heard heavy footsteps on the same stairs and in the hallways of the building. Dengler's daughter, Laura Dengler Muench, was once terrified by the sound of laughter that came from nowhere and Tru Dengler had another strange experience while painting one day. "For about four days", said John Dengler, "a French-speaking apparition seemed to delight in playing tricks of floating cigarette packs in the air and hiding them. Unexplainable too was how the KMOX radio talk show would suddenly be switched to rather unusual classical music without the dial being changed. On the fifth day of the Frenchman's visit, a baby was heard to be crying, whereupon it was soothed by a calming French voice."

So, who are the ghosts that haunt the Farmer's Home building? Are they former guests of the hotel or the spirits of those left behind from the St. Borromeo Cemetery? John Dengler has no idea but as far as he is concerned they are welcome to stay... "but they've got to behave themselves", he said with a smile.

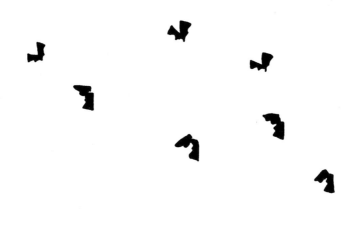

VI. SCHOOL SPIRITS

History & Hauntings of St. Louis Halls of Learning

As a "ghost writer", I have collected tales from haunted colleges and schools all over the Midwest and beyond. I have found that there are halls of learning that boast more than their share of ghosts, including a few in St. Louis. It is rare to find a school that does not boast a tale or two floating around the campus. Many of them are familiar tales of murdered coeds, whose spirits have returned to their former residences after death.

But how much truth is there to these stories? Are they merely legends that have been told over and over again for the purpose of getting a cute sorority girl to squeeze just a little closer while walking through a particularly spooky spot on campus? Or could there be something more? What if these tales of slain students just happen to be true? Are those tales so easily to dismiss?

Many have surmised that most campus ghost stories are simply the product of overactive imaginations. These same people say they are the result of students who are far too susceptible to the trappings of the supernatural. But what about the stories of ghosts that have been passed on, not only by students, but also by teachers, professors, maintenance workers and in some cases, people who claim to not even believe in ghosts? Are these school spirits simply imaginations working overtime?

Perhaps some of these stories are simply the mixture of fact and fancy. It seems that few of us can deny that we have chuckled a little over yet another report of a ghostly coed who was murdered years before and now haunts her former dorm room. In so many cases, a simple check of the local newspaper files reveals that no coed was ever murdered at the school. So how then do we explain the activity that has been reported there?

In other words, what if these academic ghosts are real? What if the energy produced by hundreds of students in one location attracts spirits who are seeking such energy to exist? Perhaps some of these ghosts really are the spirits of former students, teachers and janitors who left some sort of unfinished business in this world. Or perhaps the proverbial murdered students are sometimes real! What if their traumatic deaths have really caused them to linger behind?

Many would argue and say that these stories couldn't possibly be true but in the coming pages, I will show you that some of these stories just may be! And some of the readers know, if they have ever had their own brush with the supernatural, that there may be more to the local college campus or school building than first meets the eye! Something just may lurk in the shadows here.... but whether it is the cold image of truth or the stuff of legend is up to you to decide!

Rumors and whispers of collegiate ghosts have plagued St. Louis University for many years. The most haunted structure on campus is said to be the Cupples Mansion, a wonderful Romanesque style home that has been grandly restored by officials of the university. Samuel Cupples, a wood products manufacturer, built the mansion and according to legend, his ghost still lingers here and watches over his former residence. According to the college though, stories of a ghost here are just that, "stories", and they maintain that the house is not haunted.

Another reportedly haunted St. Louis school was actually mentioned in the last chapter, although one of the hauntings here has nothing to do with forgotten and abandoned graveyards. Roosevelt High School, located on the city's south side, has seen renovations in recent years that have wiped out a once affected area, but years ago, one of the hallways of the school was said to give chilling and uncomfortable feelings to those who passed through it. The hallway was located just outside of a lunch room where a terrible event took place in August 1977.

On the day of August 18, four off-duty firemen were working at the school, removing an old cork floor from the lunch room. Apparently, a spark appeared from the motor of a buffer the men were using and it ignited flammable cleaning fluid that was spread on the floor. The spark set off a flash fire and immediately exploded. The trained firefighters never even had time to react before they were engulfed in flames. Each of them men was literally roasted alive and one of them struggled out of the room and collapsed onto the floor in the hallway. The flames that covered him were so hot that the floor literally melted underneath him. Firefighters and rescue workers were quickly on the scene, but it was too late. Two of the men died that same day and the others died a few days later.

It was a horrific and grisly tragedy that some feel left an impression behind. Work began to try and repair the damaged lunch room, but it took more than a year to re-open it. Sources say that even when it was opened again though, students and staff members avoided it when they could. There was nothing about the room they could really put their fingers on, they simply felt uneasy and uncomfortable there. The same words could also be used to describe the hallway outside of the room. Although the floor tiles had been replaced, people stayed away from the spot where the burned fireman had fallen in the corridor. Even when the wide hallway was filled with people, the students and staff would just naturally veer around the spot, as if they sensed something there that they couldn't see.

Like St. Louis University, the McCluer High School in Florissant boasts an allegedly haunted house on its campus. The old mansion, called Taille de Noyer, was originally a log cabin that was enlarged into an antebellum home. According to stories, the ghosts of children and adults dressed in clothing from the early 1800's have been seen both inside and outside of the house.

The house is believed to be one of the oldest remaining homes in St. Louis County and it was built by a French trader at the edge of the commons in Florissant around 1790. John Mullanphy purchased the log cabin in 1805.

Born in Ireland in 1758, Mullanphy became the first true philanthropist of St. Louis. At the age of 20, he joined the Irish Brigade of the French Army but after the Fall of the Bastille, he returned home to Ireland and married Elizabeth Browne. The couple was bear 15 children together, although seven of them would die in infancy. In 1792, the Mullanphy's came to America, first settling in Philadelphia. Later, they moved to Frankfort, Kentucky, where Mullanphy opened a profitable bookstore. He moved his book business to St. Louis in 1804 and opened a shop on Second Street.

As Mullanphy spoke both fluent English and French, he made many new friends and customers in this culturally mixed city. He served the city as the justice of the peace for a time and started a number of business ventures. He bought real estate around the St. Louis area and speculated in cotton, selling it in European markets before the War of 1812. He amassed great wealth and donated large portions of it to charity. He financed the first hospital west of the Mississippi, donated property to St. Ferdinand and in 1827, presented land at Broadway and Chouteau to the Sisters of the Scared Heart. A church and a convent were constructed here and according to Mullanphy's instructions, orphaned girls were also educated here.

Mullanphy was always concerned about education and he sent his children to the best schools in New Orleans and Paris. Seven of his daughters and a son lived to be adults. His daughter Ann married Major Thomas Biddle, the paymaster at Jefferson Barracks who was killed in a duel on Bloody Island in 1831. His son, Bryan, studied law and established his own practice in St. Louis. He later served the city as an alderman, a Circuit Court Judge and the Mayor of St. Louis from 1847 through 1848. Like his father, he also donated huge portions of his estate to charity and provided housing for the homeless. He was the founder of the Traveler's Aid Society. Unfortunately, Bryan died at the age of only 42, having become eccentric and possibly insane.

John Mullanphy died on August 29, 1833 and left behind a legacy of generosity, a street named in his honor in St. Louis and of course, the Taille de Noyer house in Florissant.

The house had actually been purchased as one of Mullanphy's real estate deals but in 1817, he gave the house to his daughter Jane and her husband, Charles Chambers. He was trying to convince them to move back to St. Louis from New York. They returned and began expanding the house in 1819. Within a year, they had actually taken up residence. The Chambers' had 17 children and Taille de Noyer grew along with the family. It became a stately mansion of 22 rooms with columns and a wide veranda in front. A summer kitchen was later added near the main house.

Members of the family continuously occupied the mansion until 1960, when the property was acquired by the Ferguson-Florissant School District for the expansion of McCluer High School. The house was moved from its original site and the summer kitchen and terrace were destroyed in the process. The Florissant Historical Society managed to preserve and raise funds for the historic home though and for many years it was the headquarters for the society. The house is still open to the public and tours are regularly given of the site.

And it's likely that visitors who have attended these tours are the people who began to tell of ghostly apparitions being seen in the house. The stories say that ghosts of people in old-fashioned costumes are sometimes encountered in the mansion and are often mistaken for staff members in historical costume. One witness explained to me that he and his family had gone to the house on a tour one weekend afternoon and he saw a woman in a long dress that appeared to be from the early or middle 1800's in an upstairs bedroom. He assumed that she was supposed to be there and perhaps was a volunteer who was greeting guests in the clothing style of the period. He later learned though that no volunteers were in the house that day.

Could the ghosts be members of the Chambers family, still lingering behind at their beloved

Taille de Noyer?

Some believe this might be the case. Charles and Jane Chambers had 17 children who lived at the mansion and some of those children may also be among the resident ghosts. Witnesses have also claimed to see spectral children playing outside of the house and in its rooms on occasion. A young woman told me of an experience that she and her brother had at the house one day. As they were leaving, they heard children laughing from somewhere behind them. When they turned to look though, they found the area to be deserted. Were the sounds coming from phantom former occupants or were they echoes from some distant playground. Who knows?

The University of Missouri-St. Louis campus in Normandy once stood on the site of the old Bellerive Country Club. There have been those who have come to believe over the years that perhaps one of the former members of the country club is still hanging around the location of the college that took its place!

Dr. Dick Miller was a past director of the UMSL Library and retired from the university in the middle 1980's. He was regarded as one of the most admired and popular instructors at the college and regarded himself as a "born skeptic when it comes to the supernatural." In spite of this, he did admit a number of years ago that he had an experience at the library that simply could not be explained and as he said, "scared the hell" out of him. As soon as he arrived at the college, Miller began to hear stories about the lower level of the Thomas Jefferson Library on campus being haunted, but he didn't put any stock into the tales. The library had been built on five levels, with two of them underground, and rumors circulated that many of the librarians refused to go down to Level One alone. On the first day that he took over as Director of the Libraries, he decided to go look over the entire place. He wanted to start with Level One and go up to Level Five but when he mentioned to one of the staff members that he was going down to the basement level, she remarked, "watch out for the poltergeist." Miller said that he smiled and turned to laugh with her and then realized that she wasn't kidding. She was one of the people who took seriously the tales of Level One. According to Miller, the stories circulated of strange sounds, moaning voices and books that fell off the shelves without anyone around. It was even said that the elevators worked erratically at night, often starting their journey from Level One and traveling up and down with no one inside.

Miller decided to chance the trip alone. He had little faith in ghosts and "things that go bump in the night" and so he climbed onto the elevator and went down to the basement. His first impression of the area was that he could understand why people told ghost stories about it. Miller described the level as a long cement room with high ceilings and book stacks along one side. He was looking for storage space and so he went into a small room that was filled with old boxes and filing cabinets. Curious, he started looking through them and moments later, heard the elevator doors open in the main room and the distinct sound of footsteps walking out. They came about halfway to Miller's location and then stopped. Thinking that it might be his assistant, coming to see what he was doing, he left the room and looked around. He peered out into the gloomy space, but there was no one there. Then, from about six feet away and at the level of Miller's head, a clear voice spoke out.

"Hello, boy," it uttered.

Miller was startled to say the least. "Every hair on my body, starting on my calves, all the way to the top of my head, stood on end!", he later recalled. He stood there, just inside the doorway of the small room, for nearly ten minutes, trying to figure out where the voice had come from. When he realized there was no one else in the basement with him, he quickly returned upstairs to his office. When he got there, he told his secretary and his assistant about what had happened and made them promise not to tell anyone. He didn't want the entire staff to think that the "new boss was down in the library hearing voices." They assured him that they wouldn't mention it, especially to the many staff members who were already afraid of Level One, but within 15 minutes, the story was already making the rounds.

After that, many people refused to go into the basement at all and those who did often had their own unusual experiences. One of the library employees was working down there alone one afternoon. As she was leaning down, checking some books, she suddenly heard a very loud sound! Behind her, on a tall bookcase, was a set of very heavy, leather-bound law books. They had been on the shelf, undisturbed, for a very long time. While the staff member had been facing the other direction, one of the books had inexplicably moved from where it had been wedged between the others on the shelf and had fallen onto the floor. It landed flat, just behind where the woman was standing. She immediately fled the basement!

As Miller continued to hear stories about Level One, he had the chance to speak with one of the campus security guards about how the elevators supposedly moved by themselves. The security officer quickly agreed that it was true! He explained that they often started up in the middle of the night, around three or four in the morning. One night, the guard had been walking past the library and looked through the window to see the elevator light flashing and blinking and showing that the elevator was moving up and down between the empty floors. He told Miller that he stood there for nearly 30 minutes as the elevator "raced and bounced between floors." There was no one in the library at the time. When the security office contacted the elevator company and described to them what was going on, the company told them that what they claimed was impossible!

If any school or college in St. Louis could be labeled as "most haunted", it would undoubtedly be Washington University. The college has an interesting, and somewhat checkered, history and not surprisingly some remnants of the past have apparently lingered behind.

Washington University got its start back in the middle 1850's, thanks to the efforts of Reverend William Greenleaf Eliot, who started the first Congregational Society in St. Louis. He later became known as the organizer of the Unitarian Church in the region. He was a well-liked and popular man and was always eager to raise money for good causes. To Eliot, one of the best causes was education. In that, he found agreement with Wayman Crow, one of his most loyal supporters. Although self-educated, Crow constantly advocated the advantages of a formal education and he and Eliot often spoke of the need for a new school in St. Louis. After he was elected to the state senate, Crow carefully drafted the charter of the Eliot Seminary, which was originally a grammar school with two teachers and 30 students. The first board of directors under the charter was organized in February 1854 and it was at this meeting that the name Washington University was chosen. Three years later, the charter was changed to reflect this.

Crow then began to solicit fellow businessmen and politicians for their help in funding the college and in the winter of 1854-55, the first of Washington University's evening classes were conducted. The classes became the beginning of the O'Fallon Polytechnic Institute, which eventually became the university's engineering department. The university was officially inaugurated on April 22, 1857 and slowly began to grow. In 1859, Mary Institute was opened as part of the university (although it later became an independent school) and the St. Louis Law School was organized in 1860, although it was delayed until 1867 because of the Civil War.

The first campus of the university was developed under Dr. Eliot with help from Wayman Crow. Additions were made in 1871 and in 1879, the building of the St. Louis Institute of Fine Arts was begun. This structure, which housed both an art school and the city's first important art museum, was a gift from Wayman Crow. By the turn of the century, a number of buildings were added and at the time of the 1904 Louisiana Purchase Exposition, seven new structures stood unoccupied on the campus. These buildings were put into service for the fair.

As the years have passed many other additions have come to the university as it changes, expands and absorbs other buildings in the area. It remains a landmark in the city and one of the finest universities in the region.

And while much has changed here, some things have stayed the same. It has been said that some of the former occupants of the Washington University campus may be gone, but they are far from forgotten. The entire university complex is riddled with ghostly tales, although many are mere legends or simply small pieces of incomplete tales.

One such tale revolves around the old Shriner's Hospital that is now located on the campus. The building, which has been empty and abandoned recently, is said to be haunted by at least one ghost. This small phantom is that of a young child who presumably died in the hospital at some point in its past. She was recently seen (at the time of this writing) by a security officer who was in the building one night. As he walked down a dark and vacant corridor, he was stunned to see the image of a little girl appear ahead of him. She was wearing a white nightgown and was barefoot and didn't appear to notice him looking at her. The girl turned and walked a short distance and then vanished into the wall. The security officer did not stick around to see where she went after that!

Another legendary haunted spot at Washington University is Brookings Hall. The building was constructed as a model of Britain's Windsor Castle and it was completed in time to be used as the administration building for the 1904 World's Fair. It was built by a man named Robert Brookings, who took the place of Wayman Crow as the next great benefactor of the university.

Brookings was born in Maryland in 1850 and he came west to St. Louis as a young man as his brother was working as a salesman, or "drummer", for Cupples & Marston, a wood products company. Brookings began working as a receiving clerk for the company and later as a traveling salesman. He was so accomplished in his efforts that he was made a partner in the company at only 21 years of age. For the next 25 years, he made Cupples into a leader in the industry, expanding the company's product line and in turn, accumulating his own fortune. Brookings retired at the age of 46 and turned all of his attentions to Washington University.

He was made president of the college in 1897 and for the next number of years devoted all of his time and energy to the school. He purchased properties for the college and constructed new buildings. He convinced the board of directors to establish a medical school and even donated his own home as a residence for the chancellor. In 1920, Brookings was given honorary degrees of doctor of laws and doctor of medicine from Washington University. The degrees joined the honorary degrees he had already received from Harvard, Yale and the University of Missouri.

In 1917, President Woodrow Wilson appointed Brookings chairman of the Price Fixing

Committee of the War Industries Board and he became responsible for investigating price fixing on commodities. After World War I, he moved to Washington and was appointed by President William Taft to do a study on the president's budget plan. In 1923, he established the school that later became known as the Brookings Institute. He also authored several books on economic theory and government. Also, in 1927, Brookings married his longtime friend, Isabel Valle January. She was 26 years younger than he was but by all accounts, devoted to her husband.

Brookings passed away in Washington in November 1932. A funeral service was held in the Washington Cathedral and then a second was held at Graham Chapel of Washington University, the college so beloved by the its late benefactor.

In the years since, it has been said that a ghost now walks the top floor of Brookings Hall. It is not, as some readers might suspect, the warm presence of its builder, Robert Brookings, but rather the shade of his wife, Isabel. According to generations of students and staff members, she has been seen many times walking down the corridor of this upper floor.

Another well-known haunt on campus is the Whittemore House, which was donated to the university by the Whittemore family in the 1960's. Shortly after the house was donated, the college decided to have it renovated into Washington University's faculty club. Workmen were sent in to get started on the project, but within days, the contractors began to realize that the empty house was not so "empty" after all!

The strange happenings began shortly after a wading pool in the backyard was unearthed. It had been filled with dirt for years and the construction crew uncovered it and found a toy baby carriage, a doll and some other items had been buried in the pool. Not long after this, the workmen began to report tools disappearing from the site and then re-appearing in different places in the house. They would hear footsteps on upper floors, even when no one else was there. The men also claimed to hear loud, arguing voices that would seem to come from nowhere. Assuming at first that the voices were echoes from outside, the men would look and find no one in the yard. The workers quickly realized that even though no one else was there, they were not alone in the house.

Some time later, after the club opened, staff members and managers also began to report their own strange occurrences. They often heard unexplainable sounds in the attic, the footsteps that the workmen had also reported and slamming doors when no one was around. In fact, the attic door slammed shut so often that employees started using wooden wedges that could be jammed under the door to keep it open. Perhaps the most startling manifestations though were the wispy forms of apparitions that seem to come from nowhere and return there just as quickly. One of them reportedly took shape into the distinct form of a bearded man in a plaid shirt. Eerily, he only appeared from the waist up and then vanished. The club's manager, a man named Arthur Kleine, was working late one night and heard the boisterous sounds of a party going on. He hurried downstairs to see who was there and found the house completely empty. He had not been the only one to hear them either. The sounds had been so loud that a passerby outside had heard them and he came to the window to investigate.

After several years of this ongoing activity, staff members at the club decided to get in touch with St. Louis ghost investigators, Phillip Goodwilling and Gordon Hoener, locally known as the "Haunt Hunters". They came to the Whittemore house in May 1972 and as they did at the Lemp mansion in an earlier chapter, made plans to conduct a seance. They would either reach the ghosts present in the house or would get in touch with the unconscious mind of someone present in the house who might be causing the activity. One of those present for the seance was a young woman that Goodwilling later referred to as "Mary". She had been the person who had seen the bearded apparition in the club and the Haunt Hunters suspected that she might be influencing a portion of the activity in some way.

The seance was conducted in the attic of the house and present were Goodwilling and Hoener, Mary and another employee of the house. They placed a table in the room and lit candles to see by, as the only lighting was a bare electric bulb that was located just outside of the attic door. They also made sure that the door was propped open with one of the wooden wedges. To contact the spirits, they placed a large sheet of newsprint on the table and then a writing planchette on top of it. The planchette was a small wooden device on rollers that had a pencil attached to it. As the participants placed their fingers lightly on the device, the pencil was to record messages from the spirits by way of "automatic writing".

Just as they were beginning, and the planchette was beginning to move about on the paper, the room suddenly grew much darker. They realized that the attic door had somehow closed on its own! The wedge was worked back into place and the seance continued.

Over the next five or ten minutes, the paper began to fill with nothing more than gibberish and then all of the sudden, clear and obvious words began to be spelled out as the pencil pressed hard into the paper. Goodwilling recalled that at first the words were hard to make out and then they became frighteningly clear:

Get Out of My House ..... Death to Mary

Almost at the same moment as the words were being scrawled onto the paper, the windows in the attic suddenly banged open and an icy cold wind swept into the room! The candles were snuffed out and the room became pitch black. Even the Haunt Hunters admitted that they screamed and fled from the house.

Was the Whittemore House really haunted or were the strange happenings somehow connected to the unsuspecting "Mary", as the Haunt Hunters believed? Or were the event really a combination of both? Those questions will never be answered as Goodwilling soon learned that the seance had been conducted without the approval of officials at the university and they never returned to the house.

Another reportedly haunted building on the Washington University campus was not originally part of the college. This historic complex on Kingsland Avenue was actually constructed as the Art Academy for the People's University back in 1909. It remains today as a remnant of what may be Washington University's, and certainly University City's, most controversial period.

The People's University was the brainchild of a man named Edward Garner Lewis, the founder of University City and either a visionary or a con artist, depending on the version of the story you care to believe. Lewis was born in Connecticut, probably sometime around 1870, and attended Trinity School in Hartford. He left after only about a month to travel though and at that point, the biography of Lewis' life begins to fall into a gray area. No one really knows where he went during this period but when he returned to Trinity, he told his friends and comrades about his adventures in the American west. A short time later though, he told others that he had been traveling in South America. In fact, he claimed that natives had given him a secret herb that could cure people of smoking. Regardless of whether he was filling their cars with truth or lies, it was hard not to like Lewis. He was handsome, charming and always appeared to be sincere, no matter what tales he was spinning. He soon quit school and became a salesman, a profession that he was undoubtedly made for.

First, he went to work for a tobacco company and then tried to sell the anti-tobacco remedy that he claimed was given to him by the Indians. Next, he began selling "Anti-Skeet", a mosquito repellant in Nashville. The company that he owned fell so deeply into debt that the authorities ended up shutting him down. Lewis skipped out of Nashville one step ahead of the law and landed in St. Louis, a city that he had heard was plagued with mosquitoes. "Anti-Skeet" never really caught on, but Lewis remained in the city anyway.

His real break came when he purchased a struggling magazine called *The Winner*. He predicted (correctly) that magazines were going to come of age in the 1900's as advertising was making it possible for publishers to cut costs and the post office was giving special rates to printed matter. It was a stroke of genius that prompted Lewis to change the name of the periodical to *The Women's Magazine* and to target a market that had previously been untapped. He offered 10-cent subscriptions to the new magazine and promised romantic short stories, practical advice and columns with names like "Feminine Philosophy" and "Heart to Heart Talks with the Editor". Dimes began to pour in from all over America!

Lewis used the magazine to expound on his personal beliefs, which admittedly did give women much more power and support than they were used to in this time period. He also proposed the idea of a bank for working people and promised that future issues would give the readers the opportunity to invest in Lewis' dream town, a place called University City.

In the months to come, Lewis began to acquire more magazines and soon outgrew his offices in downtown St. Louis. He predicted (again correctly) that the city would begin to expand westward and he purchased a stretch of vacant real estate along Olive Street Road near where Washington University was laying out its new campus buildings. It was from the university that he drew the name of his "dream city" and he laid out the first streets in his subdivision and named them after Ivy League schools. He imagined a planned community of homes and businesses and began to construct an Octagon Tower, home to the "world's largest printing press", as the headquarters for his magazine publishing company. The tower was completed just in time of the 1904 Louisiana Purchase Exposition.

During the fair, Lewis helped to provide accommodations for visitors by constructing a tent camp on his property, just north of the fairgrounds. He set up 1,000 white canvas tents with wooden floors, electric lights and actual beds. He also provided a dining tent, a nursery, barber shops, reading rooms, showers and a hospital. The tent city became very popular and on Sundays, when the fair was closed, visitors toured the Octagon Tower and learned about Lewis' plans for University City. The tower, which would serve as the future city hall, was fitted with a copper dome that opened at night and shot a beacon into the sky that could be seen all over the fairgrounds and throughout St. Louis. The attention that the tent city and the tower gained for Lewis enabled him to run a contest during the fair. The challenge was to guess the correct number of people who would attend the fair and the prize was $25,000.

The contest garnered regional and national attention for Lewis and also brought about his first real brush with St. Louis authorities. City officials and others debated as to whether or not the contest was a game of skill, which was legal, or a game of chance, which was not. Many began to wonder if Lewis was really one of the fair's greatest promoters, as he claimed to be, or whether he was really just using the fair to advance his own company and magazines. One wag complained that he instructed his subscribers that "the World's Fair was an annex of his publishing company."

In 1905, Lewis finally established his planned People's Bank in what was called the "Egyptian Temple" across Delmar Boulevard from the Octagon Tower. He had promoted the bank as a way for common, working people to create some wealth for themselves and his readers had responded by purchasing $2.5 million worth of stock. Before the bank even opened though, Missouri's Secretary of State took action against it. Officials charged that the board consisted only of Lewis' friends and supporters and that it was invested too heavily in the development of University City. So, unable to do business in the Egyptian Temple, Lewis instead used it as the printing plant for his new paper, *Women's National Daily*. He planned to use it to inform his readers of the conspiracy against the People's Bank by the powerful and wealthy men who saw his bank as a threat.

While Lewis' legal problems were just beginning, his magazines were still doing quite well and his dreams of creating a model community were beginning to come together. Lewis was turning his magazine subscribers into his best salespeople. He created what he called the American Women's League" and to join for one year, a reader had to sell 520 subscriptions to Lewis' magazines. In return, the reader would receive education advantages, as well as a loan and health insurance program. They were also invited to attend the American Women's League Convention, a gathering that would be held in what Lewis dubbed "the women's capital of the United States", University City. The League managed to appeal to the feminist upsurge that marked this period, leading into the women's suffrage movement and the anti-saloon movement that would become Prohibition. Thanks to this, money began pouring into Lewis' accounts.

Lewis then launched another venture, the People's University, which was started under the auspices of the Women's League. It offered correspondence courses for women and children and Lewis also began construction on physical buildings for its campus. In 1909, he started yet another company that would be one of the first aimed at recycling. He took out patents on a process to turn waste paper into corks, hoping to interest Anheuser-Busch in the product. Unfortunately, the corks didn't hold up and the breweries were more interested in using metal bottle caps for their beer. The company soon went out of business.

At this same time, Lewis was running into other problems. His methods of turning his readers into investors had gotten the attention of the postmaster general. Officials ruled that since Lewis' magazines were really just advertisements that were disguised as periodicals, he was not entitled to special low mailing rates. The People's Bank was also prohibited from using the mail because correspondence being sent out was seen as a scheme for obtaining money through the mail by means of fraudulent representations. Lewis was tried three separate times on different charges and while never convicted, spent huge amounts of money defending himself. The struggles slowly wore him down and his existing businesses, and his plans for University City, began to suffer.

By 1912, all of his enterprises had gone into receivership. Lewis resigned as mayor of University City and packed up whatever possessions that he still had and which had not been sold at auction. He left by train and went to California, but was not quite beaten yet. He made another attempt to start a model community there with more disastrous results. He was hit with more charges of mail fraud and this time was convicted and sent to prison for six years.

It was later discovered by a subcommittee of the United States Congress that Lewis lost more than $6 million dollars for his investors. Not a single one of his companies in St. Louis had succeeded and yet Lewis has himself earned more than $182,000 over an eight-year period. The People's Bank had loaned his companies over $8 million and he had also taken more than $500,00 that had been sent to him by potential investors and had loaned it to the publishing company. After a lengthy investigation, four members of the committee chose to see Lewis as a visionary whose ideas had been wrecked by bureaucrats and big business interests. The other three members simply called him a liar and a con-artist.

Even today, no one really knows that to make of Lewis. Many believe he was simply a crook, while others feel that he was a man whose dreams just got the better of him. Regardless of what he was, it can be said that he brightened the lives of many for a period of time and has left a lasting mark on a town that still bears the name that he gave it. And if one enters University City today, you will see the lion's gates on Delmar with the names of his enterprises still etched on the pedestals and the Octagon Tower that actually serves as City Hall. (And yes, the spotlight beacon still works) His former home is now a park that bears his name and the one building that he completed for the People's University still stands. It is now a part of Washington University and is called Lewis Center.

And some say that at least one small part of the People's University still lingers here.

In the years that followed the absorption of the building by Washington University's School of Fine Arts in 1984, a long list of students and staff members began to report the sighting of a female apparition in one of the darkrooms. She was described as a young woman with long dark hair, deep-set eyes, bushy eyebrows and wearing a white blouse. The encounters were often mentioned to Stan Strembicki, a professor of art at Washington University and the head of its photography department. He assumed the stories were nothing more than overactive imaginations on the part of the students until he had an encounter of his own! He spoke about his experience to author Robbi Courtaway and described the spectral woman in the same way that so many others had. The apparition appeared to him in the darkroom, standing next to an enlarger that the department had been having problems with. That same evening, unknown to Strembicki until later, another staff member had also seen the ghost appear, standing in the same spot.

A short time later, Strembicki was in the building by himself on a cold winter's day. Suddenly, out in the corridor, he heard the echoing sound of a woman's voice. She spoke loudly enough to be heard, but not so loud that the professor could hear what she was saying. He ran out to see who was there and finding no one, went downstairs and outside. There was no one around and even though it had been snowing, there were no footprints on the ground. Puzzled, he went to the studios to see if someone was there but again, found them empty. As he came back to the base of the staircase, he again heard the woman's voice in the upper level hallway. He hurried up the stairs but the corridor was deserted.

Now, with his skepticism replaced by curiosity, Strembicki and other faculty members and students began researching the history of the building and the connections with the long defunct People's University. They discovered that the Lewis Center had been the Art Academy of the college and that it had offered correspondence courses to women all over the country. Some of the most talented among them were given scholarships that actually allowed them to come to University City and study at the school. A number of fine artists worked on the staff, including Taxile Doat of France and Adelaide Alsop Robineau and in 1911, the academy actually won the grand prize at the International Exposition in Turin, Italy. Unfortunately, Edward Lewis was charged with mail fraud about this same time and his company fell apart. He soon left the city and the university closed down in 1914.

According to the legend of the building, a famous French sculptor was on staff at the school and there was a young woman who served as his assistant. The two became involved in a love affair and after things went badly, the woman hanged herself on the third floor of the Lewis Center. It was believed that perhaps it was her ghost who haunted the building.

As was noted at the beginning of the chapter though, it usually turns out that few college ghost stories are entirely accurate but many of them do have at least a kernel of truth to them. Not surprisingly, the researchers were unable to find a police report that told of the suicide of a young woman in the building. It also turned out that there were no French sculptors on staff at the academy in those days. However (and here's where things get eerily close to the story), there was a Hungarian sculptor named George Zolnay. There was also a young farm girl named Christina Kiel who had been employed as a maid in the city but thanks to her talent for carving soap figures, she came to the school to work as Zolnay's assistant. Whether or not the two became embroiled in a love affair is unknown, but it is reported that she became depressed and committed suicide after the university closed and Zolnay returned to Hungary. Here was a legend that had much more than just a single grain of truth!

And could Christina be the spirit who still haunts the building? Could her love for the academy, or perhaps her love for the sculptor, have caused her to stay behind here after her tragic death? Perhaps we will never know the answer to that question, but you might consider asking a student of staff member at the Lewis Center what their opinion might be on the subject. They just might have an interesting story to tell!

One of the most famous haunted universities in the St. Louis region is Lindenwood College, located in St. Charles. The college was founded in 1827 by Mary Easton Sibley, the daughter of St. Louis' first postmaster and the original founder of the city of Alton, Illinois, Colonel Rufus Easton. Married at the age of only 15 to Major George Sibley, Mary never had any children of her own. Her husband was a military surveyor for the Santa Fe Trail and he began his career in western Missouri at Fort Osage. In 1825, he was chosen to lead an expedition along the Santa Fe Trail and managed to bring national attention to it. Sibley, a long-time Indian agent, also negotiated a successful treaty with the Osage Indians, who agreed to give safe passage to settlers along the trail in exchange for $800.

After his work for the military was completed, Sibley and his wife settled in St. Charles. By that time, Mary had already started taking in students. Not long after, Major Sibley was given a parcel of land as payment on a bad debt and on the land was a large hill that Mary decided to use to build a school. The hill, covered with linden trees, was called Lindenwood and it became the name for the college. The school soon opened in a large log cabin and became the first university for women west of the Mississippi River.

The school prospered and Mary remained devoted to it throughout her life. In fact, legend has even stated that Mary's ghost is said to be responsible for the good luck that has come to the school because before her death, she reportedly promised the students that she would always watch over them. Her body also remains behind as well. She is buried with her family in a small cemetery on the campus.

Not surprisingly, the most famous haunted spot on campus is Sibley Hall. This was the former Sibley family home and it later became the school's first residence hall. Back in the days when it was being used as a dormitory, many of the residents claimed to hear loud noises in the vacant rooms and could find no cause for the sounds. They also heard footsteps going up and down the stairs, the sound of music being played in the empty hall where Mary Sibley's piano was stored and they would often find furniture rearranged. It was also reported that lights would often turn on and off in parts of the building that were always closed up and locked

One summer when the school was empty, Sibley Hall was being renovated. There was no one in the building but workmen and all of the doors were kept locked. The men were busy one day on the lower floor when they heard the sound of girl's voices upstairs, loud sounds like drawers being opened and closed and noises like trunks being dragged across the floor. At quitting time, several of the men went upstairs to make sure the ladies could get out and to make sure they locked the doors as they left. They had no idea what they were going to find, assuming that several young ladies were upstairs doing some work of their own. They found no one there. The upper floors were completely vacant!

There is also a story that centers on the open staircase that rises up three floors through the building. Apparently, a young woman was hurrying down the steps one day and she tripped and then tumbled over the balcony. Rather than plunging to her death, or at least serious injury, she felt a pair of strong, but gentle, hands take hold of her and pull her back to safety. She turned to thank her rescuer and found that no one was there. The story soon began to circulate that it had been Mary Sibley who had saved her, still watching over her girls from the other side.

While many scoff at the ghostly tales of Mary Sibley (including officials of Lindenwood College), they have long been a part of the school's lore. And like many other haunted schools, there have been some unexplained happenings that have occurred, which lead many to wonder if the ghost stories may have some truth to them after all.

Years ago, campus legend stated that Mary Sibley always returned to the school every Halloween night. It was said that she would ride across the campus on her horse. Others claimed that she rose from the grave and walked through Sibley Hall. One year, a student decided to dress up in old-fashioned clothes like Mary Sibley and frighten the other girls. As she made her way into the hall where the piano was kept, she realized that she was not in the room alone. She looked up and saw a woman in a period dress and when she turned... the student saw the face of Mary Sibley! The girl screamed and fainted dead away. Her Halloween prank had apparently been interrupted by the real thing!

Such a story might sound like the stuff of campus legend to many but before the reader laughs too loudly, perhaps they should ponder a similar story that was told by a man with no connection to the university at all. One year, around the holiday season, a man was at a program in Sibley Chapel and went looking for a restroom for his young daughter. He was searching in vain until a woman in a "period costume" came downstairs and explained to him how to find the facilities. He never claimed to know who the woman was and having no knowledge of the school, he had no idea of the ghost stories told here. However, he did find out that there was no one present that evening in period clothing and no one seemed to know what he was talking about when he mentioned the incident to staff members.

Could it have been the spirit of Mary Sibley, still watching over the college that she founded?

VII. NO REST FOR THE WICKED

History & Hauntings of St. Louis Murder & Mayhem

Crime has been with St. Louis since nearly the beginning of the city. According to historical records, there was murder committed here some time in the middle 1780's when a Spanish soldier that had been garrisoned in St. Louis killed one of his fellow soldiers. As far as has been recorded, this was the only murder that occurred here during the 40 years of French and Spanish occupation. This era of peace and quiet would soon come to an end though and most would blame the arrival of the "Bostons", and the opening of the west, for ushering in the days of blood and violence to come.

In 1804, St. Louis became an American city after the signing of the Louisiana Purchase and the westward movement began. Suddenly, the streets of the once peaceful river city were no longer safe at night. There was fighting in the saloons and the alleys and public drunkenness became a common and overlooked state of order. Within a short time, the murder rate began to rise as beatings, stabbings and shootings became frequent occurrences. Those who believe that the "good old days" were always good are sadly mistaken.

Finally, the authorities of the city decided to create some laws to deal with the growing problem. An armed patrol was created to maintain order and all adult males who lived in the city had to take turns serving on it. A jail was built and a sheriff was appointed and in 1809, the first man was executed in the city. His name was John Long and he was tried and sentenced for the murder of his stepfather. He was the first, but he wouldn't be the last.

Over the course of the next few decades, St. Louis continued to grow. By this time, crime had become a recognized part of society and in the 1830's, murder was even overlooked when it was called an "affair of honor". Thousands poured into the city in the years before the Civil War and many thousands came after. Many of them passed through on their way to the western territories, but a large number stayed. St. Louis was becoming one of the great cities of the nation and the lawlessness of the late 1800's was called an "American phenomenon with no equal in the rest of the world." Crime rates began to rise all over the country, including in St. Louis, even though much of the recorded death of the time came from the west, where gun battles and murder had earned the region the description of a "great dismal swamp of civilization". The lawlessness of the cities was not as romanticized as death in the west, but the perils here were even greater to the common citizen.

Street crime came into its own in St. Louis in the 1870's. It became a good general rule for citizens to not walk anywhere except within the busiest thoroughfares at night. Many places were considered unsafe after dark and the lack of well-lighted streets added to the danger. It was suggested to travelers coming to the city that they might consider always walking in the middle of the street if possible. That way, they would be far out of reach for any hold-up man who might step out from an alley. Weapons among the criminal element could mean anything, from a club to a knife, a canvas bag filled with sand or a pistol. As there were no laws at that time against concealed weapons, any drifter or drunk who got hold of a pistol could become a deadly menace. Although the thief's object might have been to steal from a store or lift a wallet, the outcome of his "harmless" crime could easily become murder.

During the prudish time period that is often referred to as the Victorian era, prostitution ran rampant in America, including in St. Louis. While the posture of the day was one of stern resistance to human weakness, especially when it came to the carnal pleasures, the business of vice in these times tends to point to the fact that most were not practicing what was preached. Respectable standards in cities like St. Louis prescribed laws against prostitution but most of these went largely unenforced as the demands of lust and money proved more attractive than adhering to the letter of the law. In St. Louis, it was possible to find entrepreneurs who offered services for all classes and pocketbooks, from the politician on down to the riverboat workers. While the upright citizens frowned on and condemned the industry, it was practiced in the city as a commercial trade.

COPS AND ROBBERS IN ST. LOUIS

And while crime wreaked havoc in the city, many of the police officers who had been hired to offer protection for the citizens were hardly better than the criminals themselves. To modern residents of St. Louis, especially those who must travel alone at night, there is little that is more reassuring than the appearance of a policeman. Even in these times of complaints about police corruption, there is every confidence that an officer will do his public duty. In times past though, this confidence did not exist. Even after the volunteer system ended and police officers were given paid positions, the job requirements for these positions were rudimentary at best. It was necessary for the policemen on the beat to be tough and for this reason, other problems were often overlooked in favor of brutality. The behavior of many officers, which ranged from graft taking to covert alliances with criminals, generated public mistrust of policemen at large. Undoubtedly, there were many brave, upstanding and conscientious men in the ranks but a bad reputation was earned for the force by the men who were inclined toward violence or eager for a handout. The good men on the police force often faced an uphill battle in the late 1800's.

By that time, the St. Louis Police Force has been around since 1808. The original "armed patrol" mentioned earlier was made up of just four men who received no salary. This small militia served the city for ten years before it was decided to increase the size of the force to six men. Two of the officers were then assigned to night duty. One of them was a one-armed man named Gabes Warner, who was considered by most to be better qualified for the job that just about any man with two arms! At the same time, Mackey Wherry was named captain and was paid an annual salary of $400. He became the first command officer on the force and the first policemen to receive a salary.

As the city began to grow, the crime rate grew with it. It again became necessary to increase the size of the police force to combat the demands on the officers. In 1826, the city appointed a new captain and added 26 officers who were given the rank of lieutenant to the roster. In 1839, the force was increased once again. Public drunkenness, brawling and random murders were taxing the officers already on duty and it was becoming extremely difficult to maintain order after dark. Sixteen guards were added to the night watch to assist the police in preserving the peace during the evening hours. The proclamation in the streets of the hours of the night became one of their most important duties. "Twelve o'clock and all's well" was a familiar call at that time.

During the 1840's, the residents of St. Louis finally began to realize the need for the police department. As thousands of immigrants began to settle in St. Louis, the crime rate increased faster than the size of the force. With a growing population and increased river traffic, street crime became commonplace. The levee area, according to all accounts, was a busy place both day and night. Saloons, gambling and prostitution flourished along the riverfront and the police department had more than it could handle. This brought about a major re-organization in 1846 and the force became known as the "Department of Police". Even more importance was placed on making the city a less dangerous place after sunset and the night watch was comprised of a captain, six lieutenants and 48 officers. During this same period, the day watch consisted of just one lieutenant and seven officers. St. Louis could be a deadly place after dark!

As the city continued to grow out away from the riverfront district, the department began to see a need for a way to transport prisoners. The west boundary of the city extended to what is now Broadway and it was becoming impossible for officers to walk their prisoners to jail. The "Black Maria" came to St. Louis and it consisted of a wagon that was enclosed with iron bars. It saw much use during the 1850's and beyond.

Corruption was still a danger within the department and while many upstanding officers filled the ranks, there were always the few who dirtied the waters for everyone. In 1861, a decision was made to place the city police department under the control of a police board that was appointed by the governor. This would remove a level of politics and favoritism from within the police department, but many felt that it would simply move the "backroom politics" that went on to another place. Because of this, there has been no single decision in the history of the department that has caused as much controversy among citizens, politicians and police officials. To this day, the argument is still heard that the department should handle itself. Due to this change in state statute, the year 1861 is considered to be the beginning of the St. Louis Police Department as we know it today.

In that same year, the department's first Chief of Police was sworn in. Although he neither sought or expected the position, James McDonough became the first chief based on the fact that he had run a successful detective agency. During his tenure, some of the most turbulent days in St. Louis, McDonough would resign twice and serve three separate times as chief.

During these dark days of the Civil War, police officers joined average citizens in aligning themselves between the Union and Confederate forces. This created problems throughout the city and throughout the department as well. As an undercurrent of violence ran through Missouri, members of the police board began to align themselves with the Union cause. Consequently, Governor Jackson, an ardent secessionist removed each member of the board within six months of their taking their positions.

By 1866, the department had further increased in size to 225 officers. One of the major problems facing the department was the increase in crime that came from the riverboats. The city had become a major port on the Mississippi and various gangs of men joined forces and committed crimes of piracy along the levee. The problem became so bad that the department had to start a steamboat detective squad. Each steamboat captain would pay the department $1 per day and in return an officer would be assigned to the ship while it was docked. From all accounts, this plan worked well in reducing the number of crimes on the riverboats. Unfortunately, it also raised questions about the police force running a "protection racket" of sorts and so while the steamboat captains were apparently pleased, it opened the department up to what was likely undeserved criticism.

In 1867, the department implemented the first mounted patrols. During this time, the city boundary only extended to Jefferson Avenue and so officers were unable to provide protection to those who traveled beyond this point. Because of this, an increasing number of robberies and murders were occurring just outside the city limits. Farmers and merchants who traveled to and from the city were especially plagued by the violence. After these luckless men were robbed, the thieves would hide out in the caves that dotted the area. Since the bandits restricted their activity to the nighttime hours, Police Chief William F. Finn came up with the idea of having mounted officers patrol the outskirts of the city. After a few arrests and shootings, the mounted patrol was successful in controlling the problem.

In 1871, the site of the former Henri Chouteau residence became the Four Courts Criminal building. After Chouteau's pond became a railroad yard, there was little inclination to build grand residences nearby. After the Chouteau mansion was demolished, construction began on the new building and it was completed in 1871. The Four Courts Building was built to house St. Louis' four municipal courts, the Police Department and the jail. The large limestone building was designed in the Second Empire style and extended the length of Clark Street from Eleventh Street to Tucker Boulevard. Three stories high, it was visible from just about anywhere in the city, since it stood on a hill. The building's most prominent features were its three towers. The two at the east and west ends featured mansard roofs and the center tower was a large dome that was crowned by a cupola. The center section, under the dome, was faced with stone columns, making the building an impressive and intimidating place.

The jail section of the building was located in the back and was only accessible by passing through the main building. It was constructed of iron and as secure as could be made at that time. The Four Courts Building also housed the city morgue and the gallows, but unfortunately, no descriptions remain today of what these parts of the building looked like. By the 1870's, the police force boasted 305 officers and 34 men of rank. The city was divided into five districts, including the mounted patrol.

There were a number of notable trials held at the Four Courts Building, including the city's first gang murder. One gang member, Yellow Kid Mohrle, was even gunned down in the doorway of one of the courtrooms, as he was about to give testimony about his fellow criminals.

The Four Courts Building only stood for 36 years. Its short life was brought on by the fact that many citizens believed it to be the "ugliest public building ever erected in St. Louis" and by structural problems that could not be repaired. In 1905, plans were made to remove the towers on the building and replace them with a flat roof as the original roof leaked badly and nothing could be done to fix it. This was the beginning of the end however and in 1907, the building was torn down.

The police department meanwhile was making great strides toward the new century. In October 1881, one of the greatest advancements in the history of the department came about when the first police telephone system was installed. Although it used only a form of dots and dashes (much like a telegraph), it did allow the districts to be connected to one another and to the main headquarters.

In 1904, St. Louis was the fourth largest city in the nation but for most of that year, it became the most popular. The Louisiana Purchase Exposition showcased the city to the world and brought unique problems for the police department. The force at that time consisted of 1,260 officers, not including the emergency patrolmen who were sworn in to assist with the fair. While millions of ordinary people traveled to the fair that year, so did gamblers, pickpockets, swindlers and thieves. According to the accounts of the time, the department did an admirable job of policing at the World's Fair, but not without its losses. That summer, three officers were killed in a bloody shoot-out with train robbers.

The police department weathered the fair and continued to flourish over the next several years. The city also continued to expand, bringing more increases in criminal activity. But the violence of the period between 1910 and 1920 was merely a prelude to the most infamous era in the city's history, Prohibition. Crime ran rampant in the city streets with the growth of several criminal organizations (which will be explored later in this chapter) and the bloodshed that accompanied the expansion of bootlegging and gambling in St. Louis. These days of crime brought about the deaths of 46 police officers between 1920 and 1930.

The criminal activity of the day forced the department into making changes to help combat the spread of violence. The Police Band was organized in 1920 and a new Traffic Division, consisting of 122 automobiles and 44 motorcycles, was created in 1923. Forensic ballistics were adopted in 1928 and a new headquarters and academy complex opened in 1929. Recruits at the new academy were trained in these areas: patrolling, target practice, first aid, calisthenics, geography, spelling, penmanship, boxing and swimming, with the training lasting for four weeks. The days of police officers who were merely ruffians with a badge and a billy club were now gone for good.

In 1930, the department began its own radio station and 50 patrol cars were equipped with receivers. New district station houses were built throughout the decade. Police report writing was begun in 1930 and the police lab was established in 1935. By 1936, twenty-two policewomen were on the force and the Traffic Division boasted 228 automobiles and ninety-one motorcycles. The Police Library was organized in 1947 and it has developed into the largest department-owned library in the nation. In 1951, policewomen were given the power of arrest and full status as police officers. In 1958, the Canine Program was initiated in St. Louis and it is now recognized as one of the best in the country.

The 1960's and 1970's were periods of transition for law enforcement in general and the St. Louis Police Department in particular. The forty-hour week was adopted in 1963 and air conditioned cars were first purchased in 1968. In 1979, the Hostage Response Unit was formed in St. Louis. The 1980's brought about more changes, but only some were for the better. This period brought many problems to the department, including a declining budget, less manpower and additional requests for police services. To combat the drain on resources, the department responded with technological innovations and special programs to fight specific programs like auto theft, drugs in schools and drug dealing in the streets. Into the 1990's, new Mobile Data Terminals in patrol cars began to assist the officers in rapidly transferring information and revolvers were replaced with semi-automatic handguns to give the outgunned officers every advantage in their war on crime.

Once again, as in the late 1800's and in the "Roaring Twenties", St. Louis police officers are fighting an uphill battle against the criminal element in the city. As of this writing, violence has become commonplace in the city streets and the people are looking toward law enforcement officials for answers. And as with every era of the police department's history in the city, the police department must look beyond the technology and the weaponry and discover what links today's department with the past. That link is the thousands of good officers who have made the department what it had become since its inception in 1808. The foundation of the department is not police stations and data terminals but rather the courage of the officer on the street. History can teach us many things and with St. Louis criminal history, we need only to look to the police department to see that eventually justice will always prevail.

"SO PERISH ALL TRAITORS...."

During the crime-ridden days of the late 1800's, there were a number of notable murder cases that occurred in St. Louis. In these pages, I will recount one of the strangest, or at least the most unique, to give the reader a taste of the criminal activity of the day.

On April 1, 1885, W.H. Lennox Maxwell, the son of a wealthy British family, arrived in St. Louis. He was traveling throughout America for pleasure and took a room at the Southern Hotel in the city for a short stay. A short time later, another young man named C. Arthur Preller, also a traveling Englishman, registered at the hotel. The two men were given rooms next to one another but did not meet until later that day, when they were having lunch. They struck up a conversation and becoming friendly, decided to take in the St. Louis sights together. They enjoyed each other's company so much that, hotel employees learned, they intended to continue their travels together. Maxwell often spoke of this during he and Preller's two-week stay at the hotel, explaining that they would be going on to New Zealand very soon.

Within a few days, Maxwell checked out of the Southern and paid his bill in full. His friend, Preller, was nowhere to be seen but the hotel manager was not alarmed. He assumed the young man might have been caught up in some romantic escapade and would return in a few days. Besides that, Preller's clothing and belongings were still in the room.

That room became the object of concern on April 14 when hotel guests began to complain about a sickening odor that seemed to be emanating from it. A chambermaid named Maggie Cuddy entered the room and found that the smell seemed to be coming from a large zinc trunk that was fastened shut with two straps and a rope. A porter hauled the heavy trunk out onto the sidewalk and a salesman from a nearby luggage store was summoned to open it. When he arrived, he recognized the straps. He had sold them to a young Englishman named Walter Maxwell just a few days before.

The trunk was opened and those who had gathered around stepped back from the wave of odor that came forth from it. Inside of the trunk was the naked and badly decomposed body of a young man. The state of the body's decay, and the fact that the man's mustache had been crudely shaven off, made him almost unrecognizable but one of the hotel employees identified the corpse as C. Arthur Preller. A cross had been carved into his chest and a note had been crammed into his mouth. It read: "So perish all traitors to the great cause."

The police were summoned but detectives were perplexed over the mutilation and the strange message. The man's death seemed to hint at some greater conspiracy or group that was involved. Meanwhile, the newspapers were fascinated with the lurid crime and began calling it the "Hotel Horror" and the "Trunk Mystery".

Detectives began questioning staff members at the hotel and the name of Walter Maxwell immediately came to light. He was the main suspect for the murder, but where was he? They had no trouble tracing him to the train station, where he had boarded a train for San Francisco. They telegraphed the San Francisco police and learned that Maxwell had indeed boarded a ship for New Zealand, just as he announced to hotel employees that he planned to. The man was either innocent or incredibly indiscreet! They discovered that the ship Maxwell was on was still at sea and so St. Louis detectives wired the authorities in New Zealand and requested the arrest of the subject when he arrived there. He showed up a short time later and although wearing a disguise, he was immediately recognized and taken into custody. Detectives James Tracy and George Badger managed to get travel funds to retrieve the suspected killer and they returned him to St. Louis for trial in May 1886.

Things looked bad for Maxwell. When he was arrested, he still had some of Preller's underwear in his possession. He also had towels that were marked with the name of the Southern Hotel and a forged diploma from the Royal College of Physicians and Surgeons in London. He had now discarded the identity of Walter Maxwell and was claimed to be T.C. D'Auguier, a resident of Paris who had been raised in Scotland and practiced law in London. He had left a letter behind in his San Francisco hotel room that had been signed with his new identity and had been addressed to the "Le Ministre of Guerre" in Paris. The letter had been written in some sort of code and suggested that Maxwell, or D'Auguier, was a spy and that Preller's murder had been a secret assassination.

As it turned out, the man's real name was Hugh Mottram Brookes and he was English. He didn't come from a wealthy family though, as his parents had both been poor schoolteachers. Brookes attended law school but he never graduated. Instead, he stole some belongings of another student, sold them and then fled to Liverpool, where he bought a ticket to Boston. His money lasted as long as St. Louis, where he met Preller.

Preller, on the other hand, did come from a wealthy family. He was an executive for a London exporting firm who traveled widely on business. The two men became acquainted and at some point, Brookes learned the other man was traveling with a large sum of money. Over the course of several days, the two men enjoyed the saloons and restaurants of St. Louis and staff members of these places would later remember Brookes as being loud and quite talkative while Preller remained quiet and paid the bills.

When the ship carrying Brookes and the detectives docked in San Francisco, the prisoner received lively attention from the newspapers and curiosity-seekers in the city. Crowds of people came to the docks and arrived at the city jail, hoping for a look at the accused killer. The Police Chief refused to let them in and no one was more disappointed about this than Brookes himself, who was enjoying the notoriety. And even though he was dropping the facade of being a French secret agent by this time, he had new stories to take the place of that one. According to Brookes, Preller had actually been a long time friend and that the other man had recruited him to help in a scheme to defraud Preller's insurance company. It had not been Preller's body in the trunk at all, Brookes stated, as his friend had been alive and well when he'd left St. Louis. Brookes vowed to prove himself innocent at trial.

Once Brookes was returned to St. Louis and was safely in jail, the prosecution began preparing a case against him. The city had invested thousands of dollars to send detectives to New Zealand and to bring Brookes to justice and now the city attorney could not afford to fail.

He took a drastic step to insure that the jury would find Brookes guilty when he hired a private detective named Edward Furlong with his own money. Furlong was St. Louis' first private detective and had come to the city from Oil City, Pennsylvania, where he had been the chief of police. For years, he had worked for the Missouri Pacific Railroad and in 1880, opened a "secret service" company in St. Louis. Furlong began investigating the case and to gather information, he brought in an operative from out of town and had the man arrested so that he could get close to Brookes in jail. The police department was never made aware of his plans.

Furlong's operative was successful in slowly getting acquainted with Brookes (the detective remained in jail for 47 days) and eventually got the other man to admit that he had killed Preller for the money he was carrying. He had rendered Preller unconscious with an injection of morphine and then had suffocated him with chloroform so that rigor mortis would not immediately set in. Brookes had no desire to hack off the man's limbs in order to fit him into the trunk. The morphine answered some of the dangling questions in the case, such as how Brookes had managed to press a chloroform-soaked cloth over Preller's face if the other man was still conscious. It also explained why Brookes had been in possession of a used morphine syringe when he was arrested. Although why Brookes would have held onto what is presumed to have been the "murder weapon" is another puzzle entirely!

When Furlong was given this information by his operative, he turned it over to Circuit Attorney Ashley Clover, who ordered Preller's grave to be exhumed. His body was removed from Bellefontaine Cemetery and examined and not surprisingly, the medical examiner discovered the tell-tale needle mark.

The trial began on May 10, 1886 with a packed courtroom. The newspapers had generated so much interest in the case that people from all walks of life came to take part in it. The prosecutors opened and carefully began their case. A chemistry professor from Washington University was brought in to explain how Preller had been killed with chloroform and a painter from Toronto, who had done a portrait of Preller, identified the body. Shopkeepers and hotel employees testified to Brookes' strange behavior, his bragging and his proximity to the victim. Even a handwriting expert, or "professional penman" as he preferred to be called, was brought in to provide an opinion that the note found in Preller's mouth had been written by Brookes' hand.

The most damning testimony came when Furlong's jailhouse operative took the stand. He gave the same account of the murder that Brookes had given to him. He stated that the accused had been determined to kill the other man for his money and when Preller had complained of a stomach ailment, Brookes saw the perfect opportunity to "ease his pain". He knocked him out with the morphine injection and then covered his mouth and nose with the drug-soaked cloth. His first attempt didn't kill him and so Brookes went out to get more chloroform. When he returned, Preller was dead.

Furlong took the stand next and while Brookes' lawyers subjected him to intense cross-examination, it had little effect. The police department was angrier than anyone else about the fact that Furlong had taken it upon himself to gather evidence in the case without notifying them.

Finally, it was time for the defense to present their own case. After the damning testimony that had been presented already, most expected that Brookes would actually break down and admit what had happened. Those who believed this were to be sorely disappointed. Brookes had no interest in telling the truth. When he took the stand in his own defense, he had yet another lie to present. Under questioning by his attorney, he admitted that yes, he was responsible for Preller's death but the murder had been accidental. Preller, he explained, has been suffering from a disease of a personal nature and had asked Brookes to examine him. The disease, the witness inferred, was venereal and it had caused a "stricture", or a swelling of the membrane around the urethra. Brookes had offered to relive Preller's pain from this affliction by inserting a catheter. That Brookes knew absolutely nothing of medicine apparently meant nothing to the man! Preller agreed, stripped out of his clothing and lay down on the bed. Brookes, before going to work on that "most sensitive part of the human frame", wanted to make sure that his friend did not suffer, so he gave him a dose of chloroform. He had accidentally overturned the chloroform bottle, Brookes said, which is why he had gone back to purchase more. Preller passed out, as he was supposed to, but his breathing became harsh and ragged. Brookes tried to revive him, but the other man did not respond. When he saw that his friend had died, he panicked and fearing a "lynch mob" because he was a foreigner, he wrote the cryptic note that made the death appear to be part of some conspiracy and left St. Louis.

The prosecution picked Brooke's story apart on cross-examination. Brookes had arrived in St. Louis with less than $50 to his name and Preller had been carrying plenty of cash. When the other man had tired of him and refused to give him any more money, he had chloroformed him, killed him and had left with his bankroll and most of his wardrobe. The prosecutor also demanded to know what had happened to the catheter that Brookes had supposedly used. The accused stated that he had thrown it into the ocean during his passage to New Zealand.

The prosecutor scoffed, pointing out that Brookes had kept the damning syringe though. Why had he thrown away the evidence that would have proved him innocent and yet kept the one piece of evidence that highlighted his guilt? The defendant was unable to answer that question.

To make matters even worse for Brookes' case, gravediggers had returned to Bellefontaine Cemetery during his testimony and had again exhumed Preller's body. Doctors searched for any evidence of a "stricture" but found none. The chief surgeon came to the court during rebuttal testimony and reported that he had found nothing to support the defendant's story.

The jury returned a verdict of guilty on June 5 but Brookes never admitted that he had killed his friend. On August 10, he was executed and as he stood there on the scaffold with the rope about his neck, he was asked if he had any last words. "America," Brookes reportedly said, "was certainly not the land of opportunity for me."

JACK THE RIPPER & ST. LOUIS

In the year 1888, the city of London, England was terrorized by a killer who called himself "Jack the Ripper". The mysterious madman prowled the streets of the Whitechapel District in East London and slaughtered a number of prostitutes, carving his way into the historical record as the first "modern serial killer". As the years have passed, the Ripper has held the morbid curiosity of professional and amateur sleuths, armchair detectives and crime buffs alike. Having eluded capture in the 1880's, his identity has been debated ever since and while many readers may be familiar with the "bare bones" of the story, perhaps few of you are aware of the killer's possible ties to St. Louis and the fact that one viable suspect for the Whitechapel murders actually lived and died here!

Suspicion by police officials that Dr. Francis J. Tumblety may have been Jack the Ripper came about in 1913, a number of years after the murders took place. In a letter dated on September 23, Inspector John Littlechild, head of the Special Branch in England, wrote to George Sims, a journalist about a medical man who may have been the killer. He was apparently replying to Sims about other possible suspects when he wrote:

"I never heard of a Dr. D in connection with the Whitechapel murders, but amongst the suspects, and to my mind a very likely one, was a Dr. T (which sounds much like a D). He was an American quack named Tumblety and at one time was a frequent visitor to London and on these occasions constantly brought under the notice of police, there being a large dossier concerning him at Scotland Yard. Although a "Sycopathis Sexualis" [sic] subject, he was not known as a sadist (which the murdered unquestionably was) but his feelings toward women were remarkable and bitter in the extreme, a fact on record. Tumblety was arrested at the time of the murders in connection with unnatural offenses and charged at Marlborough Street, remanded on bail, jumped his bail and got away to Boulogne. He shortly left Boulogne and was never heard of afterwards. It is believed that he committed suicide but certain it is that from the time the "Ripper" murders came to an end."

And while not all of Inspector Littlechild's facts were correct, he did make an interesting case toward the American doctor being the fiendish killer. In fact, the idea was so compelling that when the letter resurfaced years later, the theory was later turned into flawed but fascinating book by two British police officers, Stewart P. Evans and Paul Gainey, called *Jack the Ripper: First American Serial Killer.*

But was the "medical man" the real Whitechapel killer? Let's look into the facts and the fancy behind the intriguing suspect.

Francis J. Tumblety was born in Canada in 1833 and moved with his family to Rochester, New York at a very young age. Although uneducated, he was a clever man and became wealthy and successful as a homeopath and a mixer of patent medicines. There is no record as to whether or not these "snake oil" cures worked or not, but it is certain that Tumblety held no medical degree. He did claim to possess Indian and Oriental secrets of healing and good health and he was described as charming and handsome, so its not surprising that he made quite a bit of money in this questionable field.

When not charming customers, Tumblety was said to have been disliked by many for his self-aggrandizing and his constant boasting. He had a penchant for staying in fine hotels, wearing fine clothes and making false claims. Often these tall tales got him into trouble and he left town on more than one occasion just a step ahead of the law.

In the late 1850's and early 1860's, Tumblety was living in Washington and from this period, the first stories of his deep-seated hatred for women began to surface. During a dinner party one night in 1861, Tumblety was asked by some guests why he did not invite any single women to the gathering. Tumblety replied that women were nothing more than "cattle" and that he would rather give a friend poison than see him with a woman. He then began to speak about the evils of women, especially prostitutes. A man who was in attendance that evening, an attorney named C.A. Dunham, later remarked that it was believed that Tumblety had been tricked into marriage by a woman who was later revealed to be a prostitute. This was thought to have sparked his hatred of woman, but none of the guests had any idea just how far the feelings of animosity went until Tumblety offered to show them his "collection". He led his guests into a back study of the house, where he kept his anatomical "museum". Here, they were shown row after row of jars containing women's uteruses!

In 1863, Tumblety came to St. Louis for the first time and took rooms at the Lindell Hotel. As he recounted in letters, his flamboyant ways did not appeal to those in St. Louis and he claimed to have been arrested in both the city and in Carondelet, an independent city at that time, for "putting on airs" and "being caught in quasi-military" dress. Regardless of his claims, Tumblety most likely caused trouble during these troubled times in the city because of his apparent southern sympathies. In 1865, he was arrested on the serious charge of what amounted to an early case of biological terrorism. Federal officers had him arrested after he was allegedly involved in a plot to infect blankets, which were to be shipped to Union troops, with yellow fever. The whole thing did turn out to be a case of mistaken identity (an alias of Tumblety's was remarkably close to a real doctor involved) but it's likely that he would not have been suspected if not for some actions on his part. Tumblety was taken to Washington and imprisoned until the confusion over the plot could be cleared up and was later released. According to British records, Tumblety was then arrested again after the death of President Abraham Lincoln, this time as a conspirator in the assassination. He was again released but this time, his reputation was destroyed in Washington and he fled to New York. After that, he began traveling frequently to London during the 1870's and 1880's.

Although there has been much debate over the years as to how many victims that Jack the Ripper claimed, and just when the murders began, it is generally believed that the first killing occurred on August 31, 1888. The victim was a prostitute named Mary Ann Nichols. Her death was followed by those off Annie Chapman and Elizabeth Stride on September 8. On September 30, the Ripper claimed Catherine Eddowes. Organs had been removed from the bodies of both Chapman and Eddowes, including the latter woman's uterus.

Just prior to the start of the murders, Dr. Tumblety had come to London and had taken lodgings in Batty Street, the heart of Whitechapel and within easy distance of the murder scenes. It is plain that he was watched closely by the police, especially after an incident involving a pathological museum. During the Annie Chapman inquest, police investigators heard information that has created the most pervasive and enduring myth of the Whitechapel murders, that of the Ripper as a surgeon. Only one medical examiner, arguing against all other expert testimony, believed that the killer had expert anatomical knowledge. He was basing his theory on a witness that claimed the killer was hunting for women's uteruses to sell to an unknown American. This bizarre bit of testimony came about because Tumblety did indeed visit a pathological museum in London and had inquired about any uteruses that might be for sale. He apparently wanted to add them to his collection.

On November 7, Tumblety was arrested, not for murder, but rather for "unnatural offences", which was usually a reference to homosexuality but could also include procuring young girls. He was later released on bail, although when exactly that was has been a matter of debate for many years. According to some records, he was released on November 16 but according to others, he was actually let go on November 8. The entire theory of whether or not he was Jack the Ripper hinges on the date that he was released from jail!

The reason for this is that on November 9, the Ripper claimed his last victim. Her name was Mary Kelly and she was mutilated in ways that cannot be imagined in her own bed. She was butchered beyond recognition and a number of her organs were removed, including her heart and uterus.

If Tumblety was actually released on November 8, then he could have easily killed Mary Kelly. One account of the days following the murder states that he was arrested on suspicion of her murder on November 12, was released without being charged and then vanished from Whitechapel. On November 24, it is alleged that he took a steamer to France and then sailed from France to New York. Scotland Yard detectives were said to have pursued him to New York and while they kept on eye on him, had no evidence to arrest him and could not have him extradited for the still outstanding indecency charges. They eventually gave up and went home.

Those who do not believe that Tumblety could have been the Ripper give a different accounting of the days after Mary Kelly was killed. According to them, Tumblety was not released on bail until November 16. As Inspector Littlechild writes, he was then believed to jump bail and escape to Boulogne with the police pursuing him. From there, he booked passage to New York, where police staked out his lodgings. He escaped them however and vanished. He was not, as far as recorded, further pursued for his part in the killings. With that said, it would have been impossible for Tumblety to be the Ripper. If he were the killer, then someone would have had to copy and exceed his previous work on Mary Kelly while the doctor was still in jail. Most would agree that this seems highly unlikely.

But our story is not quite over. Regardless of what is written about the last days of Tumblety in London, all will agree that after his escape he did end up in St. Louis. He also traveled for a time, avoiding Washington but frequently visiting Baltimore, New Orleans and St. Louis. He continued to live in hotels and established no permanent residence in any of the cities. In April 1903 though, Tumblety checked himself into St. John's Hospital and Dispensary at 23rd and Locust Streets in St. Louis. The hospital, which was then located in the old Catlin-Beach-Barney Mansion, provided care for indigents, which is how Tumblety was presenting himself at this time. The hospital is still in operation today as St. John's Mercy Medical Center, located at Interstate 64 and Ballas Road.

According to accounts, Tumblety was suffering from a long and painful illness, although what it may have been has never been specifically identified. Some have suggested that it may have been a debilitating case of syphilis, the contraction of which might have been cause for his hatred of women and especially prostitutes. Whatever it was though, Tumblety remained at St. John's until his death on May 28, 1903. However, he was far from indigent when he died. Court records showed that Tumblety left an estate of more than $135,000 when he died, some of which St. John's managed to recover. The hospital asked for about $450 to cover the room expenses and medical tests for a man who was clearly not poor. The rest of the estate, except for costs to a St. Louis undertaker, went to Tumblety's niece, Mary Fitzsimmons of Rochester, New York.

Aside from the hospital, there was one other claim to Tumblety's estate. While the hospital's costs can be seen as clearly legitimate, the additional claim was quite strange, especially in light of Tumblety's clear prejudices on the subject. The challenge to a will that Tumblety had written on May 16 came from an attorney in Baltimore named Joseph Kemp. He claimed that Tumblety had written an earlier will in October 1901 that left $1,000 from his estate to the Baltimore Home for Fallen Women... in other words, a halfway house for prostitutes! The claim was thrown out of court but it does provide an interesting final note to the life of a man who has been suspected of being the most famous killer of prostitutes in history!

ST. LOUIS GANGSTERS!

While not as famous as their counterparts in New York or Chicago, St. Louis gangsters have certainly left their mark on the city through violence and crime. They helped to create a "corridor of crime" between St. Louis and Kansas City and to bathe the city in blood during the violent days of Prohibition.

No one really knows for sure when the Mafia came to America, but it is believed to have been in the middle 1800's and to have gained a foothold here through New Orleans. As the doorway for most Italian immigrants to America, New Orleans saw a deluge of new arrivals in the late 1800's. The Italians and Sicilians brought with them their old world customs, traditions and crime. After the Civil War, Italian criminals began to spread from New Orleans to Chicago and St. Louis and there were reports of Black Hand extortion in this city as early as 1876. However, Italians would not dominate organized crime in St. Louis until after the repeal of Prohibition in 1933. By the time that the Volstead Act was passed, there were five gangs of importance in St. Louis... the Sicilian Green Ones, the Pillow Gang, Egan's Rats, the Hogan Gang and the Cuckoos.

The Green Ones were said to have garnered their name from the farming communities in Sicily where they originated. The group was led by brothers John and Vito Giannola and Alphonse Palizzola and they had financed their way to America with several robberies in 1915. Once they arrived, they went their separate ways with John going to Chicago, Vito to St. Louis and Palizzola to Springfield, Illinois. A few years later though, at Vito's urgings, they reunited in St. Louis and began to impose a tax on all goods sold in the city's Italian community. With little in the way of resistance, they established a foothold in the rackets.

In 1923, Vito decided to move into the wholesale meat industry. One distributor objected and so he was brutally murdered as an object lesson for anyone else who decided to complain. His body was found under the Kingshighway viaduct on September 16, 1923. About this time, the Green Ones decided that bootlegging would make more money than extortion and they decided to expand their operations. They soon found out the hard way though that it was not Italians who ran the liquor operations in St. Louis. Their first attempts to move alcohol ran afoul of the Egan's Rats gang and resulted in the death of Sam Palizzola, a relative of Alphonse, in September 1924. When members of Egan's Rats were sent to prison in 1925, the Green Ones soon clashed with the Cuckoos.

The Green Ones struck first and on September 1, 1925, John and Catherine Gray were murdered after complaining about having to purchase liquor for their Eagle Park resort from the Italian gang. The couple was shot to death in their automobile and then the vehicle was torched. The Cuckoos retaliated by shooting up a farm house hideout used by the Green Ones. No one was injured in this attack.

On January 29, 1926, police officers Ohmer Hockett and John Balke attempted to shake down a liquor operation that belonged to the Green Ones. They were offered $200 but they refused and demanded to wait until the "boss" arrived and speak to him. The two lawmen were greeted by four soldiers of the gang, who then beat the cops until they were unconscious. The following day, they were taken into the woods and forced to dig their own graves. As they knelt there in the freshly turned dirt, they were shot in the back of the head and then buried. Pasquale Santino fingered Alphonse Palizzola as the man behind the killings and set him up to be murdered. On September 9, 1927, four gunmen came out of nowhere and blasted away at

Palizzola on Tenth Street. He was shot to pieces and died on the sidewalk, drenched in his own blood. A ten year-old boy was also killed in the attack.

On December 28 of that same year, Vito Giannola was also killed. He was shot 37 times while hiding in the house of Augustina Cusumano. Vito had kicked Augustina's husband out of the house and was now living with her. A few days after Christmas, a knock at the door was answered to reveal two men dressed as police officers standing on the porch. They pushed their way inside and found Giannola hiding in a secret room upstairs. They opened fire and the gunshots ripped him apart in the confines of the small compartment. John Giannola went into hiding after his brother's assassination and was never involved in St. Louis crime again. He is believed to have died peacefully in his sleep in 1955.

During the short reign of the Giannola's and Palizzola, police records show that 30 people were killed and 18 were wounded. Among those shot but not killed was James Licavoli, who went on to become the boss of the Cleveland mafia. Licavoli was shot by police officers when they tried to arrest Joseph Bommarito, an associate of the Green Ones. Bommarito didn't survive the shootout that preceded the attempted arrest.

One of the earliest Italian gangs, the Pillow Gang, began operating in St. Louis around 1910. The gang's unusual name came from its leader, Carmelo Fresina, who always carried a pillow around with him to sit on. After being shot in the rear end, he found it painful to sit on wooden chairs.

Apparently, between 1910 and 1914, there was an ongoing battle between Italian factions in St. Louis that left 10 people dead and a number deported. The Italians were finally organized under Dominic Giambrioni for a time but Vito Giannola forced him out in 1924. He returned to St. Louis ten years later and was killed for it. In 1922, Fresina arrived and worked under Pasquale Santino, who was hit in 1927. After that, Fresina took over the gang and allied his men with another group that had split off from the Green Ones under Tony Russo. Together, these two factions warred with the Green Ones.

After the Giannola's had been eliminated in 1929, Fresina and two of his men attended a meeting at the home of a Russo faction member. It had been rumored that Fresina had made peace with the remaining members of the Green Ones and after hearing this, Russo felt betrayed. Fresina and his men walked into an ambush. During the shootout that followed, Fresina was wounded in the buttocks and his two associates were killed. The Pillow Gang eventually wiped out what was left of the Russo faction in 1932, but Fresina never lived to see it happen. He was killed by assassins who may have been connected to the Green Ones near Edwardsville, Illinois in 1931. He was dispatched by two bullets to the head, effectively ending his reign as gangland chief.

Perhaps the most famous of the old St. Louis gangs was Egan's Rats. Strangely, the group began as a political organization that was forged by St. Louis Fifth Ward Democratic Committeeman, Thomas Egan and Missouri State Senator Thomas Kinney. In 1907 they were dubbed Egan's Rats and their "political fund raising activities" including robbery, burglary and theft from railroad boxcars.

In April 1919, Thomas Egan passed away (natural causes) and was replaced as Fifth Ward boss by his brother, William "Willie" Egan. Around this same time, a Rats lieutenant called Max "Big Maxey" Greenberg was sent to prison on charges of interstate theft. Willie Egan managed to pull political strings, reaching all the way to President Woodrow Wilson, and managed to get Greenberg's sentence commuted. He ended up serving just six months of a five-year sentence.

According to author Allan May, Greenberg then repaid Egan for his kindness by switching his allegiance to the Hogan Gang. He went to Detroit and got involved with smuggling liquor from Canada until returning to St. Louis in 1921. Upon his return, Egan retaliated against him for his disloyalty. In March 1921, a Rat gunman opened fire on Greenberg while he was standing on a corner at Sixth Street and Chester. Political lobbyist John P. Sweeney was killed, but Greenberg was only wounded.

In fall of that same year, Greenberg hit back. Willie Egan was just walking out of a saloon at 14th Street and Franklin Avenue when he was gunned down. The Rats blamed the hit on Greenberg and the Hogan Gang and rumors had it that $30,000 had been paid for the shooting. Egan died in City Hospital, refusing to name the men who shot him. A week later, Greenberg walked into police headquarters with Hogan Gang attorney Jacob H. Mackler to provide an airtight alibi for the time of Egan's death.

Not surprisingly, the alibi didn't satisfy William "Dinty" Colbeck, the husky plumber and World War I infantryman, who had taken over Egan's spot as the leader of the Rats. He was sure that Greenberg had planned Egan's death, the attorney had been the pay-off man and that James Hogan had been one of the shooters. Those three men, plus John Doyle and Luke Kennedy, were marked for death by Colbeck.

John Doyle was killed in January 1922 and a short time later, Rat gunmen fired on an automobile containing Mackler, Kennedy and James Hogan at Eleventh and Market Streets. No one was injured that time, but Mackler was killed on February 21 when 15 bullets riddled his car as he drove along Twelfth Street. The Hogan Gang hit back and murdered Rat associate George Kurloff while he was eating in a restaurant on Franklin Avenue. Days later, bodies of Hogan gangsters Joseph Cammarata, Joseph Cipolla and Everett Summers turned up in ditches beside country roads outside of St. Louis. Those murders were followed by the death of Luke Kennedy, who was machine-gunned while driving in May 1922. Hogan gunmen retaliated again, this time gunning for the top man. As tires squealed along the street, a sedan pulled up outside of Dinty Colbeck's plumbing store on Washington Avenue and several men opened fire. Pieces of glass, wood and toilet fixtures filled the air, but no one was killed. The same could be said the following day when Rats gunmen shot up the home of Hogan gang leader, Edward "Jellyroll" Hogan.

By this time, the violence that tore apart the quiet of St. Louis streets was starting to make the public angry. Several businesses had been hit and windows had been broken out, not to mention the mess left behind by the hit on George Kurloff in the Franklin Avenue Restaurant. On another occasion, a young boy was run down in the street by a gang member's fleeing automobile. Because of the public outcry, the police were forced into action and Colbeck responded by moving the gang's headquarters outside of the city and into St. Louis County. The gang converted an 11-room house into the Maxwelton Club and then took over an abandoned horse track near St. Charles Rock Road and Pennsylvania Avenue. They spent most of them time racing on the track, shooting at cans and bottles and continually terrorizing the local residents.

At least 23 people were killed in the two-year war between Egan's Rats and the Hogan gang, but the most desirable target of Max Greenberg managed to escape from St. Louis. Shortly after the deaths of Doyle and Kennedy, Colbeck and Lewis "Red" Smith learned that Greenberg was being questioned at police headquarters. They hurried down there but were detained by officers while Greenberg was hustled out the back door. He fled to New York the next day and went back into business with an associate from his Canadian whiskey smuggling days. Someone eventually got his revenge on him though. He was shot to death in an Elizabeth, New Jersey hotel in April 1933.

The other protagonists in the bloody gang war of 1921-1923 were members of the Hogan gang, led by Edward J. "Jellyroll" Hogan, Jr. and his brother, James. Jellyroll was one of six sons born to St. Louis police officer Edward J. Hogan and had been born in 1886. Like Thomas Egan, Hogan had been intimately involved in political affairs in the city and was even elected to the legislature in 1916 as a state representative.

In March 1923, the attentions of the Rats were again aimed at Hogan. Several gunmen attempted to ambush Jellyroll and Humbert Costello as they were driving on Grand Boulevard. Two of the shooters, Rat soldiers named Elmer Runge and Isadore Londe, were arrested and Hogan was brought down to police headquarters to identify them. "I'll identify them, all right," Jellyroll reportedly told police. "I'll identify them with a shotgun!"

A few days later, another shootout took place between members of the Rats and the Hogan Gang on Lindell Boulevard. Hundreds of shots were fired, spraying cars and buildings with hot lead. Although no one was injured, the public was again enraged. Political pressure was brought to bear on both sides and peace talks were begun in April 1923. Unbelievably, Phillip Brockman, president of the Police Board, and Father Timothy Dempsey acted as mediators and got Colbeck and Hogan to agree on terms of peace between the rival factions. As amazing as this might sound to modern readers to have the police board and a priest brokering terms between criminals, the truce only lasted a few months. It was broken when Rat assassins opened fire into a crowd, trying to kill James Hogan. He managed to survive, but two bystanders were killed. One of them, William McGee, was a state representative. Colbeck claimed to be shocked when he heard the news. He denied any knowledge of it to police investigators and attributed the shooting to "boyish high spirits." He suggested that perhaps a couple of boys had a little too much to drink and might have seen Hogan in the crowd and maybe took a few shots at him "just for fun."

Colbeck may have chuckled about this incident, but by April 1923, he had more important things to worry about. On April 2, members of the Rat's crew had hijacked $2.4 million in negotiable bonds from a mail truck at Fourth and Locust Street. The following month, the crew struck again and snagged $55,000 in cash from the Staunton, Illinois post office. Egan's Rats had joined up with members of the Cuckoos to pull off the heists but when police officers began scooping up men for questions, it had been one of Colbeck's own men who had ratted out the others involved.

Former Rat member Ray Rennard spilled the beans to the government. He testified against Colbeck, David "Chippy" Robinson, Oliver Doughtery, Louis "Red" Smith, Charles "Red" Lanham, Frank Hackenthal, Gus Dietmeyer, Frank "Cotton" Eppelshelmer, Steve Ryan and Cuckoo Gang members Roy Tipton, Leo Cronin and Rudolph "Featheredge" Schmidt. He managed to help get all of them found guilty and sentenced to terms of 25 years in Leavenworth. With his testimony, he effectively destroyed Egan's Rats.

Dinty Colbeck served 16 years in prison. After his release, he tried to get back into the rackets but times had changed and he didn't last long. On February 17, 1943, Colbeck was returning home at about 10:30 that night. He had just crossed the McKinley Bridge when a car pulled up next to him around Ninth and Destrehan Streets. A man with a Thompson submachine gun suddenly opened fire on Colbeck. His car was riddled with bullets and Colbeck was hit six times. He died on the spot.

And while Egan's Rats ceased to be an organized crime power after the imprisonment of its key members in 1923, two former Rats would gain notoriety in later years. In 1929, Fred "Killer" Burke participated in Chicago's infamous St. Valentine's Day Massacre. On December 14, 1929, Burke murdered police officer Charles Shelby after he was involved in a minor auto accident. The investigation into the murder turned up a machine gun that matched bullets fired at the Massacre. Burke was never charged over that incident though but ended up with a life sentence for the murder of the cop. He died of a heart attack in July 1940.

The other notorious former Rat was Leo Vincent Brothers, who was convicted for the murder of *Chicago Tribune* reporter Jake Lingle in 1930. He received a sentence of 14 years which Brothers quipped "I could do standing on my head!" He only served eight years and many, including Chicago crime author Richard Lindberg, believe that he was paid to take the fall for the Lingle killing by associates of Al Capone, who wanted the reporter out of the way. Brothers died of natural causes in 1951.

After surviving the gang wars of the 1920's, Jellyroll Hogan continued in politics. In the 1930's, it was disclosed that one of the legislative clerks on Hogan's payroll was actually a St. Louis brewery worker who found it "unnecessary" to travel to Jefferson City even once during the 1937 legislative session. Needless to say, he got paid anyway. In 1941, Hogan was also part of the Democratic effort to prevent St. Louis Republican and Governor-Elect Forrest C. Donnell from taking office by demanding a recount but the effort failed. Hogan remained in politics for 50 years, serving five terms in the state house and four terms in the senate. He retired in 1960 after being defeated by Theodore McNeal, the first African-American to be elected to the Missouri State Senate. He passed away at age 77 in 1963 after a short illness and an amazing political career. And who says that all politicians are crooks, right?

Without much question, the most dangerous of the St. Louis gangs were the Cuckoos. They were headed by the three Tipton brothers, Herman, Ray and Roy and they earned a reputation for being "fast and willing shooters who would fight anyone, including themselves." They had few scruples and would extort money from businesses, citizens and even other criminal enterprises. They were also involved in robbery, kidnapping and "murder for fun and profit."

It was Roy Tipton who had planned the 1923 mail truck robbery that netted millions of dollars and prison sentences for himself and most of Egan's Rats. The Cuckoos only suffered minor losses from the convictions and continued on. A few months later though, the losses began to mount. Gang members Oliver Hamilton and Clarence "Dizzy" Daniels were sentenced to life in prison and August "Gus" Webbe was sent up for 10 years for the murders of St. Louis police officers Edward Griffin and John Surgant during a robbery. This was followed by the arrests of Joseph "Mulehead" Simon, Jimmy Michaels and Ben "Melonhead" Bommarito for the armed robbery of a jewelry store and the attempted robbery of a shoe company's payroll. After that, Milford Jones was implicated in a robbery with southern Illinois gangsters Carl, Bernie and Earl Shelton and Bennie Bethel was suspected in a Pine Lawn bank robbery. The authorities hit the Cuckoos again when Joseph Costello, Marvin Paul Michaels and Alfred Salvaggi were grilled over the deaths of John and Catherine Gray, the resort owners mentioned earlier. In 1925 however, the Cuckoos were rallied when Tommy Hayes was released from prison after serving time for a mail robbery in Wood River, Illinois.

In the middle 1920's, the Cuckoos went to war with the Green Ones and 13 mobsters were killed during this bloody period. It was rumored that a truce was declared after a three-day peace conference held between Herman Tipton and Green One's boss Giannola. The agreement ended when Tony Russo and his brothers broke off from the Green Ones but their leadership of the small renegade group didn't last for long. Russo and Vincent Spicuzza were later found dead outside of Chicago, each with a nickel in their hands, the trademark of Capone hitter "Machine Gun" Jack McGurn. Authorities believed that Russo and Spicuzza were killed trying to collect the $50,000 bounty that had been placed on Capone's head by his rival Joe Aiello. Some would say that it was lesson for St. Louis gangsters not to mess with the boys in Chicago!

The war continued on for another two years, during which more than a dozen more gangsters were killed, including James Russo and Mike "the Chink" Longo, who were both whacked by Cuckoo Tommy Hayes. The war finally ended on July 29, 1928 after a contingent of St. Louis police officers escorted William, Lawrence and Thomas, the last surviving Russo brothers, to the train station so that they could get out of town alive.

The Cuckoos soon became embroiled in another war, having once loaned their guns to the Shelton brothers in their battle against the Charlie Birger gang in southern Illinois. Once Birger was eliminated in 1930 however, the Shelton's ordered the Cuckoos back over to the other side of the river. Herman Tipton declined. He was enjoying the newfound bootlegging wealth from the Illinois side and continued horning in on the Shelton's operations. The Shelton's countered by convincing Tommy Hayes to come over to their operation and to turn on the Cuckoos. After that, things got even bloodier. In February 1931, Hayes led an attack on a roadhouse but managed to get three members of the Shelton gang killed in the process. Carl Shelton suspected a double-cross and so he decided to double-cross Hayes in turn. On April 15, 1932, Hayes was found in Madison, Illinois with 12 bullets in his back. As the most powerful shooter for the Cuckoos, Hayes death effectively ended the gang's presence in St. Louis organized crime. It should come as no surprise to learn though that, like the former members of Egan's Rats, many of the Cuckoos would be around for decades to come.

In the early 1950's, St. Louis became one of 14 cities where Senator Estes Kefauver held hearings about gambling and the infiltration by organized crime into interstate commerce. Colonel William L. Holzhausen, chairman of the St. Louis Police Board, was one of the first to testify before the committee and he assured them that organized gambling, facilitated by the race wire service, was one of the biggest problems for law enforcement in the city. In 1938, Southwestern Bell and Western Union Telegraph had attempted to legally cut off service for the Pioneer News Wire service and had been met with lengthy legal actions. Even when the service finally was cut off though, the company used illegal means to continue to supply race results to the local bookmaking operations. Moses Annenberg and James Ragen had once owned the wire service, but it had ended up squarely in the hands of the Capone syndicate in the late 1940's. Muscle in the St. Louis area was provided by Illinois gang boss Frank "Buster" Wortman.

The largest bookmaking operation in the area was run out of East St. Louis by J.J. Carroll and John Mooney, handling as much as $20 million annually in bets. The enterprise functioned heavily in the "layoff bet business" and employed agents to work the various racetracks, betting "come back" money at machines that would distort the track odds with the sudden placing of heavy bets just minutes before post time. Carroll refused to testify for the committee in front of cameras in St. Louis and later traveled to Washington to do so at his own expense. He saw himself as a respectable businessman and as a "betting commissioner", rather than a gambler with ties to the mob.

In the middle 1940's, crime bosses in Kansas City began to notice that there seemed to be a lack of Italian leadership in St. Louis underworld. With that in mind, they sent two representatives to oversee the rackets in the city, Thomas Buffa and Tony Lopiparo. Buffa was later murdered in Lodi, California in 1946 after testifying against the girlfriend of a Kansas City mobster.

Even with Lopiparo still in place though, leadership of organized crime in St. Louis was still shaky at best. Believed to be running the family were Lopiparo, Frank "Three Fingers" Coppola and Ralph "Shorty Ralph" Caleca. Coppola remained involved in the drug trade in Detroit and New Orleans, as well as in St. Louis, before being deported to Italy. Thanks to Coppola's contacts, St. Louis mobsters began to develop close ties to Detroit and narcotics traveled frequently back and forth between the two cities. As things began to develop, three men emerged as leaders in the St. Louis underworld from the 1950's through the early 1980's, Anthony Giordano, John Vitale and James "Jimmy" Michaels.

Anthony Giordano was born in St. Louis in June 1914 and gained a police record by 1938. He racked up more than 50 arrests that included charges for concealed weapons, robbery, income tax evasion and counterfeiting tax stamps. Giordano was groomed for a top position by his mentor, Tony Lopiparo, along with Frank Coppola and Ralph Caleca. The latter two men were former members of the Green Ones.

In 1950, Giordano became a drug courier for the St. Louis rackets. He made an unknown number of trips to Italy and it was noted that law enforcement officials were aware of at least three of them. Each time, Giordano met with Frank Coppola, the deported mobster who was competing with Lucky Luciano in the drug trade there. On the first two trips, Giordano and Detroit mobster Paul Cimino were unsuccessful in negotiating a heroin purchase. Cimino returned alone in the spring of 1951 and purchased 20 kilos of heroin, bringing it back to America in a steamer trunk with a false bottom. To the surprise of both Coppola and the Detroit mob, the heroin had been badly cut before the sale. It fell on Coppola to make good on the deal. Giordano returned to Coppola's farm in Anzio to pick up the shipment and coincidentally, he arrived in Italy at the same time that newspapers were reporting a major drug bust that had occurred in San Diego. Spooked, he returned to St. Louis empty-handed and the deal faded away.

Unbeknownst to him at the time, the three meetings that cops knew about were under the surveillance of famed narcotics agent Charles Siragusa. Years later, he wrote that Giordano had been observed during his last meeting with Coppola and had he returned to the United States with the heroin that he was supposed to bring back, he would have been arrested and sent to prison.

During his years of rising through the ranks, Giordano dressed the part of a flashy, stereotypical gangster in pinstriped, expensive suits, costly coats, shoes and rings. By the 1960's though, as he became boss of the family, he began to realize that he was drawing attention to himself and he started dressing like a blue-collar worker in work clothes and boots. He and his wife moved into a conservative house in southwest St. Louis and Giordano was often seen at one of the buildings he owned in south St. Louis doing carpentry or plumbing work. Despite this approach, he still had several brushes with the law, including a four-year stretch in 1956 for income tax charges in connection with a vending machine business. In February 1968, he was arrested as a "suspected" gambler during a citywide crackdown on illegal gaming.

Interestingly, Giordano also maintained ties with Metropolitan Towing Company, which had an exclusive contract with the St. Louis Police Department to remove vehicles from accident sites and to tow stolen or illegally parked automobiles. In November 1970, three members of the St. Teresa of Avila Church drove onto the towing lot to retrieve a stolen church vehicle. Apparently, the lot had a rule that only allowed two people onto the lot at a time and Giordano, who was in the office, ordered the van to get off his lot. Words were exchanged and one of the men in the van identified himself as a priest. Reportedly, Giordano grabbed the man by the shirt and shouted at him. "I'm a Catholic too," he allegedly yelled. "You run your church and I'll run my business!" He then (wisely) threatened to blow the heads off the three men with a shotgun. All of this took place in front of a uniformed police officer, who ignored the incident, but warrants were soon issued for Giordano's arrest anyway.

But Giordano managed to remain out of jail and under his volatile leadership, the St. Louis rackets flourished. According to the Missouri Task Force on Organized Crime, the mob in St. Louis was "engaged in labor racketeering, gambling, infiltration of legitimate businesses, loan sharking and narcotics traffic." In 1971, they named three factions who ran the rackets, with one under control of Giordano, the second headed by aging former Cuckoo Jimmy Michaels and the last group made up of remnants of the East Side gang that was once headed by Frank "Buster" Wortman. The report from the Task Force further alleged that Giordano's family was heavily dependent on gambling and that they also fenced stolen property and infiltrated legitimate businesses, like the Banana Distributing Company, which was owned by Giordano, a produce trucking company and the Metropolitan Towing Company. The towing company was also accused of being a front to launder illegal income and to provide an outlet for stolen auto parts.

Of course, all of these charges were made but never proven by law enforcement officials and the task force. The authorities seemed more concerned by the fact that the mob had infiltrated local labor unions than they were about the rest of the alleged activity. Giordano seemed untouchable, but that wouldn't last for long.

During the middle 1970's, Giordano was indicted after he attempted to gain hidden ownership in the Frontier Casino in Las Vegas. He was sent to prison in 1975, but was released two years later in December 1977. Giordano was even nominated for Nevada's infamous "Black Book" on March 4, 1975, but because he was sent to prison for his infraction, he was removed from the book in April of the following year.

Not long after Giordano's indictment, newspapers began to report that his nephews, Vincenzo "Jimmy" Giammanco and Matthew Trupiano, Jr., were in line to replace Giordano when he went away to prison. After his release, Giordano moved to Colorado, where he became involved in the local rackets there. He started working with the Smaldone family and oversaw their gambling, loan sharking, fencing and legitimate business operations. He continued to maintain connections with the family in St. Louis and in 1977, attempted to gain control of the Pueblo, Colorado police force by pushing two St. Louis candidates for the chief of police position.

In 1980, Giordano, by now gravely ill, returned home to St. Louis. On August 29, he died from cancer in his south St. Louis home. Ten days before his death, a meeting was held at the Howard Johnson's Motor Lodge at Interstate 44 and Hampton Avenue. The meeting, with members of the Colorado underworld present, was called to choose a successor. Giordano still pushed for the promotion of his nephew, Jimmy Giammanco, a move that had never come while the elder gangster was in prison. However, some of the family members protested and instead supported Joseph Cammarata, an ex-convict who had been keeping a low profile. The bickering seemed to cancel out both candidates and with the death of Giordano, government sources seemed to indicate that John Vitale became the acting boss of the St. Louis family.

Meanwhile, other factions of St. Louis organized crime had problems of their own. James "Jimmy" Michaels was heading up another gang and was encountering resistance and trouble.

Michaels' career began back in the 1920's, when he was known as "Horseshoe Jimmy" and was a member of the Cuckoos gang. At 19, he was arrested for robbing the Illinois Central freight depot in East St. Louis. He skipped out on his bond, but was captured again a year later. He was convicted of the robbery and remained in prison until 1929. After he was paroled, he was arrested as a suspect in several gangland killings but managed to stay out of prison. He was back in again for robbery a short time later though and was then out again in 1944. He quickly got involved in the gambling rackets and in 1959 was arrested for operating an after-hours joint on Hampton Avenue. And his trouble with the law continued. In December 1963, Michaels, Anthony Giordano and Kansas City mobster Max Jaben were arrested and charged with disorderly conduct in a hotel room where they had registered under the name "Mrs. Frank Wortman". In the middle 1970's, Michaels was arrested again, this time for carrying a concealed weapon, but the charges were dismissed.

Michaels' St. Louis problems had begun in the late 1970's, when a bloody struggle began escalating for the control of Laborer's Local 42. The fighting had started around 1965 when the "hoodlum element", led by Louis Shoulders Jr., George "Stormy" Harvill and William "Shotgun" Sanders, actually took control of the local union. Leadership was "officially" in the hands of Thomas "T.J." Harvill, thanks to the fact that the other three men possessed criminal records. In 1966, Stormy Harvill was gunned down and in 1972, Shoulders was killed by a car bomb. When Thomas Harvill passed away of natural causes in 1979, Jimmy Michaels backed John Paul Spica for the leadership position. Spica was a contract killer who had been released from the Missouri State Penitentiary in 1973 and was perceived as blatantly criminal by those observing from the outside.

Michaels' sponsorship of Spica brought him into opposition led by Raymond Flynn. He was determined to challenge Michaels and so he contacted more powerful Chicago mobster Joseph Aiuppa and asked for permission to do so. Flynn was then told that no one in the St. Louis family would oppose Flynn's actions as long as Michaels was not personally harmed, due to his longtime friendship with Giordano. In November 1979, Spica was blown up in his car outside his home in Richmond Heights. After this, Michaels appealed to Giordano for help against Flynn but Giordano was rebuffed by Aiuppa and told not to interfere in the struggle. He did assure him that Michaels would not be harmed though.

To Michaels' dismay, Flynn was not yet finished undermining his control. He again moved against Michaels by approaching Anthony and Paul Leisure, members of Michael's own faction, and he lured them away with high salaried jobs with the union. Michaels was no incensed. He had supported the Leisure's for years and had given Anthony an officer's position in Local 110. He flailed away at Flynn, but to no avail. Finally, Michaels' protection came to an end with the death of Giordano. He was informed by Flynn in August 1980 that any protection arrangements that he had made with his old friend had been "cancelled out" by Giordano's death.

Just 19 days later, David Leisure placed a remote-controlled bomb under the driver's seat of Michaels' black Chrysler Cordoba as it was parked outside of St. Raymond's Maronite Church.

Michaels left the church and was driving south on Interstate 55 when Anthony Leisure detonated the device. The automobile literally blew apart, lifting more than three feet into the air and scattering across the highway amidst fire and debris. The force of the explosion ripped Michaels' legs from his body and hurled his torso against a passing car.

As mentioned previously, John Vitale was thrust into a leadership position in the St. Louis family. His status had never really clear in years past. Some reports maintained that he had been Giordano's second in command, while others stated that he was the family's *consigliere*. Little is known about his early years, although he did serve two years in prison in the 1940's for narcotics violations. He had also been investigated for ties between professional boxing and the St. Louis mob. Vitale had also been a suspect in several killings, including the 1968 murder of Thomas Rodgers, owner of a mortuary supply company. He also had close ties to the Aladdin Hotel and Casino in Las Vegas and may have also been connected to the Tropicana as well. In October 1980, Vitale was stopped and searched by FBI agents at the Lambert International Airport. Agents seized $36,000 that had been secreted on his person.

After the death of Giordano and the murder of Michaels, Vitale tried to keep peace between the warring factions in the city, but he was largely unsuccessful. In 1981, Vitale followed an example set by many modern day gangsters and became an informant for the FBI. The majority of the information that he fed them involved the battles taking place between Michaels' gang and the Leisure's. He was rapidly aging though and reports claimed that he was so frail that he needed two canes to walk by this time. He died on June 5, 1982 from heart disease at Faith Hospital in Creve Coeur.

One of the gang members that Vitale tried to set up for the FBI was Jesse Stoneking, a lieutenant of Arthur Berne, the East St. Louis rackets boss who had replaced Buster Wortman. Stoneking had made a name for himself after being taken under the wing of Berne and was rumored to be a stone cold killer. However, if this was true, he was a killer with a conscience. In October 1979, he murdered a man who had raped the girlfriend of his mentor, Berne. He also killed two men who tried to set him up for a hit a few months later. When the time came for him to carry out a murder that he objected to though, he refused. When Joe Cammarata found a bomb in his truck, he ordered a hit on the man he suspected was responsible for it. That man was Tommy Callanan, a union business agent who had lost his legs to a car bomb in 1973. Stoneking refused to carry out Cammarata's orders because Callanan was confined to a wheelchair.

Stoneking's rise to the top and possible leadership of the Illinois rackets, then under Berne, went into a downturn after the death of Jimmy Michaels. First, Vitale tried to set him up for the FBI by offering him $5,000 to get a bomb. Then, on September 16, 1981, FBI agents arrested him for his part in an interstate stolen auto ring. Before he went to prison though, he attended a party at Berne's home. The wife of his boss was into astrology and at the party, she told Stoneking that one day he would "go straight". In the mob, this usually means "going straight" to the cops, which Stoneking did. Rather than spend time in prison, he decided to sing. He spent the next two years as an undercover informant for the feds and his testimony would later convict 30 members of organized crime.

The death of Jimmy Michaels continued to have repercussions in the St. Louis underworld. Less than a year after his murder, Michaels' supporters retaliated by planting a bomb under the car of Paul Leisure. It was parked outside of his mother's home on Nottingham Avenue at the time and on August 11, 1981, it was detonated as he climbed into it. Somehow, he managed to survive the blast, although it cost him his right leg and left foot and left his face severely disfigured. Members of the Flynn faction struck back a month later on September 11. They shot at and wounded Charles John Michaels, Jimmy's grandson, outside the Edge Restaurant. It should be mentioned that the younger Michaels had no connections to organized crime and was not involved in the union power struggle. This didn't seem to matter though, especially based on the next move by the Flynn gang. On October 16, George "Sonny" Faheen, Jimmy's nephew, was killed by a bomb that was wired into his car. It was detonated in the parking garage of the Mansion House Center. Once again, Faheen was not involved with the mob.

Meanwhile, investigators were still pursuing leads in the Paul Leisure attack and on March 24, 1982, they charged James A. Michaels III, another grandson of Jimmy, and Milton Schepp, a former St. George, Missouri police chief, with the bombing. Michaels was later convicted and served five years in prison.

In a separate investigation, Michael Kornhardt, who was charged with the murder of Sonny Faheen, was killed on July 31, 1982 while free on bond. Police investigators believed that he was silenced to prevent him from striking a deal with the FBI. The murder of Kornhardt turned out to be the unraveling of the Leisure faction. Paul, David and Anthony Leisure, along with Robert Carbaugh and Steven Wougamon, were all charged with the killing and in April 1983 were indicted on state capital murder and federal racketeering charges, along with three other members of the gang.

On April 2, 1985, brothers Paul and Anthony Leisure, their cousin David, Steve Wougamon and Charles Loewe were all convicted. Two other gang members pled guilty early in the trial and testified against the others. On May 1, Paul and David Leisure were sentenced to 55 years in prison. The sentence consisted of 20 years for conspiracy, 20 years for racketeering, five years for obstruction of justice and 10 years for constructing the bombs. Anthony Leisure received 40 years and Charles Loewe received 36 years. Wougamon was sentenced at a later date. Within weeks of the convictions, the men were also indicted on state murder charges. In his second trial, Paul Leisure was convicted and sentenced to life in prison without parole on December 7, 1987. Later, Anthony and David Leisure were found guilty with Anthony receiving a life sentence. David however, was sentenced to death.

Leisure's attorneys worked desperately to try and save him. They argued that he had diminished mental capacity and that it was his cousins who were the ringleaders with David as a hapless stooge. They even tried to claim that he was not responsible for his actions because he "wasn't toilet trained until age eight". It was an example of both the absurdity and the brilliance of the American legal system.

An unlikely plea for mercy came from Jimmy Michael's grandson, James Michaels III. He wrote to Missouri governor Mel Carnahan and asked that he spare Leisure's life, explaining that both he and David's families had "experienced enough grief for a lifetime". He felt that executing Leisure would bring sadness to both families. Leisure's execution was set for 12:01 am on September 1, 1999 and while his last appeal was being reviewed, Leisure tried to enjoy a last meal of a steak, baked potato, salad, apple pie, ice cream and a Pepsi.

After all of the appeals were exhausted, Governor Carnahan denied clemency and Leisure was strapped to the gurney inside of the death chamber at the Potosi Correctional Center. He gasped out a last statement, proclaiming his innocence and asking his sister, the only Leisure family member present, to "tell my children, family and relatives I love them." Leisure's sister sobbed with her head on a priest's shoulder and she watched as her brother mouthed "I love you" and then slipped away into death. Incredibly, his death was the first execution of a member of organized crime since Louis "Lepke" Buchalter was electrocuted at Sing Sing in 1944.

On July 22, 2000 Paul Leisure died from heart disease at the United States Medical Center for Federal Prisoners in Springfield, Missouri. He was 56 years old.

With the death of the "gentleman gangster" John Vitale, a new St. Louis mob boss had emerged. Matthew "Mike" Trupiano, Jr. was described as low-key and elusive and became the heir to Giordano's family after Vitale passed away. Trupiano was Giordano's nephew and was born in Detroit. After getting in over his head in the gambling racket, he was sent to St. Louis to get some guidance from his uncle. Apparently, whatever problems he suffered from as far as gambling went never got much better. In May 1986, Trupiano was fined $30,000 and sentenced to four years in prison for running an operation that took bets on college and professional football games. During his trial, witnesses testified that his bookmaking operation was so badly run that it actually lost money. It was the first time that federal agents had ever heard of an underworld bookmaking racket that operated in the red! Insiders claimed that it was because Trupiano gambled hard and lost more money than he actually won. A large part of the testimony that brought down Trupiano came from Jesse Stoneking.

Respect for Trupiano rapidly faded during his time in prison. He was cheated by other mob families during the sale of a casino and Trupiano also claimed that his own soldiers were holding out on him from their bookmaking take. By the time he was released from prison, after serving just 16 months of his sentence, the St. Louis mob "had dwindled to a handful of soldiers."

The St. Louis mob had fallen apart and the FBI relentlessly harassed Trupiano after his parole. They kept him under such close surveillance that he was arrested in 1991 for running an illegal gin rummy game in the back of a used car dealership on South Kingshighway. Prosecutors claimed that since Trupiano was an officer of Laborer's Local 100, and was playing cards on union time, that he was embezzling from the union. In June 1992, the union voted him out of office. The final insult came in October, when he was convicted on six counts and sentenced to two and a half years in prison. His health quickly deteriorated in prison. He suffered from diabetes, underwent kidney dialysis and suffered one heart attack. He died after a second attack at St. Anthony's Medical Center in south St. Louis County in October 1997.

In the wake of Trupiano's death, the St. Louis mob continues on. And while the gangsters of today may not capture the headlines of the past, don't be fooled into thinking that they aren't still out there, running the gambling operations, working the rackets and in the words of Al Capone, "giving the people what they want." Local mob watchers will tell you that you need only read the newspapers and watch the television news to see the machinations of the mob still at work. Watch carefully and if your instincts tell you that something you see does not seem quite right, well... chances are it isn't!

THE SAGA OF NELLIE MUENCH

In April 1931, one of St. Louis' most sordid and mysterious scandals began. It got its start in an unlikely spot, for the grim affair began in Portland Place, which was then (and still is) one of the city's most exclusive addresses. It is one of the dozen of so private places in the Central West

End, guarded by locked gates and lined with stately trees and magnificent mansions. It was in one of these American "palaces" that Dr. Isaac D. Kelley, an ear, nose and throat specialist, resided with his wife. On the night of April 20, Dr. Kelley was reading comfortably beside the fireplace in the library of 32 Portland Place. It was a cold, wet and stormy night and one that was to become the most harrowing of the doctor's life!

The telephone chimed about an hour after dinner and the man at the other end of the line gave his name as Holmes and he explained that he had a child with a severe earache. He had just moved to the city from Chicago, he went on, and now lived in a Clayton subdivision called Davis Place. After a few questions and a short delay, Kelley told his wife that he needed to go out for as night call. He put on his coat and drove off into the rain, arriving in Davis Place a short time later. As he looked for Holmes' address through the wet windshield and between the beating of the wipers, he noticed that another car had pulled up beside him. Two men stepped out and approached Kelley's automobile. One of them pulled a pistol from the pocket of his coat and ordered the doctor to get into the other vehicle.

And with that, the kidnapping ordeal of Dr. Isaac Kelley began.

It has already become obvious that St. Louis was infested with gangsters during the Prohibition era. The bootleggers, gamblers and racketeers fought for supremacy between the various factions, all the while stealing, killing and providing illegal alcohol. The end of Prohibition sent them into new activities, like extortion, bookmaking and the infiltration of the labor unions. Occasionally, one avenue of crime would lead to another, as with the kidnappings that sometimes rocked the region. The abduction of Dr. Kelley became the gangster's biggest success, just as the attempted kidnapping of Oscar Johnson, a wealthy shoe manufacturer, became their most daring failure.

Kelley's kidnapping was remarkably well planned. He was first lured outside of the city limits and away from the St. Louis police. After that, he was taken to a farm in St. Charles that was often used a hideout and moonshine distillery, then across the river to one safe house after another. The kidnappers held Kelley for eight days, terrorizing him, brandishing their machine guns and threatening him with retribution if he ever "opened his trap" about them. They ordered a huge ransom for the doctor and negotiations dragged out over days. Eventually, the abductors decided to unload their victim and they contacted a crime reporter for the *St. Louis Post-Dispatch* named John Rogers. More than once, the reporter had managed to solve crimes that had baffled the police and the criminal underworld had what was called a "perverse respect" for him. Kelley was shoved into a car and then dropped off on a cold and lonely Illinois road. A few moments later, another vehicle pulled up and called out to the doctor.

It was Rogers. He had received a phone call in the middle of the night, directing him to go to Grand and Finney Avenues. When he arrived, he met with a man that he knew and was told where he could find Dr. Kelley. Rogers became not only Kelley's rescuer, but his chronicler as well. The reporter and his editors wanted the whole story behind the kidnapping, and so did the public. They had to wait nearly three years for the whole story, until February 1934, but the story behind the story became a bigger sensation than the abduction itself.

When readers opened the newspaper on February 7, 1934, they were greeted with a front page photo of a man named Adolph Fiedler, a hulking and unsavory character who ran a tavern in the county that often provided shelter for local gangsters. Fiedler was connected and when he came to the writers at the *Post-Dispatch* with his story, they were willing to listen. The story was developed by the newspaper and then turned over to St. Louis County Prosecutor C. Arthur Anderson. According to Fiedler, the kidnapping has been the work of gangsters and ex-cons, including some of the same men who had also tried to kidnap Oscar Johnson. Anderson began working to get indictments against all of the men involved and against one woman who had allegedly masterminded the crime. Her name was Nellie Tipton Muench, the wife of Dr. Ludwig O. Muench, daughter of the Reverend William Tipton and the sister of Judge Ernest Tipton of the Missouri Supreme Court.

Nellie and her husband were well known in the Central West End and were even neighbors of Dr. Kelley, residing in nearby Westminster Place. She was described as a "vivacious redhead" and was the owner of the fashionable Mitzi Shop, one of the city's most expensive women's boutiques. The place was decorated with floor to ceiling mirrors, gilt furniture and with unusually attractive models. It was the kind of store where customers did not ask about prices, especially men, and which catered to not only socially prominent matrons, but to working girls of the best brothels in the city as well. In fact, it was Nellie herself who pointed out that a proper wife might actually stand next to the prostitute who was servicing her husband while in the store!

Nellie was not unknown to the police and had managed a few brushes with the law in the past. In 1919, she had been questioned about the disappearance of jewels from a hotel room and had been involved in several court cases. In one of them, the proprietor of a rival shop accused her of stealing several hundred dollars worth of dresses and in another, Nellie tried in vain to collect $7,000 from the estate of a businessman for clothing he had allegedly purchased before he died. She had also been involved in nasty dispute with a politician that she claimed had loaned her money at extortion-like interest rates. It was obvious that Nellie was chronically in need of money to support her extravagant lifestyle. She was rarely discreet about who she borrowed it from and thanks to this, got involved with gangsters. When she was unable to pay them back, they began demanding favors and information from her.

In this way, she became the "mastermind" behind the Kelley kidnapping. She had taken a look at her Central West End neighbors and had decided that the Kelley's were the most likely ones to come up with a large ransom. She "fingered him" to her mob handlers and two weeks later, he was abducted.

When the indictment against her came down, no fewer than 13 lawyers undertook to defend her. She had eluded previous convictions through charm and connections and believed this time would be no different. She had her case separated from the other defendants and even got a change of venue to Mexico, Missouri, not far from Columbia and Jefferson City, where her father had his church and her brother sat on the Supreme Court. This was where she and her husband had attended school and had gotten married and it was an area where the Tipton name was known, respected and carried political weight. Unfortunately though, back in St. Louis, Nellie's accomplices were being tried, convicted and sentenced to lengthy prison terms.

Nellie must have been rattled by this for she began to dream up a new scheme to stay out of jail. The lawyers might not be enough but if Nellie came into court cradling her new baby, she was sure to walk out a free woman. The problem was that she was already 41 years-old and had been married for more than 20 years, having never had any children. Yet on August 18, 1935, the Muench's announced the birth of a son.

The newspapers were immediately skeptical about the "blessed event" and yet the child was quite real. And so began the great "baby hoax" story. Reporters began digging into the background of the healthy, few weeks-old baby and quickly discovered the sordid tale. In July, a baby had been brought to the Muench home from the City Hospital, but it was quite ill and had died within a few days. Quickly, another baby was secured as Nellie had already started working on her story. What heartless jury could send a new mother to prison? Nellie's new baby had actually been born to an unwed Philadelphia servant girl named Anna Ware. She had been brought to St. Louis to give birth and to provide Nellie with her public relations baby. And while Nellie undoubtedly thought this plan was ingenious, she didn't stop there. She also convinced Dr. Marsh Pitzman, an eminent colleague of her husband's, that he was the father of the baby. In this way, she was able to extort a large amount of money from him!

In the early fall of 1935, newspapers managed to track down Anna Ware and they began publishing her version of the story in serialized form. The young woman had been employed in a Philadelphia suburb by Mrs. Francis Giordan, the daughter of Mrs. Rebecca Winner of St. Louis. Anna admitted to an affair with Mrs. Giordan's husband and when she became pregnant, she was sent away to St. Louis to have her baby. She was told that it was to be adopted by Giordan's aunt. She was met at Union Station by an attorney named Wilfred Jones, who took her to the Winner home, where the child was born.

Meanwhile, on October 3, Nellie Muench went to trial. In Mexico, she was treated as an honored guest and Sheriff E.S. Haycraft put only the names of personal friends on the jury list. Her brother, the Supreme Court Justice, sat beside her at the defense table and while she brought her disputed baby with her to Mexico, she did not bring him into the courtroom. As the case began, Nellie's lawyers painted a picture of her as an innocent local girl who had fallen in with bad characters in the big city. They had taken advantage of her and had blamed her for the kidnapping. The attorneys presented a skillful case and also managed to exclude just about all of the evidence that made Nellie look bad. Not surprisingly, based on the makeup of the jury, Nellie was found "not guilty" on all counts.

The acquittal though was only the first of many subsequent court appearances for Nellie. She now had to return to St. Louis and to face a writ of habeas corpus petition that had been filed by Anna Ware for the return of her baby. The young woman had been brought back to St. Louis and had been pressured by officials to reclaim her baby. Hearings in the matter were started on October 15 and a short time later, Judge William Dee Becker ordered that she bring the baby into court. The blanket-swathed baby, who had been meant to touch the hearts of jurors, had an opposite effect on the audience in this new courtroom. The spectators, mostly women, shouted and hissed at Nellie. After Anna Ware identified the baby as her own, Judge Becker announced that it would remain in the custody of the court until the matter was settled. He sent him to the St. Louis Children's Hospital and with this, Nellie lost control of her emotions and thrilled the reporters present with a hysterical, table-pounding display of grief, despair and outrage. She finally had to be led from the room. After that, even those who originally doubt the sincerity of Nellie's affections towards the baby were swayed. Her acquaintance with him had been brief, but her care for him seemed to be genuine.

A special commissioner from Cape Girardeau was assigned to hear the case. Rush H. Limbaugh (father of the radio personality) began hearings and listened to 86 witnesses in the matter. Witnesses established that Nellie Muench had purchased the baby from a "broker", attorney Wilfred Jones, and had used the child to extort money from Dr. Pitzman. (On a side note, it was later learned that Dr. Pitzman was so captivated by Nellie that he even changed his will to favor her when she told him the baby was his. Even after the scandal became front page news, he continued to give her money to help her in the legal battles against Anna Ware!) When Anna Ware was put on the witness stand, she stated that she had not wanted to give up her baby, but she had no money to care for him. Now, she wanted him back and she asserted that the child was hers, not a premature infant that had been born to Nellie Muench as was claimed. The court ruled and Anna got the baby back. She was given custody the week before Christmas and she and her son vanished from the public eye.

Nellie though was not so lucky. She escaped on the kidnapping charge but the baby hoax that she had imagined would save her, turned out to be her undoing. She was hauled into Federal Court in 1936 to face charges of mail fraud. Prosecutors presented a case that said that since she had procured the baby by correspondence, she had attempted to defraud through the mails. This little lark ended up costing her ten years in prison. Her husband, who had stood by her through everything, was ruled her accomplice and was sentenced to eight years.

Ludwig Muench was released from prison in 1943 and filed for divorce from Nellie. He also began the long and ultimately successful struggle to regain his medical license. Nellie herself was conditionally released from prison in April 1944, the same month that her divorce became final. She moved to Kansas City, assumed a new name and started a new life.

But was not the last time that St. Louis would hear the name of Nellie Muench. In 1960, a group of investors announced a plan to construct a new development at the corner of Lindell and Kingshighway that would include a 40-story hotel, a 40-story apartment building and a structure for offices and shops. The plan never came to fruition but it did grab headlines when one of the major stockholders was revealed to be Nellie Muench, now calling herself Mrs. Lee. Many years had passed, but some things had never changed... Nellie was still being talked about in St. Louis!

THE ST. LOUIS CRUCIFIXION

While this strange story is neither a bloody crime, nor a ghostly happening, it is a genuine St. Louis mystery and it remains as intriguing as it was back in 1930 when the unusual image first appeared. The story goes that this incident took place on a cold Christmas Eve in 1930, although an article that appeared in *Fate* magazine from 1959 alleged that it occurred on a less miraculous night in March 1932. Regardless, the basic facts, and the end result, of the story remain the same and just as mysterious.

According to the version of the story passed on at the St. Louis Police Library, the weather during the final days of 1930 made them cold and bitter ones. As was the custom at that time, police officers would often round up homeless men on frigid nights and let them sleep in the holdover cells at police headquarters downtown. The next morning, they were given a bologna sandwich breakfast and sent on their way.

Later on that morning, a janitor was working on cleaning out the cells. It was especially quiet that morning and he whistled Christmas melodies as he swept the floor. As the janitor entered Cell 8 though, the tune froze on his lips. With his mouth hanging open, he stared in awe at the life-sized drawing of the Crucified Christ on the dingy wall of the cell. The discovery led to what has turned out to be one of the unusual, and unsolved, mysteries of St. Louis.

Over the course of the last decades, no one had been able to learn the identity of the artist, despite a regional search for the man who might have been sleeping in Cell 8. In the years that followed the discovery, the police department opened the cell up as tourist attraction and thousands came to see the image, crowding into a cell that became a shrine. Eventually, a plate of glass was fixed over the drawing so that eager pilgrims and enthusiastic visitors would not damage it.

But not only the curious and the devout came to see the drawing. It also attracted the attention of art experts and students. It was closely studied and pronounced a work of art, but none of the experts could determine the materials used by the artist to create the work. They quickly ruled out the most likely ingredients, like oils, chalk, pencil, crayons and water colors and police procedures dismissed the idea that it had been carved or etched into the wall. All sharp objects had been taken away from the men when they were put into the cells. Artists merely examined the image and then shook their heads in bewilderment.

And a greater mystery than this was the identity of the artist. Some of the experts proclaimed that the image was the work of a genius. But how could anyone, genius or not, create such a drawing under such terrible conditions? As mentioned already, detectives put out the word that they were looking for the temporary resident of Cell 8 after a check of the department records gave no clue as to who might have occupied the cell that night. The identity of the artist remains as much a mystery today as it was in 1930.

As time has passed though, a theory has been advanced that might explain how the image was created. Officers believe that the material used to create the image was a charred piece of a shoe sole. It is believed that the artist burned the sole with matches and then used the blackened rubber to create the drawing. It would have been a laborious and unwieldy method of working, but it certainly could explain how the image was achieved. Regardless though, it is an amazing piece of work for a single night and one that you can see for yourself. The wall was later removed from Cell 8 and it is now on display in the lobby of the St. Louis Police Academy at 315 S. Tucker Boulevard. It still manages to draw thousand of visitors each year.

As one can imagine, ghosts and crime seem to go hand in hand. In 2001, I even published an entire book of chilling tales that were spawned by murder, bloodshed and mayhem and found a few such tales floating around St. Louis. Some of them were unfortunately brief, like the story that a glowing ghost haunted the Fourth District Police Station in the late 1800's. And yes, that's all that I could find about it, although I have crossed my fingers that something might turn up in the future.

On the other side of the law, there is the ghost of a bootlegger who allegedly haunts a house near Zia's Restaurant on the Hill. According to author Robbi Courtaway, the gangster operated out of a second basement in the house during Prohibition. He continues to stand watch over the grounds, even though he died during the violent era of the 1920's.

But no story of crime and ghosts in St. Louis can compare with what may be one of the most haunted places in the city, the old Newstead Avenue Police Station in the Central West End.

HAUNTED BY CRIMES PAST

In 1994, Matt and Denise Piskulic moved into a wonderful old building on Newstead Avenue in St. Louis. The place was perfect for their graphic design business with spacious rooms, hardwood floors, and a central studio with high ceilings. They had heard rumors about the place over the years but they didn't let that stop them from moving in. But little did they realize that just because people said the place was haunted, they never told them that the house was infested with ghosts!

The Newstead Avenue Police Station, which was built in 1904, was located in the Central West End of St. Louis. For years, it operated as a precinct house and jail, becoming well known for its strange and violent past. The first major tragedy struck in July 1945 when a waiter named Edward Melendes was arrested for petty theft. At some point during the night, Melendes was beaten to death in his cell. Three police officers and the victim's cellmate were indicted for manslaughter. There was no evidence to ultimately convict the men and the prosecution's case fell apart. Significantly, the accused officers resigned from the police force just two months after the murder occurred.

Horror returned to the police station in 1953 when it played a key role in the notorious Bobby Greenlease kidnapping case. The crime would shake the city of St. Louis and would have lasting repercussions for years to come.

The case became known as one of the most tragic crimes of the 1950's. The month of September 1953 marked the kidnapping and murder of 6-year-old Bobby Greenlease and also the subsequent disappearance of half the $600,000 ransom his family pointlessly paid for his release. The money disappeared at the Newstead Avenue police station.

Bobby was the son of Robert and Virginia Greenlease, residents of Mission Hills, Kansas, a prominent suburb of Kansas City. Robert Greenlease was one of the largest Cadillac dealers in the nation. In comparison to the wealth of the Greenlease family, Bobby's kidnappers, Carl Austin Hall and Bonnie Heady, were dead broke. However, both had known privilege earlier in their lives. It had been at military school that Hall had met Paul Greenlease, Bobby's older, adopted brother. Hall later inherited a large sum of money from his father, but lost it all in bad business ventures. After that, he turned to crime. He was arrested for robbing cab drivers (his total take was only $38) and he was sent to the Missouri State Penitentiary. In prison, he dreamed of the "big score" and began planning the kidnapping that would help him to retire.

After getting out of prison, Hall moved to St. Joseph, Missouri and he started dating Bonnie Heady. She was no catch, having a reputation for not only sleeping around but also for occasionally dabbling in prostitution. The good news was that she owned her own home and she and Hall often drank themselves into a stupor there, never being bothered by anyone. Hall often knocked her around though and in fact, when she was arrested for kidnapping, she still bore the bruises of her latest beating. Her willingness to put up with Hall's abuse is probably a clue as to why she agreed to go along with his kidnapping scheme.

During the summer months of 1953, Hall and Heady made repeated trips to Kansas City to follow the Greenlease family. After some debate, they decided that Bobby would be the easiest prey. At that time, the boy was enrolled at Notre Dame de Sion, a fashionable Catholic school. In the late morning of September 28, Heady entered the school and told a nun that she was Bobby's aunt. She and Virginia Greenlease had been shopping at the Country Club Plaza, she told the nun, when Virginia had suffered a heart attack. Heady said that she had come to take Bobby to the hospital. When Bobby was brought out of his class, he immediately took Heady's hand in his, as if he knew her. Heady would later say that "he was so trusting."

Heady met Hall a few minutes later at the Katz Drugstore and they drove across town and across the state line into Kansas. The crime, enacting the Lindbergh Statute (named for the famous case) had just become a matter for the Federal authorities. And it was just about to get worse....

In a vacant field in Overland Park, Heady got out of the car and walked a short distance away while Hall killed Bobby. First, he tried to strangle the little boy but the rope he used was too short. Then, he punched him in the face, knocking out one tooth. Finally, he pushed Bobby down and shot him in the head with a .38 caliber pistol. The boy was dead less than 30 minutes after he had been abducted. After that, they drove back to St. Joseph and buried the body in the back yard of Heady's home. Hall had dug the grave the night before. After the body was covered, he planted flowers in the freshly churned soil, hoping to cover all evidence of the horrific crime.

The Greenlease family got their first inkling of trouble when the nun who had released Bobby from school called to inquire about Virginia's health. Soon after, they got the ransom demands. Hall also mailed them a pin that Bobby had been wearing when he was taken. The killer demanded a ransom of $600,000 in $10 and $20 bills.

Robert Greenlease called several of his closest friends and he began putting together the money. He also called the head of the local bank, Arthur Eisenhower (brother of Dwight D. Eisenhower) and the two men put together a plan to record the serial numbers of all of the ransom bills. While the money was being accumulated, Hall called the Greenlease residence repeatedly. He continually reassured them that Bobby was alive. Finally, a week after the kidnapping, the money was delivered. Actually, it was delivered two times because Hall couldn't find it the first time.

Finally, after almost bungling another money drop on a dark country road, Hall was able to get the money. It was just after midnight on October 5 and Hall made one last phone call to a friend of Robert Greenlease, Robert Ledterman, who had been assisting with the ransom payment. He promised Ledterman that the family would have Bobby back within 24 hours.

While Robert and Virginia waited for word of where to find their son, Hall and Heady drove to St. Louis with a money bag that weighed more than 85 pounds. As they traveled, word of the kidnapping leaked to the media and it became a nationwide sensation. When they arrived in St. Louis, Hall and Heady were stunned to find themselves at the center of the story. They ditched their car and started using taxicabs. They rented a small apartment on Arsenal Street in south St. Louis and decided to lay low. Hall quickly got restless though and one afternoon, left a drunken Heady in the apartment with a few thousand dollars and vanished. He departed for the "good life".

Hall then hooked up with an ex-con cab driver and a prostitute. The three of them ended up at the Coral Courts Motel, St. Louis' legendary "no-tell motel" located along old Route 66. It was renowned as a place where a fellow could stay for awhile with no questions asked. The Coral Courts was built in 1941 by John Carr, who was long rumored to be mob-connected after operating a posh brothel in St. Louis for many years.

Hiding out in the motel, Hall began to lavish money on the cab driver and the prostitute. The hooker would later say that Hall stayed so drunk, and was so nervous, that he couldn't perform sexually. As for the cab driver, Hall had turned the man into his own personal valet. He gave the man fistfuls of money and told him to buy new clothes and whatever else he thought he might need. What the cab driver brought him was trouble. The owner of the cab company was a man named Joe Costello, a well-known local gangster. When Costello heard about the big spending customer, he contacted St. Louis police lieutenant Louis Shoulders. Since Costello and Shoulders always denied stealing the ransom money, it is unknown whether Costello figured out that Hall was the Greenlease kidnapper and gave Shoulders a tip for the arrest of a lifetime... or whether they simply conspired to rip Hall off.

However, what is known is that Hall, guided by the cab driver, rented an apartment on the edge of St. Louis. A short time after moving in, he was arrested by Shoulders and a patrolman named Elmer Dolan. Hall was picked up for questioning about the large amount of money that he was flashing around. He was then taken to the Newstead Avenue police station and after that, history becomes quite blurry about the ransom money. Shoulders and Dolan said that they brought a suitcase and a foot locker jammed with more than $550,000 in cash into the station but some later testimony stated otherwise. No one else could remember seeing what turned out to be the elusive suitcase. Regardless of what occurred, only $300, 000 was ever recovered.

Once he was arrested, Hall almost immediately broke down. Heady was quickly arrested at the small apartment where Hall had dumped her. On October 7, police officers and reporters raced for Heady's house in St. Joseph, where they dug up Bobby's body from the backyard.

And once Hall and Heady confessed to the crime, they resigned themselves to being executed for the murder. When a Federal jury in Kansas City returned the verdict, it has been said that Heady smiled. On December 18, only 81 days after the kidnapping, Hall and Heady were executed side-by-side at the Missouri State Penitentiary. The pair had declined to seek mercy at the trial and did not appeal the verdict. Missouri authorities had a second chair installed in the gas chamber so that Heady and Hall could be executed at the same time. Heady was the only woman to ever be put to death in the gas chamber and it's said that she talked cheerfully to the guards and the officials while she was being strapped in. She did not fall silent until Hall finally told her to shut up.

Amidst the widespread anger about the murder of Bobby Greenlease, there was also an immediate investigation into the money that went missing at the Newstead Avenue police station. The glory that should have led to promotions for Shoulders and Dolan became a dirty scandal that highlighted the widespread corruption of the St. Louis police department in the 1950's.

The two officers were later convicted in a Federal court on a charge of perjury, for supposedly lying about the sequence of events from the time they arrested Hall until the time the money was brought to the Newstead station and counted. Various police clerks and officers testified that they never saw the men carrying anything when they entered the station with Hall and they certainly did not see the suitcase or the foot locker. Shoulders stated that the money was outside in the car and that he brought it into the station after bringing Hall inside.

The official theory was that Shoulders and Dolan, who both left the station on personal errands after booking Hall, returned to Hall's apartment and stole half the money. They brought the remaining half (I suppose thinking that no one would notice) to the station through the rear door. Hall's statement, not surprisingly, directly contradicted that of Shoulders and Dolan. Hall maintained that the money had been left in the apartment when he was arrested.

Over time, numerous theories have been floated as to who actually took the money. Most pointed fingers at Shoulders and his connection with Joe Costello, while others blamed the corruption in the police department itself.

However, it is possible that the money vanished somewhere else entirely. It's not a far reach to think that perhaps Hall took his revenge on the two police officers that arrested him and sent him to the gas chamber. If this is true, and Shoulders and Dolan did not take the money, then a tremendous injustice was done to the officers because their careers were destroyed over the incident.

FBI agents and police detectives also targeted Costello for making off with the money. In fact, federal agents followed him for years, tapping his phones and questioning his associates. They even raided the notorious Forest Park Avenue bordello of Mary Traynor, suspecting that Costello might have hidden the money there. They delved into his mob connections as Costello was a close associate of John Vitale and they believed that if he had come into $300,000 he would have surely let Vitale know about it. All this was in vain though and it was never proven that Costello took the ransom money. However, FBI agents did manage to arrest him on unrelated weapons charges though and he was sent to prison.

So if the cops and Costello didn't have it, then where could the money have gone? Some have suggested that the mob-connected hotel owner, John Carr, may have been involved. If Carr knew about the money (and it's possible that he did), he could have entered Hall's room using a pass key and walked out with half the money, believing that Hall would never miss it. And even if he did miss it, what would he be able to do about it? When John Carr died, he was a multi-millionaire. Could any of that remaining fortune have been part of the Greenlease kidnapping money?

Obviously, we will never know. Even the old Coral Courts Motel has been torn down. The Route 66 landmark was demolished a few years ago and the land where it was once located has now been turned into a subdivision, erasing that piece of history forever.

Whoever took the money though, it was gone. For many years after, it was news whenever any of the bills linked to the missing Greenlease money turned up. But where was it coming from? No one knew and now, with so many principals in the case long dead, it can only be realized that the vanished money will always remain a mystery.

In 1960, the Newstead Avenue police station closed its doors for good. For the next five years, it sat empty until artist Howard Jones and his wife Helen, converted the place into a private residence. The former drill room was turned into a spacious studio and living quarters. Jones was an art instructor at Washington University and was famous for his "light paintings" and electronic art. The couple would soon find that the old police station was anything but a peaceful place to live.

They began to hear the sound of heavy footsteps in the studio at night, followed by a dragging sound and then more footsteps. The sounds were heard night after night, although nothing in the building was ever disturbed or moved. Stereo and electronic equipment in the place would be turned off and yet sound would still come from the speakers. The Jones' unplugged everything and yet the noises continued. The only thing that seemed to help was when Jones began leaving the light on in the studio all night long. The burning lamp seemed to keep the ghostly intruders away.

The house became one of the first investigation sites for famous psychic investigator Gordon Hoener in the 1960's. Hoener ran a small organization called "Haunt Hunters", which set the standard for many paranormal research groups that followed. Hoener ran newspaper ads and appeared on television and radio shows looking for haunted places to investigate. While he would track down many pointless cases, a few of them did turn out to be interesting. His investigations at 14 Newstead Avenue revealed at least one spirit in the building.... one who seemed to be the waiter who was killed there years before.

Hoener came to the building with a reporter named William Keenan from the *St. Louis Magazine* and a couple of independent witnesses. They say down with a Ouija board and attempted to contact the spirit who was haunting the Jones'. Hoener began to ask the presence a number of questions.

"Was the unknown presence a prisoner in this building when it was a jail?" Jones asked the Ouija board.

"YES", came the reply.

"Did he die here?" YES

"A policeman?" NO

"A prisoner?" YES

"Would the presence manifest itself for the group?" YOU - 4 - NO

The group took this to mean that the ghost wanted nothing to do with the other observers, but that it had no problem manifesting itself for the Jones'. This still left Howard Jones feeling unsettled. The only solution he could devise was to add more lamps to the rest of the house. He left them burning day and night and "for the first time, we slept undisturbed," Jones told reporter Walter Orthwein in a 1975 interview.

Between the Jones' and the Piskulic's, another artist used the building as a studio and an apartment. When he moved out of the place, he assured the Piskulic's that the stories about the house had been just that... simply stories. "About this Newstead ghost thing, I've never had any problems with it," he told Matt Piskulic when he was looking over the building to buy it. Matt didn't think anything about it at the time. He knew that it was no secret that the house had often been featured on many local radio and television specials, but the Piskulic's were determined not to let that worry them.

Unfortunately, they started having trouble shortly after they moved in. Each day, the couple heard footsteps banging up the front stairs in broad daylight. Matt first assumed that it was a delivery person, but no package was ever left behind.

The couple planned to live in the building with their company, V.I.P Graphics, until they could afford to move. They selected a small loft just a short flight of stairs away from the attic for their bedroom. One night, Denise was startled awake in the darkness because she heard a baby crying. She first believed that she imagined it and she lay there for several minutes, waiting for it to happen again. Moments later, the crying began once more. It sounded as though it was coming from inside of the walls. It soon became so loud that it woke up Matt as well. The couple tried to figure out a possible cause for the noise (the wind, an animal or anything) and then the screaming began. The sound of a man shrieking began to sound from the attic. It was a long, piercing cry of pain. The Piskulic's slept no more that night.

The following morning, Denise began calling everyone she knew to tell them of their horrifying experience. She then contacted the former owner of the house, an artist named Corey Fosmire. She told him what had happened and then asked that he tell her honestly if anything strange had occurred while he lived there.

The Fosmire's had also attempted to live in and do business at the old police station. Whatever presence was already there however did not seem to care for Fosmire and his family. Disembodied voices called out at night and they heard the same heavy footsteps that the previous occupants, and the Piskulic's, had reported. Stranger still, handprints and footprints appeared on freshly varnished floors and clean windows.... prints that matched no one in the house. Finally, the family was terrified one night by the sound of screaming that echoed throughout the entire house. It was so intense that it seemed to shake the building! The screaming drove them out into the street and they left the house that night.

Despite the bad experiences of past owners, Matt and Denise were determined to make the house and business work. They started to do some renovations that, of course, accentuated the phenomena.

In the summer of 1992, Denise heard a woman calling "hello" while she was in the bathroom. Assuming that someone had arrived on business, she told the visitor that she would be right out. But when Denise opened the door, she found no one waiting for her. She searched the building but no one was there. The footsteps were heard all summer with much of the activity being centered around the front staircase. Strangely, the footsteps sounded like hard shoe soles on the concrete staircase, even though the steps are thickly carpeted. Normal footsteps make no sound on the stairs, only the phantom ones do.

The steps continued, becoming louder and more frequent. They were sometimes accompanied by the odor of perfume and then evolved into actual apparitions. The first ghost was seen by Denise. Lars Hamilton, who did sales work for the graphics design company, had an office across the hall from Denise. One day as she happened to look across the hall toward the other office, she saw a man stand by the doorway for a moment and then duck out of sight. Assuming that this was Hamilton, Denise went across the hall to ask him a question. There was no one in the office!

Other employees had their own strange experiences. Mary Adler, a layout design artist, was working on a project one morning when she felt someone blowing on the back of her neck. Startled, she spun around to find no one behind her.

Shortly after, a visitor to the business encountered an apparition and the presence continued to show up regularly after that. Strange reports have become commonplace with the staff ever since.

On September 26, 1992, Matt and Denise invited six psychics to the building. They claimed there were many ghosts in the old station house.... some of them permanent residents and others just passing through from one plane to the next.

Eerily, the psychics had no knowledge of the past history of the building and yet they were able to reveal many hidden aspects of the place, impressing the Piskulic's. They stated that the station was filled with confused energy and most of it was centered in the attic. The basement was believed to be the part of the building where most of the violence in the place had occurred. Unknown to the mediums, this was where the prisoners had once been housed.

They also identified a number of ghosts who stayed on in the building, including police officers, jail inmates, a woman whose husband had worked at the station and even a teenaged girl.

The psychics offered to "sweep the building with light" to get the spirits to move on, but Denise declined the offer. "I told them, no, they weren't hurting anything by being here," she told author Robbi Courtaway. "It's kind of live and let live, and they've been here longer than we have, and I just didn't feel the need to do anything like that. They've never really done anything, as far as I'm concerned."

Today, the architecture firm HERA occupies the second floor of the old police station. Though the firm only moved into the place in 2001, the employees are already convinced that the place is haunted. Architect Betsy Perry told Pamela Lowney, a writer for *STL Today*, that she is certain there is a presence in the office. "It's hard to describe," she said. "It just feels like someone is looking at you." On nights when Perry has worked late, she stated that she has often felt a cold chill on the back of her neck and has heard footsteps leading up the stairs to the attic. What really disturbs her the most though are the inexplicable smells of perfume that seem to come and go without explanation. "It's an old time smell like lavender or lilac," she recalled. "Enough to make me turn around and see who's there."

Another staff member of HERA, Roxanne Gaines, agreed that the eerie smell of perfume is strong and very apparent. She also remembered coming in to work one morning to hear the sound of a crying child as she climbed the steps to the second floor. She first assumed that one of the other employees had brought her child into work with her but when she went into the other woman's office to see the boy, she discovered that he wasn't there.

And so, the haunting continues. The glimpses of the people who aren't there continue to occur as do the ghostly footsteps, the opening and closing doors, the calling voices and the water faucets that turn on and off by themselves. The ghosts, it seems, are here to stay.

But what draws the spirits to the former police station on Newstead Avenue? Is it because of the violence and strange events that took place here in the past? The answer to that is still a mystery... but one thing is sure, it may just be one of the most haunted places in St. Louis.

VIII. HAUNTED HOUSES

History & Hauntings of Some of St. Louis' Spirited Dwellings

St. Louis is a very haunted city.

That is something that I think that we have already clearly established in the preceding pages, as well as the fact that many of the hauntings that plague the city are connected to historic buildings and homes. However, there are so many haunted houses in this city that we could never begin to collect them all. Of course, with that said, we have to establish what makes a house truly haunted. Could it be the one-time, strange happening that occurred to a single occupant on a chilly winter's night... or should it be a repeated phenomena that is witnessed by a number of different people and which spans a number of years?

Everyone seems to have their own definition, but have no doubt, haunted houses do exist.. as I am sure that the unlucky people who appear in the following chapter can tell you!

And it seems as though they have been with us for many years. Even the old newspaper accounts of the city speak of haunted houses. In March 1882, a brief note appeared in the *St. Louis Globe-Democrat* that spoke of the demolition of a place called "Cottonwood Castle" in north St. Louis. The house, which was located at the corner of Broadway and Spring Streets, was being torn down to make way for a warehouse that was being constructed by the Lindell Glassworks. According to the article, the house had been built by James Ellet in 1833, but had existed as ruins for a number of years. It also went on to say that "it was a popular belief among those living in the vicinity that the castle was haunted, it being claimed that the spirits of two women, who lost their lives within its walls in 1855, roamed nightly in it and held blood-curdling revelries."

The homes of St. Louis and their ghosts will be forever intertwined.

One of the first buildings ever constructed in St. Louis was a private residence, the combination home and trading post of Pierre Laclede. Of course, this building, like all of the buildings from the Creole days in the city are long gone now. Unlike the Europeans, Americans have always torn down old buildings to make way for new ones, viewing demolition as some perverted form of progress. Because of this, much of the past of St. Louis now lies in rubble.

St. Louis has achieved a great and varied history over the years, playing important roles in the opening of the west and in the Civil War, and yet many of the homes and buildings here have been destroyed in the name of progress. There seems to be a willingness in St. Louis to ignore our own history. The former homes of important historic figures like William T. Sherman and William Clark have been gone for years, as is the house were Ulysses S. Grant married Julia Dent. In the Mill Creek Valley, literally thousands of 19th-century homes were demolished, along with scores of historic buildings and churches.

But all is not lost. Despite the staggering numbers of homes that have been lost, there are still many historic structures and sites that remain. Many areas, like Lafayette Square and the Central West End, have been rescued and restored. These old buildings still stand, noble and proud against the ravages of time and the hands of man.

For many of them however, only the spirits of the past remain.

ST. LOUIS PRIVATE PLACES

According to author Mary Bartley, there has been much debate over the years as to the origin of St. Louis' private places, including whether or not they are a derivation of the French "place" or town square. Some have also suggested that they are a continuation of the colonial St. Louis custom of surrounding homes with stockade fences to protect from attack by Indians or the British. It is more likely though that the places were a local reaction to the uncontrolled growth of St. Louis neighborhoods in the early 19th century. There was no zoning protection in those days and the free-for-all growth of the city pressed in on neighborhoods that the residents preferred to have exclusive or "private".

One of the first attempts at controlling a desirable residential area was enacted by Anne Lucas Hunt when she established Summit Square in 1828. Summit Square covered a square block that was bounded by Fifth and Sixth Streets on the east and west and by Olive and Pine Streets on the north and south. She and her brother, James H. Lucas, inherited extensive real estate holdings from their father, Jean Baptiste Charles Lucas, the largest landowner in early St. Louis. He had settled here shortly after Thomas Jefferson had appointed him land commissioner for the Louisiana Territory. Summit Square was a prominent address through the 1840's, but shortly after began to decline.

One of the most important houses here was built in 1829 for Bartholomew Berthold, who married into the Chouteau family and went into the fur business. The fine brick mansion later became the local headquarters for the Johnson and Douglas party but after they were defeated for the presidency by Abraham Lincoln, the house was given over to a group of Confederate sympathizers called the Minute Men. During their occupancy, the house was dubbed "Fort Berthold" and was used as a Confederate stronghold. On March 4, 1861, the first Confederate flag in St. Louis was flown from the roof of the house. An interested, and restless, crowd formed outside, however the cannon that had been installed on the second floor veranda kept them in the street and away from the house. The house was destroyed in 1866 to make way for a commercial building.

Summit Square was gradually destroyed and swallowed up by a developing downtown. It failed as a residential district, but made a fortune for those who invested here.

James H. Lucas began developing his own private neighborhood in 1851. In that year, he sold a parcel of land to the city to be used as a park and then used it as a buffer to protect his development of Lucas Place. The area was not deeded to the city and instead was controlled by the investors in the property. Lucas executed all of the deeds here himself and mandated that all construction had to take place at least 25 feet from the street. In addition, only private vehicles were permitted on the street, which was maintained and lighted from a fund created by the place property owners.

1858 Image of Lucas Place (Courtesy Missouri Historical Society)

All of the residents here were among the wealthiest in the city and the homes were constructed in a variety of architectural styles from Greek Revival to the newly fashionable Italianate design.

In the years following the Civil War, Lucas Place was the most conspicuously elegant street in St. Louis but by the 1880's, it was on serious decline. Lucas had been unable to control the encroaching of businesses and industry along the outer edges of the place and the address began to become undesirable. Many of the residents moved out, some to Vandeventer Place, others to Chouteau Avenue and the most daring went all the way west to the new streets being developed near Forest Park. The final blow came in 1883 when the city constructed a new Exposition Hall in the park next to Lucas Place. This new hall was the scene of several national political conventions and offered music for as many as 3,524 people at a time. The Hall was demolished in 1906, but by then, Lucas Place was a thing of the past. In 1893, it had officially become Locust Street.

VANDEVENTER PLACE

While many of St. Louis' private places still exist today, perhaps the one most sorely missed is Vandeventer Place, which is almost considered the stuff of legend today. The heyday of this district, which came in the 1890's, is still spoken of in the city today, even though not a single trace remains of this street in its original location.

Vandeventer Place extended west from Grand Avenue to Vandeventer between Enright and Bell Avenues. It was home to 86 of the city's wealthiest individuals, businessmen and politicians. The subdivision was platted by a noted surveyor named Julius Pitzman after William Vandeventer sold a portion of his farmland to three prominent citizens, Charles H. Peck, Napolean Mulliken and John S. McCune, in 1870. They immediately began to fashion their exclusive enclave.

The homes in Vandeventer Place were built on a scale unlike anything St. Louis had seen, before or since. Mansions filled all of the available lots here by 1890 and in 1894, two sets of circular white granite gates replaced the original cast-iron ones to guard the east and west entrances of the place. A landscaped center parkway was fitted with an ornamental pool and fountain. Restrictions here forbade tanneries, museums, breweries and schools and forced owners to have their front steps scrubbed at least twice a week. Three sets of curtains were required for each front window. Homes had to cost a minimum of $30,000 to build and had to be placed at least 30 feet back from the street. All main entrances had to face Vandeventer Place and all kitchens had to be located in the basement. No non-family member could spend more than one night in a Vandeventer Place mansion and "for rent" or "for sale" signs were completely out of the question.

The largest and most pretentious house here was built for Henry Clay Pierce, who had converted an outdated whale oil business into the Waters Pierce Oil Company, which was large enough to rival Standard Oil. He also had interests in railroads, coal mines and steamships. Pierce's rough-cut stone and brick mansion had 26 rooms and took three years to complete. He employed 22 servants for the house, who were required to hold a daily dress parade before the "master of the manor". The servants lived in a separate house, which was located behind the main house and across the street on Enright Avenue, and it was connected to the Pierce mansion by way of an underground tunnel.

After Pierce's first wife died in 1910, he moved to New York and never lived in the Vandeventer for an extended time again. It was maintained though as if he planned to return at any time. It was during this period that Pierce ran into problems. He was accused of having a "behind the scenes" role in the Mexican Revolution and he was indicted for massive antitrust violations. It turned out that Waters Pierce Oil Co. was in an alliance with Standard Oil, not a competitor.

Pierce died in 1927 after spending some time in prison. A year later, the furnishings of the mansion were sold at auction and in 1933, the house was deeded to the U. S. Fidelity and Casualty Company in payment for default federal income taxes. In 1936, the fixtures were sold off and the house was demolished.

In 1889, architect George I. Barnett designed a Victorian brick mansion for Jordan Wheat Lambert, a native of Alexandria, Virginia who came to St. Louis in 1873. Lambert was a chemist and pharmacist by trade. He discovered an antiseptic that he called "Listerine" and it became the backbone of the Lambert Pharmacal Company, which enjoyed great success.

Ironically, Lambert died of an infection in 1889 and his six children were orphaned six months later when his wife Lily died of pneumonia, shortly after the birth of their youngest child. The children were raised in the homes of guardians and relatives and enjoyed some success of their own.

The eldest son, Albert Bond Lambert, was an aviation pioneer who put up a considerable amount of money to finance Charles Lindgergh's flight to Paris. Lambert International Airport is named in his honor. Another son, Gerard, continued the growth of the family company and made Listerine a product that could be found in almost every home in America. He also became president of the Gillette Company.

Among the largest and most prominent homes in Vandeventer Place was built for Joseph

Gilbert Chapman in 1892. The yellow brick mansion stood at the corner of Vandeventer Place and Spring Avenue. Chapman was a native of New York state and had come to St. Louis to work in his father's company, Chapman and Thorp, a large lumber manufacturing company. He married Emma Bridge, the daughter of Hudson Bridge, a prominent businessman, and became a leading citizen of St. Louis. He became the director of the St. Louis National Bank, the Bridge and Beach Manufacturing Co. and the Bellefontaine Railroad. He served as a trustee for Washington University and on the board of the St. Louis Museum and School of Fine Arts. Chapman passed away in 1897, after only living in his extraordinary mansion for only five months.

Two years later, his daughter married architect John Lawrence Mauran. They moved into the house and remained there for many years. Mauran died in 1933, but his widow remained and became one of the last members of the original families in Vandeventer Place.

Emily Eaton also remained. She had grown up in a home that had been built for her mother and after she had married, she and her husband bought the mansion and never moved. It was Emily Eaton who began a campaign in the middle 1930's to save Vandeventer Place. The economy was terrible by this time, as the country was in the midst of the Depression, but she believed the old, and now crumbling, houses in the place could be saved. Unfortunately, Eaton overlooked the economic and social forces working against Vandeventer Place. She neglected the fact that the creation of Portland Place, Westmoreland Place and other private places in the Central West End had begun offering an alternative to Vandeventer years before. Many of the residents had been gone for years, many of them leaving once the growth of the city began to creep up to the place's borders.

Vandeventer Place had begun to lose its premier status back in 1922. By that time, many of the original residents had died and others had escaped from the crowded conditions of the city. The first attempt to break the single-family deed restrictions in the place occurred that year when a new owner opened a boarding house. It was reported that shocked residents had seen men lounging on the front porch in their shirt sleeves! Worse yet, some of the men were without collars and even had their sleeves rolled up. The boarding house was quickly put out of business, but it signaled the beginning of the end.

A little earlier in this same period saw resentments begin to appear toward the upper class residents of Vandeventer Place. When rumors of a threatened strike by the cooks here and stories of the street's coachmen demanding regular hours reached nonresidents in the early 1910's, many were delighted. The residents' seeming disregard for others and their opulent lifestyles did little to endear them to the common people Two decades later, this same feeling would do nothing to garner public sympathy when it came time to try and save the street and restore the houses here.

Emily Eaton did all she could but it was likely the attitudes of Vandeventer's remaining residents that brought about the end of the place. In the 1930's, a few proposed breaking deed restrictions and erecting an apartment complex and the city even suggested turning the place into a public park in 1935. They already owned several properties on the street because of nonpayment of back taxes and suggested that the WPA do the work to convert the area. Remaining residents held firm though and refused to let the park be built. By the end of the Great Depression, many of the houses that had been empty and could not be sold, along with others whose owners wanted to save on taxes and maintenance costs, were demolished. Ten years later, there were only 36 houses left and four of those were empty. Vandeventer Place was lost.

In 1947, the easternmost block of Vandeventer Place was chosen by the Veterans Administration as the site of a new hospital. The residents at the western end of the area found their fate sealed as well, although most of the decaying mansions stood until 1958. At that time, the city condemned the last of the Vandeventer houses, had them torn down and built the Juvenile Detention Center over their remains.

There is nothing left of Vandeventer today, save for memories, but the gates that once guarded the west entrance of the place can still be seen today. They were removed and now stand just east of the Jewel Box in Forest Park. There is also a parkway fountain that rests in Shaw Place, standing as a relic to times long past.

SPIRITS OF SOULARD

The Soulard section of south St. Louis is one of my favorite areas of the city. In times past, it was filled with breweries, beer gardens, caves and industry and even today it boasts an eclectic mix of homes, antique stores, restaurants and bars. It is a thriving area and essential place to visit for anyone who wants to capture the real spirit of St. Louis.

Soulard is named for a prominent early family who began subdividing their land in 1836. Antoine Soulard was born in France and came to St. Louis in 1794. He was the King's Surveyor of Spanish Upper Louisiana and a man of great wealth. He purchased a considerable amount of land in St. Charles County, in Jefferson County and in St. Louis itself. In 1795, he married Julie Cerre, the daughter of a prosperous Kaskaskia merchant. The couple moved into a Creole house that Soulard owned between Main and Second Streets and settled to raise four children together. They remained in this house until the death of Julie's mother in 1800. She inherited land that belonged to her father and she and her husband moved into a stone house on the farm.

In 1825, Soulard passed away and Julie and the children remained in the house until 1836, when the large piece of land was subdivided. The house and the block were left intact and the building was rented to the Vauxhall Gardens, a restaurant and park.

In 1837, Julie Soulard constructed an elaborate home on land that was part of her husband's estate at Ninth and Marion Streets. Soulard had been given the land by Spanish governor Charles Dehault Delassus in payment for surveying services rendered. The house was an odd attraction to many, who were used to the Colonial French architecture of the time, as Julie had it built of red brick in the American style that was more familiar in eastern cities. The house was two and one-half stories tall with a full basement and had a stone wall that surrounded it.

As time passed, Julie expanded her holdings through her children, giving them generous gifts of land and homes. Her second son, Henry, bought a large section of land near the confluence of the Mississippi and Missouri Rivers and his mother also gave him a parcel at Hamtrack Street (now Tucker Avenue) and Soulard Street (now Lafayette Avenue). He built a house that was similar to his mother's here in 1841. In 1843, she passed on her home at Ninth and Marion to her son Benjamin, but he only lived in it until February 1844. At that time, the house was sold to St. Vincent's Church, which was built on the northeast corner of the Soulard property. In 1845, the St. Louis Seminary occupied the house but rented it out to Edward Chouteau in 1864. Later, it was divided into two dwellings to provide extra income for the church.

Sadly, in 1949, the state of Missouri purchased the house and land and demolished it three years later because it rested on a highway right-of-way. No thought was ever given to slightly altering the highway to save one of the most historic homes in St. Louis.

In addition to the gifts given to her children, Julie also donated two city blocks to use as a public market (Soulard Market) and donated another block, bounded by Ninth, Decatur, Carroll and Eighth Streets, to be used as the site for Holy Trinity Church. The church site turned out to be a "cursed" location. When the walls of Holy Trinity were nearly completed, a mass was said at the site in hopes of being able to raise the money to complete the project. Unfortunately, a cyclone came along and destroyed the completed portion of the structure. Later, St. Vincent's Insane Asylum was built on the site but it was destroyed by the Great Cyclone of 1896.

The unusual mix of industry in south St. Louis and Soulard attracted a rich diversity of people who came to live here because of the job opportunities offered. Italians came to work in the clay pit and brick yards and the Germans came because of the breweries. Many laborers and business owners found the area to their liking but it was perhaps the breweries that made the greatest impact on the area. In previous chapters, I have already chronicled the history of beer and brewing in this part of the city but there is one tale of a haunted house than combined not only the brewing history, but the ghosts as well.

Located in the Soulard section is a mansion that was dubbed "Lion House" after it was built in 1865. It was the first home in St. Louis to feature a pair of stone lions to guard its entrance but it boasted other refinements as well. The house had been patterned after a German castle and originally featured three sets of doors, a large pipe organ, ornate plasterwork, the city's first residential burglar alarm, a third-floor cupola, two beer lagering cellars and an entrance into the Sidney Street Cave, which was mentioned in an earlier chapter. According to a previous owner of the house, who purchased the mansion in 1983, another startling addition to the place is its resident ghost! Just who that ghost might be remains a mystery, although some believe that it might be the owner of the house, Max Feurbacher.

Feurbacher was one of the founders of the Green Tree Brewery, which began operations on Sidney Street in 1863 between Eighth and Buel Streets. This operation was a actually a branch of the original Green Tree Brewery, located on Second Street and started by Feurbacher and his brother-in-law, Joseph Schnaider. The new brewery was larger and better equipped and did very well for many years. After Fuerbacher's death, Henry Nicholas took over operations until the brewery was absorbed by the St. Louis Brewing Association in 1889. For many years, the company was very successful though and it enabled Feurbacher to build the "Lion House" just three blocks away from the brewery site itself.

The house gained a reputation for being haunted a number of years ago. Residents often complained of hearing the doorbell or the sound of someone knocking on the front door when no one was there. In addition, footsteps have been heard and the son of one of the past owners once reported seeing the ghost of a man in the dining room. The couple's daughter once heard a toilet flushing in the empty house and a collection of old dolls that were once displayed in the former drawing room often changed positions. It was as if someone had picked the dolls up, looked at them and then carelessly laid them back down again in a different spot. There were also stories told about an old clawfoot bathtub on the second floor. For some reason, witnesses claim that they have felt a rush of cold air wash over them as they are taking in bath. Attempts to try and explain where the chill comes from haven't amounted to anything, as they are no vents or fans nearby.

Another Soulard house is a private residence that is located not far from the Feurbacher mansion. While it certainly is not of the historic significance of a Soulard beer baron's home, it still manages to maintain a vintage air about it and provides a comfortable home to its current owners, who told me about the strange happenings in their house in 1999. At that time, they had been living there for about five years but unusual things had started to occur shortly after they moved in.

On their first night in the house, they were awakened by a loud thumping noise that seemed to come from downstairs. Ron (names have been changed to protect the owner's privacy) was startled out of bed and went to the steps, thinking that someone was at the door. Oddly, the noise could no longer be heard on the first floor. He looked outside, but seeing no one, he went back upstairs again. About an hour later, the same thing happened again. He described the sound to me as being "like someone was banging on a wall or a door with their hands." Ron's wife, Connie, had also been awakened by the sound but she didn't believe that it had come from downstairs. To her, it seemed as though someone was knocking on the door in the next room.

While things didn't seem to be off to a great start, Ron and Connie soon settled into their new home. Neither one of them was a really a believer in ghosts, but both claimed to harbor an open-minded skepticism about things they didn't understand. This open-mindedness quickly became useful as more and more odd things began to happen in the house.

They soon began to notice what seemed to be footsteps walking back and forth at odd hours and lights that sometimes switched on an off under their own power. Connie also reported the scent of a "stale and musty" perfume outside the bedroom one morning. "I knew that it wasn't my perfume," she said, " and no one else had been wearing anything like that in the house. I had no idea where it could have come from."

In addition, the thumping sounds continued during the night, but it was no longer a mystery as to where they were coming from. One warm night in July, Ron was again awakened by the mysterious sounds. This time, he decided to prowl around on the second floor and to see if he could figure out where they originated. Right next to Ron and Connie's bedroom was a spare room that they used for storage. They had talked of trying to do something with it but never had. Connie later told me that she was always uncomfortable in there, but blamed that on the fact that the room seemed very hard to heat. As Ron walked down the upstairs hallway on that summer night, he was curious to discover that the thumping sound seemed to be coming from inside of this room. He listened carefully and realized that the sound was not coming from the walls or a door, but from the floor of the room! It sounded like someone was positioned on his or her knees and then kept falling down over and over again. He opened the door and quickly entered the room to find it empty. However, the noise immediately ceased!

The couple was intrigued by the weird goings-on, but even with assorted cold spots, erratic lights and footsteps, they were not yet willing to consider ghosts. "I have several friends who are in the construction field," Ron explained to me, "and I wanted to have them check things out with the house. We were sure there was an explanation for the stuff that was happening." Ron called two friends who were contractors and had them check the wiring of the house, as well as to check and see if water pipes or anything ran beneath the floor of the spare room. He thought that perhaps that might explain the knocking noises. The two men thoroughly inspected the house but found nothing that would explain what Ron and Connie were experiencing.

"At that point, I guess I was willing to concede that the house might be haunted," Ron told me with an uncertain grin.

It turned out that Ron and Connie had bought the house from a friend of Connie's sister and so they didn't have far to go when it came to looking into the history of the place. They wanted to know if anyone in the past had also had problems in the house, especially with the spare room. "I called my sister's friend," Connie recalled, "and asked her if she or anyone else had ever noticed anything weird about the house. Immediately, the first thing that she asked me was 'are you talking about the sounds in the cold room upstairs?'"

The other woman began to tell Connie about her own experiences in the house, which she had shared with two female roommates in the early 1990's. They had also noticed the problems with the lights, with doors that locked and unlocked and opened and closed and with the icy cold temperature of the spare room. The three women had never used the room either, mostly because of the odd drafts that seemed to blow through it. One night, one of her roommates had been awakened by a thumping sound and when she went to the door of her bedroom, she saw what appeared to be the shape of a person dart across the hallway. It seemed to come from the spare room, even though the door was locked at the time. Her frightened screams had disturbed the other occupants of the house but a search of the place revealed that everything was locked up tight and there was no one else there.

"The story that she had heard was that there was a woman who was murdered in the house back some time in the early 1900's. She was supposed to have been killed by her lover in that upstairs room," Connie explained. "After that, her ghost haunted the house."

"That was the story that she was told," Ron interjected, "but when we tried to find some record of it, we couldn't find anything. I think we both just figured that it was folklore about the house... or at least that's what we thought at the time."

In 1998, Ron left his former job and went into business for himself. He needed a home office and the only room available for it was the spare room, the scene of so many unusual incidents over the years. He was determined not to let these things bother him though and he began remodeling and painting the room to suit his needs. One of the first things that he decided to do was to remove the old carpet that was on the floor and to reveal the hardwood floors beneath it. When he tore up the dusty carpet pad, he got the surprise of his life!

"Right in the middle of the floor," he told me, "there were these dark, almost black stains. They were really just big smears and marks, except for two of them. Those two marks were the really clear handprints. All that I could think of was that it must have been blood. I could see where someone had tried to clean the floor in the past, but the stains were really soaked into the wood."

Connie spoke up. "I think it was at that point when we started to wonder if maybe the story about the woman being killed in the house was true," she said quietly. "Her ghost might certainly explain the bumps and noises and maybe even that weird perfume smell that we sometimes have."

"She doesn't seem to hurt anything though," Ron finished. "It's like she just wants us to know she's there."

GHOSTS OF THE CENTRAL WEST END

During the late 1800's, St. Louis was a bustling and spreading city that looked forward to wondrous events like the 1904 World's Fair and the glory days of the coming new century. The city had survived cholera epidemics, a disastrous fire and the horrific days of the Civil War. Things were changing and prospering in this "Gilded Age". St. Louis was the fourth largest city in the nation, new industry was arriving every week and even the newly established Forest Park was rivaling any like it in the larger eastern cities. Unexpectedly, the city had begun to spread to the west, rather than to the north and south along the Mississippi River. This unplanned outgrowth required the relocation of several cemeteries and the extension of the city limits, but St. Louis adapted, just as it always had.

The central corridor area west of Grand Avenue out to the city limits was simply known as the west end in those days and in the 1950's, became known as the Central West End. It was here, and in Vandeventer Place, that the opulent architecture of the times began to appear. Large, elegant homes and mansion were built along public and private streets and Lindell Boulevard began to boast both amazing homes and businesses. The thoroughfare became the most prominent of the broad avenues, lined with mansions, universities and clubs. It was well traveled by the increasing number of visitors to Forest Park and was also the scene of the first speeding tickets ever issued by the police department. Apparently, the broad, yellow gravel street was just too big a temptation to young men with fast horses and quick carriages.

In 1901, the street was improved and upgraded in preparation for the upcoming fair and during the event, Lindell, and the adjacent public and private streets gained international recognition from fair visitors. In 1903, a national magazine ranked this part of St. Louis as first-rate, stating that the houses were "veritable palaces in every particular richness, appointment and setting."

Lindell Boulevard had been named for Peter Lindell, an early businessman who made his fortune on the Ohio River and later in the real estate market in St. Louis. The small path that later became the busy street was likely claimed from the prairie by French colonials as they journeyed from town to Montaigne a Marie to drink, visit and relax. The spring, then owned by Alexis Marie, was located on land now bordered by Newstead, Lindell, Maryland and Euclid. None of these early colonists could have had any idea how important that dusty footpath would someday become.

In addition to all of the mansions and wonderful homes that appeared along Lindell Boulevard, it also played a large part in the social and fraternal building boom that hit St. Louis between the early 1890's and the middle 1920's. These organizations wanted to be located near the residences of their members and so many came to the West End. These included the Scottish Rite, the Moolah Temple of the Mystic Shrine, the Masonic Temple, the Medical Society, the St. Louis Club and the Columbian Club. The latter was the first of these massive buildings as the Columbian Club was completed in 1894. It was a huge building with banquet halls and ballrooms, theaters and even athletic facilities like a gym, swimming pool and four bowling alleys. This building was demolished back in 1975, but many of the others remain today.

Located near Lindell and scattered throughout the Central West End are the many private and public places where clusters of old homes stand proudly against the passage of time. In the middle 1800's, the land now occupied by Westmoreland and Portland Places was a dairy farm owned by the Cabanne family. In the early 1870's, the Cabanne's sold a portion of their land to William Griswold but in 1872 and 1874, part of his newly acquired land, as well as land belonging to others on the west side of the city, was selected as the site of a new park by the city. The landowners fought it, but in 1876, Forest Park was dedicated anyway.

Griswold was one of the few landowners who ended up making money from the forced deal with the city. He also owned land to the north of the new park and also owned the St. Louis

Transfer Company, which stood to make a fortune transporting visitors from the city to the new recreation area. In 1887, he was approached by a group of investors who wanted to buy 78 acres of his land to establish an exclusive residential area. These investors recognized that many of the private places that preceded them had been destroyed by the encroachment of the city. The park, they realized, would protect the southern flank of the enclave and would also stimulate positive residential real estate development for the remaining borders. Today, most of this area, now called Westmoreland Place, Portland Place and Forest Park Terrace, has survived. The area, like most of the Central West End, managed to get through the social and economic changes of the 1900's, especially the Great Depression, which ravaged other private places in the city. The lack of industrial development in the surrounding area has also helped and has given the Central West End a longevity that was not enjoyed by the earlier neighborhoods.

There are many fascinating stories to be told of this area and tales that tie in to both St. Louis and American history.

One of the grandest mansions ever built in St. Louis was constructed in Forest Park Terrace for Colonel Charles Spear Hills in 1899. Hills was a tobacco millionaire who was awarded the rank of brevet-colonel by Abraham Lincoln for gallantry during the Civil War. He moved to St. Louis and earned his fortune, first in wholesale grocery and then as the manager of the Daniel Catlin Tobacco Company.

His amazing house was built from brick and faced with Carthage marble. The exterior had three columned porticos on separate sides of the house. The main entrance featured a balcony over the doorway, oval-shaped first floor and attic windows and a low, flat roof that was covered in tile. The building was so magnificent that it truly looked like a landmark government building rather than a private home. Inside, each of the 15 rooms was paneled with a different type of imported wood and had a broad, central staircase made from bird's-eye maple. Further touches included art glass on the landing that was illuminated by electric light after dark and silver-plated bathroom fixtures. A luxurious ballroom occupied most of the third floor.

Hills passed away in 1902 and his death was attributed to poor health that had been caused by "a thrilling experience with robbers in Assyria" in 1879. He married twice but had no children and left his estate to his second wife. When she died in the late 1920's, the house was rented to an inventor named James J. Maccallum. He had patented a gas gauge that was supposed to provide him with a steady income and a substantial fortune, but hard times in the 1930's destroyed any chance of this. He and his wife became increasingly unhappy and eventually divorced. He moved out of the Hills mansion soon after and it was never occupied again. The house was demolished in 1939.

The mansions of Portland Place have had a much better survival rate than those of Westmoreland Place and thankfully, all but a few remain. One of those lost belonged to carpet millionaire Samuel M. Kennard. Born in Kentucky in 1844, Kennard ran away from home and joined the Confederate Army as a teenager. He fought in a number of battles and was later captured at Vicksburg by Grant's army. He was eventually paroled and moved to St. Louis after the war ended. He and his father soon founded J. Kennard & Sons, which was dubbed "the largest carpet house in the world."

In 1889, Kennard built a massive, limestone mansion in Portland Place. The house had steep gabled roofs and a rounded tower that was located to the right of the main entrance. The front door was graced with two large arches and another steep tower rounded out from another portion of the structure. The house had the look of a small castle and the interior design managed to stay in that theme. The entrance hall was huge, with a carved staircase and large arches at the landing. On the east side of the first floor was a drawing room and there was also a conservatory, or sun room, filled with plants and furniture. The second floor featured eight connecting bedrooms and three bathrooms, a great luxury for the time period.

In addition to his carpet company, Kennard was also the president of the St. Louis and Suburban Railway and the first president of the Autumnal Festivities, which became the Veiled Prophet Fair. He was also a trustee of Barnes Hospital, the Methodist Orphan's Home, Kingdom House and St. John's Methodist Church.

Kennard died in 1916 and his wife died in 1930. His children had fine homes elsewhere and so the Portland Place house stayed empty for the next 28 years. It was said that it was never sold because Kennard's sons could never bear to have anyone else living in it. One family member had a rather odd memory of going through the house near the time of its demolition and seeing that each of the rooms was "painted in a garish color, each stronger than the last." The house was eventually torn down in 1958, having been recognized as too large and too expensive to repair.

Interestingly, one former resident of this neighborhood recalled that the Kennard house was (in his words) "Portland Places' original haunted house". As a boy, he recalled stories being told about the empty house being haunted. Neighbors claimed that lights were often seen moving past the windows, when there was no one in the house and no electricity either. Local children also spoke of seeing the figure of a woman in the house on occasion. Could she have been Kennard's late wife? Or merely the imaginings that often surround the local abandoned house?

In addition to Portland and Westmoreland Places, there are a number of other private places in the Central West End, like Washington Terrace, Kingsbury Place, Fullterton Place and many others. However, there is no private place in this area with as ghostly a reputation as Hortense Place. This private enclave boasts three very different ghostly locations. One of these is the home that was once occupied by Elsa Lemp. It was in this house where she committed suicide in 1920 and it is also where her ghost reputedly still lingers today. Unfortunately, this "ghost story" remains merely a rumor as no witness has come forward to verify the tales that have been told for many years.

One of the other homes here was built in 1902 for Marion L.S. Lambert and a number of years later, it became the home of the late KMOX radio host Jack Carney. His son, John Carney, a wonderful on-air personality in his own right, told author Robbi Courtaway that while he actually grew up in San Francisco, he often spent the summers in this house. He moved to St. Louis when he was 13. One of the odd things that he remembered from when he was a boy was that they seemed to have a constantly changing household staff. The maids never seemed to stay very long, thanks to the odd noises in the house, the voices that were sometimes heard and the fact that the doorbell frequently rang when no one was at the door. Carney remembered that one summer they actually went through seven housekeepers!

Carney even had his own strange encounter in the house one early summer morning. Unable to sleep, he left his room and went out in the hallway toward his father's room. When he stepped into the dimly lit corridor, he noticed a flicker of movement that he first believed to be his imagination. When he turned to confront it though, he saw the brief movement had turned into the shape of a woman! She was moving down the hallway in an almost smoky haze. The woman never really took full form, but moved through the mass of white and blue mist, swirling and changing along with it. Finally, the specter vanished into the wall between his father's room and a guest room next door. Carney later admitted that while he was frightened by what he saw, he never felt that he was in danger from it.

When he told his father about the strange experience, they checked over some old blueprints of the house and discovered that the spot where the apparition had disappeared into the wall had once been the doorway to another bedroom!

Perhaps the most famous ghost of Hortense Place though is the small phantom that haunts that house that became known as "the Castle" many years ago. Hortense Place itself is actually dedicated to the memory of this young girl and it still bears her name today. She was devoutly loved by her father and when she died, he built a monument to memorialize her for all time.

Jacob Goldman was a German immigrant who was born in 1845 and came to America in the 1860's to make his fortune. He began in the cotton industry of Arkansas and New Orleans and eventually settled in St. Louis. He started the Lesser-Goldman Cotton Co. and it became one of the largest in the world at that time. He married and had four children and began to enjoy a prosperous and successful life. Unfortunately, fate had other plans for Jacob Goldman.

In 1894, Goldman's wife passed away, leaving him alone with the four children. To make matters worse, his favorite daughter, Hortense, died two years later in 1896. She was only a young girl at the time and Goldman was grief-stricken over the loss.

Before tragedy struck, the Goldman family had been living in the city, but Jacob wanted quite badly to move out to the west end, near Forest Park and into one of the new enclaves like Westmoreland Place. However, because he was Jewish, he was not accepted into any of the private neighborhoods, so he decided to build his own. He bought an entire tract of land between Kingshighway and Euclid and he named it Hortense Place, in honor of the daughter who had just died. He purchased a huge quantity of stone from Carthage, Missouri and set to work, completing a set of grand entrance gates in 1899. One year later, in 1900, he hired architect William Levy and began construction of his home from the same stone.

The house was one of the finest in the Central West End with a large, stone arch over the entry way, rounded towers and gabled roofs. The entry way and grand staircase were carved from oak and a stained glass window was added to the landing. The music room was of bird's-eye maple and boasted an intricately carved fireplace. The second floor had four huge bedrooms and the third floor was one of the largest ballrooms in the city at that time. Goldman spent more than $35,000 on the furnishings of the house and it was said that even those who had snubbed him socially when he wanted to moved into their private places were anxious to receive invitations to one of his lavish parties.

Goldman began to sell off the surrounding lots to influential and eminent residents of the city, including to Burt Walker, the great-grandfather of President George W. Bush. He had surrounded himself with opulence and society but no accounts exist to say whether or not he was happy in his new home. That part of the story, even after the death of his wife and daughter, seems to have been forgotten.

The Goldman's lived in the house until the 1930's and at that time, the Henry Miller family purchased it. They set about modernizing the place, as it was considered gloomy by 1930's standards. It would be during the ownership of the Miller family that the house was first considered to be haunted. The Miller servants were the first to speak of odd things going on.

Without ever realizing the sad history behind the house, they spoke of a ghostly little girl who could be heard calling near the staircase at night. Her mournful cries echoed through the landing and the entry way as she searched desperately for her father. Her voice was heard calling over and over again but there was no little girl to be found. Confused, one of the servants looked to see which one of Henry Miller's daughters needed assistance, but neither of the girls was home at the time. After this continued to occur, the servants began to realize that the house was haunted.

According to later accounts, Mr. Miller seemed to take these reports seriously, although whether he believed there was a ghost or whether he believed that someone had gotten into the house to try and scare the family is unknown. What is for sure is that on Halloween night, he hired an armed guard to patrol the house!

After the Miller's moved out, the Castle fell on hard times. Through the 1940's and 1950's, it mostly sat forlorn and abandoned, save for incursions by vandals, who broke in and stole the chandeliers and the fireplace mantels. The yard became overgrown and the house itself crumbled into disrepair. It saw occupancy again for a brief time in the 1960's when an artist tried to turn it into a rooming house, but that didn't last for long.

In 1971, Barry Alexander purchased the house and while he saved the house by restoring and renovating, he didn't do much to preserve the original look of the place. For instance, he raised the floor in the front parlor and covered it with brown shag carpeting to create a "conversation pit". He also put in a Spanish style kitchen, which, while great in the "swinging" 1970's, didn't do much for the architectural integrity of the grand Victorian mansion.

In the 1980's, the house was sold again and this time the owners made a concerted effort to renovate the mansion back to its former glory days. They restored much of the earlier woodwork and design, like the stained glass and the hand-stenciled border in the library. Not surprisingly, restoring the house back to its heyday seemed to bring back the ghost.

One night, the owners had house guests from out of town who arrived very late in the evening. There hardly time for more than a few words of conversation before they went right to bed. The guests had been sleeping for some time when they were awakened by a voice outside of their room, coming from the direction of the main staircase. It seemed to be a little girl who was calling for her father. Assuming that their hosts would take care of the child's needs, the guests turned over and went back to sleep. Oddly, the incident came up as a topic at breakfast the next morning when one of the guests remarked that they were not aware that the hosts had any children, let alone a little girl who might be calling for her father in the middle of the night.

As the reader might have guessed already, the hosts had no children!

While Lindell Boulevard and the private places of the Central West End have long been known for their fine mansions, these are not the only locations where grand homes can be found. Many of the public streets in this area have their share as well.

In 1876, Baker Avenue was a wide and easily traveled road that ran from the city to Forest Park, passing through a wooded area where few homes were located. In the 1890's, the name of the street was changed to West Pine Boulevard and as the city moved westward, many wealthy residents chose to build homes here, away from the clutter and decay of the city. The houses were large and comfortable, although mostly not as grand as those that could be found in the nearby private places. A handful of them though, like the mansion built for newspaperman Daniel Houser, could easily stand alongside the most extravagant homes in the secluded enclaves.

The Houser mansion was built in 1893 and sprawled out over 30 rooms. It boasted 11 fireplaces and a wedding or holiday capacity of 250 guests. Of course, this space was well used as Houser married twice and have seven children. The main entrance of the house was located beneath two curved archways and it rose to a looming two stories with a gabled attic. There was a rounded tower at the east end of the house, nestled next to a window-lined conservatory. The main door opened into an entry hall with shoulder-high mahogany paneling and led to a broad staircase with a large newel post and carved banisters.

There was a huge kitchen with a massive cooking range and a breakfast room that held a large table, 12 chairs and a large oak sideboard. The second floor had seven bedrooms, six bathrooms, six fireplaces and a full library. Eerily, one of the upper floor bedrooms was decorated completely in gargoyles.

The Houser's lived in grand style in the West Pine mansion, but rarely found happiness there. A series of tragic deaths and illnesses rocked the family, including one son who was forced to move to Arizona with his health destroyed, the suicide of another son's wife and a third son that died of typhoid fever in the mansion. According to legend, his spirit never left the house....

In 1916, the Houser family sold the house to Mrs. and Mrs. Alan Baker, who moved in with their huge family. At one point, the mansion was home to four generations of the family at the same time. During World War II, they also moved their rather large menagerie of animals into the house and around the property. The horses and some of the other animals were brought into the city from the Baker's farm. Gas rationing during the war made it impossible for the family to get back and forth to their country property.

The horses, which were stabled in the old carriage house, were walked in the alleyway behind the house and exercised in the nearby city streets. Among the farm animals brought into the city was a goat that the family called "Tony". One day, the goat disappeared and Mrs. Baker was so worried that she called the police. A short time later, police officers called back to say that they had located Tony. He had managed to climb the fire escape of the Kingsway/Ambassador Hotel, then located at Kingshighway and West Pine, and a female guest had called the hotel office to complain that "an ugly old man with a filthy beard" was peeping into her bedroom window. When the woman screamed, Tony ran away and then boarded a streetcar, from which the driver soon ejected him. Even though he broke his leg when he was tossed from the streetcar, the goat was soon returned home and he never roamed again.

The Baker's and their extended family were the only owners of the house besides the Houser's and consequently, the only residents to allegedly encounter the resident ghost. For a number of years, this restless phantom (presumably that of the young man who died from typhoid fever) was believed to roam the house, sometimes appearing on the grand staircase, in the upstairs hallway, his former bedroom and most often in the spooky basement of the house.

The family remained in the house until 1963, when the mansion had to be sold to pay inheritance taxes. The new owners bought the house in order to demolish it and to make room for a parking lot. The Baker clan moved out of the place on the same day the salvage and wrecking crew arrived. As the bulldozers and trucks pulled up, the family sat down on the front steps and offered a toast to their years of happiness in the house and to a lonesome ghost who would soon have nowhere to live.

Which poses an interesting question to ponder.. just where do the ghosts go when the wrecking ball comes for the house they inhabit?

As readers of this book have undoubtedly already realized from the preceding pages, I have a tendency to focus the majority of my tales of St. Louis' historical and haunted houses on residences that no longer exist. This is unfortunately a shortcoming of mine that can be directly connected to my fascination with old homes and vanished architecture. I have always been steadfastly opposed to the "progress by destruction" plan of urban development. For this reason, I have always liked to look at our history through the things that we have lost. They may be gone, I have always believed, but they are not forgotten.

I mention this because I don't want the reader to fall under the impression that every haunted house in the Central West End has fallen prey to the demolition crew. In fact, this is far from the case. There are undoubtedly many haunted houses here that I am not aware of, as well as houses about which only isolated tales have been told. There are other houses though that have been haunted for years... and remain quite haunted today.

One such house is located just blocks off of Kingshighway and along a quiet street that the present owners of the house asked not be identified. Their names have been changed in the story that follows but the strange things that occurred have not been altered in any way.

The Tucker family moved into the house in 1986, delighted with the Victorian era mansion that had been constructed in 1901. The rambling house was built of brick and stone and boasted a wide front entrance, graced with an elaborate arch and a large round window to the right of the carved wooden door. The aging mansion boasted 22 rooms and the Tucker's made good use of them with their six children and Janet Tucker's mother, who often stayed with them during the summer months.

The neighbor children wasted no time in informing the Tucker kids about the legends of the house. According to their stories, the house was haunted by a woman who had died there many years before. A wealthy physician had originally built the house and the story had it that the woman had been a patient who had come to him for help one night. The doctor and his family were seated to dinner when one of the housekeepers came in to explain that a caller had come to the back door. She was the niece of one of the servants and she was badly ill. The doctor, being a kind and compassionate man, left his dinner and went to the kitchen to check on the young girl. Legend has it that the girl was burning with fever and deathly ill from the flu. The doctor had her put to bed in one of the guest rooms but she didn't live through the night. She died before morning and the doctor's wife was so upset over what happened that the family paid for the young woman's funeral.

She died in the house but she never left it. In the years that followed, the doctor's family, as well as two other families who had also lived in the mansion, claimed to see the ghost of the young woman in the guest room where she died and in the downstairs kitchen. On some nights, there would come a knocking on the back door but when it was opened, there would be no one there. They also said that they heard footsteps that would pace back and forth in the guest room, echoes of the past from when the worried maid watched over her dying relative.

David Tucker admitted to me that he naturally did not believe the stories that the children were told by the neighbors. "No one seemed to know what year this happened, or even what room this girl died in. Naturally, my wife and I were a little skeptical," he told me and then added with a grin, "but the kids swallowed it hook, line and sinker."

Before long, all of the children were talking of doors that opened and closed by themselves, eerie whispers, knocking sounds and finally, the apparition of a woman that appeared in the hallway. Even after this, Janet and David refused to believe any of it. They were convinced the "incidents" were nothing more than the overactive imaginations of their children, spooked by the house's ghost stories. It would not be until Janet's mother, Doris, had her own encounter that the Tucker's began to consider that there might be something to the stories after all.

One summer night, the family went downtown to attend the VP Fair (now called Fair St. Louis) and after the fireworks, they all returned home. Doris later recalled being very tired and going straight upstairs to bed. At some point, she believed around 2:00 am, she was awakened by the sound of someone coughing loudly in her room. Thinking that perhaps one of the children was sick and had come into her room by mistake, she switched on the bedside lamp. As the room flooded with light, she was startled (and perhaps even terrified) when she found herself staring into the face of a pale and ghastly-looking young woman!

"Janet's mom let out a scream that woke up everyone of us in the house," David Tucker told me.

Doris said that the girl was very thin and drawn. Her cheeks were sunken and there were dark circles around her eyes. She had pale yellow hair that was pulled back and yet loose enough that it fell around her face and over her ears. She was only there for a moment and then she was gone. Doris later recalled that the room seemed very cold when she woke up, which was odd considering that it was a warm night and she had gone to sleep with the window open. She had heard the stories that the children had been telling and she no longer had any doubts that the house was haunted!

"And she never slept in that room again," David said. "We had to move all of her stuff into another room and it was a long time before she came back that summer."

After that, even the ever-skeptical David Tucker had to admit that there might be something strange going on in the house. Even after all of these years, he has never seen anything like what Doris described but he did confess to me about an unsettling experience that occurred to him a few years ago.

"I was working late one night and came home after everyone else had gone to bed. I hadn't had anything to eat for dinner, so I decided to make myself a sandwich," he remembered.

Tucker managed to find some dinner leftovers in the refrigerator, along with some lunch meat and some bread, and put himself together a midnight snack. When he was finished, he closed the icebox door, turned off the kitchen light and went into the library to watch television while he ate. Just as he sat down and balanced his plate on the ottoman, he remembered that he had left his bottle of beer on the kitchen table. With a sigh, he climbed out of the chair and hurried down the corridor to the kitchen... where light spilled out of the room and onto the floor of the hallway. Even though he remembered turning the light off, it was back on again!

With a frown, David looked into the kitchen. He was sure that everyone else was in bed, but he still expected to see his wife or one of his children in the room. He glanced around but the room was empty. And not only had the lights been turned back on, but the door to the refrigerator was also standing wide open. "I may have forgotten to turn off the light," Tucker assured me, "but I knew for a fact that I had closed that door."

He shook his head with a smile. "I have to admit that I think we have a family ghost," he added, "but she is welcome to stay. There's more than enough room in that house for all of us!"

Another historic mansion of the Central West End once belonged to the most famous St. Louis citizen of the early 1900's. His name was David Rowland Francis and he was a millionaire before the age of 30. He originally built a home in Vandeventer Place, which was a fitting backdrop for a man who was elected mayor of the city in 1885. During the time he served in office, he convinced the city to buy the Chain of Rocks waterworks site and brought several major conventions and national recognition to St. Louis. In 1887, he hosted President and Mrs. Grover Cleveland in his Vandeventer Place home and one year later, he was elected governor of Missouri and left Vandeventer Place for good.

In 1893, Francis returned to St. Louis and bought a five-acre parcel of land that was bounded by Maryland, Newstead and Pershing Avenues. The site had been the location of the Coleman house since 1869. Francis engaged an architectural firm called Eames and Young to create a house that would be "the most beautiful in St. Louis". The architects retained only four rooms from the original house and created a large mansion with front columns that reminded many of the White

The David Francis Mansion

(Courtesy of Missouri Historical Society)

The squared-off building had a front portico with a pitched roof and side entrances with rounded roofs above them. While the house is gone now, the entrance gates to the residence still stand on Newstead Avenue, one block west of Lindell Boulevard and the St. Louis Cathedral.

The most unique additions to the interior of the house were the large reception hall with a central staircase that led to two balconies overlooking the hall, two living rooms, a double drawing room and a huge dining room. These areas were the scenes of numerous parties, galas and festivities, held by the Francis' for presidents, governors and even foreign dignitaries.

In 1896, Francis left St. Louis to serve the country as the Secretary of the Interior. During this time, he was responsible for adding millions of acres to the nation's forest reserves. He returned to St. Louis in 1897 and began to assemble the Louisiana Purchase Exposition Company, which would run the 1904 World's Fair. Part of his responsibilities during this time included serving as president of the 118-member board and convincing the government that St. Louis would be a better location for the fair than New Orleans. The financing that he arranged for the fair from city, state and national sources was about $15 million, the same amount that was paid to Napoleon for the entire Louisiana Territory!

He also traveled throughout Europe, visiting emperors, kings and presidents and convincing them to come and exhibit at the fair. Most of them came and those who did visited and spent time at the Francis home. According to accounts from the time, visitors to the house included many foreign officials, as well as three American presidents, Grove Cleveland, Theodore Roosevelt and William Howard Taft.

In 1916, Francis again left St. Louis for public service when President Woodrow Wilson appointed him ambassador to Russia. The Great War was being fought in Europe at the time and terrifying changes were coming to Imperial Russia. Francis arrived in Petrograd (formerly St. Petersburg, then Leningrad and now St. Petersburg again) when Tsar Nicholas II had only one turbulent year left in his reign. Francis carefully watched the events of the day as the nation unraveled and when the American embassy was besieged by a revolutionary mob, he held them off and managed to disperse the crowd with a shotgun and with the aid of only his valet! He warned Secretary of State Robert Lansing of the seriousness of the Russian situation, in terms of both war and revolution, but even he could not have guessed the bloody fate of the tsar and his family.

Tired and discouraged, Francis came back to St. Louis in 1918. He did not return to the mansion at Maryland and Newstead though, but rather took up residence in the St. Regis Apartments, then on Ellenwood Avenue. The mansion never had a full-time occupant again, although Francis often loaned it out for meetings of the Boy Scouts and the Junior Chamber of Commerce. The last major event to be held there was the funeral of David Francis in 1927.

In 1929, the St. Louis Board of Education voted to locate Central High School on the site, but the deal never went through. The house then decayed until 1936 when the Sisters of Mercy purchased the land. They built a "business women's home" (McCauley Hall) on the site and the Francis home was lost forever. Only the large gate that faces Newstead remains today, a sad reminder of another time and place and of the home of one of the city's most famous residents.

LAFAYETTE SQUARE

Throughout this chapter of the book (and elsewhere), much has been written of the lost history and destroyed buildings of St. Louis. It should be stressed again though that not all of the historic sites of the city have been lost. Many of the old and beautiful homes remain and in no place in the city is this more true than in the area known as Lafayette Square. The original houses here have survived time, natural disaster and neglect to make up one of the most wonderfully preserved parts of St. Louis.

And perhaps the longevity of the structures explains the fascinating concentration of ghosts that seem to exist here....

Lafayette Square had its beginnings far back in St. Louis history. In the early 1800's, when the city was still was still quite small and nestled alongside the Mississippi River, an area was set aside to the south of the settlement for the pasturing and herding of cattle. The commons were later to be converted into a neighborhood that would be designated as Lafayette Square. Housing lots around the commons were offered for sale to the public in 1835. Later, in order to attract buyers for the lots, an ordinance was passed that 30 acres of the land would be devoted to a park that would be bounded by 100-foot wide streets. The park, which was in time called Lafayette Park, would become the center of the grand and fashionable neighborhood that would spring up in this area before and after the Civil War.

The first lots were sold in the commons in 1836 and the buyers were mostly affluent residents who hoped to escape from the crowded conditions of the city proper. During the decade between 1840 and 1850, St. Louis grew enormously and consequently, the population of the Square increased as well. Construction was halted during the Civil War but in the decade that followed it, most of the houses facing Lafayette Park were constructed. In 1866, Montgomery Blair, who served as postmaster general under Abraham Lincoln, laid out Benton Place. It was named for famed politician Thomas Hart Benton and the section would become an integral part of the district's history.

In order to continue to enhance the desirability of the area, further improvements were made to Lafayette Park between 1865 and 1896. In 1868, a statue of Thomas Hart Benton, designed by Harriet Hosmer, was unveiled to a crowd of about 40,000 people and erected in the park. The next year, an ornate iron fence was built at great expense to surround the park and in 1870, gazebos, bandstands, a boathouse and an aquarium were added. When the Great Cyclone of 1896 struck the park, almost all of the foliage and buildings here were wiped out. The only exception was the statue of Thomas Hart Benton, which somehow withstood the storm.

As mentioned earlier in the book, the tornado had more of a tragic impact in Lafayette Square than in any other part of the city. The Great Cyclone of May 27, 1896 was a part of a deadly series of tornadoes that swept through Missouri and southern Illinois. It first struck St. Louis in the southwest part of the city and then ripped across Shaw's Gardens, devastating an area just south of Tower Grove and Vandeventer Avenues. The tornado then headed uphill toward Compton Heights. Nearly every house in this area lost its roof and in some neighborhoods, especially to the east toward Jefferson Avenue, houses were completely destroyed. Whole blocks of homes and buildings lost their upper floors and walls were ripped away and reduced to splinters.

Lafayette Square Area in the Early 1890s

(Courtesy Swekosky Collection / School Sisters of Notre Dame)

As it reached Jefferson Avenue, the neighborhood around Lafayette Park was laid waste. The park and square are located on the summit of a hill and that seemed to offer a particularly attractive target to the tornado. By the time the center of the storm was directly over Lafayette Avenue, the tail of it had begun to swing to the north. It swept past Grand Avenue and then descended onto Jefferson. It pushed up against the side of the hill, with the tail of the storm now swinging around toward Chouteau, and ripped a path along Jefferson Avenue from Chouteau to Russell. The tail of the storm continued to move from north to south, while the dense body of the tornado remained in the area, revolving in the direction of Geyer Avenue. All the while, the winds that accompanied it wreaked havoc on the homes and the neighborhoods in the path.

The tornado moved above the Scullin power plant and as it did, the tail of the cyclone came along, swept beneath it and ravaged the streetcars, men, machinery and buildings located here. Then, it swung toward the South Side racetrack and literally obliterated all trace of it. The storm them rolled on, flashing lightning in its belly, destroying more homes and then stripping Lafayette Park.

By the time that the storm reached Lafayette Square, its path had widened to nearly three-quarters of a mile. The Benton statue was the tallest thing remaining in the park as the trees around it were torn to pieces. Those not torn out by the roots were broken and splintered and stripped of their leaves and branches. The massive iron fence was flat on the ground and the horticulture wonder of the park had been turned into a wasteland. Obviously, the houses that surrounded the park and along the avenues where the private places were located fared no better. The mansions and churches here were unroofed and their walls demolished. Broken bits of wood, brick and stone were scattered in the streets and across lawns. Survivors wandered about the area in the aftermath of the storm, bemoaning the destruction of the once beautiful neighborhood.

Almost every home was damaged and many others were wrecked beyond repair. Accounts of the day listed the most tragic of the disasters. The Soderer House, located on the corner of Missouri and Park, was badly broken. The stable was simply a ruin and their horse and driver were buried under the rubble. Dr. Soderer's brother, Julius, who lived further down Park Avenue, had a "house not fit to live in". Two of the houses next to his, owned by his mother-in-law, were totally wrecked.

The Alexander Selkirk house was also destroyed and the family lost everything they owned.

The home belonging to cotton magnate Jerome Hill was nearly dismantled. Great gaps had been ripped throughout the house, the roof was gone and the glass had been blown out of the windows.

John Endres, who lived next door to Hill, ended up with his home devastated but according to a contemporary account, he "good-naturedly said that he was only glad that nobody in the house was hurt." As he directed the removal of belongings from the house, he took the time to spread a luncheon on the parlor mantle, along with some bottles of wine that had been salvaged from the cellar. He insisted that everyone in the house sit down and eat before his daughters were sent off to stay with their grandmother. Endres spent the night on the floor of the Carr residence next door and got up every half-hour to go and make sure that the remains of the house were undisturbed. The accounts went on to say that "Mr. Endres' courage and philosophy over his loss did much to inspire his neighbors with the same sort of feelings."

Next door to Endres was the home of Mrs. James Carr, the widow of Judge Carr. She and her children resided in what turned out to be the least damaged home on that side of the street. The structure had been relatively untouched, although not a single pane of glass remained in it. Her sons spent most of the night after the storm replacing windows and helping Endres restore some amount of order to the immediate neighborhood. In addition to Endres, Mrs. Carr also housed other homeless people from around the Square and nursed those who were injured or cut and bleeding from flying debris. Fortunately, the entire family escaped from the disaster unscathed, although Mrs. Carr's daughters were almost not so lucky. The young women had just returned from a wedding at a nearby church. The guests had barely left the church when the roof blew off, sending everyone running for their lives. The Carr's sought refuge from the storm in a cellar "between two large brick piers", which swayed and rocked but didn't give away.

One of the most horrifying stories of the neighborhood came from the John Bene home, located just off Park Avenue, where the house was first wrecked and then burned. Mrs. Bene and her two children, ages five and two, were buried under the debris from the residence and the youngest child actually burned to death in the fire that followed. The older child was also badly burned but rescuers managed to dig him out from beneath the rubble before the fire could claim him. Mrs. Bene had been pinned beneath several heavy timbers but she refused to be removed until those who came to her assistance had saved her children first. When she was finally taken out, she was found to have been badly burned about the legs, hips and feet. She had been struck in the head by falling bricks and wood and when she learned of the fate of her youngest child, she fainted dead away.

In the end, the murderous storm lasted less than a half-hour and yet it created such destruction that its repercussions would last for years. After the tragedy was over, many of the homeowners here fled to the Central West End. It took until the early 1900's for the Square to recover from both the cyclone and the abandonment by so many of the residents, but the recovery would be a brief one. By the 1920's, the area had lost its fashionable image and it became apartments and boarding houses for the working class. The decline continued through the Great Depression and World War II and the once stately houses became residences for the impoverished. Lafayette Square became a crime-riddled ghetto and the once elegant neighborhood simply began to be called "Slum D".

All of that slowly began to change in 1945 when architect and historian John Albury Bryan purchased the house at #21 Benton Place. He renovated the house and then began a fierce, and at first quite lonely, battle to take back and restore Lafayette Square. Through the 1960's and 1970's, things started to happen, first at a tedious snail's pace and then much faster. Little by little, brave people began moving into the neighborhood and they organized the Lafayette Restoration Committee. A campaign was launched to restore the area and to bring Lafayette Square back to its former glory.

And undoubtedly, their efforts have been successful. To visit Lafayette Square today is to take a trip back in time and to recapture a bit of an era that has long been forgotten. If you get a chance, take a short trip to this area some day and take a stroll around Lafayette Park and past the mansions and homes that have been so gloriously restored.

Who knows? You might get the chance to meet one of the former residents face to face!

Ghost stories have long been a part of the history of the Lafayette Square neighborhood. There are a number of houses here that boast otherworldly dwellers. Some of them are well-known, while others are seldom spoken of, even in a whisper. Here is a sampling of such tales but I warn you, there are many more that are unrecorded from where these came from!

Marie and Michael Davies are the owners of an unusual house that is located in Benton Place. The 1893 mansion is today the Lehmann House Bed & Breakfast, but it started out as the home of wealthy businessman Edward Rowse. Unfortunately though, Rowse was only able to enjoy his opulent home for a short time. He died within a year of it being completed from what was believed to be stomach cancer. This would not be the new home's only taste of tragedy either, for also within that same year, both the architect and the construction foreman of the house also died.

Despite this unnerving beginning, later occupants of the house enjoyed many happy years here. The current bed and breakfast was named in honor of Frederick and Nora Lehmann, who owned the house from 1899 to the 1930's. Lehmann was a well-known attorney and during the time he lived here with his wife, they played host to three presidents and a many other notable guests. During the years of Lafayette Square's decline, the mansion was used as a boarding house from 1941 to 1968. The Davies family purchased it in 1992 and began a lengthy restoration that ended with the opening of the inn.

The ghostly activity that has come to be associated with the house is mainly centered around the bedroom that is located directly above the dining room. It was here that Edward Rowse died back in 1894. However, other activity has been reported in other spots in the house as well and as with many older homes, it seems to be more prevalent during times of renovation or remodeling. The owners have stated that the ghost seems to be much quieter when nothing is going on. The odd happenings usually seem to be footsteps that are heard from the floor below, even when the upstairs is empty, the sounds of something rolling across the floor and crashing noises in an upstairs room that is normally kept locked. And on at least a couple of occasions, Mr. and Mrs. Davies have seen the ghost of Edward Rowse himself!

Marie Davies stated that she has been in bed at night and has felt the presence of someone else in the room with her. One night, she awakened from a sound sleep to see a man standing at the end of the bed. In the gloom, she was able to recognize Rowse from a photograph that she had seen of him. Of course, she had never expected to actually see him in person! On another occasion, she saw Rowse and his wife, Anne Eliza, standing at the end of the bed.

In spite of the sometimes spine-tingling experiences though, the Davies' don't seem upset about having the spirits of the former owners still hanging around the place. Everyone is welcome here, guests and ghosts alike!

One location that is no longer haunted today, but was very unnerving when it was first restored back in the 1970's, is a former apartment house that is located directly on the site of the stables that once belonged to Alois Soderer. In the earlier account of the Great Cyclone of 1896, readers will remember that the destruction of the stables took the life of the driver that was employed by the family. The coachman's name was William Taylor and he had been with the family for many years. As the storm approached, Taylor had gathered in the basement of the Soderer home with the family but over the sound of the wind and the house ripping itself apart, he heard the cries of the family's horse, Bess. She had been left out in the stable and it was said that he was passionately devoted to the animal.

Even though the Soderer's urged him to stay, Taylor ran outside and to the stable. He arrived just as the storm was reaching its peak, but he was unable to free the horse in time. The roof of the building collapsed, killing both the coachman and the horse.

Year later, the foundation of the stable was used to construct an apartment building on the site, which later became a rooming house. And while there were rumors of a murder that took place in the building at one point in its history, it seems to have been the storm of 1896 that left the greatest ghostly impression on the place. Shortly after the building was restored in the early 1970's, residents began to complain about eerie sound that they heard around it. Many of them were unnerved and frightened about living here, especially during thunderstorms, when they would claim to hear the sound of a horse crying and hooves beating on the pavement outside.

Wild imaginations or some imprint of time from the past? It's impossible to say, but according to residents today, the house is no longer haunted. Whatever odd happenings may have occurred here no longer seem to trouble the residents of the three condominiums that now rest here. Perhaps the haunting from the past merely faded away....

Another house on Lafayette Square is also haunted by remnants of the past. The owners here moved into the place in the early 1990's and began renovations that continued until the time they moved out in six years later. During this period of remodeling, they experienced a number of frightening events that most likely played a part in their decision to move to St. Charles, Missouri a few years later. And while they can look back on these events with less trepidation today, they certainly seemed scary to them at the time!

Bob and Linda Smith (names have been changed to protect their privacy) moved into the historic home in 1993, excited at the prospect of bringing the old place back to its former glory. The house had been built in 1895 and was rather simple in comparison when compared to some of the mansions located nearby. It was three stories tall and constructed with brick, with a gabled roof and a front entrance at the lower right corner of the house. Not long after moving in and starting work on the place, the first of the eerie incidents took place.

Early one morning, Bob was working in the downstairs portion of the house, repairing a portion of the floor that has been damaged by the neglect of past residents. As he was working, he heard the sounds of someone walking down the upstairs hallway. The footsteps walked from where Bob knew was the top of the staircase, down a short hallway and into a bedroom at the back of the house. He knew that Linda was not there, and his brother-in-law, who often helped at the house, had not yet arrived. He could only assume that an intruder had broken into the house and was now upstairs!

Cautiously, he removed a hammer from his toolbox and went up the stairs. He could still hear the heavy-soled footsteps as they paced down the hall and then walked back and forth in the bedroom, even over the creak of his own feet on the steps. As he reached the top of the staircase, he nervously peered down the hall, but he saw no one. This meant that the intruder could only be in the bedroom, but Bob couldn't see inside of the room because the door had been shut! He rounded the corner around the stair post and crept down the hall. His knuckles had turned white as he was gripping the hammer so tightly. He reached out and turned the knob on the bedroom door and then quickly slammed it open! The sound of the door hitting the wall behind it was almost deafening in the silent room and even though Bob had clearly heard the sound of someone walking in the room just moments before... it was now totally empty! There was no one there!

Perplexed, Bob went into the room and looked around. He even went to the narrow closet and opened it to see if anyone was inside, but it too was empty. As he stood there scratching his head, he looked down and noticed something peculiar on the floor. In the thick dust that had gathered from years of the house being empty, and from the work being done by the Smith's, Bob could clearly see the footprints of his shoes... but only his shoes and only one set of prints! Where were the footprints of the man who had been walking around up here? Bob looked back out in the hallway and saw that only a single line of footprints made a path from the staircase to the bedroom and they were his own!

With that, he made a hasty retreat to the lower floor and waited for his brother-in-law to arrive before getting back to work again.

And this would not be the last time the phantom boots would march through the house. On another occasion during the renovations, the footsteps upstairs were so heavy that they caused a trickle of dust to fall through a part of the ceiling Linda's brother was repairing. A quick search of the upper floor once again revealed that the house was empty though. After the Smith's took up residence in the house, the footsteps continued to be heard in the hallway and in that same bedroom. No identity was ever found for the phantom intruder, although Linda started referring to him as "Doc Martin", thanks to the weighty tread of his boots.

Readers might come to think that because the Smith's nicknamed the ghost that they found his antics humorous, but this couldn't be further from the truth. While the ghostly footsteps, and later the doors that opened and closed and lights that turned on and off, were relatively harmless, Bob and Linda were genuinely terrified by what was happening. They didn't see the events as charming in the least, but rather chilling and a sure sign that something "evil" was in the house. Based on their accounts, I wouldn't be quick to agree with this, but regardless, they were quite frightened by what was going on. If it had happened more often than it did, I am sure that their residency in the house would have been considerably shorter than it was.

In 1995, the Smith's were re-plastering a wall in what was to be the dining room of the house and they discovered five playing cards and several pieces of old paper money inside of the wall. The money was all dated from the 1930's and the cards appeared to be quite old and were brittle with age. A further check in that section of the wall also revealed a number of yellowed newspapers (which crumbled when handled) and a pocket watch on a chain. No explanation was ever discovered as to why these items were found in the wall or who they might have belonged to, but the Smith's later told me that their discovery set off a new round of weird happenings in the house.

The phantom footsteps on the second floor began to increase in frequency and one night, they marched up and down the hallway as many as seven times. On another night, they were awakened in the early morning hours by the slamming of the bedroom door at the end of the hall (which had been turned into a guest room) and then footsteps that ran down the corridor and descended the steps. Even though he had heard the ghostly sounds on many occasions before this, they seemed so real this time that Bob sprang out of bed, absolutely convinced that a flesh and blood burglar had broken into the place. He made it to the bedroom door, he recalled, before the footsteps had even reached the bottom of the stairs. He followed the sounds to the first floor and just as he reached the lower landing, he heard the front door slam so hard that it seemed to shake the whole building. Bob ran through the darkened house, sure that he was on the heels of the intruder, only to collide with the still-locked front door! He was sure that it had just been slammed, but according to the fact that it was locked, it had never even been opened! He turned the lock anyway and ran outside, only to find that the street and the area around the house was completely empty.

In the years that followed, the strange events declined in frequency but never really stopped. Eventually, the Smith's had gotten more than their fill of the house and moved to St. Charles, where they have since renovated another old home, which is completely free of ghosts! And as for the house in Lafayette Square, it seems to be ghost-free as well these days. In the course of researching book, I contacted the current owners of the house by mail and they were kind enough to telephone and assure me that nothing strange had occurred during the two years they had been living in the house.

They weren't surprised to hear about the ghost though, they told me, as they had heard many such stories since moving to the neighborhood. "Many of the houses here were apparently what you might call 'haunted' at one time," said the owner. "The ghostly stuff all started when the houses were first being rehabbed but most of them seem to wear down after awhile. Before long, your haunted house isn't haunted anymore. Maybe that's what happened in this place."

OTHER HAUNTED HOUSES

There are two other legendary haunted houses of St. Louis that should be mentioned in this chapter, the former St. Louis Museum of Science and Natural History that was once located in Clayton and the Bissell Mansion, located in the city's Hyde Park neighborhood.

The old mansion that once housed the museum and is now owned by the city of Clayton was (along with another home) formerly a part of the Charles Rise and Alvin Goldman estates. The area was established back in 1913 and in those days, was out in the country and far from the lights of St. Louis. There are varying stories as to how the museum house became haunted but all of the stories date back to the days when the area was a functioning estate. According to one version of the tale, a husband shot and killed his wife in the third floor bathroom of the house. A newspaper report from 1975 stated that the man had been a chauffer at the estate and had accidentally shot his wife while she was taking a bath. A similar version of the tale states that the accidental killer was a houseguest at the estate. He was shooting crows on the grounds one day and one of his bullets hit a tree limb, ricocheted and went through the third floor bathroom window. A woman who was taking a bath was stuck and killed by the bullet. There are apparently no police records about the incident because the estate was in an unincorporated area at the time.

Regardless of how exactly the murder happened, the end result was the same in that the mansion became haunted. After the woman's death, footsteps, crashes and thuds began to be heard on the third floor, lights would turn on an off by themselves and the toilet in that room would inexplicably flush when no one was around. On one occasion, a housekeeper at the estate was frightened one evening by a woman's piercing scream. And she was not the only one who heard it. Another staff member was reportedly so scared by the sound that she did not return to work for nearly a week!

In 1959, the house was turned into the Science and Natural History Museum (which moved to new quarters in 1985) and the grounds became Clayton's Oak Knoll Park. Soon after, during the remodeling work that was going on, workers would arrive early in the morning to discover that a light was always burning on the third floor. When they approached what they believed to be an unoccupied building, the light would suddenly turn off. They would then search the house, only to discover that no one was there.

Staff members and volunteers at the house began to have their own odd encounters. Two employees were shocked to see a dumbwaiter, left over from the old mansion, suddenly take off and start operating by itself. Others reported being touched on the back of the neck, feeling cool breath on their face and hearing phantom footsteps prowling through the house. One of the museum's original volunteers was a retired military officer who took no stock in his fellow volunteer's stories of the supernatural. Early one Saturday morning, before anyone else arrived, he was in the house alone and was startled to hear someone walking across the unoccupied second floor. Sure that someone had entered the museum without authorization, he hurried upstairs to catch them. What followed was a ghostly chase throughout the building! No matter where he went he never seemed to be able to get closer to the quickly moving intruder. By the time that he stopped, exhausted from having run up and down stairs and through the corridors, he reluctantly admitted that the house might be haunted after all!

In the Hyde Park neighborhood of north St. Louis stands the elegant and well-preserved Bissell Mansion. Located along Randall Place, the house is the oldest surviving brick residence in

St. Louis, even though it was far out in the countryside when Captain Lewis Bissell built it back in 1823. The stories say that Bissell was very proud of his towering mansion and in fact, so proud that he continues to watch over it today.

The Bissell Mansion in the 1940s (Courtesy of Missouri Historical Society)

Used as a private residence for years, the home was located in the center of a 2,000 acre farm. The land around it dwindled over time and today it is surrounded by homes and apartments and is used as a restaurant and a dinner theater. The second floor of the mansion, which is used for overflow dining and for private parties is said to be the most haunted portion of the house.

Unexplained noises are frequently heard in the mansion and it has long been home to ghosts, according to a former owner who was the last to live in the house before it was turned into a restaurant. This older woman stated that she was constantly in touch with many spirits here, most of which were her children who had died years before. Current employees wonder if there may be some truth to the woman's tales because around holidays, and especially Christmas Eve, the sounds of children laughing, running and playing can he heard echoing throughout the house! And some ghosts here are seen rather than heard. For instance, Captain Bissell's ghost has been seen frequently over the years, standing and staring at the house from what is now the parking lot. In addition, a waiter once had a ghostly encounter with a woman in white one night on the second floor. He was entering the upstairs room when he glanced up and saw a woman in a long, flowing gown in the center of the room. He later told other staff members that he was frightened at first and then a feeling of calm came over him. The woman then turned and left the room, taking a moment to smile back at him over her shoulder as she departed!

In 1986, the dinner theater was started at the restaurant and employees began to notice that other odd things were taking place. The manager at that time began to realize that each night after a performance, wine glasses were vanishing from the racks. She would find a different number each night and occasionally that number would change from week to week. Several might be missing one night and then the next night, the entire rack might be full! She investigated to see if another staff member might be playing a trick on her, but she was the first and last person to see the glasses each day and she began to wonder if it were the ghosts who were playing tricks on her and not those who were still among the living!

THE HOUSE ON PLANT AVENUE

Aside from the Lemp Mansion, there is probably no haunted house in St. Louis as famous as that of the former Henry Gehm house in Webster Groves. This private residence is located along the 300 block of Plant Avenue, a quiet suburban street where nothing much out of the ordinary happens. If you were driving along this street, with no hint of the history of the homes here, it is unlikely that you would imagine any of them to be haunted. You would mainly find large old bungalows with neat yards and carefully trimmed shrubbery.

One of the houses though hides a secret. It is a place with a strange past, although on the outside, it looks no different from the others on the street. It is made from brick and wood and it possesses no unique style to set it apart from the others. It is simply a house, with a large yard that sets it back from the street and a short staircase that leads into the front door. Like many of the other houses on the street, it has a large living room and a kitchen with a door that exits into the backyard. From the living room, there is a winding set of steps that ascends to the second floor, where the bedrooms are located.

It is a house and in most ways, it is simply a house like all of the others on Plant Avenue. There is one difference however, this house is haunted.

Bart Adams originally built the house on Plant Avenue as a summer retreat in 1890. As mentioned though, it is best remembered as belonging to its second occupant, a slightly eccentric man named Henry Gehm, who resided in the house from 1906 to 1944. Gehm was involved in the railroad car business and his company was actually responsible for building the first gondola car. He also leased many of his cars to traveling circuses, which all journeyed by rail in the early 1900's. Because of his connections to the circus folk, many have come to believe over the years that Gehm was somehow involved with that business, but this is apparently inaccurate. It is also not true that Henry Gehm died in the house on Plant Avenue. Despite tales to the contrary, he died an excruciating death from cancer of the spine and passed away in a hospital.

There is a part of the legend of the house (the importance of which will be apparent later in our study) that was true though and it was that Gehm did hide gold coins in various places around the property. He was said to have often dealt in gold coins and because of the bank failures during the Depression, he preferred to keep his valuables at home. This story about Henry Gehm was told and re-told so many times over the years that even the current owners have been plagued by visitors to their home who ask to look for "buried treasure".

But what of the ghosts? And how did this come to be considered such a haunted house?

The ghostly tales that have made this house famous have their beginnings in 1956, when the S.L. Furry family purchased the house. It was Fannie Furry who first noticed some of the peculiarities about the new house. It started quite suddenly and eerily as Mrs. Furry began to be awakened each night, literally shaken awake by unseen hands, at precisely 2:00 in the morning. On one occasion, she clearly heard a hammering sound on the headboard of the bed that was so loud that when she turned on the light, she expected to see that it had been broken and splintered into pieces. However, it looked as though it had never been touched. Soon this strange sound, as well as the shaking, was joined by the sound of something beating against the windows as night. She could find nothing that could be causing the noises.

One morning, she came downstairs to find that a heavy light sconce that had been attached to the wall was now mysteriously lying on the floor. This seemed impossible, as it had been securely attached to the wall the night before, but she could find no reason that it had fallen. Her two young daughters were much too small to have removed it and it was certain that her husband would have mentioned it if he had done it.

These strange incidents were followed by the sounds of footsteps that paced up and down the stairs, day and night, as if someone were looking for something and could not find it. The footsteps always ended on the upstairs landing. Fannie would have assumed that the sounds were nothing more than her imagination if she had not experienced the other bizarre happenings.

At first, she hesitated to mention any of these things to her husband. Mr. Furry was a practical man with no interest in anything that smacked of the occult. He soon noticed how upset she was though and questioned her as to what was bothering her. When she finally explained, he scoffed at her concerns and told her simply that he had experienced nothing to disturb his sleep. He had heard no phantom footsteps on the stairs. He advised her to ignore the problem and it would surely go away.

That was what he told her in the evening but at the breakfast table the following morning, he had a change of heart. He sheepishly told her that he too had heard some strange noises. "Of course, there must be a logical explanation," he told her and then added that old houses make all sorts of noise. And while he seemed satisfied with that explanation, Fannie was most assuredly not happy about it. She still heard the searching, scurrying noises on the staircase and they certainly did not sound like noises caused by the house settling to her.

Eventually though, Furry did not continue to insist on his convenient explanation. He had a change of heart one night when he was awakened in the night and saw a wispy, white shape that passed directly through the door to the hallway and vanished into one of his daughter's rooms. He jumped out of bed and peered into the dark bedroom but he could see nothing. He tried to tell himself that it had been the reflection of headlights from a car that passed by the house but when a vehicle drove down the street, and the strange light did not re-appear, he was no longer so sure.

The years passed and the Furry's managed to get used to the strangeness of the house. Too much work, money and care had gone into the place for them to simply give it up and they were reluctant to admit that they could be chased out by a ghost. A wave of shock must have passed through the parents though when their three year-old daughter suddenly spoke up with a chilling question one morning at breakfast. "Who is the lady in black who comes into my room at night?" she asked them.

Her mother demanded to know what lady she was talking about, as they had received no visitors, and the little girl replied that she was an old lady in a black dress who led a little boy with her by the hand. A little later, she began to speak about the lady in black again. She told her mother that the lady would sometimes spank her with a broom, "but it doesn't hurt".

As any parent would be, Mrs. Furry was upset by these new and startling revelations. After nine years of residing on Plant Avenue, the Furry's found another house and moved. The house was once again for sale but it didn't remain empty for long.

In November 1965, the Walsh family rented the house and moved in with two of their three children, ten year-old Wendy and 20 year-old Sandy. They had not been told anything about the house by the previous residents and noticed nothing about it that was out of the ordinary... at least at first.

A short time after moving in, Clare Walsh was preparing dinner one night in the kitchen. She was alone in the room except for the family dog, who suddenly began to behave very strangely. She glanced over to see the animal cowering and shaking with fear. Disturbed, she tried to see what was causing the animal to behave in such a way and that's when she saw the image in the doorway. It was white and hazy and roughly the same shape and size as a person. It shimmered into the living room, wavered for a second and then vanished. She was immediately convinced that she had seen a ghost!

Unlike most people, she was not frightened. More than a decade later, she would write: "I have a master's degree in science and am not inclined to believe things without proof. All I can be sure of is that there was something in that house besides our family... from the moment that I walked into that empty house I felt that it was not empty."

After a little time passed, Clare put the apparition in the kitchen out of her mind, especially after nothing similar happened in the days that followed. She couldn't forget about the weird sounds that seemed to roam the house at night though, or the unmistakable presence that she felt in the house with her. After one more night of footsteps roaming up and down the stairs, she became determined to find out about the background of the house.

She broached the subject with a neighbor couple over dinner in February 1966. She casually asked them if anyone in the past had ever mentioned anything odd about the place. When questioned herself, she confessed the weird things that had been happening, including the footsteps that wandered through the house. It's almost like they are searching for something, she added.

The neighbors, Mr. and Mrs. Kuru nodded in understanding. They told Clare that they had almost bought the house she was living in a couple of years before but the man who lived across the street had talked them out of it. He had once been a frequent guest in the home and had been there often enough to come to believe the house was haunted. The Kuru's then decided to buy the house next door instead.

Clare continued her investigation by talking with the man across the street. He had his own ideas about what was going on there. He explained that a past owner of the house had hidden valuables in a number of places all over the house. He was convinced that the man's ghost had come back and was now searching for the treasure.

Clare began watching for out of the ordinary things to happen in the house and she remembered that the attic door refused to stay closed. She began searching the area and discovered that the stairs to the attic had a step whose tread would lift off, revealing a hiding place beneath it. Perhaps the stories of secret hiding places and treasure were true?

In the days and weeks to come, Clare kept a careful eye on the attic door. On one occasion, Mr. Walsh came down with the flu and slept in a separate bedroom from his wife. While Clare was resting, she heard the attic door open and close four times during the night. She believed that it was her husband rising from his sickbed, mistakenly thinking that the door she heard was the spare bedroom rather than the attic. She discovered the next morning however that her husband had only gotten up once!

More time passed and Mrs. Walsh, her husband and her children continued to hear footsteps and the door to the attic creaking open. Once she realized that the empty hiding place was there, Clare began to realize that the steps on the stairs paused at that tread each time. The following morning, the attic door, which had been securely closed the night before, was standing wide open.

One morning, Clare went up to the attic and closed the door again, then continued preparing breakfast in the kitchen. For some reason though, she had the urge to return to the attic again. She found the door once again standing open and she stepped into the room that they had always just used for storage. The last time that she had seen it, everything had been carefully arranged, but on this morning, Clare was startled to find that everything had been moved about. The heavy chest of drawers that was sitting against one wall had been opened and one of the drawers was hanging loosely on its slide. Clare stepped over to it and saw that it was filled with blueprints. She picked up one of them and saw the name at the bottom that said "Henry Gehm."

As she stood there holding the blueprints, she again felt a compulsion to act. She felt that she should go to the other side of the attic, where the furniture had also been moved about. Who had been here? She knew that it had been no one in her family, so had it been moved by other than human hands? She felt a chill pass down her spine and it intensified when she saw the vague outlines of a door behind the furniture. It seemed as though someone had revealed the door for her but she refused to look and see what was behind it. She simply didn't want to know!

Strange events continued to occur. The footsteps went on marching up and down the stairs at night. One morning, the breakfront in the dining room was found open and the drawers had been re-arranged. Clare's dresser was found open and her clothing scattered one morning. This seemed to mean that her youngest daughter's account of seeing someone opening and closing her mother's dresser was true after all. Oddly, she later learned that her and her husband's bedroom had once been the bedroom of Henry Gehm. If it was his ghost who was searching the house, perhaps he had mistaken her furniture for his own and had gone through on a quest for his missing gold coins.

In early March 1966, Clare was in the basement and her daughter, Wendy, was out back in the garden playing. Then, Clare heard the sound of a child running through the dining room and into the kitchen. Thinking that Wendy had come in from outside, she called out to her. When there was no answer, she went upstairs to see what was going on. The house, she discovered, was empty and quiet. Wendy was still outside and Sandy was not at home.

Five days later, the entire family, save for Mr. Walsh, was out of the house and attending church. He slept in that morning but after the family had left for church, he came downstairs and fixed himself something for breakfast. He was making coffee when he heard the sound of a child walking across the floor upstairs. He thought perhaps Wendy had taken sick and had stayed home from church and worried, he went upstairs to see if she was okay. He went into her room, but he found it empty. There was no child in the house.

When his family came home, they all sat down to discuss the situation. As far as they could tell, there were at least two ghosts in the house. There was the man with the solid feet who searched the house (Henry Gehm?) and apparently a child. Of course, the Walsh family had no idea about the woman in the black dress that had been seen by the Furry's daughter or the little boy that she led about by the hand.

A week or so later, Clare again awakened early in the morning and found that the attic door was once again standing open. The furniture in the storage room had again been moved about and she seemed to have a vague recollection of hearing a dull thudding sound from the attic the night before. She deduced that the sound had been made by a trunk that had been moved into the center of the floor. It had not been sitting in that space before. Not only that, but she clearly saw fresh markings that had been made in the dust on the floor. They looked like writings...

writings that had been attempted by a child's hand! It was as if someone had tried to write his or her name in the dust, but she knew that it had not been her children. Both girls were too frightened to even come into the room. So who could it have been? With that question still lingering in her mind, she fled from the attic.

She couldn't forget about the writing though and she went back to the attic the next day. The writing was still there but something else had been added next to it. Just inches away from the crude words was the distinct imprint of a small hand... a child's hand! As she stared at it, memories of small running footsteps and a child's cries came washing over her. They were things that both she and her family had experienced while living in the house. There were truly more ghosts here than she could have ever imagined. It seemed to be an entire family from the past, apparently unaware that time had moved on and that the house on Plant Avenue was no longer theirs.

More months passed and the incidents continued. The door to the attic swung open and closed, the footsteps wandered the staircase, muffled cries were sometimes heard in the darkness, a typewriter in Wendy's room began operating by itself, lights turned on and off and the family dog, who had been a peaceful animal during the entire seven years they had owned him, had become an addled and frightened shadow of his former self.

It finally got to be too much for the Walsh's. The ghosts could have the place if they wanted it. The Walsh's decided that they would build a new house, an "unhaunted" one, that no one else had ever lived in before. They never planned to inherit the ghosts of previous owners again!

Soon after, they contacted the owner about their intentions to leave and as soon as their new home was completed, they moved out. Even on the last day though, they heard the sound of footsteps climbing the stairs, pausing at the hidden tread and then fading into oblivion.

Today, the house on Plant Avenue is owned by June and Robert Wheeler, who have raised three children in the home and rescued the place the place from the dim prospects of rental property. In addition, they have also researched the history and haunts of the house and have corrected some of the myths and misconceptions of the place, like the fact that Henry Gehm was not the builder of the place and that he did not work for the circus. They were also able to track down the fact that he often used gold coins and had apparently hidden them around the house.

The Wheeler's have no doubt that the house is haunted and at one time, had a dog who behaved in the same way the Walsh's dog once acted. He would sometimes stand at the top of the stairs, nose pointed and tail in the air, as if he were glaring at something that no one else could see.

Their son, Jack, also once saw the apparition of a man in old-fashioned clothing in his bedroom and also reported (long before he knew anything about the haunted history of the house) that he had been awakened in the night by his bed shaking. The other members of the family have had experiences of their own, including strange sounds in the attic, moving bed covers, indentions on the mattress and a hazy shape that appeared one day in the pantry and had June Wheeler convinced that someone had dumped flour all over the floor. She was stunned when the white haze vanished!

And so the haunting of the house on Plant Avenue continues. Is one of the ghosts here Henry Gehm? Or is it another phantom altogether? And who are the other spirits? Are they Henry's wife and perhaps a child who perished long ago? Records do show that Gehm lost a six year-old grandson during the time that he resided in the house. Could he still linger here, perhaps looking for a playmate among the children who have come here over the years?

The mysteries remain.. as does the reputation of one of the most renowned haunted houses in St. Louis.

IX. THE DEVIL CAME TO ST. LOUIS

Exploring St. Louis' Greatest Unsolved Mystery

In 1949, the Devil came to St. Louis.... Or at least, if you believe the stories that have been told for the last fifty-odd years, a reasonable facsimile of him did.

This is the story that has been told for three generations and it is the story that has inspired books, films and documentaries. It is, without question, the greatest unsolved mystery of St. Louis. And, let's face it, a story that has become a confusing and convoluted mess over the years. There are so many theories, legends, tales and counter-stories that have been thrown into the mix that it's become very hard to separate fact from fantasy. So, let's see if we can get to the bottom of what happened here in 1949, despite all of the unanswered questions that have been left behind.

What happened at the old Alexian Brothers hospital that still has former staff members whispering about it in fear today? What really happened to bring a young boy and his frightened family from Maryland to St. Louis? And most of all, was this boy really possessed by demon?

The story began not in St. Louis, but in the small Washington, D.C. suburb of Cottage City, Maryland (not Mount Rainier as has been erroneously reported in so many books and articles). As most readers already know, what has come to be known as the "St. Louis Exorcism Case" would go on to inspire William Peter Blatty's 1971 best-selling book and the movie based on it, *The Exorcist.* In the novel, a young girl is possessed by a demon and is subjected to an exorcism by Catholic priests. In the true story though, the subject of the alleged possession was not a girl but a boy who has been identified in various accounts as "Roland" or "Robbie Doe". Robbie (as we will call him here) was born in 1935 and grew up in Cottage City. He was the only child of a dysfunctional family and had a troubled childhood.

In January 1949, the family of 13-year-old Robbie began to be disturbed by scratching sounds that came from inside of the walls and ceilings of the house. Believing that the house was infested with mice, the parents called an exterminator but he could find no sign of mice. To make matters worse, his efforts seemed to add to the problem. Noises that sounded like someone walking in the hallway could be heard and dishes and objects were often found to be moved without explanation.

And while the noises were disturbing, they weren't nearly as frightening as when Robbie began to be attacked. His bed shook so hard that he couldn't sleep at night. His blankets and sheets were torn from the bed. When he tried to hold onto them, he was reportedly pulled off the bed and onto the floor with the sheets still gripped in his hands.

Those who have come to believe the boy was genuinely possessed feel that he may have been invaded by an invisible entity after experimenting with a Ouija board. He had been taught to use the device by his "Aunt Tillie", a relative who took an active interest in Spiritualism and the occult. Tillie had passed away a short time before the event began and it has even been suggested that it was her spirit who began to plague the boy. This seems unlikely though, especially considering the timing of her death. She lived in St. Louis and had died of multiple sclerosis on January 26, 1949... a number of days after the phenomena surrounding Robbie began. However the family did feel there was some connection, as was evidenced in the written history of the mystery.

Many of the early events in the case were chronicled by the Jesuit priests who later performed the exorcism. Apparently, a diary was kept and it was the same diary that was heard about by author William Peter Blatty when he was a student at Georgetown University in 1949. He first became interested in the story after reading about in newspaper articles and discussed it with his instructor, the Rev. Thomas Bermingham, S.J.. The "diary" of the Robbie Doe case came to light in the fall of 1949 under rather odd circumstances. Fr. Eugene B. Gallagher, S.J., who was on the faculty of Georgetown, was lecturing on the topic of exorcisms when one of his students, the son of a psychiatrist at St. Elizabeth's Hospital in Washington, spoke of a diary that had been kept by the Jesuits involved in the Robbie Doe exorcism. Father Gallagher asked the psychiatrist, who may have been one of the professionals involved in the early stages of the case, for a copy of the diary and eventually received a 16-page document that was titled "Case Study by Jesuit Priests". It had apparently been intended to be used a guide for future exorcisms. Blatty asked to see a copy of the diary, but he was refused.

He later turned back to newspapers for information about the case and discovered that one of them actually listed the name of the priest involved. His name was Rev. William S. Bowdern, S.J. of St. Louis. Bowdern refused to comment on the case for the newspaper reports, as priests who perform exorcisms are said to be sworn to secrecy. Blatty tried contacting him anyway but the priest refused to cooperate. Out of respect, Blatty changed the identity of the possession victim in his book to a young girl, but the exorcist of the novel remains an apparently thinly veiled portrait of Bowdern.

Father Bowdern passed away in 1983, never publicly acknowledging the fact that he was involved in the St. Louis case. He had talked with other Jesuits though and eventually these stories reached a man named Thomas Allen, an author and contributing editor to *National Geographic*. He managed to find one of the participants in the case, Walter Halloran, S.J., who was then living in a small town in Minnesota. Halloran was suspicious at first but he did admit that there had been a diary. But was it the diary that fell into the hands of Father Gallagher? Maybe or maybe not...

According to legend, the diary that Halloran had access to later turned up as a 26-page document of the case that was literally snatched out of the old Alexian Brothers hospital just before it was demolished, so where did the 16-page diary come from? And what happened to it? Accounts have it that Father Gallagher later loaned his 16-page diary to Fr. Brian McGrath, S.J., then dean of Georgetown University, in the spring of 1950. When Gallagher later tried to retrieve the diary, he was told that seven pages of the diary had been lost. Only nine of the 16 pages remained and they were only photocopies.

And what about the later 26-page diary? Sources say that this longer document was found in the Alexian Brothers Hospital on South Broadway in St. Louis. The old psychiatric wing of the hospital was being torn down in 1978 and workmen were sent in to remove furniture from that part of the building. One of these men found the document in a desk drawer of a locked room and he gave it to his supervisors, who in turn passed it on to hospital administrators. It was eventually identified as the work of Rev. Raymond Bishop, S.J., a priest who had participated in the exorcism. The manuscript was locked away but Father Halloran had access to it. He made a copy of the diary and sent it to Allen, who published a book about it in 1993.

As it has turned out, the only details that we have about the case have come through the "diary" and from witnesses who were present at the time. The Catholic Church has never released details of the story. The diary does reveal details though, many of which have been overlooked and forgotten over the years.

As mentioned already, the strange noises and scratching in the house progressed into actual witnessed attacks on Robbie himself. Worried that the incidents might have something to do with Aunt Tillie, Robbie's mother attempted to make contact with her spirit. According to the priest's diary, she asked questions aloud and implored Tillie's spirit, if it was really her, to knock three times and make herself known. Allegedly, Robbie, his mother and his grandmother all felt a wave of air pass over them and then heard three knocks on the floor. Robbie's mother asked again, this time for four knocks and they again came in reply. They were followed by scratching sounds on the bed mattress, which then began to shake and vibrate onto the floor. And while these events must have certainly been chilling, it still seems unlikely that they could have been involved with Aunt Tillie, or her ghost.

There are other explanations for what was going on. Many believe that Robbie may have been the victim of "poltergeist-like phenomena", where unknowing people actually manifest a form of psychokinesis that causes objects to move about in their presence. It often centers around troubled young people and has been documented many times over the years. Other principals in the case would further explore this explanation.

Another explanation, and one offered by more people that you might imagine, was that the boy truly was possessed and that the invisible presence wreaking havoc in the house was not connected to Aunt Tillie at all!

By this time, the family was becoming desperate. They began seeking help for Robbie and according to one account from 1975, called in two Lutheran ministers and a rabbi. Robbie had been baptized a Lutheran at birth, so one has to wonder why a rabbi was called to the house, although some have suggested that perhaps one of the ministers had asked him along. The account goes on to say that while the rabbi was examining the boy, Robbie suddenly began to shout in an unknown tongue. After listening for a few moments, the rabbi announced that he was speaking in Hebrew! Not only that, but the reports adds that a professor from Washington University would later hear the boy's speech and he insisted that Robbie was speaking Aramaic, an ancient language of Palestine! If this account is accurate, we have to ask how a 13-year boy from Maryland would have learned to speak Aramaic?

Rev. Luther Schulze, one of the Lutheran ministers and the pastor from the family's own church, tried praying with Robbie and his parents in their home and then with Robbie alone. He took the boy to the church to pray with him and he begged whatever was bothering him to leave. It didn't help though and the strange afflictions continued. The weird noises continued to be heard in the house and Robbie's bed went on shaking and rocking so that he was unable to get any sleep at night. Finally, in February, Schulze decided to question whether the house was haunted, or the boy was. He offered to let Robbie spend the night in his home and his parents quickly agreed. They were anxious to try anything that might help by this time.

That night, Mrs. Schulze went to the guest room and Robbie and the minister retired to the twin beds located in the master bedroom. About ten minutes later, Schulze reported that he heard the sound of Roland's bed creaking and shaking. He also heard strange scratching noises inside of the walls, just like the ones that had been heard at Robbie's own house. Schulze quickly switched on the lights and clearly saw the vibrating bed. When he prayed for it to stop, the vibration grew even more violent. He stated that Robbie was wide awake but he was completely still and was not moving in a way that would cause the bed to shake.

Schulze then suggested that Robbie try and sleep in a heavy armchair that was located across the room. While Schulze watched him closely, the chair began to move. First, it scooted backward several inches and its legs jolted forward and back. The minister told Robbie to raise his legs and to add his full weight to the chair but that wasn't enough to stop the chair from moving. Moments later, it literally slammed against the wall and then it tipped over and deposited the boy unhurt onto the floor.

Trying not to be frightened or discouraged, Rev. Schulze made a pallet of blankets on the floor for Robbie to sleep on. As soon as the boy fell asleep though, the pallet began to slide across the floor and under one of the beds! When Robbie was startled awake by the movement, he raised up and struck his head on one of the bedposts. Again, the minister made up the pallet, only to this time have it whip across the floor and slide under the other bed. Robbie's hands were visible the entire time and his body was taut with tension. The blankets didn't even wrinkle at all!

Schulze was now both puzzled and a little afraid. He suggested that Robbie's parents take the boy to see a doctor and a psychologist to rule out any kind of physical or mental problems that might be causing the phenomena to take place. The minister also contacted J.B. Rhine, the famed founder of the parapsychology laboratory at Duke University. He explained what was going on and Rhine and his partner and wife, Louisa Rhine, drove from North Carolina to Cottage City to see the boy. Unfortunately, no activity took place while the investigator was present, but Rhine did deduce that it sounded like a classic poltergeist case in which the boy's unconscious abilities were influencing the objects around him. The details fit well with other experimental results that Rhine had been obtaining.

And while the explanation suggested by Rhine must have appealed to the minister (as he had contacted the investigator in the first place), he did an abrupt about-face a short time later when the phenomena took another turn. A week or so after the incident at Schulze's home, bloody scratches began to appear on the boy's body. Perhaps startled by this new turn of events, Schulze suggested that the family contact a Catholic priest.

And here's where things get (if possible) even more confusing.

According to some sources, Robbie's family then turned to the Catholic Church for help and his father went to the nearby St. James Church in Mount Rainier, Maryland. Here, he met with a young priest named Edward Albert Hughes. He was the assistant pastor of the church at the time. He was skeptical and reluctant to get involved in the matter, but he did agree to go and see Robbie. During the visit, Robbie allegedly addressed the priest in Latin, a language that he did not know. Shaken, Hughes was said to have applied to his archbishop for permission to conduct an exorcism. The sources go on to say that the ritual was performed at Georgetown Hospital in in February. Robbie seemed to go into a trance and he thrashed about and spoke in tongues. Hughes ordered the boy to be put into restraints but he somehow managed to work a piece of metal spring loose from the bed and he slashed the priest with it. The stories say that Hughes subsequently left St. James, suffered a nervous breakdown and during masses that he held later in life, he could only hold the consecrated host aloft in in one hand.

That was the story anyway, although according to research done by Mark Opsasnick in 1999, none of this may have happened at all. This incident appears only in the book *Possessed* by Thomas Allen. Opsasnick's work actually pointed out a number of other suppositions and possible problems in the book, including the fact that Allen often refers to the possessed boy's home in Mount Rainier. He apparently never considered the fact that the priests in the case may have used this town as a cover to discourage reporters from looking for the boy in Cottage City.

The stories about Father Hughes were apparently not accurate either. Father Hughes became assistant pastor of St. James Church under Rev. William Canning in June 1948 and he served without a break until June 1960. (He was later reassigned to St. James in 1973 and stayed there until his death in 1980.) Church records do not indicate that he ever suffered a breakdown, nor that he ever even made an attempt to exorcize Robbie at Georgetown University Hospital. However, Robbie was checked into the hospital under his real name for several days during the period when the alleged exorcism attempt took place, but that is all. Records say that he underwent extensive medial and psychological evaluations.

Father Hughes also never actually visited Robbie in his home. In truth, his mother brought him to St. James for the only consultation. There is nothing to suggest that Robbie spoke to the priest in Latin and no evidence to say that Father Hughes was ever slashed with a bedspring. Those who knew Hughes personally remember him suffering no injuries during this period and the fact is, the church social calendar showed him quite busy during the weeks after Robbie's release from the hospital.

It's possible that the confusion about Hughes' part in the case came from the assistant pastor that he had later in life. According to this pastor, Frank Bober, Hughes confided in him about the first exorcism attempt. Bober later became an important figure in the case, being very accessible to journalists. He has appeared in literally dozens of articles, books and documentaries about the case and Thomas Allen cited him as being "extremely reliable" about Hughes' role in the incidents. Journalist Mark Opsasnick believed that Bober "dramatized" many of the re-tellings of the events and also may have been the person who first perpetrated the idea that Robbie and his family lived in Mount Rainier. Who knows?

But even if we consider the idea that this part of the story didn't actually happen, what was documented as occurring around this same time was strange enough that all of that becomes almost irrelevant!

Robbie's hospital stay was documented as occurring between February 28, 1949 and March 2, 1949 but according to the priest's "diary", strange things began to happen on February 26.

The statement records that "there appeared scratches on the boy's body for about four successive nights. After the fourth night words were written in printed form. These letters were clear but seemed to have been scratched on the body by claws."

At about this same time, Robbie's mother began to suggest that perhaps a trip away from Maryland might free the boy from the strange happenings. She thought that perhaps they could leave their troubles behind by visiting St. Louis. Robbie's mother was a native of the city and still had many relatives there. The more she considered this, the better the idea seemed. And apparently, the haunting entity agreed because the word "LOUIS" inexplicably appeared on Robbie's rib cage. When this "skin branding" occurred, Robbie's hands were always visible and his mother specifically notes that he could not have scratched the words himself. He had been under observation at the time and the words, according to witnesses, had simply appeared.

The priest's diary even noted that the writing also appeared on Robbie's back. Later on, while in St. Louis, there was some question raised about sending Robbie to school while in the city but the message "NO" appeared on his wrists. A large letter "N" also appeared on each of his legs and his mother feared disobeying what she saw as a supernatural order. It has been suggested that perhaps Robbie created the writing himself with his mind, either consciously or unconsciously. With that in question, it should be noted that before his parents consulted a priest, they also had him examined by a psychiatrist. He reported that the boy was quite normal, as did a medical doctor who gave him a complete physical.

At this point, records do indicate that Robbie's mother took him to consult with Father Hughes at the St. James Church. During this one documented visit, he suggested that the family use blessed candles, holy water and special prayers and to perhaps rid the boy of his problems. Robbie's mother began the use of the blessed candles and on one occasion, a comb flew violently through the air and struck them, snuffing out the flames. Later, an orange and a pear flew across Robbie's room. The kitchen table once overturned in the boy's presence, but without his aid, and milk and food flew off of counters and onto the floor. At another time, a coat jerked from a hanger and a bible landed at Robbie's feet. A chair that the boy was sitting in spun around so fast that he was unable to stop it. Finally, he was said to have discontinued attending school because his desk refused to remain in the same place.

The priest's diary went on to add that "the mother took the bottle of holy water and sprinkled all of the rooms." She then took the bottle and placed it on a shelf but it snapped into the air and flew onto the floor, although it did not break.

A 1975 report stated that attempts were also made to baptize Robbie into the Catholic faith in order to help him. The press mentioned that one of these attempts was made during Robbie's hospital stay (not an exorcism as was later reported) and then later in St. Louis. Another baptism attempt was allegedly made in February 1949. It was said that as Robbie's uncle was driving him to the rectory for the ceremony, the boy suddenly glared at him, grabbed him by the throat and shouted, "You son of a bitch, you think I'm going to be baptized but you are going to be fooled!"

The Catholic baptism ritual usually only takes about 15 minutes but for Robbie, it reportedly lasted for several hours. It was said that when the priest asked "Do you renounce the devil and all his works?" Robbie would go into such a thrashing rage that he had to be restrained.

In early March, after being released from the hospital and found normal, Robbie boarded a train to St. Louis with his parents. The family was graciously taken in by relatives in Normandy, Missouri and here, the boy's mother hoped that he might be freed from the strange and horrifying events. For those readers who are convinced that nothing was occurring in this case aside from overactive imaginations and silly superstition, they may want to consider the trip to St. Louis itself as evidence that something (supernatural or not) was taking place. The fact that Robbie's parents would uproot the boy from his home, his father would often abandon his employment and they would all travel halfway across the county in a last ditch effort to find help is suggestive (if not downright convincing) that terrible things were indeed happening.

Unfortunately, Robbie did not improve in St. Louis. His aunt and uncle in Normandy, as well as various other relatives, witnessed more of the "skin brandings", as well as saw his bed and mattress shaking on many occasions. On March 8, 1949, the shaking of the mattress and scratching continued. A stool that was sitting near the bed was seen flying across the room by Robbie's cousin. The boy was so concerned about Robbie that he even tried lying down on the bed beside him to stop the mattress from shaking. To his dismay, it didn't work. Finally, one of the relatives, who had attended St. Louis University, went to see her old teacher there, Rev. Raymond J. Bishop, S.J. She asked him if he might be able to assist Robbie and while we have no idea what his initial reply may have been, he did agree to look into the case. It was Bishop who brought William Bowdern into the case.

Bowdern was not on the faculty of St. Louis University. In 1949, he was the pastor of St. Francis Xavier Church, located at the corner of Grand and Lindell. He was a native of St. Louis and had served as a chaplain during World War II. He had many years experience dealing with people and their problems and he listened carefully to the story that Bishop told him. Then, he and Bishop went to Paul Reinert, S.J., the president of the university. All of them were skeptical about the case and concerned with bringing embarrassment to the church and the college but decided that it might be well to have the boy say some prayers and to give him the priestly blessing.

Apparently, Father Bishop first went to the house alone. He came to bless the house and the room in which Robbie slept. A second-class holy relic of St. Margaret Mary was pinned on the boy's bed. But even after the blessing and in spite of the relic, the bed still shook and swayed and the scratches still appeared all over the boy's body. Bishop then sprinkled holy water on the bed in the form of a cross and the movement suddenly ceased. Moments later, it started up again after Bishop stepped out of the room. Then, a sharp pain allegedly struck Robbie in the stomach and he cried out. His mother pulled back the bed covers and lifted the boy's pajama top to reveal red lines that zigzagged across the boy's abdomen. During this entire time, Robbie was in clear view of at least six witnesses.

The next two nights passed in the same way, with a shaking mattress, scratching and objects being thrown about. On March 11, Father Bishop returned to the home and this time brought Father Bowdern with him. The Jesuits were still skeptical about the case but open-minded enough to observe the boy and also to study the literature available about demonic attacks on humans. The priests came and prayed again and this time, the activity did not respond. However, as soon as Bishop and Bowdern left, a loud noise was reportedly heard in Robbie's room and five relatives rushed to see what had happened. They discovered that a 75-pound bookcase had swiveled in a complete circle, a bench had turned over and a crucifix that one of the priests had left under Robbie's pillow had moved to the end of the bed! As they rushed into the room, the mattress was violently shaking and bouncing once more.

Unfortunately, there is no reliable, clear-cut information about how the decision was reached by the Jesuits to perform an exorcism. According to church doctrine, there are a number of different conditions that have to be met to show that someone is truly possessed. Whether or not these conditions were met is not for me to say or judge but regardless, Bowdern and Bishop went to Archbishop Joseph E. Ritter for permission to perform an exorcism on March 16. Ritter had a reputation as a down-to-earth progressive and earlier in the decade, he had campaigned hard to integrate the St. Louis schools and parishes. Later, he would also have a large role in the sweeping reforms that came to the church as Vatican II. The Jesuits, who already have a tense history with the regular church, had no idea how Ritter would respond to the request. Surprisingly, he prompted agreed.

And the exorcism began...

The chronology throughout the remainder of the case is extremely confusing. It is not clear how long Robbie stayed at his relative's house but it is known that he was taken to the Alexian Brothers Hospital in south St. Louis, possibly for as long as a month, and that portions of the exorcism were also carried out in the rectory of the St. Francis Xavier Church. The rectory has since been demolished and replaced.

It also isn't clear how many people were actually actively involved in the exorcism. The names of the exorcists given out in St. Louis were Father Bowdern, Father Bishop and Father Lawrence Kenny. Father Charles O'Hara of Marquette University in Milwaukee was also present as a witness (he later passed on information about what he saw there to Father Eugene Gallagher at Georgetown) and there were undoubtedly a several hospital staff members and seminary students who were also in attendance.

One of these students was Walter Halloran, the priest who passed along the 26-page diary to Thomas Allen. At that time, he was a strapping young former football player who had been asked along to hold Robbie down. Exorcisms were known for being often violent rituals and the Jesuits must have felt that the young man would prove to be very useful. For reason though, Halloran was removed from the exorcism about one week before it came to end, leaving his accounts of it rather incomplete.

And while Halloran would go on to have his own uncertain recollections of the case, hospital staff members would remember the events with fear. Steve Erdmann, who wrote about the case in 1975, personally knew at least one of the nurses involved. The man's name was Ernest Schaffer and he was barely able to talk about the case more than two decades later. He stated that the priests had a "terrible time" during Robbie's hospital stay. He had many conversations with the priests and believed that what he saw was supernatural in origin. He said that he cleaned vomit out of the boy's room on several different occasions.

The exorcism apparently started at the home of Robbie's relatives. The priests came late in the evening and after Robbie went to bed, the ritual began. The boy was said to go into a trance, his bed shook and welts and scratches appeared on his body. Bishop was said to have wiped away blood that welled up in the scratches while Halloran attempted to hold the boy down. An exorcism is said to be a dire spiritual and physical struggle. The demon that takes control of the person also tries to break the faith of the exorcist involved. Father Bowdern had prepared himself for the exhausting events through a religious fast of prayer, bread and water. It is said that from the time he first learned of Robbie's plight until the exorcism had run its course, Bowdern lost nearly 40 pounds.

As the prayers commanding the departure of the evil spirit began, Robbie winced and rolled in a sudden seizure of pain. Over the next two hours, the boy was branded and scratched 30 times on his stomach, chest, throat, thighs, calves and back. When Bowdern demanded that the demon reveal itself, the words "WELL" and "SPITE" appeared on the boy's chest. Another time, the word "HELL" appeared in red welts as the boy rocked back and forth, apparently in pain. All the while, he reportedly cursed and screamed obscenities in a voice that "ranged from deep bass to falsetto". The ritual came to an end that night near dawn but little progress had been made.

The ordeal continued for many weeks and through many readings of the exorcism ritual. According to the witnesses, the boy's responses became more violent and repulsive as time went on. He was said to speak in Latin, in a variety of voices, in between bouts of screams and curses. He spat in the faces of the priests who knelt and stood by his bed and his spittle and vomit struck them with uncanny accuracy and over great distances. He punched and slapped the priests and the witnesses. He constantly urinated and he belched and passed gas that was said to have an unbelievable stench. He was even said to have taunted the priests and to have confronted them with information about themselves that he could not possibly have known. His body thrashed and contorted into seemingly impossible shapes and would continue during the nighttime hours. Each morning though, he would appear to be quite normal and would profess to have no memory of the events that took place after dark. He usually spent the day reading comics or playing board games with the student assistants.

Father O'Hara told Father Gallagher something even stranger. "One night the boy brushed off his handlers," he reportedly said, "and soared through the air at Father Bowdern standing some distance from the bed with a ritual book in his hands. Presumably Bowdern was about to be attacked but the boy got no further than the book. And when his hands hit that - I assure you, Gene, I saw this with my own eyes - he didn't tear the book, he dissolved it! The book vaporized into confetti and fell in small fine pieces to the floor!"

The ritual continued with the prayers being recited every day, despite Robbie's rabid reaction to them. The exorcism seemed virtually useless and so the priests requested permission to instruct Robbie in the Catholic faith. They felt that his conversion would help to strengthen their fight against the entity controlling the boy. His parents consented and he was prepared for his first communion. During this time of instruction, Robbie seemed to quiet somewhat and he was moved to the rectory. He seemed to be enjoying his lessons in the Catholic faith but this time of peace would not last. As Robbie prepared to receive communion, the priests literally had to drag him into the church. He broke out in a rage that was worse than anything the exorcists could remember.

The family was exhausted and was ready to give up.

Father Bowdern began searching for a new approach and so he made arrangements to return Robbie to Maryland and continue the ritual. It was said that during the train ride, Robbie became maniacal and struck Bowdern in the testicles. He reportedly cried "that's a nutcracker for you, isn't it?" The others present wrestled with Robbie until he finally fell asleep.

Bowdern found no accommodations to continue with Robbie in Maryland. No one would have anything to do with the boy and so he returned with him to St. Louis. Robbie's instructions in the Catholic faith continued. It was now Holy Week, the week before Easter, and Robbie was taken to White House, a Jesuit retreat overlooked the Mississippi River. As they walked the Stations of the Cross, located outside, Robbie suddenly became nervous and agitated. He ran away from the priests and launched himself toward the bluffs that loomed over the river. Halloran, the seminary student, tackled the boy and managed to subdue him. Shortly after, they returned the boy to the hospital.

The exorcism was now at an impasse. Seeking a solution, Bowdern again plunged into the literature regarding possession. He learned of an 1870 case that took place in Wisconsin that seemed similar to Robbie's plight and he devised a new strategy. On the night of April 18, the ritual resumed. Bowdern forced Robbie to wear a chain of religious medals and to hold a crucifix in his hands. Suddenly, Robbie became strangely contrite and he began to ask questions about the meaning of certain Latin prayers. Bowdern ignored him though, refusing to engage the entity in conversation, and he instead demanded to know the name of the demon and when he would depart.

Robbie exploded in a rage. Five witnesses held him down while he screamed that he was a "fallen angel" but Bowdern continued on with the ritual. He recited it incessantly for hours until Robbie suddenly interrupted in a loud, masculine voice, identifying himself as "St. Michael the Archangel". The voice ordered the demon to depart. Robbie's body then went into violent contortions and spasms. Then, he fell quiet. A moment later, he sat up, smiled and then spoke in a normal voice. "He's gone", Robbie said and then told the priests of a vision that he had of St. Michael holding a flaming sword.

The exorcism was finally over.

Robbie left St. Louis with his parents 12 days later and returned to Maryland. He wrote to Father Bowdern in May 1949 and told him that he was happy and had a new dog. He was, by last report, still living in Maryland and is a devout Catholic with three children. He has only dim recollections of what happened in 1949.

Father Bowdern believed until the end of his life that he and his fellow priests had been battling a demonic entity. His supporters in this maintain that there were many witnesses to the alleged supernatural events that took place and that no other explanations existed for what was seen. A full report that was filed by the Catholic Church stated that the case of Robbie Doe was a "genuine demonic possession." According to Father John Nicola, who had the opportunity to review the report, he noted that 41 persons had signed a document attesting to the fact that they had witnessed paranormal phenomena in the case.

So, what possessed Robbie Doe? Many believe that Robbie may have been faking the whole thing. Mark Opsasnick, during his research into the boy's troubled childhood, began to feel that the case may have started as a way to get attention, or to get out of school, and that it snowballed into the mess that it became. While he does some great investigative work into the early stages of the case, and does have many relevant points about Robbie's childhood and the many flaws in the chronicling of the case, he is too quick to dismiss some of the strange things that occurred in front of multiple witnesses. His report never really delves at all into the events in St. Louis and in this way, leaves out just about everything that took place that was so hard to explain.

And there are other theories. Some would agree that while Robbie was not possessed, he was afflicted with another unexplainable paranormal disturbance. Earlier in this chapter, I briefly mentioned "poltergeist-like" activity and how it can sometimes be associated with disturbed teenagers. While medical doctors have no interest in this, a few more adventurous scientists have grudgingly speculated that perhaps the human mind has abilities and energies that are still unrecognized. These energies just might be able to make objects move, writing to appear and beds to shake. If it can really happen, it just might explain what happen to Robbie Doe.

Many are not willing to believe in any of this however and not surprisingly, skepticism runs rampant when it comes to the "St. Louis Exorcism Case". Many feel that Robbie suffered from a mental illness and not demonic possession. He may have been hallucinating or suffering from some weird psychosomatic illness that caused him to behave so strangely, to curse and scream and to thrash about so violently.

It should be noted though that people who have suggested that all of this was nothing more than a hoax or a mental illness are all people who were in no way involved in the case. Even Father Walter Halloran, who now serves as the assistant pastor of the St. Joseph's Cathedral in San Diego, California, has stated that while he is not expert enough in the field to make the determination about whether the possession officially genuine, he does feel that it was real. "I have always thought in my mind that it was," he said. As he was present during much of the events that took place, his opinion has to be considered and acknowledged far beyond those who speculate and yet were not even born in 1949.

In spite of the skeptics though, there were (and are) many who believe the events were real. They have no explanation for what took place in 1949 and while none of the buildings directly involved in the exorcism remain today.... memories of them still linger today.

For years after the exorcism, people who were involved in the case, or who worked at the hospital, shared stories of things they heard and saw during the several week ordeal. Orderlies spoke of cleaning up pools of vomit and urine in the boy's rooms. Staff members and nurses claimed to hear the sounds of someone screaming and the echoes of demonic laughter coming from Robbie's room. Most especially though, they spoke of the cold waves of air that seemed to emanate from the room. No matter how warm the rest of the hospital was, the area around the door to the boy's room was always ice cold!

And even after the exorcism ended, something apparently remained behind. Was it some remnant of the entity that possessed Robbie or perhaps the impression of the horrific events that occurred in the room? Whatever it was, it was enough to keep staff members from ever using the room again. It was locked and sealed off after the exorcism ended and was never re-opened. According to witnesses, the lights refused to stay on in the room and the heat would not work. It was always cold and on occasion, foul odors would drift from beneath the door. The entire section of the hospital was eventually closed but whether or not this was because of the "exorcism room" is unknown. What is known is that the wing was eventually razed in 1978, but not without difficulty. Workers on the demolition crew claimed to be unable to control the wrecking ball when that floor was taken off. The ball swung around and hit a portion of a new building but luckily did not damage. This incident seemed to further enhance the legend of the room!

And the legend grew... When the wrecking crew came in to remove furniture and any other items that could be re-sold from the wing, they broke into the "exorcism room" to find that it had been untouched since 1949. Inside of a desk in the room was a copy of the exorcist's diary from the case, which was given to hospital administrators and later became the basis for the public's fascination with the story.

But that was not the strangest thing to happen when the room was opened! According to crew members who worked for the Department of Transportation, "something" was seen emerging from the room just moments before the wrecking ball claimed it. Whatever it was, the men likened it to a "cat or a big rat or something". I wouldn't begin to suggest what this creature might have been, natural or supernatural, but I will say that it has continued to add to the legend of the "St. Louis Exorcism Case" over the years!

In closing, I will not ask again what the reader believes occurred in St. Louis in 1949. The case, whether you believe in possession, demons and exorcisms or not, remains unsolved. There is simply no way to adequately dismiss every unusual thing that was reported in this case without just saying that everyone involved was a liar, drunk or insane. For myself, I can't say that young Robbie Doe was possessed, or not possessed, but what I can say is that this is one of the few cases of alleged "possession" that has left me with many lingering questions.

The reader, of course, is advised to judge for himself but as for this author, well, I think I paraphrased my thoughts best in the opening segment of this book..

There are certainly more things in heaven and earth than are dreamt of in our philosophies!

- SELECT BIBLIOGRAPHY -
& RECOMMENDED READING

Allen, Thomas B. - Possessed (1993 / 2000)

Amsler, Kevin - Final Resting Place: Lives & Deaths of Famous St. Louisans (1997)

Barringer, Fifield & Herb Weitman - Seeing St. Louis (1987)

Bartley, Mary - St. Louis Lost (1994)

Bettmann, Otto - The Good Old Days, They Were Terrible (1974)

Brown, John Gary - Soul in the Stone (1994)

Carlson, Bruce - Best of the Mississippi River Ghosts (1997)

Clevenger, Martha R. - "Indescribably Grand" (1996)

Corbett, Katharine T. & Howard S. Miller - St. Louis in the Gilded Age (1993)

Courtaway, Robbi - Spirits of St. Louis (1999)

Curzon, Julian - The Great Cyclone at St. Louis & East St. Louis, May 27, 1869 (1896/1997)

Deakin, James - A Grave for Bobby (1990)

Ebon, Martin - Exorcism: Fact Not Fiction (1974)

Ebon, Martin - They Knew the Unknown (1971)

Elz, Ron - Red-Haired Ghost Lady of Suite 304 (1984)

Erdmann, Steve - The Truth Behind "The Exorcist" - *Fate* Magazine (January 1975)

Evans, Stewart P. & Paul Gainey - Jack the Ripper: First American Serial Killer (1995)

Faherty, William Barnaby, S.J. - St. Louis: A Concise History (1989)

Ferguson, H.N. - Mystery Painting in St. Louis Jail - *Fate* Magazine (March 1959)

Gilbert, Joan - Missouri Ghosts (1997)

Goodwin, David - Ghosts of Jefferson Barracks (2001)

Graham, D. Douglas - The Most Haunted House in Town - *Fate* Magazine (October 1994)

Graham, Shellee - Tales from the Coral Court (2000)

Groth, Bert - The Strange Case of Patience Worth - *Fate* Magazine (April 1965)

Guiley, Rosemary Ellen - Encyclopedia of Ghosts & Spirits (2000)

Hauck, Dennis William - Haunted Places: The National Directory (1996)

Hernon, Peter & Terry Ganey - Under the Influence (1991)

Holland, Gerald - The King of Beer - *American Mercury* Magazine (October 1929)

Holleman, Joe - Did Jack the Ripper Have Ties to St. Louis? (2001)

Holzer, Hans - Gothic Ghosts (1970)

Jakubowski, Maxim & Nathan Braund - Mammoth Book of Jack the Ripper

Jarvis, Sharon - Dark Zones (1992)

Kirschten, Ernest - Catfish & Crystal (1960)

Lowney, Pamela - The Phantom Menace (2001)

May, Allan - The St. Louis Family (2001) (www.crimelibrary.com)

Missouri Historical Society - The Chatillon- DeMenil House (1966)

Linzee, David - Infamous St. Louis Crimes & Mysteries (2001)

Longo, Jim - Haunted Odyssey (1986)

Loughlin, Caroline & Catherine Anderson - Forest Park (1986)

McNulty, Elizabeth - St. Louis Then & Now (2000)
Montesi, Albert & Richard Deposki - Lafayette Square, St. Louis (1999)
Nash, Jay Robert - Bloodletters & Badmen (1995)
Nash, Jay Robert - Murder, America (1980)
Norman, Michael & Beth Scott - Historic Haunted America (1995)
Opsasnick, Mark - The Haunted Boy - *Strange* Magazine (December 1998)
Riccio, Dolores & Joan Bingham - Haunted Houses USA (1989)
Rother, Hubert & Charlotte - Lost Caves of St. Louis (1996)
Roussin, Donald & Kevin Kious- William J. Lemp Brewing Company: A Tale of Triumph &
        Tragedy in St. Louis, Missouri - American Breweriana Journal (March-April 1999)
St. Louis Globe-Democrat Newspaper
St. Louis Police Library
St. Louis Post-Dispatch Newspaper
Samuel, Ray , Leonard Huber & Warren Ogden - Tales of the Mississippi (1955)
Sauer, Georgia - The Castle: Mystery in the West End (1989)
Scott, Beth & Michael Norman - Haunted Heartland (1985)
Sifakis, Carl - The Mafia Encyclopedia (1987)
Silverberg, Robert - Home of the Red Man (1963)
Somerlott, Robert - "Here, Mr. Splitfoot" (1971)
Speer, Lonnie - Portals to Hell (1997)
Stulce, Corey - Based on a True Story (2000)
Sugnden, Phillp - The Complete History of Jack the Ripper (1994)
Taille de Noyer (brochure) - Florissant Valley Historical Society
Taylor, Troy - Beyond the Grave (2001)
Taylor, Troy - Haunted Alton (2000)
Taylor, Troy - No Rest for the Wicked (2001)
Walker, Stephen - Lemp: The Haunting History (1988)
Wayman, Norbury L. - St. Louis Union Station & Its Railroads (1987)
Windham, Kathryn Tucker - 13 Tennessee Ghosts & Jeffrey (1977)
Winter, William C. - The Civil War in St. Louis (1994)
Witherspoon, Margaret Johanson - Remembering the St. Louis World's Fair (1973)

Personal Interviews & Correspondence

Special thanks to David Goodwin, Stacy Deist and to Ray Nelke, long-time Fortean of St. Louis,
for all of their assistance in the preparation and research of this book.

ABOUT THE AUTHOR: TROY TAYLOR

Troy Taylor is the author of 21 previous books about ghosts and hauntings in America, including HAUNTED ILLINOIS, SPIRITS OF THE CIVIL WAR, THE GHOST HUNTER'S GUIDEBOOK. He is also the editor of GHOSTS OF THE PRAIRIE Magazine, a travel guide to haunted places in America. A number of his articles have been published here and in other ghost-related publications.

Taylor is the president of the "American Ghost Society", a network of ghost hunters, which boasts more than 450 active members in the United States and Canada. The group collects stories of ghost sightings and haunted houses and uses investigative techniques to track down evidence of the supernatural. In addition, he also hosts a National Conference each year in conjunction with the group which usually attracts several hundred ghost enthusiasts from around the country.

Along with writing about ghosts, Taylor is also a public speaker on the subject and has spoken to well over 100 private and public groups on a variety of paranormal subjects. He has appeared in literally dozens of newspaper and magazine articles about ghosts and hauntings. He has also been fortunate enough to be interviewed over 300 times for radio and television broadcasts about the supernatural. He has also appeared in a number of documentary films like AMERICA'S MOST HAUNTED, BEYOND HUMAN SENSES, GHOST WATERS, NIGHT VISITORS and in one feature film, THE ST. FRANCISVILLE EXPERIMENT.

Born and raised in Illinois, Taylor has long had an affinity for "things that go bump in the night" and published his first book HAUNTED DECATUR in 1995. For six years, he was also the host of the popular, and award-winning, "Haunted Decatur" ghost tours of the city for which he sometimes still appears as a guest host. He also hosts the "History & Hauntings Tours" of Alton, Illinois.

In 1996, Taylor married Amy Van Lear, the Managing Director of Whitechapel Press, and they currently reside in a restored 1850's bakery in Alton.

ABOUT WHITECHAPEL PRODUCTIONS PRESS

Whitechapel Productions Press is a small press publisher, specializing in books about ghosts and hauntings. Since 1993, the company has been one of America's leading publishers of supernatural books. Located in Alton, Illinois, they also produce the "Ghosts of the Prairie" internet web page.

In addition to publishing books on history and hauntings, they also host and distribute the Haunted America Catalog, which features over 500 different books about ghosts and hauntings from authors all over the United States. A complete selection of these books can be browsed in person at the "History & Hauntings Book Co." Store in Alton.

Visit Whitechapel Productions Press on the internet and browse through our selection of over ghostly titles, plus information on ghosts and hauntings; haunted history; spirit photographs; information on ghost hunting and much more. Visit the internet web page at:

www.prairieghosts.com

Or visit the Haunted Book Co. in Person at:

515 East Third Street
Alton, Illinois t2002
(618)-456-1086

For More on Haunted St. Louis, see David Goodwin's Book -

Ghosts of Jefferson Barracks
History & Hauntings of Old St. Louis

Printed in the United States
4972

9 781892 523204